Lecture Notes in Computer Science 6705

Commenced Publication in 1973
Founding and Former Series Editors:
Gerhard Goos, Juris Hartmanis, and Jan van Leeuwen

Judith Bishop   Antonio Vallecillo (Eds.)

Objects, Models, Components, Patterns

49th International Conference, TOOLS 2011
Zurich, Switzerland, June 28-30, 2011
Proceedings

 Springer

Volume Editors

Judith Bishop
Microsoft Research
One Microsoft Way, Redmond, WA 98052-6399, USA
E-mail: jbishop@microsoft.com

Antonio Vallecillo
University of Málaga
ETSI Informática
Bulevar Louis Pasteur, 35, 29071 Málaga, Spain
E-mail: av@lcc.uma.es

ISSN 0302-9743   e-ISSN 1611-3349
ISBN 978-3-642-21951-1   e-ISBN 978-3-642-21952-8
DOI 10.1007/978-3-642-21952-8
Springer Heidelberg Dordrecht London New York

Library of Congress Control Number: Applied for

CR Subject Classification (1998): F.3, D.2, D.3, D.1, C.2, D.2.4

LNCS Sublibrary: SL 2 – Programming and Software Engineering

Typesetting: Camera-ready by author, data conversion by Scientific Publishing Services, Chennai, India

Printed on acid-free paper

Springer is part of Springer Science+Business Media (www.springer.com)

Preface

Now that object technology is mainstream, it can be studied in combination with other technologies devoted to achieving high-quality software. TOOLS Europe is a long-standing conference that brings together researchers, practitioners and students to discuss all aspects of object technology and related fields, in particular model-based development, component-based development, language implementation and patterns, in a holistic way. TOOLS Europe has a strong practical bias, without losing sight of the importance of correctness and performance.

The 49th International Conference on Objects, Models, Components and Patterns (TOOLS Europe 2011) was held during June 28–30, 2011 at the Swiss Federal Institute of Technology (ETH) in Zurich, Switzerland, organized by the Chair of Software Engineering.

TOOLS Europe 2011 received 68 abstract submissions of which 66 were submitted as full papers. The Program Committee suggested 19 papers for presentation and inclusion in these proceedings. This corresponds to a 28% acceptance rate, which indicates the level of competition that occurred during the selection process. All submissions were peer-reviewed by at least three members of the Program Committee. Submissions and the reviewing process were administered by EasyChair, which greatly facilitated these tasks. Continuing with the tradition started by Jan Vitek last year, a face-to-face PC meeting was held in Zurich on Saturday March 19 to discuss all papers and decide the final program. Twelve members attended in person and the other 19 joined by Skype. The meeting significantly contributed to a better analysis of the papers and a more thorough selection process.

The TOOLS Europe 2011 keynote speakers were Oscar Nierstrasz and Frank Tip. Abstracts of their talks are included in these proceedings. We thank them very much for accepting our invitation and for their enlightening talks.

Finally, we would like to acknowledge the work of the many people that made this conference possible. In the first place we would like to thank the Publicity Chair, Esther Guerra, for handling so efficiently all the dissemination activities and for taking care of the website. We would also like to thank the authors for their submissions, whether accepted or not, and the Program Committee members and their subreviewers for their thorough and professional reviews. Alfred Hofmann and the Springer team were really helpful with the publication of this volume. Finally, we would like to warmly thank the TOOLS series General Chair, Bertrand Meyer, and the local organizing team, "Max" Pei Yu, Hans-Christian Estler and Claudia Günthart, from the ETH in Zurich, for their continuous support and great help with all logistic issues.

April 2011

Antonio Vallecillo
Judith Bishop

Organization

Program Committee

Uwe Assmann	TU Dresden, Germany
Alexandre Bergel	University of Chile, Chile
Lorenzo Bettini	Università di Torino, Italy
Judith Bishop	Microsoft Research, USA
William R. Cook	University of Texas at Austin, USA
Juan De Lara	Universidad Autonoma de Madrid, Spain
Wolfgang De Meuter	Vrije Universiteit Brussel, Belgium
Julian Dolby	IBM T.J. Watson Research Center, USA
Sophia Drossopoulou	Imperial College London, UK
Catherine Dubois	ENSIIE-CEDRIC, France
Stephane Ducasse	INRIA Lille, France
Gregor Engels	University of Paderborn, Germany
Erik Ernst	University of Aarhus, Denmark
Benoît Garbinato	University of Lausanne, Switzerland
Jesús García-Molina	Universidad de Murcia, Spain
Angelo Gargantini	University of Bergamo, Italy
Jeff Gray	University of Alabama, USA
Thomas Gschwind	IBM Research, Switzerland
Matthias Hauswirth	University of Lugano, Switzerland
Nigel Horspool	University of Victoria, Canada
Gerti Kappel	Vienna University of Technology, Austria
Doug Lea	State University of New York at Oswego, USA
Welf Löwe	Linnaeus University, Sweden
Peter Müller	ETH Zurich, Switzerland
James Noble	Victoria University of Wellington, New Zealand
Aditya Nori	Microsoft Research, India
Nathaniel Nystrom	University of Texas at Arlington, USA
Manuel Oriol	University of York, UK
Richard Paige	University of York, UK
Ralf Reussner	Karlsruhe Institute of Technology (KIT), Germany
Peter Thiemann	Universität Freiburg, Germany
Nikolai Tillmann	Microsoft Research, USA
Laurence Tratt	Middlesex University, UK
Antonio Vallecillo	Universidad de Málaga, Spain
Arie Van Deursen	Delft University of Technology, The Netherlands
Jan Vitek	Purdue University, USA
Jules White	Vanderbilt University, USA
Manuel Wimmer	Vienna University of Technology, Austria

Additional Reviewers

Arcaini, Paolo
Balzer, Stephanie
Bieniusa, Annette
Bono, Viviana
Brosch, Franz
Burger, Erik
Burroughs, Neil
Capecchi, Sara
Cech, Sebastian
Christ, Fabian
Delaware, Ben
Denker, Marcus
Dietl, Werner
Dolby, Julian
Espinazo-Pagán, Javier
Figueiredo, Eduardo
Geisen, Silke
Gonzalez Boix, Elisa
Grau, Brigitte
Heidegger, Phillip
Heidenreich, Florian
Jacob, Ferosh
Karol, Sven
Koziolek, Anne
Kuehne, Thomas

Küster, Martin
Liegl, Philipp
Liu, Qichao
Loh, Alex
Lombide Carreton, Andoni
Luckey, Markus
Marr, Stefan
Marshall, Stuart
Mayrhofer, Dieter
Mostinckx, Stijn
Nagel, Benjamin
Noorshams, Qais
Pearce, David
Pena, Vanessa
Pierantonio, Alfonso
Riccobene, Elvinia
Scholliers, Christophe
Schreiber, Hendrik
Sánchez Cuadrado, Jesús
Thywissen, John A.
Troya, Javier
Van Der Storm, Tijs
Van Der Straeten, Ragnhild
Wende, Christian
Wieland, Konrad

Table of Contents

Synchronizing Models and Code
(Invited Talk)

Oscar Nierstrasz

Software Composition Group
University of Bern, Switzerland
`http://scg.unibe.ch`

Abstract. Object-oriented development promotes the view that "programming is modeling". Nevertheless, it remains difficult to correlate domain concepts and features with source code, to reconcile static and dynamic views of object-oriented code, and to evolve software of a running system. There continues to be a significant gap between high-level models of software applications and the code that realizes these models. We review some recent research of the Software Composition Group that attempts to address these shortcomings, and we put forward some challenges for future object-oriented development systems.

J. Bishop and A. Vallecillo (Eds.): TOOLS 2011, LNCS 6705, p. 1, 2011.
© Springer-Verlag Berlin Heidelberg 2011

Finding and Fixing Bugs in Web Applications (Invited Talk)

Frank Tip

IBM Thomas J. Watson Research Center
Hawthorne, NY USA
ftip@us.ibm.com

Abstract. Today's society is critically dependent on the existence of web applications. From online purchases to personal banking to mobile devices, web applications are the backbone of the 21st century's economy. However, web applications have a number of characteristics that make them highly fragile and prone to bugs that threaten the important applications they enable. In particular, they are typically written in a combination of multiple languages, they often rely on low-level manipulation of string values to generate dynamic web page content, and the flow of control in web applications usually depends strongly on interactive input from the user. In this presentation, I will present an overview of the Apollo project at IBM Research, which aims to make web applications more robust by assisting programmers with finding and fixing bugs, using automated techniques for test generation, fault localization, and program repair.

J. Bishop and A. Vallecillo (Eds.): TOOLS 2011, LNCS 6705, p. 2, 2011.
© Springer-Verlag Berlin Heidelberg 2011

Test Suite Quality for Model Transformation Chains

Eduard Bauer[1], Jochen M. Küster[1], and Gregor Engels[2]

[1] IBM Research - Zurich, Säumerstr. 4
8803 Rüschlikon, Switzerland
{edb,jku}@zurich.ibm.com
[2] Department of Computer Science, University of Paderborn, Germany
engels@upb.de

Abstract. For testing model transformations or model transformation chains, a software engineer usually designs a test suite consisting of test cases where each test case consists of one or several models. In order to ensure a high quality of such a test suite, coverage achieved by the test cases with regards to the system under test must be systematically measured. Using coverage analysis and the resulting coverage information, missing test cases and redundant test cases can be identified and thereby the quality of the test suite can be improved. As test cases consist of models, a coverage analysis approach must measure how complete models cover the domains of the transformations in the chain and to what degree of completeness transformations are covered when executing the test suite. In this paper, we present a coverage analysis approach for measuring test suite quality for model transformation chains. Our approach combines different coverage criteria and yields detailed coverage information that can be used to identify missing and redundant test cases.

1 Introduction

Model transformations are used nowadays in model-driven engineering for model refinement, model abstraction, and for code generation. Model transformations can either be implemented directly in programming languages (such as Java) or using one of the available transformation languages that have been developed in recent years (e.g. [6,14]). For complex model transformations, several smaller model transformations can be concatenated to build a model transformation chain [22]. Besides reducing the complexity, this enables reuse and distributed development of individual model transformations. One example for such a model transformation chain is a solution for version management of process models in the IBM WebSphere Business Modeler [1].

For testing model transformations or model transformation chains, systematic software testing has to be applied in order to ensure a high quality of the model transformation chain. In this context, a software engineer usually designs a test suite consisting of test cases where each test case consists of one or several models. One important aspect of testing is to measure and ensure a high coverage level which is used to be certain that the test suite and the system under test are of a high quality.

Measuring the coverage level of a test suite requires a coverage analysis approach which allows measuring the coverage achieved by a test case with regards to the model

J. Bishop and A. Vallecillo (Eds.): TOOLS 2011, LNCS 6705, pp. 3–19, 2011.

transformation chain. The result of coverage analysis can then be used to identify missing and redundant test cases. Application of traditional code coverage analysis techniques usually leads to information about non-covered code. However, such information is not sufficient for identifying missing and redundant test cases: It cannot be directly used for constructing new test cases which yield higher coverage and it does not take into account whether test cases cover the domains of model transformations sufficiently.

Existing work on testing model transformations (cf. [4]) shows how a metamodel of the input language of one single model transformation can be used to determine the quality of this model transformation. To the best of our knowledge, there is currently no approach known for measuring test suite quality for model transformation chains. In particular, there exists no means of identifying missing and redundant test cases.

In this paper, we present an approach for measuring test suite quality of model transformation chains. Our approach measures coverage achieved by a test case in the model transformation chain by computing a footprint which contains the main characteristics of the test case execution. Based on the footprints, it is then possible to identify missing and redundant test cases in a test suite. We have validated our approach using a large model transformation chain for version management of process models in the IBM WebSphere Business Modeler [1].

The paper is structured as follows. We first give some fundamentals concerning model transformation chains and coverage analysis, and establish requirements for measuring test suite quality in Section 2. Section 3 introduces a coverage analysis approach for model transformation chains which is then used in Section 4 for identifying missing and redundant test cases. In Section 5 we present our coverage analysis tool which has been used on a larger model transformation chain to improve the quality of a test suite. We discuss related work in Section 6 and conclude.

2 Background and Motivation

A model transformation chain is composed of several individual model transformations. Each model transformation itself transforms one or more source models into one or more target models. To design a model transformation, a software engineer has to define the metamodels that specify the source and target models and implement the transformation definition which contains the logic to transform the models [7]. In addition to the transformation definitions, transformation contracts [8] are used to specify declaratively what a transformation has to do. Such an approach is inspired by the design-by-contract approach [18], adapted for model transformations. To design a model transformation chain, several model transformations are composed so that models produced by one transformation are used for a consecutive model transformation.

In general, a metamodel used to specify the domain of a model transformation can be defined by a standard (i.e. the UML language definition) or it can be domain-specific. In the latter case, the software engineer can define an own domain-specific metamodel, specifying the input/output language of the model transformation. The transformation definition can be expressed using one of the numerous model transformation languages (e.g. QVT [10] or ATL [14]) or using a programming language such as Java. In the case when source and target metamodels are the same, the model transformation is called endogenous model transformation, otherwise it is called exogenous model transformation [7]. Transformation contracts are defined independently of the implementation of the model transformation. They consist of different kinds of contract rules which specify conditions for the models used and created by the model transformation: A precondition rule specifies conditions that have to hold for the source models. A transformation condition rule specifies conditions for the relation between source and target models. A postcondition rule specifies conditions that have to hold for the target models. A variety of possibilities exist to express transformation contracts. Cariou et al. [8] use Object Constraint Language (OCL) to define transformation contracts. Guerra et al. [11] define a separate visual language to specify transformation contracts.

In this paper we use as a case study the complex model transformation chain Compare/Merge Model Transformation Chain (CMTC) that is used in the IBM WebSphere Business Modeler [1] for version management of process models. Given two business process models expressed in Business Process Modeling Notation (BPMN) [19], this model transformation chain computes their differences in the form of a Difference Model. A simplified BPMN metamodel that is used in this paper is shown in Figure 1.

The models of the CMTC and their relation are shown in Figure 2. The rounded rectangles represent models, the arrows show which models are transformed into which other models. The two BPMN models $bpmn_1$ and $bpmn_2$ are transformed into Workflow Graph (WFG) models

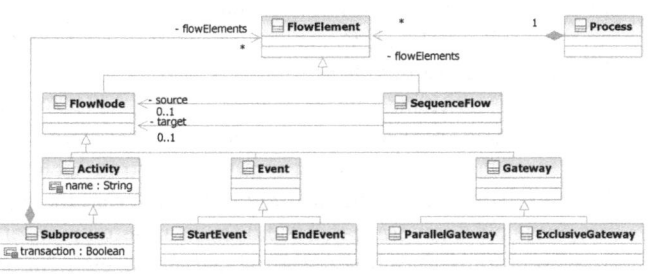

Fig. 1. BPMN Metamodel (Simplified)

wfg_1 and wfg_2. These models are transformed by an endogenous model transformation to models that are called Process Structure Trees (PSTs) (pst_1 and pst_2). The PST models conform to the same metamodel as WFG models but have different properties which are more suitable for difference detection. Comparing the PST models pst_1 and pst_2 yields the model $comp_1$, which maps the model elements that are similar in the two PST models to each other. Finally, based on these PST models and the $comp_1$ model, the $diff_1$ model is computed which represents the difference between the two initial BPMN models. The whole test suite of the model transformation chain CMTC consists of 188 different test cases. A detailed overview of the CMTC is given by Küster et al. [15].

In addition to specifying the domains of the model transformations by metamodels, the CMTC makes use of transformation contracts to specify what the transformations have to do. For the transformation of BPMN

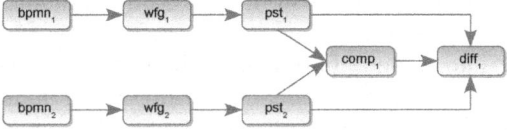

Fig. 2. Models of the CMTC

models into WFG models, one transformation condition rule is that each `Activity` without outgoing edges is transformed into a node in the WFG that is connected to the end of the WFG model.

A complex model transformation chain, such as the CMTC, has to be systematically tested in order to achieve a high quality. Software testing is usually done by creating a number of test cases, consisting of input values and expected results, which define how a software component should behave for a given input. For a model transformation chain, a test suite consists of test cases where each test case consists of models. Two sample test cases for the CMTC are shown in Figure 3, each in a separate column. As the CMTC is used for difference detection for two process models, each test case consists of two process models. The expected Difference models are not shown.

In the context of coverage analysis [2], one uses the concept of a test requirement in order to represent a particular element of the System Under Test (SUT), like for example a statement or a class of the SUT, that has to be tested. The elements that are used as test requirements are defined by coverage criteria. One very common coverage criterion is statement

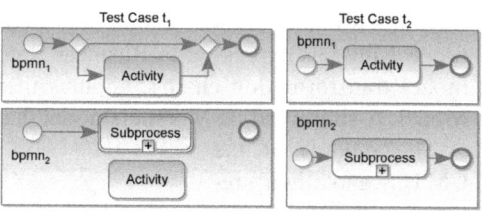

Fig. 3. Test Case 1 and Test Case 2

coverage, which derives a test requirement from each statement of the SUT. Another coverage criterion deriving test requirements from the input domain of model transformations is class coverage that yields a test requirement for each class of the metamodel. A test requirement is covered, if the according element is executed/used by a test case in the test suite. If for example a model contains an instance of a particular class of the metamodel, the according test requirement derived from this class is covered. The result of coverage analysis contains information about covered and non-covered test requirements. This information is called coverage information. Nonetheless, it has to be mentioned that covering all test requirements does not imply absence of faults in the SUT.

For coverage analysis, the SUT is also called coverage artifact. Based on the distinction between source code or specification as two kinds of coverage artifacts, coverage criteria are divided into specification-based and code-based coverage criteria. For model transformation chains, metamodels can be considered as part of the specification as they specify all possible input and output models. Transformation contracts specify the logic of the model transformation by preconditions and postconditions for models.

When analyzing test suite quality for model transformation chains, an approach is required that measures coverage of the domains of the separate model transformations that build the transformation chain. In addition, the coverage of the transformation contracts resulting from models created during the execution of the test suite has to be taken into account. Information about missing test cases should be given in such a way that a tester can use this information to create new test cases which cover a certain part. In this context, endogenous as well as exogenous model transformations have to be supported. For determining redundant test cases, the behavior of test cases in the whole model transformation chain has to be taken into account. The removal of such test cases should not affect the fault detection effectiveness of the test suite.

3 A Combined Coverage Approach

In this section, we present a combined coverage approach [5] for measuring test suite quality of model transformation chains. The combined coverage approach combines different specification-based coverage criteria for model transformation chains. We start by explaining relevant coverage criteria and then elaborate on how coverage analysis is performed.

3.1 Coverage Criteria

Based on the specification of the model transformation chain, test requirements are derived by different coverage criteria from metamodels and transformation contracts.

Metamodel. In the following, we describe coverage criteria for metamodels (partially based on Fleurey et al. [9]). The following examples make use of the BPMN metamodel shown in Figure 1 and one particular instance of this metamodel, shown in Figure 4.

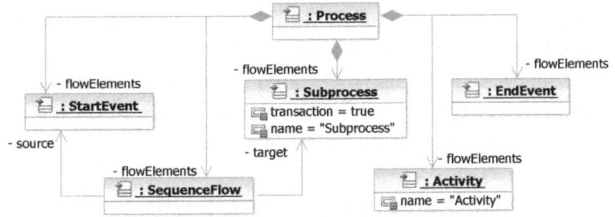

Fig. 4. Abstract Syntax of the *bpmn$_2$* Model of t_1

Class Coverage. The coverage criterion *class coverage* [9] uses the classes of a metamodel to derive test requirements: For each class c in a metamodel, a test requirement is derived. Such a test requirement for a class c is satisfied, if a model (being an instance of the metamodel) contains an object of class c. As instances of the classes StartEvent, Activity, and Process, belong to the BPMN model, the test requirements derived from these classes are satisfied.

Attribute Coverage. The coverage criterion *attribute coverage* [9] derives test requirements from the attributes of the classes of a metamodel. For this, the common software testing technique equivalence partitioning [2] is used. For an attribute a, let D be the domain of the attribute a. Assuming an equivalence partitioning E of D, attribute coverage derives a test requirement for each block $e \in E$. As an example, the equivalence partitioning for attributes with the data type Boolean with the domain $D = \{true, false\}$ is $E = \{\{true\}, \{false\}\}$. This yields two test requirements, one for each block. The BPMN model shown in Figure 4 covers the test requirement derived from the block $\{true\}$ for the attribute Subprocess.transaction.

Association Coverage. The coverage criterion *association coverage* [9] uses associations of a metamodel to derive test requirements. Each association has a multiplicity, which defines the lower and upper number of instances of the association's target class which are allowed to be referenced. Since this can be seen as the domain of associations, equivalence partitionings can again be used in this situation. Let an association a with the lower bound l and upper bound u be given. This yields the domain $D = \{n \in \mathbb{N} \mid l \leq n \leq u\}$. Given an equivalence partitioning E for D, we derive a test requirement for each block $e \in E$ of the equivalence partitioning E for association a. A possible equivalence partitioning for the association `Subprocess.flowElements` is $E = \{\{0\}, \{n \mid n \in \mathbb{N} \land n \geq 1\}\}$, yielding two test requirements. The test requirement for the block $\{0\}$ is covered by the BPMN model shown in Figure 4, as the `Subprocess` does not contain any elements.

Feature Coverage. A feature can be seen as a particular characteristic of a model, such that the model can be considered as a special case. Since models consists of model elements, a feature is a particular combination of several model elements of that model. The coverage criterion feature coverage uses the features defined in the context of a metamodel to derive test requirements. For a feature f defined in the context of a metamodel, a test requirement is created that requires the instances of the metamodel to have the particular combination of model elements defined by feature f. A possible feature for the shown metamodel is the nesting of subprocesses. Describing features by OCL expressions yields the OCL expression `self.flowElements->exists(x | x.oclIsTypeOf(Subprocess))`, defined in the context of the class `Subprocess`. None of the BPMN models shown in Figure 3 cover the test requirement derived from this feature.

Transformation Contract. Transformation contract coverage uses the contract rules of a transformation contract to derive test requirements. For each contract rule cr of a transformation contract, a separate test requirement is created. We call the result of the evaluation of a transformation contract for a sequence of models a contract result. The contract result contains the evaluation of each contract rule which is called contract rule result. A contract rule result is a number which counts how often the condition stated by the contract rule is fulfilled.

For the exemplary contract rule (Each `Activity` without outgoing edges is transformed to a node in the WFG that is connected to the end of the WFG model, cf. Section 2) evaluated on the BPMN model shown in Figure 4, we see that the contract rule result is two as the condition is evaluated twice successfully. The test requirement derived from this contract rule is then satisfied if the contract rule result has a positive value.

3.2   Test Requirements for Model Transformation Chains

The coverage criteria for metamodels and transformation contracts are used to derive test requirements from the specification of a model transformation chain. The combined coverage approach distinguishes between two levels of the specification of model transformation chains, called *type level* and *composition level*. The type level contains all distinct metamodels and transformation contracts. The composition level describes the assembly of these metamodels and transformation contracts and by this defines the structure of the model transformation chain. Here, a metamodel or a transformation contract from the type level can be used at several positions in the structure of

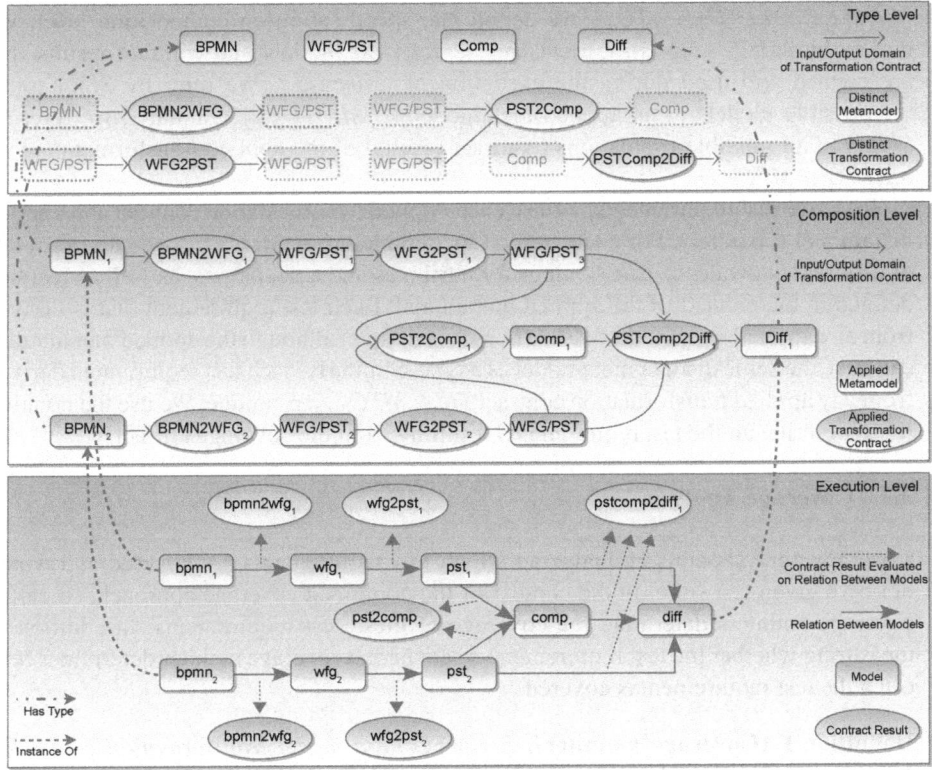

Fig. 5. Specification and Execution Level of CMTC

the model transformation chain. Metamodels and transformation contracts belonging to the composition level are referred to as applied metamodels and applied transformation contracts, respectively.

Figure 5 shows the type level, the composition level and the execution level for the CMTC. The execution level here refers to the models and contract results created and used during one sample execution of the CMTC (cf. Figure 2). The CMTC makes use of four distinct metamodels and four distinct transformation contracts (top of Figure 5). As a transformation contract specifies a model transformation, it refers to the metamodels specifying the domain of the model transformation chain. An incoming arrow to a transformation contract originates from a metamodel specifying the input domain, an outgoing arrow connects to a metamodel specifying the output domain.

On the composition level, the distinct metamodel *BPMN* is applied twice, yielding the two applied metamodels $BPMN_1$ and $BPMN_2$. Similarly, the applied transformation contracts $BPMN2WFG_1$ and $BPMN2WFG_2$ have the transformation contract *BPMN2WFG* as type. During execution, each applied metamodel is instantiated once, each applied transformation contract is evaluated once. For the sake of clarity, we omit some of the dashed lines describing the *has type* and *instance of* relations in Figure 5.

We denote by $MTC_{type} = \{M_1, .., M_k, TC_1, .., TC_l\}$ the set of distinct metamodels and transformation contracts of the model transformation chain *MTC*. With MTC_{comp}

$= \{M_1, ..., M_n, TC_1, ..., TC_m\}$ we denote the specification on composition level. We denote by $MTC_{exec}^t = \{m_1, ..., m_n, tc_1, ..., tc_m\}$ all models and contract results that are created and used during the execution of test case t. We refer by $S(M)$ to all the possible models of an applied metamodel $M \in MTC_{comp}$. Similarly, we refer by $S(TC)$ to all possible evaluations (contract results) of the applied transformation contract $TC \in MTC_{comp}$.

To derive test requirements, we use each applied transformation contract and applied metamodel separately. For each applied metamodel $M \in MTC_{comp}$, we can make use of different equivalence partitionings for attributes and associations, as well as features defined in the context of the applied metamodel. Each test requirement that is derived from any applied metamodel $M \in MTC_{comp}$ is unique, although the applied metamodels can have the same distinct metamodel as a type. Similarly, each test requirement derived from any applied transformation contract $TC \in MTC_{comp}$ is unique. We use the notation R^X to describe all the test requirements resulting from the coverage artifact X.

3.3 Coverage Analysis

Coverage analysis aims at analyzing which test requirements are covered and which not by a given test suite. In the context of the combined coverage approach, so-called coverage counters determine the coverage of these test requirements. In addition to measuring whether the test requirement is satisfied, a coverage counter determines how often the test requirement is covered.

Definition 1 (Coverage Counter). *Let MTC be a model transformation chain. Let* $MTC_{comp} = \{M_1, ..., M_n, TC_1, ..., TC_m\}$ *be the set of applied metamodels and applied transformation contracts for MTC. Let* R^{MTC} *be the set of test requirements derived from* MTC_{comp}*. Let* $r \in R^{MTC}$ *be a test requirement derived from* $X \in MTC_{comp}$*. A coverage counter* c_r*, which measures the coverage of test requirement r, is a function that determines a coverage count for the test requirement r using* $x \in S(X)$*.* c_r *is defined as follows:*

- $c_r : S(M) \rightarrow \mathbb{N}$ *for applied metamodel* $M \in MTC_{comp}$*, from which r is derived.*
- $c_r : S(TC) \rightarrow \mathbb{N}$ *for applied transformation contract* $TC \in MTC_{comp}$*, from which r is derived.*

We say that c_r *accepts a model* $m \in S(M)$*,* $M \in MTC_{comp}$*, if r is derived from M. We say* c_r *accepts* $tc \in S(TC)$*,* $TC \in MTC_{comp}$*, if r is derived from TC.*

As an example, consider the class Activity in the applied metamodel $BPMN_1$ that has the type $BPMN$ (cf. Figure 1 and Figure 5). The coverage of the resulting test requirement r is measured by a coverage counter c_r which counts how often the class Activity is instantiated by a model $bpmn_1$. For the test case t_1, the resulting coverage count is 1 because the test case only contains one instance of type Activity.

Aggregating all coverage counts for all test requirements during the execution of a test case yields the footprint of a test case, which is the central concept representing coverage information in the context of the combined coverage approach. The footprint f_t for a test case t characterizes t in terms of coverage counts for test requirements. By this, the footprint f_t contains information about the parts of the applied metamodels

Table 1. Footprints for Test Cases shown in Figure 3

Model	Test Requirement	t_1	t_2
bpmn1	Activity	1	1
	Subprocess	0	0
	Gateway	2	0
	ParallelGateway	0	0
	ExclusiveGateway	2	0
	($\{true\},\{\{true\},\{false\}\}$, Subprocess.transaction)	0	0
	($\{false\},\{\{true\},\{false\}\}$, Subprocess.transaction)	0	0
	($\{0\},\{\{0\},\{n \mid n \in \mathbb{N} \land n \neq 0\}\}$, Subprocess.flowElements)	0	0
	($\{n \mid n \in \mathbb{N} \land n \neq 0\},\{\{0\},\{n \mid n \in \mathbb{N} \land n \neq 0\}\}$, Subprocess.flowElements)	0	0
	Each Activity without outgoing edges is transformed to a node that is connected to the end of the WFG	0	0
bpmn2	Activity	2	1
	Subprocess	1	1
	Gateway	0	0
	ParallelGateway	0	0
	ExclusiveGateway	0	0
	($\{true\},\{\{true\},\{false\}\}$, Subprocess.transaction)	1	0
	($\{false\},\{\{true\},\{false\}\}$, Subprocess.transaction)	0	1
	($\{0\},\{\{0\},\{n \mid n \in \mathbb{N} \land n \neq 0\}\}$, Subprocess.flowElements)	1	1
	($\{n \mid n \in \mathbb{N} \land n \neq 0\},\{\{0\},\{n \mid n \in \mathbb{N} \land n \neq 0\}\}$, Subprocess.flowElements)	0	0
	Each Activity without outgoing edges is transformed to a node that is connected to the end of the WFG	2	0

and applied transformation contracts that are covered by the test case t. The test requirements and their coverage counts describe the behavior of the test case during the execution of the model transformation chain. Formally, we define:

Definition 2 (Footprint). *Let a model transformation chain MTC be given. Let R^{MTC} be the set of test requirements derived from MTC_{comp}. Let $t \in T$ be a test case of the test suite T. Let $MTC^t_{exec} = \{m_1, ..., m_n, tc_1, ..., tc_m\}$ be the set of models and contract results used or created during the execution of t in MTC. A footprint f_t for the test case t is a function $f_t : R^{MTC} \rightarrow \mathbb{N}$ that maps each $r \in R^{MTC}$ to its coverage count: $f_t(r) = c_r(x)$, with $x \in MTC^t_{exec}$ and c_r accepts x.*

For evaluating the coverage of the test requirement $r \in R^X$ derived from $X \in MTC_{comp}$ only exactly one $x \in MTC^t_{exec}$, with $x \in S(X)$, exists. This results from the construction of the composition level specification. For example, for an applied metamodel $M \in MTC_{comp}$ only exactly one model $m \in MTC^t_{exec}$, with $m \in S(M)$, exists that can cover $r \in R^M$. As a consequence, only one model/contract result $x \in MTC^t_{exec}$ is used by the coverage counter for computing the coverage of a test requirement r.

An extract of footprints for the test cases t_1 and t_2 shown in Figure 3 is presented in Table 1. We use triples for describing the block of an equivalence partitioning for an association or attribute. The first element of the triple describes the block, the second element the equivalence partitioning, and the third element addresses the attribute/association. As an example, for both t_1 and t_2 the coverage count for the test requirement derived from Subprocess is 0 for $bpmn_1$ which shows that both do not contain subprocesses.

During coverage analysis of a given test suite, a footprint is created for each test case. This coverage information is used afterwards for measuring the quality of the test suite which we will describe in the following.

4   Ensuring Test Suite Quality

Test suite quality targets the adequacy and minimality of a test suite. Test suite adequacy is concerned with determining which parts of the model transformation chain are tested by the test suite and which parts remain untested. In contrast to this, analyzing the minimality of a test suite involves identifying redundant test cases that do not yield any new insights for finding faults in the model transformation chain and removing these unnecessary test cases.

4.1   Test Suite Adequacy

To determine the adequacy of a test suite, the information represented by the footprint of each test case is used. One footprint contains information about the parts of the model transformation chain that are executed by one test case–in terms of test requirements derived from applied metamodels and applied transformation contracts and their coverage counts. Combining the footprints of the test cases belonging to the test suite yields information about the parts of the model transformation chain that are tested by the test suite. Untested parts are identified by test requirements, for which the coverage counts are 0 for all test cases of the test suite:

Definition 3 (Unsatisfied Test Requirement). *Let a model transformation chain MTC be given. Let R^{MTC} be the set of test requirements derived from MTC_{comp}. Let $T = \{t_1, ..., t_m\}$ be a test suite for MTC. Let $f_{t_1}, ..., f_{t_m}$ be the footprints of $t_1, ..., t_m$. A test requirement $r \in R^{MTC}$ is called unsatisfied if and only if $\forall t_i \in T : f_{t_i}(r) = 0$.*

As test requirements are derived from applied metamodels and applied transformation contracts, testers of model transformation chains receive feedback from unsatisfied test requirements that is close to the terms and concepts used in the domain of model transformation chains. Accordingly, test cases that are currently missing in the test suite can be easily created by the tester of model transformation chains.

As an example, assume a test suite consisting of the test cases shown in Figure 3. The resulting footprints are shown in Table 1. The table shows several unsatisfied test requirements that we describe in the following:

– The first BPMN models of the two test cases do not contain any Subprocesses, yielding the unsatisfied test requirements derived from the class Subprocess and its attributes and associations which belong to the applied metamodel $BPMN_1$. Due to this, test cases with a model $bpmn_1$ should be created that contain Subprocesses in order to increase coverage.
– The BPMN models do not contain parallel gateways and lead to unsatisfied test requirements for the element ParallelGateway. Here, new test cases which contain parallel gateways should be created.

Based on these observations, a tester can now create a new test case in order to increase the coverage level. Figure 6 shows a possible new test case where the previous deficits have been removed.

In general, if the unsatisfied test requirement is derived from one of the source metamodels, a model from the input language of the model transformation chain can be used to satisfy the test requirement. For satisfying an unsatisfied test requirement that is derived from one of the target metamodels, a model has to be created which is transformed into a target model that covers the test requirement. This can in some cases be difficult as it requires a detailed knowledge of the model transformation chain itself.

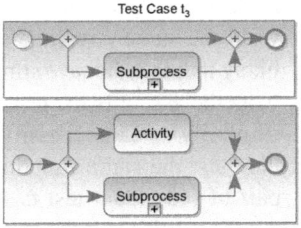

Fig. 6. Test Case t_3

In the context of increasing coverage systematically, the concept of a composition level (which makes use of applied metamodels and applied transformation contracts) has several important advantages:

- For endogenous model transformations, unsatisfied test requirements can be mapped to the source or the target metamodel of the endogenous model transformation.
- The concept of applied metamodels also has advantages for defining features and equivalence partitionings: For example, for the model transformation that transforms WFG models to PST models, we use different features for the source and the target metamodel (which has the same metamodel as type). One feature, for example, requires PST models with exclusive fragments to exist which is meaningless for the same metamodel for WFG models. The reason for this is that WFG models do not make use of combinations of model elements that represent exclusive gateways.

In spite of the support achieved by our approach to systematically increase coverage, it is important to note that the adequacy of a test suite depends on equivalence partitionings for attributes and associations, as well as features defined in the context of applied metamodels. Since the equivalence partitionings and features are defined by the tester/developer of the model transformation chain, the knowledge of these actors influences the adequacy of the test suite.

4.2 Test Suite Minimality

For determining the minimality of the test suite as well as for reducing the test suite, the information provided by footprints of test cases is used. Finding unnecessary test cases that do not yield any insights for finding faults in the model transformation chain is based on comparing the footprints of test cases. If footprints are seen as vectors, the distance between footprints can be used as an indicator for their similarity. We use the Manhattan distance between these vectors to define the distance between footprints:

Definition 4 (Distance Between Footprints). *Let a model transformation chain MTC be given. Let R^{MTC} be the set of test requirements derived from MTC_{comp}. Let $t_1, t_2 \in T$ be two test cases belonging to the test suite T. Let f_{t_1}, f_{t_2} be the footprints of the test cases t_1, t_2. Then the distance $d_{f_{t_1}, f_{t_2}}$ between the footprints f_{t_1} and f_{t_2} is defined as*
$$d_{f_{t_1}, f_{t_2}} = \sum_{r \in R^{MTC}} |f_{t_1}(r) - f_{t_2}(r)|.$$

In the case when the distance between footprints of two test cases is zero, the test cases yield the same coverage counts for all test requirements. As a consequence it is very likely that they behave similarly during the execution of the model transformation chain. Nonetheless, only the tester of the model transformation chain can approve the complete similarity and unnecessity of such test cases. We call these test cases redundant since they test the same functionality of the model transformation chain. An example for a pair of redundant test cases for the CMTC is the test case t_2 shown in Figure 3 and the test case t_4 shown in Figure 7. These test cases have the same footprints for the CMTC (distance between footprints: 0) because the difference detection is based on the structure of the graph and not on the names of the activities.

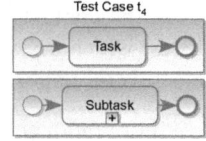

Fig. 7. Test Case t_4

One test case of a pair of redundant test cases can be removed from the test suite without affecting the fault detection effectiveness of the test suite. Extending this idea to partition the test suite into partitions of mutually redundant test cases and using one test case out of each partition yields the redundancy reduction algorithm.

The pseudo code for this algorithm is given in Algorithm 1. The input of the redundancy reduction is a test suite T and the set of footprints F, which contains a footprint f_t for each test case $t \in T$. The result of the algorithm is the reduced test suite T', which does not contain any redundant test cases. The `for each` loop in lines 4-10 creates partitions of mutually redundant test cases $p \in P$. All test cases that are redundant to each other belong to one partition p. Observe that the `for each` loop iterates over each pair of footprints f_{t_i} and f_{t_j} with a distance of 0. This also holds true for any single footprint $f_{t_i} \in F$. Thus, in the case when t_i is not redundant to any other test case t_j, this yields a partition $p = \{f_{t_i}\}$.

The problem of reducing the size of the test suite while maintaining the satisfied test requirements is called the test suite reduction problem [12]. The solution to this problem is a so-called smallest reduced test suite that covers the same test requirements as the whole test suite. Compared to the known test suite reduction heuristics our redundancy reduction has two advantages:

First of all, by retaining redundant test cases that do not yield any new insights for finding faults in the model transformation chain, the fault detection effectiveness of the test suite should usually not be affected. This is different for the fault detection effectiveness of the reduced test suites that are computed by test suite reduction heuristics (e.g. [21,13]).

Secondly, redundancy reduction does not favor large test cases, which subsume other test cases. For example, it does not favor test cases whose footprints have higher coverage counts for each test requirement compared to other footprints. Keeping large test cases in the reduced test suite is usually a property of the test suite reduction heuristics, as large test cases tend to subsume small test cases in terms of covered test requirements. Accordingly, the reduced test suite resulting from the redundancy reduction does not necessarily consist of test cases consisting of large models which are usually poorly maintainable.

Algorithm 1. Redundancy Reduction

    Input : $T = \{t_1, ..., t_n\}$ test suite
    Input : $F = \{f_{t_1}, ..., f_{t_n}\}$ footprints of test cases $T = \{t_1, ..., t_n\}$
    Output: $T' \subseteq T$ reduced test suite

1 `redundancyReduction`(T, F)
2 | $T' \leftarrow \emptyset$;
3 | $P \leftarrow \emptyset$;
4 | **foreach** $f_{t_i}, f_{t_j} \in F$ with $d_{f_{t_i}, f_{t_j}} = 0$ **do**
5 | | **if** $\exists p \in P : \exists f \in p : d_{f, f_{t_i}} = 0$ **then**
6 | | | add f_{t_i}, f_{t_j} to p
7 | | **else**
8 | | | $P \leftarrow P \cup \{\{f_{t_i}, f_{t_j}\}\}$
9 | | **end**
10 | **end**
11 | **foreach** $p \in P$ **do**
12 | | $t \leftarrow t_i \in T$ for exactly one $f_{t_i} \in p$;
13 | | $T' \leftarrow T' \cup t$;
14 | **end**
15 | **return** T';
16 **end**

---

5 Tool Support and Validation

For supporting the combined coverage approach, we have created the Test Suite Analyzer for model transformation chains, which consists of a set of Eclipse plug-ins. The Test Suite Analyzer supports obtaining coverage information as well as investigating the coverage information. Figure 8 shows a screenshot and illustrates the obtained coverage information (bottom of figure) and one particular footprint (top of figure). The supported use cases are shown in Table 2.

Table 2. Summary of Applications of the Combined Coverage Approach

Use Case	Description
Coverage Analysis	
Adjustment of coverage analysis	For performing the coverage analysis, the user is provided with functionality to express equivalence partitionings for attributes and associations, define features in the context of applied metamodels, and specify transformation contracts for transformation definitions.
Performing coverage analysis	During performing coverage analysis, the actual calculation of the coverage information in terms of footprints for test cases is created and persisted. An overview of the results is shown in the view at the bottom of Figure 8.
Investigation of coverage information	
Display/Compare Footprints	Different views are provided for the analysis of separate footprints as well as for the comparison of different footprints.
Redundancy Computation	Computation of pairs of redundant test cases.
Reduction of Test Suite	Application of the redundancy reduction algorithm. Removal of redundant test cases.
Identification of unsatisfied test requirements	The information about unsatisfied test requirements is shown to the user.

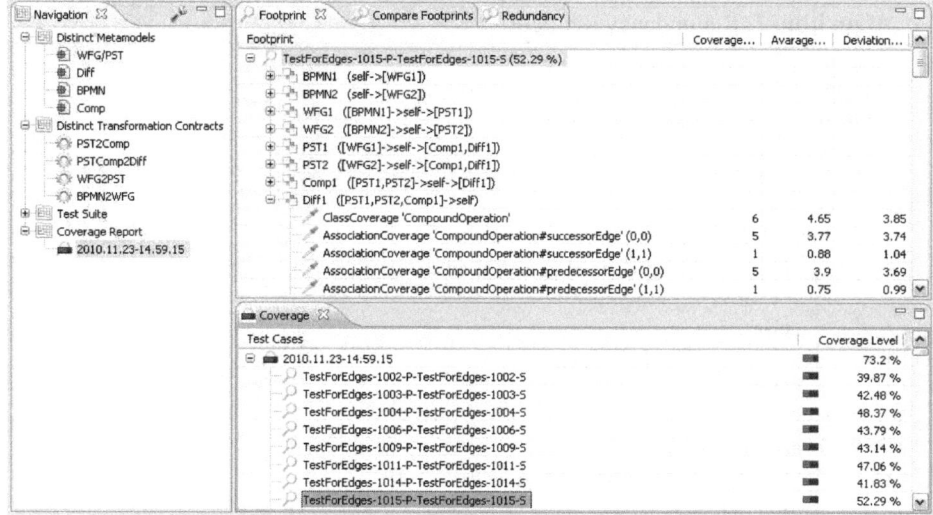

Fig. 8. Test Suite Analyzer for model transformation chains

Applying the combined coverage approach to the model transformation chain CMTC had the following results: Analyzing the adequacy of the test suite provided information about several unsatisfied test requirements. For example, nested subprocesses were identified as missing. The subsequent creation of test cases containing nested subprocesses uncovered some faults in the model transformation chain. Concerning the minimality of the test suite, 27 pairs of redundant test cases have been identified. The main reason for such a high number is the creation of the test suite by different people and the lack of maintenance of the test suite throughout the years. The redundancy reduction algorithm allowed us to remove 19 test cases from the overall 188 test cases. A manual investigation showed that only those test cases that behaved similarly to other test cases were removed. Accordingly, the fault detection effectiveness of the reduced test suite should be comparable to the fault detection effectiveness of the whole test suite. The Test Suite Analyzer has already been successfully used when evolving the CMTC for supporting another input language for the process models.

6   Related Work

In the domain of software testing, several coverage criteria exist to determine the adequacy of test suites. McQuillan et al. [17] introduces a code-based coverage criterion for model transformations to derive test requirements from transformation definitions composed in ATLAS Transformation Language (ATL). In contrast to their work, we focus on specification-based coverage analysis as this facilitates the derivation of test cases for increasing coverage.

Specification-based coverage analysis has been studied by Andrews et al. [3]. They define coverage criteria for models composed in Unified Modeling Language (UML), including coverage criteria for UML class diagrams. Andrews et al. define three coverage criteria, which are called association-end multiplicity criterion, generalization criterion, and class attribute criterion. Fleurey et al. [9] adapt the approach of Andrews et al. for deriving test requirements from the source metamodel of a model transformation. In our approach, we extend metamodel coverage to applied metamodels that are used at any position of the model transformation chain. Furthermore, we introduce transformation contract coverage which allows us to analyse coverage also for the transformation logic.

To determine similarity between test cases, the domain of software profiling makes use of execution profiles for test cases. Leon et al. [16] as well as Yan et al. [23] detect similar test cases by defining metrics for computing the distance between execution profiles. Yan et al. [23] use the euclidean distance between execution profiles for this computation. In contrast to using euclidean distance, we make use of the Manhattan distance, although both possibilities yield the same results for finding redundant test cases.

Reducing the size of the test suite based on coverage information is a common problem in software testing–the test suite reduction problem [12]. Solving this problem requires finding the smallest possible subset of test cases which satisfies the same test requirements as the whole test suite. Harrold et al. [12] formulate this problem mathematically and show that finding such a subset is NP-hard. They present the first heuristic to solve this problem. In recent years, several different test suite reduction heuristics have been published (see e.g. [20]). A drawback of such heuristics is the potentially decreased fault detection effectiveness of the reduced test suite. Empirical experiments (see e.g. [21]) yield the conclusion that the simple reduction of the test suite, based on the test suite reduction problem and the test suite reduction heuristics, decreases the fault detection effectiveness of the test suite significantly. In contrast to these reductions, we make use of redundant test cases to reduce the test suite, which does not decrease the fault detection effectiveness of the test suite. In addition, other than test suite reduction heuristics, our approach does not tend to retain large test cases in the test suite which are difficult to understand and maintain.

7 Conclusion

Coverage analysis achieved by test cases for a model transformation chain is important for ensuring the quality of the test suite. In particular, such coverage analysis must allow the software engineer to discover missing and redundant test cases. In this paper, we have introduced the combined coverage approach for measuring the quality of a test suite. Our approach is independent of a specific model transformation language and computes a so-called footprint of a test case. This footprint allows a detailed analysis and is also used for identification of missing and redundant test cases. We have validated our approach on a large model transformation chain where it has been used for discovering several missing and redundant test cases.

Future work includes the automatic generation of missing test cases based on the result of coverage analysis. Another direction of future work is a detailed investigation of how results from our coverage analysis approach relate to traditional code coverage analysis approaches.

References

1. IBM WebSphere Business Modeler,
   http://www.ibm.com/software/integration/wbimodeler/
2. Ammann, P., Offutt, J.: Introduction to Software Testing. Cambridge University Press, New York, NY, USA (2008)
3. Andrews, A., France, R., Ghosh, S., Craig, G.: Test Adequacy Criteria for UML Design Models. Software Testing, Verification and Reliability 13(2), 95–127 (2003)
4. Baudry, B., Dinh-Trong, T., Mottu, J.-M., Simmonds, D., France, R., Ghosh, S., Fleurey, F., Le Traon, Y.: Model Transformation Testing Challenges. In: Proceedings of IMDT workshop in conjunction with ECMDA 2006, Bilbao, Spain (2006)
5. Bauer, E.: Analyzing Test Suites for Model Transformation Chains. Master's thesis, University of Paderborn (2010)
6. Csertán, G., Huszerl, G., Majzik, I., Pap, Z., Pataricza, A., Varró, D.: VIATRA: Visual Automated Transformations for Formal Verification and Validation of UML Models. In: ASE 2002: 17th IEEE International Conference on Automated Software Engineering, pp. 267–270. IEEE Computer Society Press, Los Alamitos (2002)
7. Czarnecki, K., Helsen, S.: Feature-based Survey of Model Transformation Approaches. IBM Systems Journal 45(3), 621–645 (2006)
8. Cariou, E., Marvie, R., Seinturier, L., Duchien, L.: OCL for the Specification of Model Transformation Contracts. In: Workshop OCL and Model Driven Engineering of the Seventh International Conference on UML Modeling Languages and Applications UML 2004, Lisbon, Portugual, October 12 (2004)
9. Fleurey, F., Baudry, B., Muller, P., Le Traon, Y.: Qualifying Input Test Data for Model Transformations. Software and Systems Modeling 8(2), 185–203 (2009)
10. Object Management Group (OMG). Meta Object Facility (MOF) 2.0 Query/View/Transformation Specification Version 1.1 (January 2011)
11. Guerra, E., de Lara, J., Kolovos, D., Paige, R.: A Visual Specification Language for Model-to-Model Transformations. In: IEEE Symposium on Visual Languages and Human-Centric Computing, vol. 0, pp. 119–126. IEEE Computer Society Press, Los Alamitos (2010)
12. Harrold, M.J., Gupta, R., Soffa, M.L.: A Methodology for Controlling the Size of a Test Suite. ACM Transactions on Software Engineering and Methodology 2(3), 270–285 (1993)
13. Heimdahl, M., George, D.: Test-suite Reduction for Model Based Tests: Effects on Test Quality and Implications for Testing. In: Proceedings of the 19th IEEE International Conference on Automated Software Engineering (ASE), pp. 176–185. IEEE Computer Society, Los Alamitos (2004)
14. Jouault, F., Allilaire, F., Bézivin, J., Kurtev, I.: ATL: A Model Transformation Tool. Science of Computer Programming 72(1-2), 31–39 (2008)
15. Küster, J.M., Gerth, C., Förster, A., Engels, G.: Detecting and Resolving Process Model Differences in the Absence of a Change Log. In: Dumas, M., Reichert, M., Shan, M.-C. (eds.) BPM 2008. LNCS, vol. 5240, pp. 244–260. Springer, Heidelberg (2008)
16. Leon, D., Podgurski, A., White, L.: Multivariate Visualization in Observation-based Testing. In: ICSE 2000: Proceedings of the 22nd International Conference on Software Engineering, pp. 116–125. ACM Press, New York (2000)
17. McQuillan, J., Power, J.: White-Box Coverage Criteria for Model Transformations. In: 1st International Workshop on Model Transformation with ATL, Nantes, France, July 8-9 (2009)
18. Meyer, B.: Applying "Design by Contract". Computer 25(10), 40–51 (1992)
19. Object Management Group (OMG). Business Process Modeling Notation, V2.0 Beta 2 (June 2010)

20. Parsa, S., Khalilian, A., Fazlalizadeh, Y.: A New Algorithm to Test Suite Reduction Based on Cluster Analysis. In: International Conference on Computer Science and Information Technology, vol. 0, pp. 189–193 (2009)
21. Rothermel, G., Harrold, M.J., Ostrin, J., Hong, C.: An Empirical Study of the Effects of Minimization on the Fault Detection Capabilities of Test Suites. In: ICSM 1998: Proceedings of the International Conference on Software Maintenance, pp. 34–43. IEEE Computer Society Press, Los Alamitos (1998)
22. von Pilgrim, J., Vanhooff, B., Schulz-Gerlach, I., Berbers, Y.: Constructing and Visualizing Transformation Chains. In: Schieferdecker, I., Hartman, A. (eds.) ECMDA-FA 2008. LNCS, vol. 5095, pp. 17–32. Springer, Heidelberg (2008)
23. Yan, S., Chen, Z., Zhao, Z., Zhang, C., Zhou, Y.: A Dynamic Test Cluster Sampling Strategy by Leveraging Execution Spectra Information. In: ICST 2010: Proceedings of the 2010 Third International Conference on Software Testing, Verification and Validation, pp. 147–154. IEEE Computer Society Press, Washington, DC, USA (2010)

Automated Translation of Java Source Code to Eiffel

Marco Trudel[1], Manuel Oriol[2], Carlo A. Furia[1], and Martin Nordio[1]

[1] Chair of Software Engineering, ETH Zurich, Switzerland
{marco.trudel,carlo.furia,martin.nordio}@inf.ethz.ch
[2] University of York, United Kingdom
{manuel@cs.york.ac.uk}

Abstract. Reusability is an important software engineering concept actively advocated for the last forty years. While reusability has been addressed for systems implemented using the same programming language, it does not usually handle interoperability with different programming languages. This paper presents a solution for the reuse of Java code within Eiffel programs based on a source-to-source translation from Java to Eiffel. The paper focuses on the critical aspects of the translation and illustrates them by formal means. The translation is implemented in the freely available tool J2Eif; it provides Eiffel replacements for the components of the Java runtime environment, including Java Native Interface services and reflection mechanisms. Our experiments demonstrate the practical usability of the translation scheme and its implementation, and record the performance slow-down compared to custom-made Eiffel applications: automatic translations of *java.util* data structures, *java.io* services, and SWT applications can be re-used as Eiffel programs, with the same functionalities as their original Java implementations.

1 Introduction

Code reuse has been actively advocated for the past forty years [12], has become a cornerstone principle of software engineering, and has bred the development of serviceable mechanisms such as modules, libraries, objects, and components. These mechanisms are typically language-specific: they make code reuse practical within the boundaries of the same language, but the reuse of "foreign" code written in a specific language within a program written in a different "host" language is a problem still lacking universally satisfactory solutions. The reuse of foreign code is especially valuable for languages with a small development community: some programmers may prefer the "host" language because its design and approach are more suitable for their application domain, but if only a small community uses this languages, they also have to wait for reliable implementations of new services and libraries unless there is a way to reuse the products available, sooner and in better form, for a more popular "foreign" language. For example, the first Eiffel library offering encryption[1] was released in 2008 and still

---

[1] http://code.google.com/p/eiffel-encryption-library/

J. Bishop and A. Vallecillo (Eds.): TOOLS 2011, LNCS 6705, pp. 20–35, 2011.
© Springer-Verlag Berlin Heidelberg 2011

is in alpha status, while Java has offered encryption services in the *java.security* standard package since 2002.

A straightforward approach to reuse foreign code is to wrap it into components and access it natively through a bridge library which provides the necessary binding. This solution is available, for example, in Eiffel to call external C/C++ code—with the *C-Eiffel Call-In* Library (CECIL)—and Java code—with the *Eiffel2Java* Library; the Scala language achieves interoperability with Java using similar mechanisms. Such bridged solutions execute the foreign code in its native environment which is not under direct control of the host's; this introduces potential vulnerabilities as guarantees of the host environment (provided, for example, by its static type system) may be violated by the uncontrolled foreign component. More practically, controlling the foreign components through the interface provided by the bridge is often cumbersome and results in code difficult to maintain. For example, creating an object wrapping an instance of *java.util.LinkedList* and adding an element to it requires six instructions with Eiffel2Java, some mentioning Java API's signatures encoded as strings such as *method_id := list.method_id* ("**add**", "**(Ljava/lang/Object;)Z**").

A source-to-source translation of the foreign code into the host does not incur the problems of the bridged solutions because it builds a functionally equivalent implementation in another language. The present paper describes a translation of Java source into Eiffel and its implementation in the tool J2Eif [8]. While Eiffel and Java are both object-oriented languages, the translation of one into the other is tricky because superficially similar constructs, such as those for exception handling, often have very different semantics. In fact, correctness is arguably the main challenge of source-to-source translation: Section 3 formalizes the most delicate aspects of the translation to describe how they have been tackled and to give confidence in the correctness of the translation.

As shown by experiments in Section 4, J2Eif can translate non-trivial Java applications into functionally equivalent Eiffel ones; the system also provides replicas of Java's runtime environment and a precompiled JDK standard library. The usage of the translated code is, in most cases, straightforward for Eiffel programmers; for example, creating an instance *l* of *java.util.LinkedList* and adding an element *e* to it becomes the mundane (at least for Eiffel programmers):

create *l.make_JAVA_UTIL_LINKEDLIST* ; *r := l.method_add_from_object* (*e*)

Since Eiffel compiles to native code, a valuable by-product of J2Eif is the possibility of compiling Java applications to native code. The experiments in Section 4 show that Java applications automatically translated into Eiffel with J2Eif incur in a noticeable slow-down—especially those making an intense use of translated data-structure implementations. The slow-down is unsurprising, as a generic, automated translation scheme is no substitute for a carefully designed re-engineering that makes use of Eiffel's peculiarities. Using J2Eif, however, enables the fast reuse of new Java libraries in Eiffel applications—a valuable service to access Java's huge codebase in a form congenial to Eiffel programmers. Performance enhancement belongs to future work.

Section 2 gives an overview of the architecture of J2Eif; Section 3 describes the translation in detail; Section 4 evaluates the implementation with four experiments and points out its major limitations; Section 5 discusses related work; Section 6 concludes.

2   Design Principles

J2Eif [8] is a stand-alone compiler with graphical user interface that translates Java programs to Eiffel programs. The translation is a complete Eiffel application which replicates the functionalities of the Java source application by including replacements of the Java runtime environment (most notably, the Java Native Interface and reflection mechanisms). J2Eif is implemented in Java.

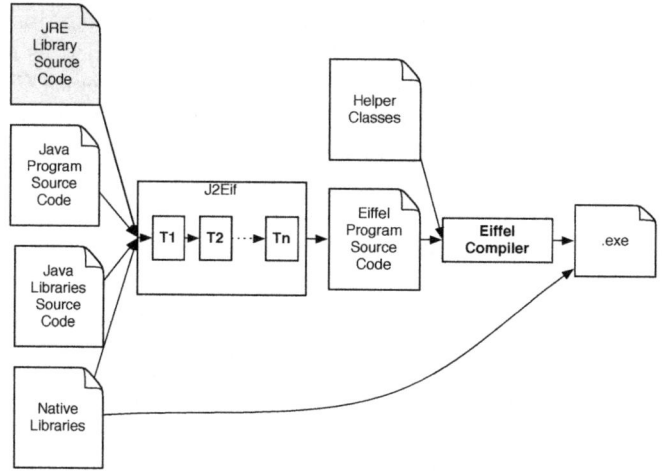

Fig. 1. High-level view of J2Eif

High-level view. Figure 1 shows the high-level usage of J2Eif. To translate a Java program, the user provides the source code of the program, its Java dependencies, as well as any external native libraries referenced by the program. J2Eif produces Eiffel source code that can be compiled by an Eiffel compiler such as EiffelStudio. Native libraries called by native methods in Java are then directly called from Eiffel. While J2Eif can compile the complete code of the Java Runtime Environment (JRE) library source, it comes with a precompiled version which drastically reduces the overall compilation time.

Translation. J2Eif implements the mapping $\mathcal{T}$: Java $\rightarrow$ Eiffel of Java code into Eiffel code. Both languages follow the object-oriented paradigm and hence share several notions such as objects, classes, methods, and exceptions. Nonetheless, the semantics of the same notion in the two languages are often quite different.

Section 3 describes all the aspects taken into account by the translation and focuses on its particularly delicate features by formalizing them.

J2Eif implements the translation $\mathcal{T}$ as a series $T_1, \ldots, T_n$ of successive incremental transformations on the Abstract Syntax Tree. Every transformation T_i takes care of exactly one language construct that needs adaptation and produces a program in an intermediate language L_i which is a mixture of Java and Eiffel constructs: the code progressively *morphs* from Java to Eiffel code.

$$\mathcal{T} \equiv T_n \circ \cdots \circ T_1, \text{ where } \begin{cases} T_1 : & \text{Java} \rightarrow L_1 \\ T_2 : & L_1 \rightarrow L_2 \\ & \cdots \\ T_n : & L_{n-1} \rightarrow \text{Eiffel} \end{cases}$$

The current implementation uses 35 such transformations (i.e., $n = 35$). Combining small transformations has some advantages: several of the individual transformations are straightforward to implement and all are simple to maintain; it facilitates reuse when building other translations (for example into a language other than Eiffel); the intermediate programs generated are readable and easily reviewable by programmers familiar with Java and Eiffel.

3 Translating Java to Eiffel

This section describes the salient features of the translation $\mathcal{T}$ from Java to Eiffel, grouped by topic. Eiffel and Java often use different names for comparable object-oriented concepts; to avoid ambiguities, the present paper matches the terms in the presentation, whenever possible without affecting readability, and uses only the appropriate one when discussing language-specific aspects. Table 1 lists the Java and Eiffel names of fundamental object-oriented concepts.

Table 1. Object-oriented terminology in Java and Eiffel

Java	Eiffel	Java	Eiffel
class	class	member	feature
abstract/interface	deferred	field	attribute
concrete	effective	method	routine
exception	exception	constructor	creation procedure

3.1 Language Features

We formalize some components of $\mathcal{T}$ by breaking it down into simpler functions denoted by ∇; these functions are a convenient way to formalize $\mathcal{T}$ and, in general, different than the transformations T_i discussed in Section 2; the end of the present section sketches an example of differences between ∇'s and T_i's. The following presentation ignores the renaming scheme, discussed separately (Section 3.4), and occasionally overlooks inessential syntactic details. The syntax of Eiffel's exception handling adheres to the working draft 20.1 of the ECMA Standard 367; adapting it to work with the syntax currently supported is trivial.

Classes and interfaces. A Java program is defined by a collection of classes; the function ∇_C maps a single Java class or interface into an Eiffel class or deferred (abstract) class.

$$\begin{aligned}
\mathcal{T}(C_1, ..., C_n) &= \nabla_C(C_1), \ldots, \nabla_C(C_n)\\
\nabla_C(\textbf{class } name \text{ extend } \{ \text{ body } \}) &= \textbf{class } name \ \nabla_I(\text{extend}) \ \nabla_B(\text{body}) \ \textbf{end}\\
\nabla_D(\textbf{interface } name \text{ extend } \{ \text{ body } \}) &= \textbf{deferred class } name \ \nabla_I(\text{extend}) \ \nabla_{iB}(\text{body}) \ \textbf{end}
\end{aligned}$$
where $name$ is a class name; $extend$ is a Java inheritance clause; and $body$ a Java class body.

∇_I translates Java inheritance clauses (**extends** and **implements**) into Eiffel **inherit** clauses. The translation relies on two helper classes:

JAVA_PARENT is ancestor to every translated class, to which it provides helper routines for various services such as access to the native interface, exceptions, integer arithmetic (integer division, modulo, and shifting have different semantics in Java and Eiffel), strings. The rest of this section describes some of these services in more detail.

JAVA_INTERFACE_PARENT is ancestor to every translated interface.

Java generic classes and interfaces may have complex constraints which cannot be translated directly into Eiffel constraints on generics. $\mathcal{T}$ handles usages of genericity with the same approach used by the Java compiler: it erases the generic constraints in the translation but enforces the intended semantics with explicit type casts added where needed.

Members (features). ∇_B and ∇_{iB} respectively translate Java class and interface bodies into Eiffel code. The basic idea is to translate Java fields and (abstract) methods respectively into Eiffel attributes and (deferred) routines. A few features of Java, however, have no clear Eiffel counterpart and require a more sophisticated approach:

Anonymous classes are given an automatically generated name.
Arguments and attributes can be assigned to by default in Java, unlike in Eiffel where arguments are read-only and modifying attributes requires setter methods. To handle these differences, the translation $\mathcal{T}$ introduces a helper generic class *JAVA_VARIABLE* [G]. Instances of this class replace Java variables; assignments to arguments and attributes in Java are translated to suitable calls to the routines in the helper class.
Constructor chaining is made explicit with calls to **super**.
Field hiding is rendered by the naming scheme introduced by $\mathcal{T}$ (Section 3.4).
Field initializations and initializers are added explicitly to every constructor.
Inner classes are extracted into stand-alone classes, which can access the same outer members (features) as the original inner classes.
JavaDoc comments are ignored.
Static members. Eiffel's **once** routines can be invoked only if they belong to effective (not deferred) classes; this falls short of Java's semantics for static members of abstract classes. For each Java class C, the translation $\mathcal{T}$ introduces a class *C_STATIC* which contains all of C's static members and is inherited by the translation of C; multiple inheritance accommodates such helper classes. *C_STATIC* is always declared as effective (not deferred), so that static members are always accessible in the translation as **once** routines.

Varargs arguments are replaced by arguments of type array.

Visibility. Eiffel's visibility model is different than Java's, as it requires, in particular, to list all names of classes that can access a non-public member. $\mathcal{T}$ avoids this issue by translating every member into a *public* Eiffel feature.

Instructions. ∇_M maps Java method bodies to Eiffel routine bodies. As expected, ∇_M is compositional: $\nabla_M(\text{inst}_1 \ ; \ \text{inst}_2) = \nabla_M(\text{inst}_1) \ ; \ \nabla_M(\text{inst}_2)$, hence it is sufficient to describe how ∇_M translates Java instructions into Eiffel. The translation of many standard instructions is straightforward; for example, the Java conditional **if** (*cond*){*doThen*} **else** {*doElse*} becomes the Eiffel conditional **if** $\nabla_E(cond)$ **then** $\nabla_M(doThen)$ **else** $\nabla_M(doElse)$ **end**, where ∇_E maps Java expressions to equivalent Eiffel expressions. The following presents the translation of the constructs which differ the most in the two languages.

Loops. The translation of *loops* is tricky because Java allows control-flow breaking instructions such as **break**. Correspondingly, the translation of **while** loops relies on an auxiliary function $\nabla_W : \text{JavaInstruction} \times \{\top, \bot\} \rightarrow \text{EiffelInstruction}$ which replicates the semantics in presence of **break** (with $\mathsf{t} \in \{\top, \bot\}$):

$$
\begin{aligned}
\nabla_M(\textbf{while (stayIn) \{body\}}) &= \textbf{from } breakFlag := \textbf{False} \\
&\quad \textbf{until not } \nabla_E(\text{stayIn}) \textbf{ or } breakFlag \\
&\quad \textbf{loop } \nabla_W(\text{body}, \bot) \textbf{ end} \\
\nabla_W(\textbf{break}, \mathsf{t}) &= breakFlag := \textbf{True} \\
\nabla_W(\text{inst}_1 \ ; \ \text{inst}_2, \mathsf{t}) &= \begin{cases} \nabla_W(\text{inst}_1, \mathsf{t}) \ ; \ \nabla_W(\text{inst}_2, \top) & \text{if inst}_1 \text{ contains } \textbf{break} \\ \nabla_W(\text{inst}_1, \mathsf{t}) \ ; \ \nabla_W(\text{inst}_2, \mathsf{t}) & \text{if inst}_1 \text{ doesn't contain } \textbf{break} \end{cases} \\
\nabla_W(\text{atomicInst}, \top) &= \textbf{if not } breakFlag \textbf{ then } \nabla_M(\text{atomicInst}) \textbf{ end} \\
\nabla_W(\text{atomicInst}, \bot) &= \nabla_M(\text{atomicInst})
\end{aligned}
$$

The **break** instruction becomes, in Eiffel, an assignment of **True** to a fresh boolean flag *breakFlag*, specific to each loop. Every instruction within the loop body which follows a **break** is then guarded by the condition **not** *breakFlag* and the loop is exited when the flag is set to **True**. Other types of loops (**for**, **do..while**, **foreach**) and control-flow breaking instructions (**continue**, **return**) are translated similarly.

Exceptions. Both Java and Eiffel offer exceptions, but with very different semantics and usage. The major differences are:

- Exception handlers are associated to whole routines in Eiffel (**rescue** block) but to arbitrary (possibly nested) blocks in Java (**try..catch** blocks).
- The usage of control-flow breaking instructions (e.g., **break**) in Java's **try.. finally** blocks complicates the propagation mechanism of exceptions [15].

The function ∇_M translates Java's **try..catch** blocks into Eiffel's agents (similar to closures, function objects, or delegates) with **rescue** blocks, so that exception handling is block-specific and can be nested in Eiffel as it is in Java:

$\nabla_M(\textbf{try} \{\text{doTry}\} \ \textbf{catch} \ (t \ e) \ \{\text{doCatch}\}) = skipFlag := \textbf{False}$
$\qquad\qquad (\textbf{agent} \ (args) \ \textbf{do}$
$\qquad\qquad\qquad \textbf{if not} \ skipFlag \ \textbf{then} \nabla_M(\text{doTry}) \ \textbf{end}$
$\qquad\qquad \textbf{rescue}$
$\qquad\qquad\qquad \textbf{if} \ e.conforms\_to \ (\nabla_T(t)) \ \textbf{then}$
$\qquad\qquad\qquad\qquad \nabla_M(\text{doCatch}) \ ; Retry := \textbf{True} \ ; skipFlag := \textbf{True}$
$\qquad\qquad\qquad \textbf{else} \ Retry := \textbf{False end}$
$\qquad\qquad\qquad \textbf{end}).call$
$\nabla_M(\textbf{throw} \ (exp)) \qquad = (\textbf{create} \ \{EXCEPTION\}).raise \ (\nabla_E(exp))$

The agent's body contains the translation of Java's try block. If executing it raises an exception, the invocation of *raise* on a fresh exception object transfers control to the **rescue** block. The **rescue**'s body executes the translation of the **catch** block only if the type of the exception raised matches that declared in the **catch** (∇_T translates Java types to appropriate Eiffel types, see Section 3.2). Executing the **catch** block may raise another exception; then, another invocation of *raise* would transfer control to the appropriate outer **rescue** block: the propagation of exceptions works similarly in Eiffel and Java. On the contrary, the semantics of Eiffel and Java diverge when the **rescue/catch** block terminates without exceptions. Java's semantics prescribes that the computation continues normally, while, in Eiffel, the computation propagates the exception (if *Retry* is **False**) or transfers control back to the beginning of the **agent**'s body (if *Retry* is **True**). The translation ∇_M sets *Retry* to **False** if **catch**'s exception type is incompatible with the exception raised, thus propagating the exception. Otherwise, the **rescue** block sets *Retry* and the fresh boolean flag *skipFlag* to **True**: control is transferred back to the **agent**'s body, which is however just skipped because *skipFlag* = **True**, so that the computation continues normally after the **agent** without propagating any exception.

An exception raised in a **try..finally** block is normally propagated after executing the **finally**; the presence of control-flow breaking instructions in the **finally** block, however, cancels the propagation. For example, the code block:

$b=2; \ \textbf{while(true)}\{\textbf{try}\{\textbf{throw new} \ Exception();\}\textbf{finally}\{b++; \ \textbf{break};\}\}$
$b++;$

terminates *normally* (without exception) with a value of 4 for the variable b.

The translation ∇_M renders such behaviors with a technique similar to the Java compiler: it duplicates the instructions in the **finally** block, once for normal termination and once for exceptional termination:

$\nabla_M(\textbf{try} \{\text{doTry}\} \ \textbf{finally} \ \{\text{doFinally}\}) = skipFlag := \textbf{False}$
$\qquad\qquad (\textbf{agent} \ (args) \ \textbf{do}$
$\qquad\qquad\qquad \textbf{if not} \ skipFlag \ \textbf{then} \nabla_M(\text{doTry} \ ; \text{doFinally}) \ \textbf{end}$
$\qquad\qquad \textbf{rescue} \ \nabla_M(\text{doFinally})$
$\qquad\qquad\qquad \textbf{if} \ breakFlag \ \textbf{then}$
$\qquad\qquad\qquad\qquad Retry := \textbf{True} \ ; skipFlag := \textbf{True}$
$\qquad\qquad\qquad \textbf{end}$
$\qquad\qquad\qquad \textbf{end}).call$

A **break** sets *breakFlag* and, at the end of the **rescue** block, *Retry* and *skipFlag*; as a result, the computation continues without exception propagation. Other control-flow breaking instructions are translated similarly.

Other instructions. The translation of a few other constructs is worth discussing.

Assertions. Java's **assert** *exp* raises an exception if *exp* evaluates to **false**, whereas a failed **check** *exp* **end** in Eiffel sends a signal to the runtime which terminates execution or invokes the debugger. Java's assertions are therefore translated as **if not** *exp* **then** ∇_M(**throw** (**new** *AssertionError* ())) **end**.

Block locals are moved to the beginning of the current method; the naming scheme (Section 3.4) prevents name clashes.

Calls to parent's methods. Eiffel's **Precursor** can only invoke the parent's version of the overridden routine currently executed, not any feature of the parent. The translation $\mathcal{T}$ augments every method with an extra boolean argument *predecessor* and calls **Precursor** when invoked with *predecessor* set to **True**; this accommodates any usage of **super**:

$$\nabla_B(\text{type } method \text{ (args) \{ body \})} = method \text{ (args ; predecessor: BOOLEAN): } \nabla_T(\text{type}) \textbf{ do}$$
$$\textbf{if } predecessor \textbf{ then Precursor } (args, \textbf{False})$$
$$\textbf{else } \nabla_M \text{ (body) } \textbf{end}$$
$$\textbf{end}$$
$$\nabla_E (method(\text{exp})) = method \text{ } (\nabla_E(\text{exp}), \textbf{False})$$
$$\nabla_E (\textbf{super}.method(\text{exp})) = method \text{ } (\nabla_E(\text{exp}), \textbf{True})$$

Casting and type conversions are adapted to Eiffel with the services provided by the helper class *JAVA_TYPE_HELPER*.

Expressions used as instructions are wrapped into the helper routine *dev_null* (*a: ANY*): $\nabla_M(\text{exp}) = dev\_null \text{ } (\nabla_E \text{ (exp)})$.

Switch statements become **if..elseif..else** blocks in Eiffel, nested within a loop to support fall-through.

How J2Eif implements $\mathcal{T}$. As a single example of how the implementation of $\mathcal{T}$ deviates from the formal presentation, consider J2Eif's translation of exception-handling blocks **try**{doTry} **catch**(*t e*){doCatch} **finally**{doFinally}:

```
skipFlag := False ; rethrowFlag := False
(agent (args) do
    if not skipFlag then ∇M (doTry)
    else if e.conforms_to (∇T (t)) then ∇M (doCatch) else rethrowFlag := True end end
    skipFlag := True ; ∇M (doFinally)
    if rethrowFlag and not breakFlag then (create {EXCEPTION}).raise end
    rescue if not skipFlag then skipFlag := True ; Retry := True end
    end).call
```

This translation applies uniformly to all exception-handling code and avoids duplication of the **finally** block, hence the **agent**'s body structure is more similar to the Java source. The formalization ∇_M above, however, allows for a more focused presentation and lends itself to easier formal reasoning (see Section 4.1). A correctness proof of the implementation could then establish that ∇_M and the implementation J2Eif describe translations with the same semantics.

3.2   Types and Structures

The naming scheme (Section 3.4) handles references to classes and interfaces as types; primitive types and some other type constructors are discussed here.

Primitive types with the same machine size are available in both Java and Eiffel: Java's **boolean, char, byte, short, int, long, float**, and **double** exactly correspond to Eiffel's *BOOLEAN*, *CHARACTER_32*, *INTEGER_8*, *INTEGER_16*, *INTEGER_32*, *INTEGER_64*, *REAL_32*, and *REAL_64*.

Arrays in Java become instances of Eiffel's helper *JAVA_ARRAY* class, which inherits from the standard EiffelBase *ARRAY* class and adds all missing Java functionalities to it.

Enumerations and annotations are syntactic sugar for classes and interfaces respectively extending *java.lang.Enum* and *java.lang.annotation.Annotation*.

3.3   Runtime and Native Interface

This section describes how J2Eif replicates, in Eiffel, JRE's functionalities.

Reflection. Compared to Java, Eiffel has only limited support for reflection and dynamic loading. The translation $\mathcal{T}$ ignores dynamic loading and includes all classes required by the system for compilation. The translation itself also generates reflection data about every class translated and adds it to the produced Eiffel classes; the data includes information about the parent class, fields, and methods, and is stored as objects of the helper *JAVA_CLASS* class. For example, $\mathcal{T}$ generates the routine *get_class* for *JAVA_LANG_STRING_STATIC*, the Eiffel counterpart to the static component of *java.lang.String*, as follows:

```
get_class: JAVA_CLASS once ("PROCESS")
    create Result.make ("java.lang.String")
    Result.set_superclass (create {JAVA_LANG_OBJECT_STATIC})
    Result.fields.extend (["count" field data])
    Result.fields.extend (["value" field data])
    ...
    Result.methods.extend (["equals" method data]))
    ...
end
```

Concurrency. J2Eif includes a modified translation of *java.lang.Thread* which inherits from the Eiffel *THREAD* class and maps Java threads' functionalities to Eiffel threads; for example, the method *start()* becomes a call to the routine *launch* of class *THREAD*. *java.lang.Thread* is the only JRE library class which required a slightly *ad hoc* translation; all other classes follow the general scheme presented in the present paper.

Java's **synchronized** methods work on the implicit *monitor* associated with the current object. The translation to Eiffel adds a *mutex* attribute to every class which requires synchronization, and explicit locks and unlocks at the entrance and exit of every translated **synchronized** method:

$$\nabla_B(\textbf{synchronized } type\ method(\text{args})\{\text{body}\}) = method\ (\text{args}): \nabla_T(type)$$
$$\textbf{do } mutex.lock\ ;\ \nabla_M(\text{body})\ ;\ mutex.unlock\ \textbf{end}$$

Native interface. Java Native Interface (JNI) supports calls to and from precompiled libraries from Java applications. JNI is completely independent of the rest of the Java runtime: a C **struct** includes, as function pointers, all references to native methods available through the JNI. Since Eiffel includes an extensive support to call external C code through the CECIL library, replicating JNI's functionalities in J2Eif is straightforward. The helper class *JAVA_PARENT*— accessible in every translated class—offers access to a **struct** *JNIEnv*, which contains function pointers to suitable functions wrapping the native code with CECIL constructs. This way, the Eiffel compiler is able to link the native implementations to the rest of the generated binary.

This mechanism works for all native JRE libraries except for the Java Virtual Machine (*jvm.dll* or *jvm.so*), which is specific to the implementation (OpenJDK in our case) and had to be partially re-implemented for usage within J2Eif. The current version includes new implementations of most JVM-specific services, such as *JVM_FindPrimitiveClass* to support reflection or *JVM_ArrayCopy* to duplicate array data structures, and verbatim replicates the original implementation of all native methods which are not JVM-specific (such as *JVM_CurrentTimeMillis* which reads the system clock). The experiments in Section 4 demonstrate that the current JVM support in J2Eif is extensive and sufficient to translate correctly many Java applications.

Garbage collector. The Eiffel garbage collector is used without modifications; the marshalling mechanism can also collect JNI-maintained instances.

3.4   Naming

The goal of the renaming scheme introduced in the translation $\mathcal{T}$ is three-fold: to conform to Eiffel's naming rules, to make the translation as readable as possible (i.e., to avoid cumbersome names), and to ensure that there are no name clashes due to different conventions in the two languages (for example, Eiffel is completely case-insensitive and does not allow in-class method overload).

To formalize the naming scheme, consider the functions η, ϕ, and λ:

- η normalizes a name by successively (1) replacing all "_" with "_1", (2) replacing all "." with "_", and (3) changing all characters to uppercase—for example, $\eta(java.lang.String)$ is *JAVA_LANG_STRING*;
- $\phi(n)$ denotes the fully-qualified name of the item n—for example, $\phi(String)$ is, in most contexts, *java.lang.String*;
- $\lambda(v)$ is an integer denoting the nesting depth of the block where v is declared—for example, in the method **void** *foo*(**int** a){**int** b; **for**(**int** c=0;...)...}, it is $\lambda(a) = 0$, $\lambda(b) = 1$, $\lambda(c) = 2$.

Then, the functions $\Delta_C, \Delta_F, \Delta_M, \Delta_L$ respectively define the renaming scheme for class/interface, field, method, and local name; they are defined as follows, where $\oplus$ denotes string concatenation, "className" refers to the name of the class of the current entity, and ϵ is the empty string.

$$\Delta_C(\text{className}) = \eta(\phi(\text{className}))$$
$$\Delta_F(\text{fieldName}) = \text{``}field\text{''} \oplus \lambda(\text{fieldName}) \oplus \text{``\_''} \oplus \text{fieldName} \oplus \text{``\_''} \oplus \Delta_C(\text{className})$$
$$\Delta_L(\text{localName}) = \text{``}local\text{''} \oplus \lambda(\text{localName}) \oplus \text{``\_''} \oplus \text{localName}$$
$$\Delta_M(\text{className(args)}) = \text{``}make\_\text{''} \oplus \Delta_A(\text{args}) \oplus \Delta_C(\text{className})$$
$$\Delta_M(\text{methodName(args)}) = \text{``}method\_\text{''} \oplus \text{methodName} \oplus \Delta_A(\text{args})$$
$$\Delta_A(t_1\ n_1, \ldots, t_m\ n_m) = \begin{cases} \epsilon & \text{if } m = 0 \\ \text{``}from\_\text{''} \oplus \delta(t_1) \oplus \ldots \oplus \delta(t_m) & \text{if } m > 0 \end{cases}$$
$$\delta(t) = \begin{cases} \text{``}p\text{''} \oplus t & \text{if } t \text{ is a primitive type} \\ t & \text{otherwise} \end{cases}$$

The naming scheme renames classes to include their fully qualified name. It labels fields and appends to their name their nesting depth (higher than one for nested classes) and the class they belong to; similarly, it labels locals and includes their nesting depth in the name. It pre-pends "*make*" to constructors—whose name in Java coincides with the class name—and "*method*" to other methods. To translate overloaded methods, it includes a textual description of the method's argument types to the renamed name, according to function Δ_A; an extra p distinguishes primitive types from their boxed counterparts (e.g., **int** and *java.lang.Integer*). Such naming scheme for methods does not use the fully qualified name of argument types. This favors the readability of the names translated over certainty of avoiding name clashes: a class may still overload a method with arguments of different type but sharing the same unqualified name (e.g., *java.util.List* and *org.eclipse.Swt.Widgets.List*). This, however, is extremely unlikely to occur in practice, hence the chosen trade-off is reasonable.

4   Evaluation

This section briefly discusses the correctness of the translation $\mathcal{T}$ (Section 4.1); evaluates the usability of its implementation J2Eif with four case studies (Section 4.2); and concludes with a discussion of open issues (Section 4.3).

4.1   Correctness of the Translation

While the formalization of $\mathcal{T}$ in the previous sections is not complete and overlooks some details, it is useful to present the translation clearly, and it even helped the authors find a few errors in the implementation when its results did not match the formal model. Assuming an operational semantics for Java and Eiffel (see [17]), one can also reason about the components of $\mathcal{T}$ formalized in Section 3 and increase the confidence in the correctness of the translation. This section gives an idea of how to do it; a more accurate analysis would leverage a proof assistant to ensure that all details are taken care of appropriately.

The operational semantics defines the effect of every instruction I on the program state: $\sigma \xrightarrow{I} \sigma'$ denotes that executing I on a state σ transforms the state to σ'. The states σ, σ' may also include information about exceptions and non-terminating computations. While a Java and an Eiffel state are in general different, because they refer to distinct execution models, it is possible to define an equivalence relation $\simeq$ that holds for states sharing the same "abstract" values [17], which can be directly compared. With these conventions, it is possible to prove correctness of the formalized translation: the effect of executing a translated Eiffel instruction on the Eiffel state replicates the effect of executing the original Java instruction on the corresponding Java state. Formally, the correctness of the translation of a Java instruction I is stated as: "For every Java state σ_J and Eiffel state σ_E such that $\sigma_J \simeq \sigma_E$, if $\sigma_J \xrightarrow{I} \sigma'_J$ and $\sigma_E \xrightarrow{\nabla_M(I)} \sigma'_E$ then $\sigma'_J \simeq \sigma'_E$."

The proof for the the Java block B: **try** $\{\text{doTry}\}$ **catch** $(t\ e)\{\text{doCatch}\}$, translated to $\nabla_M(B)$ as shown on page 26, is now sketched. A state σ is split into two components $\sigma = \langle v, e \rangle$, where e is ! when an exception is pending and $\star$ otherwise. The proof works by structural induction on B; all numeric references are to Nordio's operational semantics [17, Chap. 3]; for brevity, consider only one inductive case.

doTry raises an exception handled by doCatch. $\langle v_J, \star \rangle \xrightarrow{\text{doTry}} \langle v'_J, ! \rangle$, the type τ of the exception raised conforms to t, and $\langle v'_J, ! \rangle \xrightarrow{\text{doCatch}} \langle v''_J, e \rangle$, hence $\langle v_J, \star \rangle \xrightarrow{B} \langle v''_J, e \rangle$ by (3.12.4). Then, both $\langle v_E, \star \rangle \xrightarrow{\nabla_M(\text{doTry})} \langle v'_E, ! \rangle$ and $\langle v'_E, ! \rangle \xrightarrow{\nabla_M(\text{doCatch})} \langle v''_E, e' \rangle$ hold by induction hypothesis, for some $v'_E \simeq v'_J$, $v''_E \simeq v''_J$, and $e' \simeq e$. Also, $e.conforms\_to\ (\nabla_T(t))$ evaluates to false on the state v'_E. In all, $\langle v_E, \star \rangle \xrightarrow{\nabla_M(B)} \langle v''_E, e' \rangle$ by (3.10) and the rule for **if..then**.

4.2 Experiments

Table 2 shows the results of four experiments run with J2Eif on a Windows Vista machine with a 2.66 GHz Intel dual-core CPU and 4 GB of memory. Each experiment consists in the translation of a system (stand-alone application or library). Table 2 reports: (1) the size in lines of code of the source (J for Java) and transformed system (E for Eiffel); (2) the size in number of classes; (3) the source-to-source compilation time (in seconds) spent to generate the translation ($\mathcal{T}$, which does not include the compilation from Eiffel source to binary); (4) the size (in MBytes) of the standard (s) and optimized (o) binaries generated by EiffelStudio; (5) the number of dependent classes needed for the compilation (the SWT snippet entry also reports the number of SWT classes in parentheses). The rest of the section discusses the experiments in more detail.

Table 2. Experimental results

	Size (locs)		#Classes		Compilation (sec.)	Binary Size (MB)		#Required Classes
	J	E	J	E	$\mathcal{T}$	s	o	
HelloWorld	5	92	1	2	1	254	65	1208
SWT snippet	34	313	1	6	47	318	88	1208 (317)
java.util.*	51,745	91,162	49	426	7	254	65	1175
java.io tests	11,509	28,052	123	302	6	255	65	1225

HelloWorld. The *HelloWorld* example is useful to estimate the minimal number of dependencies included in a stand-alone application; the size of 254 MB (65 MB optimized) is the smallest footprint of any application generated with J2Eif.

SWT snippet. The SWT snippet generates a window with a browsable calendar and a clock. While simple, the example demonstrates that J2Eif correctly translates GUI applications and replicates their behavior: this enables Eiffel programmers to include in their programs services from libraries such as SWT.

java.util.* classes. Table 3 reports the results of performance experiments on some of the translated version of the 49 data structure classes in *java.util.* For each Java class with an equivalent data structure in EiffelBase, we performed tests which add 100 elements to the data structure and then perform 10000 removals of an element which is immediately re-inserted. Table 3 compares the time (in ms) to run the test using the translated Java classes (column 2) to the performance with the native EiffelBase classes (column 4).

Table 3. Performance of translated *java.util* classes

Java class	Java time	Eiffel class	Eiffel time	Slowdown
ArrayList	582	*ARRAYED_LIST*	139	4.2
Vector	620	*ARRAYED_LIST*	139	4.5
HashMap	1,740	*HASH_TABLE*	58	30
Hashtable	1,402	*HASH_TABLE*	58	24.2
LinkedList	560	*LINKED_LIST*	94	6
Stack	543	*ARRAYED_STACK*	26	20.9

The overhead introduced by some features of the translation adds up in the tests and generates the significant overall slow-down shown in Table 3. The features that most slowed down the translated code are: (1) the indirect access to fields via the *JAVA_VARIABLE* class; (2) the more structured (and slower) translation of control-flow breaking instructions; (3) the handling of exceptions with agents (whose usage is as expensive as method call). Applications that do not heavily exercise data structures (such as GUI applications) are not significantly affected and do not incur a nearly as high overhead.

java.io test suite. The part of the Mauve test suite [11] focusing on testing input/output services consists of 102 classes defining 812 tests. The tests with J2Eif excluded 10 of these classes (and the corresponding 33 tests) because they relied on unsupported features (see Section 4.3). The functional behavior of the tests is identical in Java and in the Eiffel translation: both runs fail 25 tests and pass 754. Table 4 compares the performance of the test suite with Java against its Eiffel translation; the two-fold slowdown achieved with optimizations is, in all, usable and reasonable—at least in a first implementation of J2Eif.

Table 4. Performance in the *java.io* test suite

	Overall time (s)	Average time per test (ms)	Slowdown
Java	4	5	1
Eiffel standard	21	27	5.4
Eiffel optimized	9	11	2.2

4.3 Limitations

There is a limited number of features which J2Eif does not handle adequately; ameliorating them belongs to future work.

Unicode strings. J2Eif only supports the ASCII character set; Unicode support in Eiffel is quite recent.

Serialization mechanisms are not mapped adequately to Eiffel's.

Dynamic loading mechanisms are not rendered in Eiffel; this restricts the applicability of J2Eif for applications heavily depending on this mechanism, such as J2Eif itself which builds on the Eclipse framework.

Soft, weak, and phantom references are not supported, because similar notions are currently not available in the Eiffel language.

Readability. While the naming scheme tries to strike a good balance between readability and correctness, the generated code may still be less pleasant to read than in a standard Eiffel implementation.

Size of compiled code. The generated binaries are generally large. A finer-grained analysis of the dependencies may reduce the JRE components that need to be included in the compilation.

5 Related Work

There are two main approaches to reuse implementations written in a "foreign" language within another "host" language: using wrappers for the components written in the "foreign" language and bridging them to the rest of the application written in the "host" language; and translating the "foreign" source code into functionally equivalent "host" code.

Wrapping foreign code. A wrapper enables the reuse a foreign implementation through the API provided by a bridge library [5,4,19,13]. This approach does not change the foreign code, hence there is no risk of corrupting it or of introducing inconsistencies; on the other hand, it is usually restrictive in terms of the type of data that can be retrieved through the bridging API (for example, primitive types only). J2Eif uses the wrapping approach for Java's native libraries (Section 3.3): the original Java wrappers are replaced by customized Eiffel wrappers.

Translating foreign code. Industrial practices have long encompassed the manual, systematic translation of legacy code to new languages. More recently, researchers proposed semi-automated translation for widely-used legacy programming languages such as COBOL [2,14], Fortran-77 [1,21], and C [23]. Other progress in this line has come from integrating domain-specific knowledge [6], and testing and visualization techniques [18] to help develop the translations.

Other related efforts target the transformation of code into an extension (superset) of the original language. Typical examples are the adaptation of legacy code to object-oriented extensions, such as from COBOL to OO-COBOL [16,20,22], from Ada to Ada95 [10], and from C to C++ [9,24]. Some of such efforts try to go beyond the mere execution of the original code by refactoring it to be more conforming to the object-oriented paradigm; however, such refactorings are usually limited to restructuring modules into classes.

As far as fully automated translations are concerned, compilation from a high-level language to a low-level language (such as assembly or byte-code) is of course a widespread technology. The translation of a high-level language into another high-level language with different features—such as the one performed by J2Eif—is much less common; the closest results have been in the rewriting of domain-specific languages, such as TXL [3], into general-purpose languages.

Google web toolkit [7] (GWT) includes a project involving translation of Java into JavaScript code. The translation supports running Java on top of JavaScript, but its primary aims do not include readability and modifiability of the code generated, unlike the present paper's translation. Another relevant difference is that GWT's translation lacks any formalization and even the informal documentation does not detail which features are not perfectly replicated by the translation. The documentation warns the users that "subtle differences" may exist,[2] but only recommends testing as a way to discover them.

6   Conclusions

This paper presented a translation T of Java programs into Eiffel, and its implementation in the freely available tool J2Eif [8]. The formalization of T built confidence in its correctness; a set of four experiments of varying complexity tested the usability of the implementation J2Eif.

Future work includes more tests with applications from different domains; the extension of the translation to include the few aspects currently unsupported (in particular, Unicode strings and serialization); and the development of optimizations for the translation, to make the code generated closer to original Eiffel implementations.

Acknowledgements. Thanks to Mike Hicks and Bertrand Meyer for their support and advice, and to Louis Rose for comments on a draft of this paper.

---

[2] `http://code.google.com/webtoolkit/doc/latest/tutorial/JUnit.html`

References

1. Achee, B.L., Carver, D.L.: Creating object-oriented designs from legacy FORTRAN code. Journal of Systems and Software 39(2), 179–194 (1997)
2. Canfora, G., Cimitile, A., Lucia, A.d., Lucca, G.A.D.: A case study of applying an eclectic approach to identify objects in code. In: IWPC, pp. 136–143 (1999)
3. Cordy, J.R.: Source transformation, analysis and generation in TXL. In: PEPM, pp. 1–11 (2006)
4. de Lucia, A., Di Lucca, G.A., Fasolino, A.R., Guerra, P., Petruzzelli, S.: Migrating legacy systems towards object-oriented platforms. In: Proc. of ICSM, pp. 122–129 (1997)
5. Dietrich, W.C., Nackman Jr., L.R., Gracer, F.: Saving legacy with objects. SIG-PLAN Not. 24(10), 77–83 (1989)
6. Gall, H., Klosch, R.: Finding objects in procedural programs: an alternative approach. In: WCRE, pp. 208–216 (1995)
7. Google Web toolkit (2010), http://code.google.com/webtoolkit/
8. J2Eif. The Java to Eiffel translator (2010), http://jaftec.origo.ethz.ch
9. Kontogiannis, K., Patil, P.: Evidence driven object identification in procedural code. In: STEP, pp. 12–21 (1999)
10. Llamosí, A., Strohmeier, A. (eds.): Ada-Europe 2004. LNCS, vol. 3063. Springer, Heidelberg (2004)
11. Mauve project (2010), http://sources.redhat.com/mauve/
12. Mcilroy, D.: Mass-produced software components. In: ICSE, pp. 88–98 (1968)
13. Meyer, B.: The component combinator for enterprise applications. In: JOOP, vol. 10(8), pp. 5–9 (1998)
14. Millham, R.: An investigation: reengineering sequential procedure-driven software into object-oriented event-driven software through UML diagrams. In: COMPSAC, 2002, pp. 731–733 (2002)
15. Müller, P., Nordio, M.: Proof-Transforming Compilation of Programs with Abrupt Termination. In: SAVCBS 2007, Dubrovnik, Croatia, pp. 39–46 (2007)
16. Newcomb, P., Kotik, G.: Reengineering procedural into object-oriented systems. In: WCRE, pp. 237–249 (1995)
17. Nordio, M.: Proofs and Proof Transformations for Object-Oriented Programs. PhD thesis, ETH Zurich (2009)
18. Postema, M., Schmidt, H.W.: Reverse engineering and abstraction of legacy systems. Informatica, 37–55 (1998)
19. Serrano, M.A., Carver, D.L., de Oca, C.M.: Reengineering legacy systems for distributed environments. J. Syst. Softw. 64(1), 37–55 (2002)
20. Sneed, H.M.: Migration of procedurally oriented cobol programs in an object-oriented architecture. In: Software Maintenance, pp. 105–116 (1992)
21. Subramaniam, G.V., Byrne, E.J.: Deriving an object model from legacy Fortran code. In: ICSM, pp. 3–12 (1996)
22. Wiggerts, T., Bosma, H., Fielt, E.: Scenarios for the identification of objects in legacy systems. In: WCRE, pp. 24–32 (1997)
23. Yeh, A., Harris, D., Reubenstein, H.: Recovering abstract data types and object instances from a conventional procedural language. In: WCRE, pp. 227–236 (1995)
24. Zou, Y., Kontogiannis, K.: A framework for migrating procedural code to object-oriented platforms. In: APSEC, pp. 390–399 (2001)

A Generic Solution for Syntax-Driven Model Co-evolution

Mark van den Brand, Zvezdan Protić, and Tom Verhoeff

Eindhoven University of Technology
P.O. Box 513, 5600 MB Eindhoven, The Netherlands
{M.G.J.v.d.Brand,Z.Protic,T.Verhoeff}@tue.nl

Abstract. In this paper we discuss, and provide a generic solution to the problem referred to as *model co-evolution*: How to evolve models in case their metamodels evolve?

We solve this problem by extending a traditional three-step approach. In the first step, differences between an original and an evolved metamodel are determined. Unlike traditional approaches, we treat metamodels as models conforming to a special metamodel, thus the same difference representation and calculation mechanisms for metamodels as for models are used in our approach. In the second step, metamodel differences are classified into four groups based on their possible influence on co-evolving models, and the possibilities of handling them automatically. We adopt two of these groups (*non-breaking* and *breaking and resolvable* differences) from the existing co-evolution approaches, and we introduce two new groups (*breaking and semi-resolvable* and *breaking and human-resolvable* differences). In the third step, based on the determined metamodel differences, a generic co-evolution transformation is invoked. This transformation takes the metamodel differences, and a model as arguments, and returns an adapted model.

We validated our approach by incorporating our method into a prototype tool for generic model co-evolution, and by testing this tool on a large set of metamodels and models.

1   Introduction

Model evolution is a frequent research topic in the context of model-driven engineering. Modelers often need to determine the extent and the nature of changes between different versions of the same model. To understand the evolution of a model, modelers compare two versions of that model, and visualize the resulting differences.

Traditionally, models are described as instances of metamodels that, in turn, are instances of a selected metametamodel. Without exception, metametamodels (e.g. MOF [20] or Ecore [9]) allow for the representation of models as hierarchical labeled attributed graphs, i.e. each model can be represented as a tree[1].

---

[1] Model elements are nodes of the tree, and edges of the tree are aggregation relations between model elements.

J. Bishop and A. Vallecillo (Eds.): TOOLS 2011, LNCS 6705, pp. 36–51, 2011.
© Springer-Verlag Berlin Heidelberg 2011

The model differences are also considered as trees in [4,18,15,10,1], and the comparison of models [17,1] is based on tree comparison techniques [3].

There are two conceptually different types of approaches to the representation and calculation of model differences. In the *state-based* approaches, the model differences are calculated between two states of a model, i.e. between two versions of a model. In the *operation-based* (also called *change-based*) approaches, the model differences are represented by a set of *operations* which when applied to the initial model produce the final model. Thus, in the *operation-based* approaches, all the tools used to develop models must supply the *operations* in a predefined form, while in the *state-based* approaches this is not necessary. Visualization of the model differences is usually accomplished by superimposing the model differences on the old version of a model, and by using different colors to denote different types of differences (e.g. green for added, red for deleted, and blue for changed model elements) [24,2].

Often, the metamodels also evolve in the modeling process, either during development or during maintenance[2]. This raises the question of *co-evolution of models*[3]: how to adapt models conforming to the original version of a metamodel such that they conform to the target (evolved) version of that metamodel? Since metamodels in model-based engineering correspond to languages in language-based engineering, model co-evolution can be compared to the situation in language-based engineering, where a new version of a programming language requires adaptation of the source code written in the old version of a language. Similar problems also exist in database schema evolution, where evolution of a database schema (which corresponds to a metamodel of the underlying data) induces evolution of the related database content.

The basic idea of existing approaches to model co-evolution, which we also adopt here, is: first calculate the differences between an evolved metamodel and an original version of the same metamodel, and then, based on those differences, (semi-)automatically generate model differences. The schematic of our approach is depicted in Figure 1.

In this paper we consider model co-evolution in the context of model configuration management systems. Therefore, we have specified a set of requirements that a co-evolution process should satisfy in order to be efficiently usable in such systems, and we have defined our co-evolution process to satisfy these requirements:

1. The co-evolved models are syntactically correct, i.e., conforming to the new metamodel.
2. The difference between the old model and the new (co-evolved) model is minimal, i.e., only 'necessary' changes are carried through.
3. The co-evolution process allows for (user-defined) extensions to preserve semantic correctness.

---

[2] Similarly to *model difference*, a *metamodel difference* denotes the change set between an old and a new version of a metamodel.

[3] Also called *coupled evolution of models* or *coupled evolution of metamodels and models*.

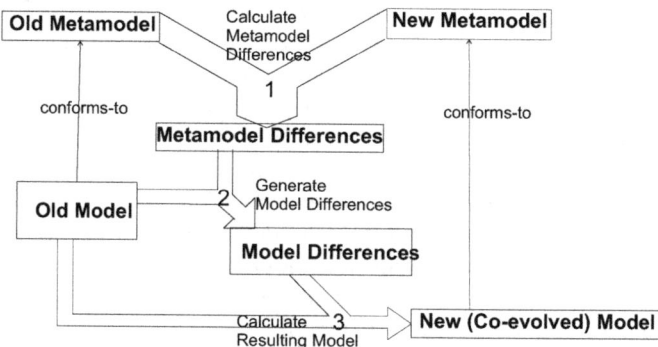

Fig. 1. The schematic of our approach to co-evolution of models

4. The co-evolution process itself maximizes automation, i.e., minimizes human intervention, and where intervention is unavoidable it should be well-defined.

In order to satisfy the *first* requirement our process of co-evolution is guided by syntax. We decided to focus on syntax because in co-evolution approaches which deal with *state-based* (meta)model differences, it is very hard to correctly infer the intention of a developer in case of complex changes. Thus, in the *state-based* co-evolution approaches it is much harder to reason about the influence of metamodel changes on models, than in the co-evolution approaches that deal with *operation-based* model differences, where the intent of the model developer is discernible from the nature and the order of the operations supplied by tools. Therefore, in our approach we consider only the syntactic structure and the static semantics of models as a basis of the *automated* part of the co-evolution process, and do not take into account dynamic semantics of models. By dynamic semantics we mean a formal system of rules (e.g. Structured Operational Semantics), that allows reasoning about the behavior of systems represented by models. Thus, in contrast to approaches to database schema evolution, which are geared towards automatic resolution of semantic issues (i.e. retaining the relations between data items), but are constrained only to schema evolution, we loosen the requirement of *automatic resolution* of semantic issues, in order to be more generic and to support arbitrary metamodels. Hence, our approach can support the co-evolution of databases, ontologies, state machines, petri-nets, etc. Nonetheless, as specified in the *third* requirement, it is possible to define user extensions to ensure the semantic correctness of the co-evolved models. This means that advanced algorithms for schema evolution or petri-net evolution can be applied as extensions to our approach.

The *second* requirement states that the co-evolved model should be changed as little as possible to conform to the new metamodel, thus allowing efficient implementation of our approach in configuration management systems.

The *fourth* requirement states that the co-evolution process should be as automatic as possible, and that the reasons for, and extent of, human interventions should be well-specified and minimized. In this regard, existing approaches to model co-evolution [13,11,6,23,8,14] classify metamodel differences based on how they affect both the co-evolving models and the possibility to automate the co-evolution process. Three groups can be distinguished: non-breaking differences, breaking but resolvable differences, and breaking but non-resolvable differences. *Non-breaking differences* (NBD) to a metamodel do not require any change in the models. *Breaking but resolvable differences* (BRD) require a transformation of the model, which can be automated. *Breaking but non-resolvable differences* (BNRD) require user intervention and are almost impossible to automate. Next, the existing approaches define, depending on which metametamodel is used (e.g. MOF or Ecore), all possible metamodel differences, and relate these differences to the three defined groups. Furthermore, the non-breaking differences, and breaking but resolvable differences, are used to automatically generate model differences, and the breaking but non-resolvable differences are resolved with the help of a human.

We split the possible differences into four groups based on their influence on the *syntactic structure* of co-evolving models and based on the possible automation of the co-evolution process. In particular the group of *breaking but non-resolvable* differences is split into two groups: *breaking and semi-resolvable differences* (BSRD) and *breaking and human-resolvable differences* (BHRD). *Breaking and semi-resolvable differences* are differences which can be automatically resolved by configuring the co-evolution process. These differences also encompass the semantic differences which can be resolved by taking into account the semantics of the models. *Breaking and human-resolvable differences* can only be resolved by a user in a differences-resolution environment and cannot be fully automated. For example, if a reference, which has a lower bound of 1, is added to a metamodel, in order to obtain the correct resulting models, concerning the intention of a metamodel developer, a user needs to connect the correct objects in models.

As already mentioned, although our approach is not geared towards automatic resolution of semantic problems, the specified tool architecture is extensible and can be extended to deal with the semantic issues. For example, a logic-based conflict resolver such as Aleph used in [7], a generic model transformation method like Viatra [22], or, in case of database schemas, a database schema matching algorithm like Cupid [19] can be used to resolve possible semantic problems.

The outline of the rest of the paper is as follows. In Section 2, we discuss some preliminaries necessary to understand our approach. Then, in Section 3, we discuss the evolution of metamodels. Next, in Section 4 we discuss the process of co-evolution of models. Furthermore, we describe the tool we built that faithfully implements our approach, and we describe an experiment we performed to validate our approach. Finally, in Section 6, we conclude the paper and give some directions for further research.

2   Preliminaries

In this section we give some preliminaries necessary for understanding our method for model co-evolution. We first describe a special *domain-specific* metametamodel which we use in describing our method. This metametamodel is simple, but allows formal reasoning on metamodels, models, and their relation. Next, we describe a generic differences metamodel, which is based on the described metametamodel. This differences metamodel is used to capture the differences between two models, and, in our approach, also the differences between two metamodels[4].

2.1   Domain-Specific Metametamodel

We approached the problem of generic model differences by designing a domain-specific metametamodel, that exposes not only the details of metamodels, but also the details of models, and the relations between metamodels and models. Metamodels are obtained by instantiating the *Metamodel* element (non colored elements in Figure 2), and models are obtained by instantiating the *Model* element (grey elements in Figure 2). Each metamodel can contain a set of named elements. Each of these elements can contain named and typed attributes, and labeled references to other metamodel elements. Each model can contain a set of model elements, that must be related to a conforming metamodel elements. Moreover, each model element can contain attribute instances (containing values), and reference instances (referencing other model elements). Unlike in traditional metametamodeling approaches (e.g. MOF or Ecore), in our approach models are not considered instances of metamodels, but models only *conform-to* metamodels. However, both models, metamodels, and their relationships, are instances of the introduced metametamodel. Notice that although our metametamodel is designed for a specific domain of model differences, it allows for description of labeled attributed graphs, and thus is quite generic (i.e. it allows for description of all graph-based systems)[5]. The architecture of the metametamodel allows the specification of a metamodel-independent differences metamodel [1], which is discussed in the following section.

2.2   Model Differences

Our approach to the representation of model differences satisfies all of the requirements specified in [5]. These requirements allow model differences to be seamlessly used in model configuration management systems. The differences between two models are represented by a differences model that conforms to a differences metamodel. The differences metamodel is an extension of the metametamodel introduced in the previous section and is depicted in Figure 3. Differences

---

[4] The details of both metametamodel and the differences model can be found in [1].

[5] For example, we have developed transformations from metamodels conforming to Ecore, and models conforming to those metamodels, to our formalism. This makes it possible to use our co-evolution approach with the Ecore-based metamodels and models.

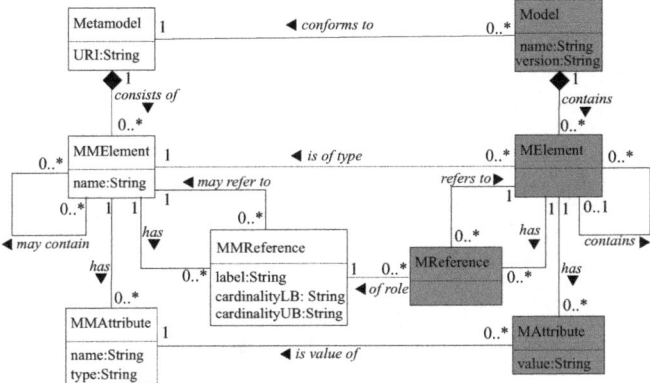

Fig. 2. Metametamodel

models are instances of the *DifferencesModel* element. The building blocks of the differences models are instances of *ChangedElement*, *DeletedElement*, *AddedElement*, and *MovedElement*. Assuming that the differences model represents the differences between models *A* and *B*, then the instances of the *AddedElement* are elements that are in model *B* and not in model *A*, the instances of the *DeletedElement* are elements that are in model *A* but not in model *B*, and the instances of the *ChangedElement* are elements that represent the *same entities* in both models but are not structurally identical. Since a differences model contains only references to models, this differences metamodel is generic (metamodel-independent).

3   Metamodel Evolution

Traditional approaches to metamodel evolution define special mechanisms for representing, calculating and visualizing metamodel differences. These methods are usually based on techniques for representing, calculating and visualizing model differences, but there is a clear separation between metamodels and models, and thus also between metamodel differences and model differences.

In our approach, the techniques for representing, calculating and visualizing model differences are applied directly to metamodel differences. Our key idea is to represent metamodels as models conforming to a special metamodel. In this way, all the techniques for model comparison can be directly applied to metamodel comparison.

In order to represent metamodels as models, we define a special metamodel for metamodels (MMfMM). The metamodels can now be interpreted as (i.e. transformed to) the models conforming to the MMfMM. Consequently, the differences between metamodels are obtained by transforming metamodels to models, and by calculating the differences between the resulting models. This approach is particulary useful in the context of a model configuration management systems, because it allows a unified treatment of models and metamodels.

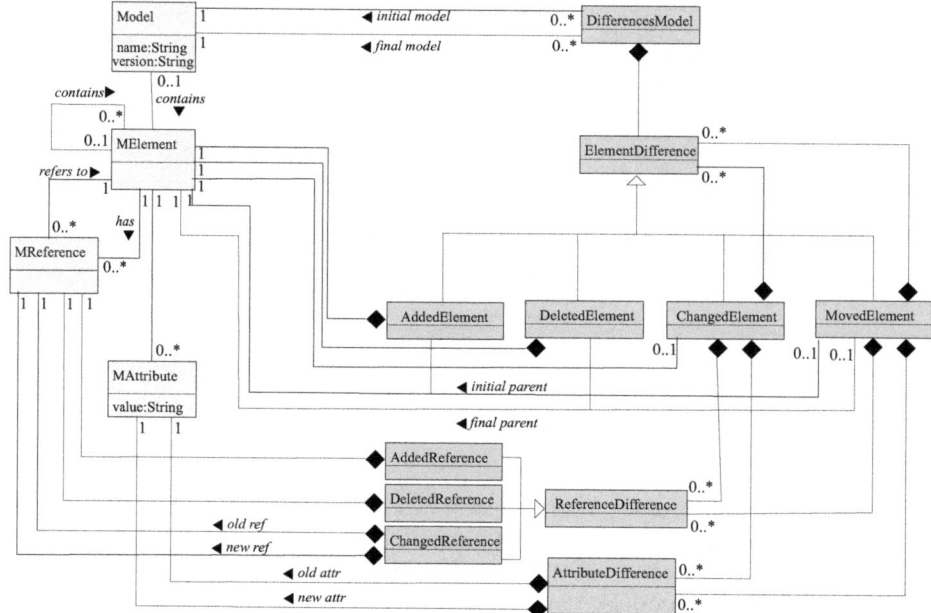

Fig. 3. Differences metamodel

In the next section we describe our metamodel for metamodels (MMfMM). By consulting this metamodel, it is possible to specify all the possible types of metamodel differences, and their influence on co-evolving models, which is discussed in Section 3.2.

3.1   Metamodel for Metamodels - MMfMM

In this section we discuss a metamodel for metamodels (MMfMM), depicted in Figure 4. Since MMfMM is a metamodel, it is an instance of the *Metamodel* element from our *domain-specific* metametamodel (depicted in Figure 2). Models that conform to the MMfMM represent metamodels. Thus, each metamodel has two representations: its *natural* representation (instance of the *Metamodel* element), and a *transformed* representation (instance of the *Model* element that conforms to the MMfMM)[6]. However, we designed MMfMM in such a way that a transformation from a *natural* representation of a metamodel to a *transformed* representation is trivial. For example, a MMfMM element named *MMElement* represents metamodel elements. Elements in models that are instances of MMfMM, and that conform to MMfMM element named *MMElement* represent metamodel elements.

---

[6] In EMF terminology, MMfMM corresponds to a metamodel *Ecore.ecore. Ecore.ecore* is an Ecore-based metamodel that allows for the creation of Ecore-based models such that there is a bijection between any of those models and an Ecore-based metamodel.

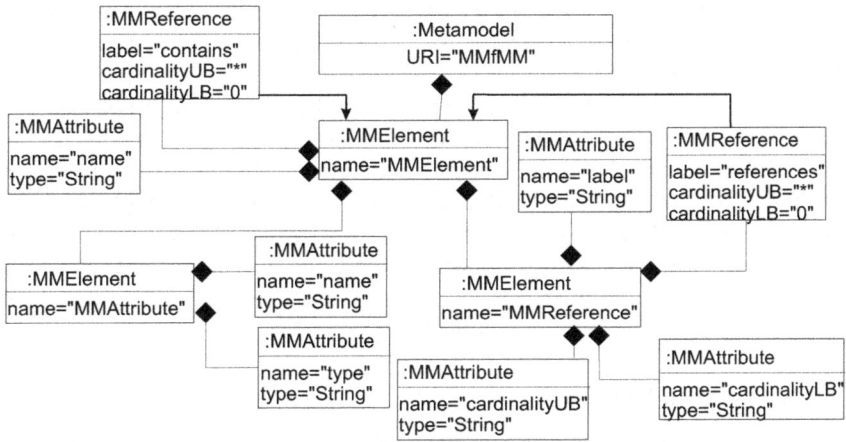

Fig. 4. A metamodel for metamodels - MMfMM

A *natural* representation of an example metamodel, and a *transformed* representation of the same metamodel, are depicted in Figure 5.

A natural representation of a metamodel (top left part of the Figure 5) is named *example*, and has two metamodel elements named *State* and *Transition*. Both the State element, and the Transition element, have an attribute Name of type String. Moreover, a Transition element has a reference that has a label Connects. In the transformed (i.e. model) representation of a metamodel (lower

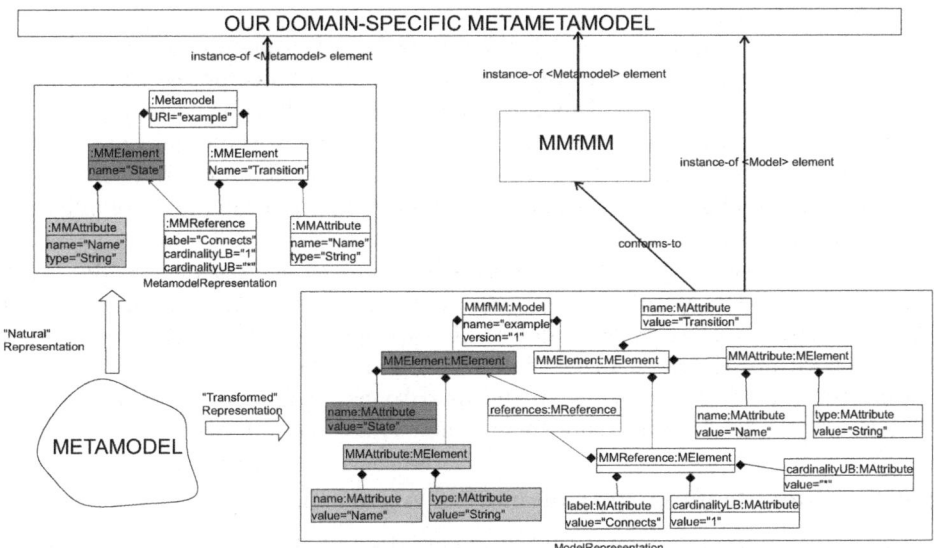

Fig. 5. Example metamodel represented both as an instance of a *Metamodel* element and as an instance of a *Model* element conforming to the MMfMM

right part of the Figure 5), the rectangles represent instances of model elements conforming to specific MMfMM elements. The labels of those rectangles can be split into two parts, before and after the token ":". The first part denotes the MMfMM element that the element represented by the rectangle conforms to. The second part represents the type of the model element (*MElement, MAttribute or MReference*). For example, a metamodel element named State is represented with one model element, and with one attribute of that model element that has a value *State* (dark grey part of Figure 5). The attribute Name of a metamodel element named State is also represented with one model element. However, this element has two attributes having values Name and String, representing the name and type of the Name attribute.

3.2 Metamodel Differences

As already mentioned, in this paper we focus on automatic processing of syntactic changes (differences) to metamodels. The list of all detectable metamodel differences, and the consequences of these differences are given in Appendix A. In some cases we mention the relation of differences to the (static) semantic of models, and these relations guided our reasoning in many cases. However, since we did not choose any semantic formalism for interpreting the behavior of models conforming to a certain metamodel, we did not formally reason about semantics.

4 Model Co-evolution

In this section we present a method for calculating model differences, based on metamodel differences.

In order to obtain the model differences from the metamodel differences, a necessary prerequisite is the existence of formal methods for the representation of metamodels, models and model differences, as well as a method for the calculation of model differences. As mentioned before, without loss of generality we use the metametamodel depicted in Figure 2 for the representation of metamodels and models, and a metamodel for the representation of model differences depicted in Figure 3.

Next, we assume that the differences between the *evolved* and *original* metamodel have been calculated and are presented as a differences model labeled *differences*. Then, for each model M that conforms to the *original* metamodel, the algorithm described in the following section can be used to calculate the differences model DM, that can be used to patch model M to obtain a new (evolved) model M' that conforms to the *evolved* metamodel.

4.1 Model Differences Calculation Algorithm

The calculation algorithm is an implementation of the causal relations between metamodel differences and model differences described in Appendix A. The algorithm traverses the graph representation of a model (actually a tree representation, where the edges are instances of the containment relation, is traversed), and for each model element checks if the metamodel element that that element conforms to has changed. If this was the case, then, based on the changes to the metamodel element, the model differences for that particular element are generated, otherwise nothing happens.

For solving *breaking and human-resolvable differences* we introduced two special functions in the algorithm. The first of these functions is *warningrequest(name, id)*. This function first checks for the presence of conflicts (*breaking and human-resolvable differences*) of the specified *name* in all model elements that conform to the metamodel element of the specified *id*. If there are no conflicts then the function terminates, and if there are conflicts, an environment for manual conflict resolution is started. This function is used in case of possible conflicts, for example if the references bounds change, this function checks if the model is in a conflicting state, and starts an environment for manual conflict resolution if this is the case. The second function is *conflictrequest(name, id)*. This function denotes that there is a conflict, having a *name* as specified in the argument of the function, and that it is necessary to start an environment for manual conflict resolution, for all model elements that conform to the metamodel element identified by the specified *id* argument. This function is used in case of affirmed conflicts, for example if the type of a reference changes.

4.2 Validation

In order to validate our co-evolution method we built a tool that faithfully implements our method, and we systematically tested this tool with a large set of metamodels and models.

The tool consists of two parts. The first part is responsible for the completely automatic transformation of models by considering non-breaking differences, or the breaking differences which are resolvable by providing a configuration file. The second part is a graphical application, that allows manual resolution in case of breaking changes which are not resolvable automatically. The tool is extensible, and thus users can define additional (e.g. metamodel specific) transformations in order to solve semantic issues that may arise during the co-evolution process. The tool can be configured to call the user-defined transformation functions before, during, or after the part of the co-evolution process that is fully automated.

Our goals in testing the tool were:

– Assessing the capability of a tool in detecting metamodel differences;
– Assessing the functional correctness of a tool in cases of both automatic and semi-automatic processing of differences;
– Assessing the extent of user involvement in adaptation of a larger set of co-evolved models.

For the testing we selected 10 metamodels, and for each metamodel 10 conforming models, giving rise to one hundred models altogether[7]. In order to make our experiment transparent, we decided to co-evolve the selected models by using the co-evolution scenarios specified in previous research in this area. For this reason, we selected 9 operations from the set of 61 co-evolution operations defined in [16], and we applied each operation to each metamodel, thus obtaining 90 co-evolved metamodels. These operations were selected such that they ensure coverage of all cases of possible resolution scenarios as specified in Section 3.2. Next, we applied our co-evolution tool to each evolved metamodel, co-evolving models accordingly.

For each operation we measured: the number of metamodels for which the tool correctly detected the co-evolution operation, the number of fully automatically co-evolved models, the number of semi-automatically co-evolved models, the number of models that need to be manually co-evolved, and the number of models that did not need to change. The results are given in Table 1.

Table 1.

Operation	Correctly Detected in Metamodels	Automatically adapted models	Semi-automatically adapted models	Manually adapted models	Unaffected models	Total models
Create Class	10	0	0	0	100	100
Create Attribute	10	0	80	0	20	100
Create Reference	10	0	0	100	0	100
Delete Reference	10	100	0	0	0	100
Rename Attribute	10	0	0	0	100	100
Make Reference Composite	10	0	100	0	0	100
Change Attribute Type	10	0	90	0	10	100
Move Feature Over Reference	10	0	73	0	27	100
Reference To Class	10	0	74	0	26	100
TOTALS	100	100	417	100	283	900

The interpretation of the results is as follows: *Create Class* and *Rename Attribute* operations are completely automated, and the models do not need adaptation. *Delete Reference* operation is also completely automated, but models are affected. *Create Reference* operation requires user intervention in specifying possible instances of the created reference. *Create Attribute* operation is semi-automated by defining the configuration entry specifying the default value of the created attribute. *Change Attribute Type* operation is semi-automated by defining the configuration entry specifying a function for transforming the values of attributes of the original type, to attributes of the new type. *Make Reference Composite, Move Feature Over Reference* and *Reference To Class* operations are semi-automated by specifying specific model transformations that deal with semantic issues of these operations. In particular, these operations are built up of many atomic metamodel differences, thus detecting these operations requires pattern matching on model differences[8]. Furthermore, the resolution of these operations requires more complex algorithms than those provided by a tool.

---

[7] The metamodels used in the tests are generated by using a metamodel-generator tool that we developed, and models used in the tests are generated by using a model-generator tool that we developed. The output metamodels and models are Ecore-based, but are transformed to our metamodeling formalism for the purpose of this validation study.

[8] In a state-based approach to model differences, which is employed by us.

Our conclusion is that while most models require some form of intervention, this intervention can usually be specified on a per-operation, or on a per-metamodel basis, and not on a per-model basis.

The developed tool, as well as the test metamodels and models, are available online [21][9].

5 Related work

Our approach is applicable in case of a *state-based* representation and calculation of model differences [1]. In contrast to approaches that deal with *operation-based* representation and calculation of model differences, such as COPE [15], our approach can also be used for modeling tools that have as output only complete (meta)models and not the set of *operations*[10].

In our approach, we represent metamodels as models conforming to a meta-model specifically designed for this purpose[11]. The first advantage of our approach with respect to the existing approaches featuring *state-based* model co-evolution is that we do not need to invent a special representation mechanism for metamodel differences, but we represent the metamodel differences as model differences. This allows us to use generic techniques for the representation and calculation of model differences as described in [1], to represent and calculate *meta*model differences. For example in [4,7], for each metamodel a custom differences metamodel must be specified, whereas in our approach only one differences metamodel is used. Furthermore, our differences metamodel provides a more detailed representation of model differences than, for example, the ones used in [4,7] (for details see [1]).

Another advantage of our approach is that, since our technique for representing (and calculating) differences is state-based, it does not require special modeling-tool support like operation-based approaches [14,13], but can be used also with the tools that provide this support.

Furthermore, most existing co-evolution approaches [12,11], use a single heuristic algorithm for metamodel comparison, where we reuse a generic declarative model-differences calculation algorithm, which is based on tree-comparison techniques, and can be configured such that it does not use heuristics at all [1]. Therefore, in our approach it is possible to easily configure the comparison algorithm, such that it suits the needs of the users.

Finally, we introduce a metametamodel which involves only two metamodeling levels. Because of this we do not require the use of higher-order model transformations for calculating co-evolved model differences [11,4,7], but the differences are obtained by an ordinary, first-order model transformation. The advantage of this is that the tool based on our co-evolution approach is easy to build and maintain.

---

[9] http://www.win.tue.nl/~zprotic/coevol.html

[10] Thus, our approach is most useful if a company uses multiple tools for managing its models. However, if a company uses only one tool for managing all its models, and if that tool can provide operations, an operation-based approach would be preferred.

[11] Thus, metamodels need to be transformed to equivalent models in order to be used in this manner.

6   Conclusion

In this paper we define a method to support the co-evolution of models as induced by the evolution of metamodels. Our main contributions are:

- We show that by representing metamodels as models conforming to a special metamodel, existing techniques for representing and calculating model differences can be directly applied to calculation of metamodel differences;
- We show that the group of *breaking and non-resolvable metamodel differences* can be further split into two sub-groups based on further possibilities for automation of the resolution process;
- We show that it is possible to have only one, generic, transformation for co-evolving models, which is an improvement to the previous approaches where higher-order transformations were employed;
- We execute a large validation study, showing that it is possible to automate most of the co-evolution process, and that for only a small percentage of changes to metamodels, the co-evolution requires manual intervention.

Our method ensures syntactic correctness of the resulting models. Ensuring semantic correctness of the co-evolved models is supported by providing an extension mechanism for user-defined transformation functions. An example of a semantic issue that can be solved by a user-defined transformation is the introduction of an attribute in a metamodel element whose value in the corresponding model element is to be obtained by combining multiple values of attributes in other model elements.

Since our method uses a *state-based* approach to representation and calculation of model differences, and since it is independent of a specific framework and (meta)metamodel, it is directly applicable in an industrial context for companies that use a variety of tools and that would like to co-evolve models developed with those tools. The stand-alone tool that we developed supports this claim.

Future work includes conducting an even larger and more thorough case study based on an industrial case. Furthermore, it would be interesting to adapt our approach to more popular metamodeling formalisms like MOF [20] or EMF [9].

Acknowledgements. This work has been carried out as part of the FALCON project under the responsibility of the Embedded Systems Institute with Vanderlande Industries as the industrial partner. This project is partially supported by the Netherlands Ministry of Economic Affairs under the Embedded Systems Institute (BSIK03021) program.

References

1. van den Brand, M., Protić, Z., Verhoeff, T.: Fine-grained metamodel-assisted model comparison. In: Proceedings of the 1st International Workshop on Model Comparison in Practice, IWMCP 2010, pp. 11–20. ACM, New York (2010)
2. Brand, M.v.d., Protić, Z., Verhoeff, T.: Generic tool for visualization of model differences. In: Proceedings of the 1st International Workshop on Model Comparison in Practice, IWMCP 2010, pp. 66–75. ACM, New York (2010)

3. Chawathe, S.S., Rajaraman, A., Garcia-Molina, H., Widom, J.: Change detection in hierarchically structured information. SIGMOD Rec. 25, 493–504 (1996)
4. Cicchetti, A.: Difference Representation and Conflict Management in Model-Driven Engineering. PhD thesis, Universita' degli Studi dell'Aquila (2007)
5. Cicchetti, A., Di Ruscio, D., Eramo, R., Pierantonio, A.: A metamodel independent approach to difference representation. JOT: Journal of Object Technology, 165–185 (2007)
6. Cicchetti, A., Di Ruscio, D., Eramo, R., Pierantonio, A.: Automating co-evolution in model-driven engineering. In: Proceedings of the 2008 12th International IEEE Enterprise Distributed Object Computing Conference, pp. 222–231. IEEE Computer Society Press, Washington, DC, USA (2008)
7. Cicchetti, A., Di Ruscio, D., Eramo, R., Pierantonio, A.: Meta-model differences for supporting model co-evolution. In: Proceedings of the 2nd Workshop on Model-Driven Software Evolution - MODSE 2008, Athene, Greece (2008)
8. Cicchetti, A., Di Ruscio, D., Pierantonio, A.: Managing dependent changes in coupled evolution. In: Paige, R.F. (ed.) ICMT 2009. LNCS, vol. 5563, pp. 35–51. Springer, Heidelberg (2009)
9. Ecore, http://download.eclipse.org/modeling/emf/emf/javadoc/2.5.0/org/eclipse/emf/ecore/package-summary.html#details
10. EMF compare, wiki.eclipse.org/index.php/EMF_Compare
11. Garces, K., Jouault, F., Cointe, P., Bezivin, J.: Practical adaptation of models to evolving metamodels. INRIA Technical Report No 6723, INRIA (2008)
12. Garcés, K., Jouault, F., Cointe, P., Bézivin, J.: Managing model adaptation by precise detection of metamodel changes. In: Paige, R.F., Hartman, A., Rensink, A. (eds.) ECMDA-FA 2009. LNCS, vol. 5562, pp. 34–49. Springer, Heidelberg (2009)
13. Gruschko, B., Kolovos, D., Paige, R.: Towards synchronizing models with evolving metamodel. In: Proceedings of the 1st International Workshop on Model-Driven Software Evolution - MODSE (2007)
14. Herrmannsdoerfer, M., Benz, S., Juergens, E.: COPE - automating coupled evolution of metamodels and models. In: Drossopoulou, S. (ed.) ECOOP 2009. LNCS, vol. 5653, pp. 52–76. Springer, Heidelberg (2009)
15. Herrmannsdoerfer, M., Koegel, M.: Towards a generic operation recorder for model evolution. In: Proceedings of the 1st International Workshop on Model Comparison in Practice, IWMCP 2010, ACM, New York (2010)
16. Herrmannsdoerfer, M., Vermolen, S.D., Wachsmuth, G.: An extensive catalog of operators for the coupled evolution of metamodels and models. In: Malloy, B., Staab, S., van den Brand, M. (eds.) SLE 2010. LNCS, vol. 6563, pp. 163–182. Springer, Heidelberg (2011)
17. Kelter, U.: A generic difference algorithm for UML models. In: Liggesmeyer, P., Pohl, K., Goedicke, M. (eds.) Software Engineering. LNI, vol. 64, pp. 105–116. GI (2005)
18. Konemann, P.: Model-independent differences. In: Proceedings of the 2009 ICSE Workshop on Comparison and Versioning of Software Models (CVSM 2009), pp. 37–42. IEEE Computer Society Press, Washington, DC, USA (2009)
19. Madhavan, J., Bernstein, P.A., Rahm, E.: Generic schema matching with cupid. In: VLDB 2001: Proceedings of the 27th International Conference on Very Large Data Bases, pp. 49–58. Morgan Kaufmann, San Francisco (2001)
20. MetaObject Facility (MOF), http://www.omg.org/mof
21. Model co-evolution tool, http://www.win.tue.nl/~zprotic/coevol.html
22. Viatra.: http://wiki.eclipse.org/VIATRA2_Transformation_Language

23. Wachsmuth, G.: Metamodel adaptation and model co-adaptation. In: Bateni, M. (ed.) ECOOP 2007. LNCS, vol. 4609, pp. 600–624. Springer, Heidelberg (2007)
24. Wenzel, S.: Scalable visualization of model differences. In: Proceedings of the 2008 international workshop on Comparison and versioning of software models, pp. 41–46. ACM, New York (2008)

A   Possible Metamodel Differences

In this Appendix we describe all the possible types of atomic metamodel differences and (separated by → symbol) the possible impact of those differences to the co-evolving models. This set of atomic differences is sound and complete. Notice that each type of metamodel difference is related to one group of metamodel differences introduced in Section 1. This relation is denoted by an abbreviation of a group (BRD, NBD, BSRD or BHRD).

1. In the *new* metamodel, an **element** was **deleted** (BRD) → The conforming model elements should be deleted from all the models.
2. In the *new* metamodel, an **element** was **added** (NBD) → Nothing should change in co-evolving models.
3. In the *new* metamodel, the **name** of an element was **changed** (NBD) → This change does not have any influence on the conforming models.
4. In the *new* metamodel, an **attribute** of an element was **deleted** (BRD) → The instance of that attribute should also be deleted from all model elements conforming to that metamodel element.
5. In the *new* metamodel, an **attribute** was **added** to an element (BSRD) → The instance of added attribute should be added to all the model elements conforming to the changed metamodel element. However, a default value should be provided for all added attributes. This value can be provided in a static (per-metamodel) configuration file, making this *Breaking and semi-resolvable difference*.
6. In the *new* metamodel, an **attribute** of an element was **changed**; the following options are possible:
   (a) In the *new* metamodel, the **name** of the attribute was **changed** (NBD) → Nothing should be changed in the models, because models do not reference attributes by name.
   (b) In the *new* metamodel, the **type** of the attribute was **changed** (BSRD) → The values of that attribute in models might not be valid anymore. Thus, a transformation function that transforms the old values of the attributes to the new values of the new type should be provided in a configuration file.
7. In the *new* metamodel, a **reference** of an element was **deleted** (BRD) → All instances of it should also be deleted from all of the model elements conforming to the changed metamodel element.
8. In the *new* metamodel, a **reference** was **added** to an element (BHRD) → The changes to model elements depend on the lower bound of the added reference. If the lower bound of the reference is zero (0), then, syntactically, the models are correct without any change. If the lower bound on the reference is not zero, then the appropriate instances of the reference should be added by a user.
9. In the *new* metamodel, a **reference** of an element was **changed**:
   (a) In the *new* metamodel, the **label** of the reference was **changed** (NBD) → Nothing should change in models.

(b) In the *new* metamodel, the **bounds** of the reference were **changed** (BHRD) → A syntactic check should be invoked in the target model and appropriate warnings/errors should be issued in case the new bounds of the references are not respected in the model elements conforming to the changed metamodel element.

(c) In the *new* metamodel, the **reference** was **changed** to refer to a different element (BHRD) → The reference instances do not point to the right type of elements, and a user should resolve the conflict.

10. In the *new* metamodel, a **contained element** was **deleted** (BRD) → All instances of the deleted subelement should be deleted from the instances of the model elements conforming to the changed metamodel element.

11. In the *new* metamodel, a **contained element** was **added** (NBD) → Nothing should change in models.

If in the *new* metamodel the contained element has been changed, then for each changed subelement the defined differences should be processed recursively.

From UML Profiles to EMF Profiles
and Beyond*

Philip Langer[1], Konrad Wieland[2], Manuel Wimmer[2], and Jordi Cabot[3]

[1] Johannes Kepler University Linz, Austria
philip.langer@jku.at
[2] Vienna University of Technology, Austria
{wieland,wimmer}@big.tuwien.ac.at
[3] INRIA & Ecole des Mines de Nantes, France
jordi.cabot@inria.fr

Abstract. Domain-Specific Modeling Languages (DSMLs) are getting more and more attention as a key element of Model Driven Engineering. As any other software artefact, DSMLs should continuously evolve to adapt to the changing needs of the domain they represent. Unfortunately, right now evolution of DSMLs is a costly process that requires changing its metamodel and re-creating the complete modeling environment.

In this paper we advocate for the use of EMF Profiles, an adaptation of the UML profile concept to DSMLs. Profiles have been a key enabler for the success of UML by providing a lightweight language-inherent extension mechanism which is expressive enough to cover an important subset of adaptation scenarios. We believe a similar concept for DSMLs would provide an easier extension mechanism which has been so far neglected by current metamodeling tools. Apart from direct metamodel profiles, we also propose reusable profile definition mechanisms whereby profiles are defined independently of any DSML and, later on, coupled with all DSMLs that can benefit from these profiles. Our approach has been implemented in a prototype integrated in the EMF environment.

Keywords: language extensions, UML profiles, language engineering.

1   Introduction

Domain-Specific Modeling Languages (DSMLs) have gained much attention in the last decade [7]. They considerably helped to raise the level of abstraction in software development by providing designers with modeling languages tailored to their application domain. However, as any other software artifact, DSMLs are continuously subjected to evolution in order to be adapted to the changing needs of the domain they represent. Currently, evolving DSMLs is a time-consuming and tedious task because not only its abstract and concrete syntax but also

---

* This work has been partly funded by the Austrian Federal Ministry of Transport, Innovation and Technology (BMVIT) and FFG under grant FIT-IT-819584.

J. Bishop and A. Vallecillo (Eds.): TOOLS 2011, LNCS 6705, pp. 52–67, 2011.

all related artifacts as well as all DSML-specific components of the modeling environment have to be re-created or adapted.

UML has avoided these problems by promoting the use of profiles. Indeed, the profile mechanism has been a key enabler for the success and widespread use of UML by providing a lightweight, language-inherent extension mechanism [14]. Many UML tools allow the specification and usage of user-defined profiles and are often shipped with various pre-defined UML Profiles. Induced by their widespread adoption, several UML Profiles have even been standardized by the OMG[1].

In the last decade, many debates[2] on pros and cons of creating new modeling languages either by defining metamodels from scratch (with the additional burdens of creating a specific modeling environment and handling their evolution) or by extending the UML metamodel with UML Profiles (which provide only a limited language adaptation mechanism) have been going on.

However, in this paper we propose a different solution to combine the best of both breeds. We advocate for adapting the UML Profiles concept as an annotation mechanism for *existing* DSMLs. We believe the usage of profiles in the realm of DSMLs brings several benefits:

(1) Lightweight language extension. One of the major advantages of UML Profiles is the ability to systematically introduce further language elements without having to re-create the whole modeling environment such as editors, transformations, and model APIs.

(2) Dynamic model extension. In contrast to direct metamodel extensions, also already existing models may be dynamically extended by additional profile information without recreating the extended model elements. One model element may further be annotated with several stereotypes (even contained in different profiles) at the same time which is equivalent to the model element having multiple types [2]. Furthermore, the additional information introduced by the profile application is kept separated from the model and, therefore, does not pollute the actual model instances.

(3) Preventing metamodel pollution. Information not coming from the modeling domain, can be represented by additional profiles without polluting the actual domain metamodels. Consider for instance annotating the results of a model review (as known from code reviewing) which shall be attached to the reviewed domain models. Metaclasses concerning model reviews do not particularly relate to the domain and, therefore, should not be introduced in the domain metamodels. Using specific profiles instead helps to separate such concerns from the domain metamodel and keeps the metamodel concise and consequently, the language complexity small.

(4) Model-based representation. Additional information, introduced to the models by profile applications, is accessible and processable like ordinary model information. Consequently, model engineers may reuse familiar model engineering

---

[1] http://www.omg.org/technology/documents/profile_catalog.htm

[2] Consider for instance the panel discussion "A DSL or UML Profile. Which would you use?" at MoDELS'05 (http://www.cs.colostate.edu/models05/panels.html)

technologies to process profile applications. Due to their model-based representation, profile applications may also be validated against the profile definition to ensure their consistency as it is known from metamodel/model conformance.

Until now, the notion of profiles has not been adopted in current metamodeling tools. Thus, the contribution of this paper is to adapt the notion of UML profiles to arbitrary modeling languages residing in the Eclipse Modeling Framework[3] (EMF) which is currently one of the most popular metamodeling frameworks. Thanks to this, existing modeling languages may easily be extended by profiles in the same way as it is known from UML tools. Besides this, we propose two novel techniques to enable the systematic reuse of profile definitions across different modeling languages. First, we introduce *generic profiles* which are created independently of the modeling language in the first place and may be bound later to *several modeling languages*. Second, we propose *meta profiles* for immediately reusing them for *all modeling languages*. Finally, we present how our prototype called EMF Profiles is integrated in EMF.

2   From UML Profiles to EMF Profiles

In this section, we present the *standard profile* mechanism (as known from UML) for EMF. Firstly, we disclose our design principles. Secondly, we discuss how the profile mechanism may be integrated in EMF in a way that profiles can seamlessly be used within EMF following the previous design principles. Finally, we show how profiles as well as their applications are represented based on an example.

2.1   Design Principles

With EMF Profiles we aim at realizing the following five design principles. Firstly, annotating a model should be as *lightweight* as possible, hence, no adaptation of existing metamodels should be required. Secondly, we aim at avoiding to *pollute* existing metamodels with concerns not directly related to the modeling domain. Thirdly, we aim at *separating annotations from the base model* to allow importing only those annotations which are of current interest for a particular modeler in a particular situation. Fourthly, the annotations shall be *conforming to a formal and well-known specification* such as it is known from metamodel/model conformance. Finally, users should be enabled to intuitively attach annotations using environments and editors they are familiar with. Consequently, annotations shall be created either on top of the concrete (graphical) syntax of a model or on top of the abstract syntax using e.g., generic tree-based editors.

2.2   Integrating Profiles in the EMF Metalevel Architecture

The profile concept is foreseen as an integral part of the UML specification. Therefore, the UML package *Profiles*, which constitutes the language for

---

[3] http://www.eclipse.org/modeling/emf

specifying UML Profiles, resides, in terms of the metamodeling stack [9], at the meta-metalevel M_3 [13] as depicted in Fig. 1. A specific profile (*aProfile*), as an instance of the meta-metapackage *Profile*, is located at the metalevel M_2 and, therefore, resides on the same level as the UML metamodel itself. Thus, modelers may create profile applications (*aProfileApplication* on M_1) by instantiating *aProfile* just like any other concept in the UML metamodel.

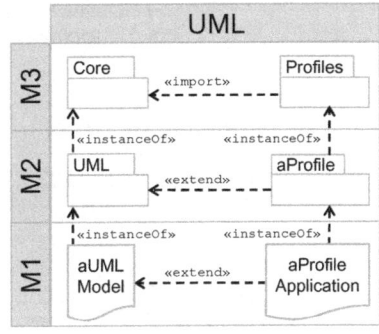

Fig. 1. UML Architecture

To embed the profile mechanism into EMF, a language (equivalent to the package *Profiles* in Fig. 1) for specifying profiles is needed as a first ingredient. This is easily achieved by creating an Ecore-based metamodel which is referred to as *Profile MM* (cf. column *Profile Definition* in Fig. 2). Specific profiles, containing stereotypes and tagged values, may now be modeled by creating instances, referred to as *aProfile*, of this profile metamodel. Once a specific profile is at hand, users should now be enabled to apply this profile to arbitrary models by creating *stereotype applications* containing concrete values for tagged values defined in the stereotypes. As already mentioned, in UML, a stereotype application is an instance—residing on M_1—of a stereotype specification in M_2 (cf. Fig. 1).

Unfortunately, in contrast to the UML architecture, in EMF no profile support exists in M_3. The level M_3 in EMF is constituted only by the metamodeling language Ecore (an implementation of MOF [12]) which has no foreseen profile support. Extending Ecore on level M_3 to achieve the same instantiation capabilities for profiles as in UML is not a desirable option, because this would demand for an extensive intervention with the current implementation of the standard EMF framework. Therefore, in EMF, our profile metamodel (*ProfileMM* in column *Profile Definition* of Fig. 2) is defined at level M_2 and the user-defined profiles (*aProfile*) reside on M_1. As an unfortunate result, a defined stereotype in *aProfile* cannot be instantiated for representing stereotype applications (as in UML), because *aProfile* is already located on M_1 and EMF does not allow for *instantiating an instance* of a metamodel, i.e., EMF does not directly support multilevel modeling [1].

Therefore, more sophisticated techniques have to be found for representing stereotype applications in EMF. In particular, we identified two strategies for lifting *aProfile* from M_1 to M_2 in order to make it instantiable and directly applicable to EMF models.

(1) Metalevel Lifting By Transformation. The first strategy is to apply a model-to-model transformation which generates a metamodel on M_2, corresponding to the specified profile on M_1. The generated metamodel, denoted as *aProfile as MM* in the first column of Fig. 2, is established by implementing a mapping from Profile concepts to Ecore concepts. In particular, the transformation generates for each `Stereotype` a corresponding `EClass` and for each

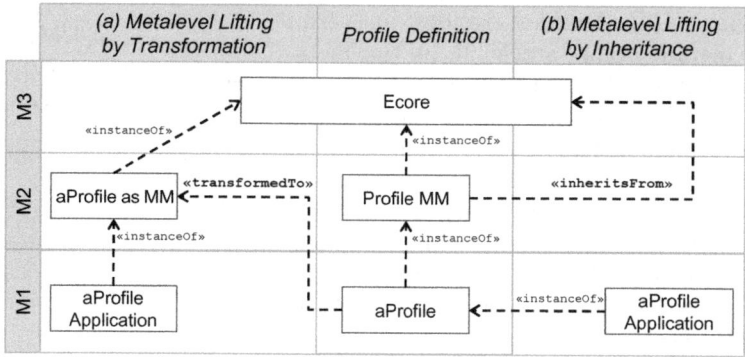

Fig. 2. EMF Profile Architecture Strategies

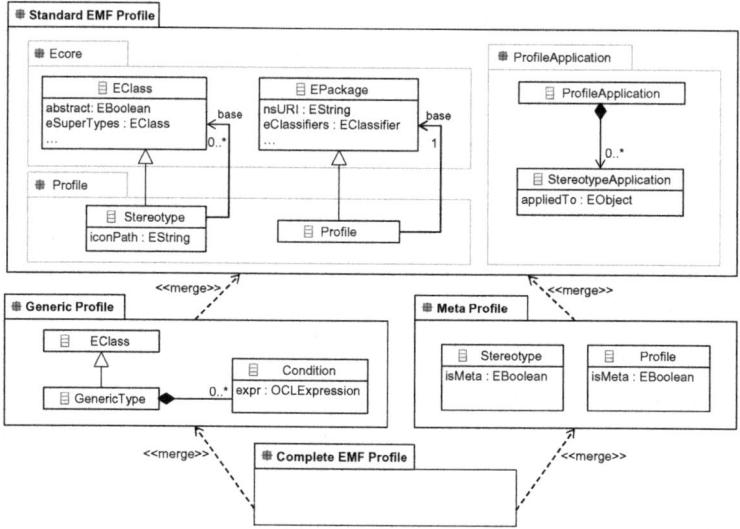

Fig. 3. EMF Profile Metamodel

`TaggedValue` a corresponding `EStructuralFeature`. The resulting metamodel is a direct instance of Ecore residing on M_2 and therefore, it can be instantiated to represent profile applications.

(2) Metalevel Lifting By Inheritance. The second strategy allows to *directly* instantiate profiles by *inheriting instantiation capabilities* (cf. «*inheritsFrom*» in the right column of Fig. 2). In EMF, only instances of the meta-metaclass `EClass` residing on M_3 (e.g., the metaclass `Stereotype`) are instantiable to obtain an object on M_1 (e.g., a specific stereotype). Consequently, to allow for the direct instantiation of a defined stereotype on M_1, we specified the metaclass `Stereotype` in *Profile MM* to be a *subclass of* the meta-metaclass `EClass`. By this, a stereotype inherits EMF's capability to be instantiated and thus, a stereotype application may be represented by a direct instance of a specific stereotype.

We decided to apply the second strategy, because of the advantage of using only one artifact for both, (1) defining the profile and (2) for its instantiation. This is possible because by this strategy, a profile is now a dual-faceted entity regarding the metalevels which is especially obvious when considering the horizontal «*instanceOf*» relationship between *aProfile* and *aProfileApplication* (cf. Fig. 2). On the one hand, a profile is located on M_1 when considering it as an instance of the profile metamodel (*ProfileMM* on M_2)). On the other hand, the stereotypes contained in the profile are indirect instances of `EClass` and are therefore instantiable which means that a profile may also be situated on M_2. Especially, when taking the latter view-point, the horizontal «*instanceOf*» relationship between profile and profile application shown in Fig. 2 will become the expected vertical relationship as in the UML metalevel architecture.

2.3 The EMF Profile Metamodel

The metamodel of the profile definition language is illustrated in package *Standard EMF Profile* of Fig. 3. As a positive side effect of choosing the metalevel lifting strategy 2, the class `Stereotype` may contain, as an `EClass`, also `EAttributes` and `EReferences` which are reused to represent tagged values. Thus, no dedicated metaclasses have to be introduced to represent the concept of tagged values. Please note that stereotype applications also require to have a reference to the model elements to which they are applied. Therefore, we introduced an additional metamodel package, namely *ProfileApplication* in Fig. 3. This metamodel package contains a class `StereotypeApplication` with a reference to arbitrary `EObjects` named `appliedTo`. Whenever, a profile (instance of the *Profile* package) is saved, we automatically add `StereotypeApplication` as a superclass to each specified stereotype. To recall, this is possible because each `Stereotype` is an `EClass` which may have superclasses. Being a subclass of `StereotypeApplication`, stereotypes inherit the reference `appliedTo` automatically. In the following subsection, we further elaborate on the EMF Profile metamodel by providing a concrete example. Please note that the so far unmentioned packages *Generic Profile* and *Meta Profile* in Fig. 3 are discussed in Section 3.

2.4 Applying the EMF Profile Metamodel

To clarify how profiles and profile applications are represented from a technical point of view, we make use of a small example. In particular, a simplified version of the well-known *EJB profile* is applied to an Entity-Relationship (ER) model [4]. Fig. 4(a) depicts an excerpt of the ER metamodel and the EJB profile. The EJB profile contains the stereotypes `SessionBean` and `EntityBean`, which both extend the metaclass `Entity` of the ER metamodel. Besides, the profile introduces the stereotype `IDAttribute` extending the metaclass `Attribute` to indicate the ID of an `Entity`.

As already mentioned in the previous subsection, internally, we use the *ProfileApplication* metamodel (cf. Fig. 4(b)) to weave the necessary concepts for

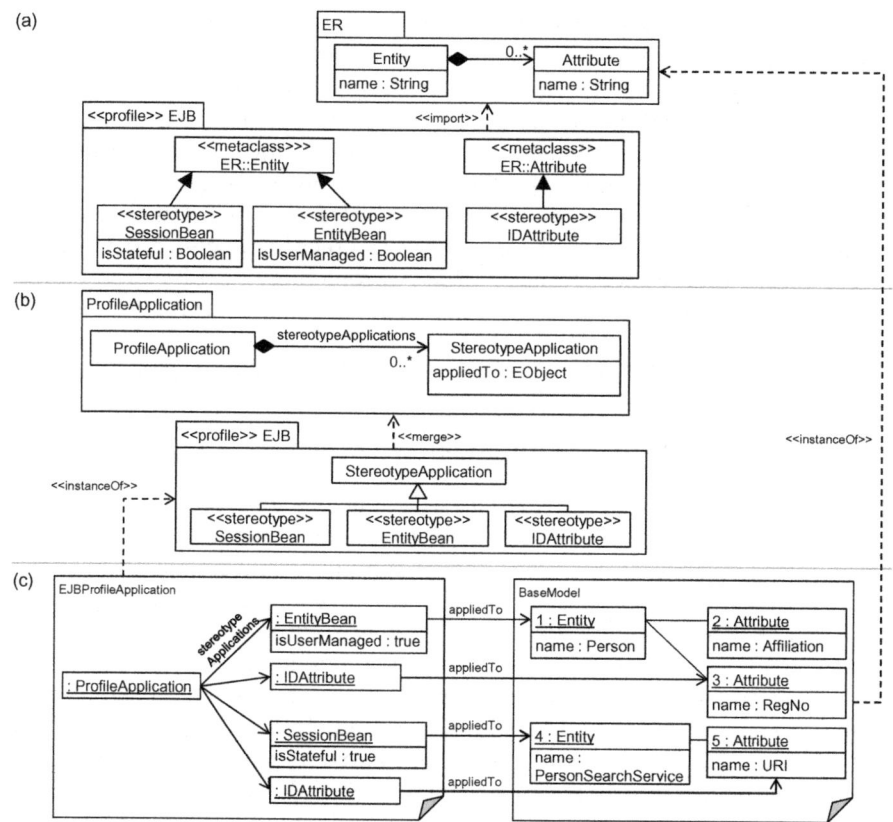

Fig. 4. EMF Profiles by Example: (a) Profile definition user-view, (b) Internal profile representation, (c) Profile application

a profile's application into a profile model. In particular, the class `Profile-Application` acts as root element for all `StereotypeApplications` in a profile application model. Furthermore, all `Stereotypes` inherit the reference `appliedTo` from `StereotypeApplication`. When instantiating (i.e., applying) the EJB profile, a root element of the type `ProfileApplication` is created which may contain stereotype applications as depicted in Fig. 4(c). For determining the applicability of a stereotype `s` to a particular model element `m`, it is checked whether the model element's metaclass (`m.eClass()`) is included in the list of metaclasses that are extended by the stereotype (`s.getBase()`). If so, the stereotype `s` is applicable to model element `m`. Each stereotype application is represented as a direct instance of the respective stereotype (e.g., *≪EntityBean≫*) and refers to the model element in the *BaseModel* to which it is applied by the reference `appliedTo` (inherited from the class `StereotypeApplication`). Please note that the EJB profile application resides in a separated model file and not in the original ER model denoted with *BaseModel* in Fig. 4.

3   Going Beyond UML Profiles

Originally, the profile mechanism has been specifically developed for UML. Hence, profiles may only extend the UML metamodel. In the previous section, we showed how this lightweight extension mechanism is ported to the realm of DSMLs. However, in this realm a whole pantheon of different DSMLs exists which are often concurrently employed in a single project. As a result, the need arises to reuse existing profiles and apply them to *several DSMLs*. Thus, we introduce two dedicated reuse mechanisms for two different scenarios:

(1) Metamodel-aware Profile Reuse. The first use case scenario is when users aim to apply a profile to a *specific set of DSMLs*. Being aware of these specific DSMLs' metamodels, the user wants to take control of the applicability of stereotypes to a manually selected set of metaclasses.

(2) Metamodel-agnostic Profile Reuse. In the second use case scenario, users intend to use a profile for *all DSMLs* without the need for further constraining the applicability of stereotypes. Therefore, a stereotype shall—agnostic of the DSMLs' metamodels—be applicable to every existing model element.

To tackle scenario (1), we introduce *generic profiles* allowing to specify stereotypes that extend so-called generic types. These generic types are independent of a concrete metamodel and may be bound to specific metaclasses in order to reuse the generic profile for several metamodels. For tackling scenario (2), we propose *meta profiles* which may immediately be applied to all DSMLs implemented by an Ecore-based metamodels.

3.1   Generic Profiles

The goal behind generic profiles is to reuse a profile specification for several "user-selected" DSMLs. Therefore, a profile should not depend on a specific metamodel. Inspired by the concepts of generic programming [10], we use the notion of so-called *generic types* instead. In particular, stereotypes within a generic profile do not extend concrete metaclasses as presented in the previous section, they extend generic types instead. These generic types act as placeholders for concrete metaclasses in the future. Once, a user decides to use a generic profile for a specific DSML, a binding is created which connects generic types to corresponding concrete metaclasses contained in the DSML's metamodel. For one generic profile there might exist an arbitrary number of such bindings. Consequently, this allows to reuse one generic profile for several DSMLs at the same time. Furthermore, it enables users to first focus on the development of the profile and reason about the relationship to arbitrary DSMLs in a second step.

As example, consider the same EJB profile which has been specified in terms of a concrete profile in Section 2. Now, we aim at specifying the same profile in a generic way to enable its use also for other DSMLs. In particular, we show how the EJB profile may first be specified generically and we subsequently illustrate the binding of this generic profile again for ER models. We get the same modeling expressiveness as before but now in a way that allows us to reuse the EJB profile when using other data modeling languages. The original EJB profile for ER extends two metaclasses, namely the stereotypes `SessionBean` and

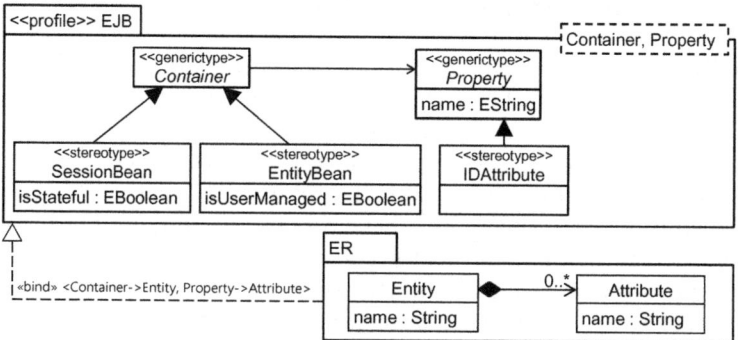

Fig. 5. Generic EJB Profile and its Binding to the ER metamodel

EntityBean extend the metaclass Entity and the stereotype IDAttribute extends Attributes (cf. Fig. 4). To turn this concrete profile into a generic one, we now use two generic types, named Container and Property in Fig. 5, instead of the two concrete types Entity and Attribute.

Before we describe how generic profiles may be bound to concrete DSMLs, we first discuss conditions constraining such a binding. When developing a concrete profile, the extended DSML is known and consequently only suitable metaclasses are selected to be extended by the respective stereotypes. For instance, in the concrete EJB profile for ER, Entities can be annotated with the stereotype EntityBean. For marking the Entity's ID attribute, the EJB profile introduces the stereotype IDAttribute which extends Attributes. This is reasonable, because we are aware of the fact that Entities *contain* Attributes in the ER metamodel, otherwise it obviously would not make any sense to extend the metaclass Attribute in this matter. However, generic profiles are developed without a concrete DSML in mind. Hence, profile designers possibly need to specify conditions enforcing certain characteristics to be fulfilled by the (up to this time) unknown metaclasses to which a generic type might be bound in future.

Therefore, EMF Profiles allows to attach conditions to generic profiles. Such conditions are specified by simply adding references or attributes to generic types. This is possible because, as a subclass of EClass, generic types may contain EReferences and EAttributes. By adding such a reference or attribute in a generic type, a profile designer states that there must be a corresponding reference or attribute in the metaclass which is bound to the generic type. Internally, these references and attributes are translated to OCL constraints which are evaluated in the context of the metaclass a user intends to bind. Furthermore, the profile designer must specify which meta-features, such as the cardinality of the reference or attribute in a generic type, shall be enforced. In our example in Fig. 5, the profile designer specified a reference from the generic type Container to Property as well as an attribute name in Property. To enforce this, the OCL constraints in Listing 1.1 are generated. These constraints must be satisfied by each metamodel on which we want to apply this profile on.

Listing 1.1. OCL Constraints generated for `Container` and `Property`

```
1 context Container inv:
2 self.eReferences->exists(r | r.eType = Property)}
3 context Property inv:
4 self.eAttributes->exists(a | a.name = "name" and a.eType = EString)
```

Once the stereotypes and generic types are created, the profile is ready to be bound to concrete DSMLs. This is simply achieved by selecting suitable meta-classes of a DSML for each generic type. In our example depicted in Fig. 5, the generic types `Container` and `Property` are bound to the metaclasses in the ER metamodel `Entity` and `Attribute`, respectively, in order to allow the application of the generic EJB profile to ER models. When the binding is established, it can be persisted in two different ways. The first option is to generate a concrete profile out of the generic profile for a specific binding. This concrete profile may then be applied like a normal EMF profile as discussed in Section 2. Although this seem to be the most straightforward approach, the explicit trace between the original generic profile and the generated concrete profile is lost. Therefore, the second option is to persist the binding directly in the generic profile definition. Whenever a user intends to apply a generic profile to a concrete DSML, the EMF Profile framework searches for a persisted binding for the concrete DSML's metaclasses within the profile definition. If a binding exists, the user may start to apply the profile using this persisted binding. Otherwise, the user is requested to specify a new binding.

To support generic profiles, we extended the EMF Profile metamodel by the class `GenericType` (cf. Fig 3). Generic types inherit from `EClass` and may contain `Conditions` representing more complex constraints going beyond the aforementioned enforced references and attributes for bound metaclasses.

3.2   Meta Profiles

With meta profiles we tackle a second use case for reusing profiles for more than one DSML. Instead of supporting only a manually selected number of DSMLs, with meta profiles we aim at reusing a profile for *all* DSMLs without the need of defining an explicit extension for each DSML. This is particularly practical for profiles enabling general annotations which are suitable for every DSML. In other words, stereotypes within a meta profile must be agnostic of a specific metamodel and shall be applicable to *every model element* irrespectively of its metaclass, i.e., its type.

In EMF, every model element is an instance of a metaclass. Each metaclass is again an instance of Ecore's `EClass`. Therefore, meta-stereotypes in a meta profile do not extend metaclasses directly. Instead, they are configured to be applicable to *all instances of instances* of `EClass` and, consequently, to every model element (as an instance of an instance of `EClass`). This approach is inspired by the concept of potency known from multilevel metamodeling [1]. Using the notion of potency, one may control on which metamodeling level a model element may be instantiated. By default, the potency is 1 which indicates that a model element may be instantiated in the next lower metamodeling level. By

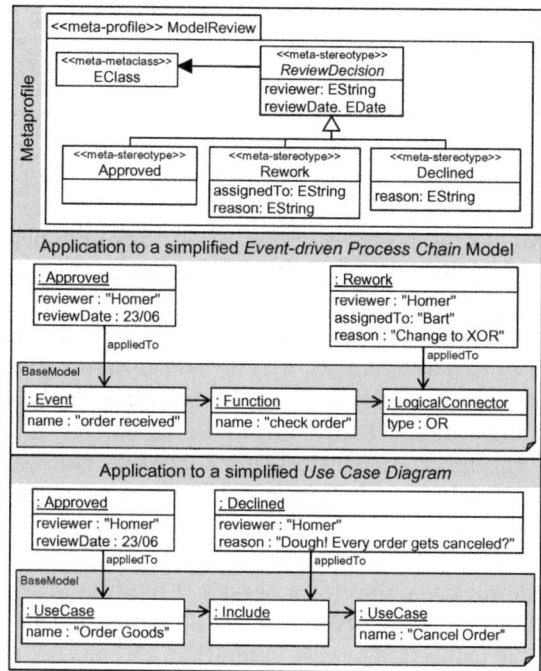

Fig. 6. Meta profile Example: The Model Review Profile

a potency $p \geq 1$ on a metamodeling level n, a model element may also be configured to be instantiable on the level $n - p$ instead of the next lower level. In terms of this notion of potency, a meta-stereotype has a potency of $p = 2$.

Meta profiles are created just like normal profiles. However, a new attribute, namely isMeta, is introduced to the profile metamodel for indicating whether a stereotype is a meta-stereotype (cf. Fig. 3). The Boolean value of this attribute is regarded by EMF Profiles when evaluating the applicability of stereotypes. In particular, if isMeta is true, a stereotype is always considered to be applicable to every model element, irrespectively of its metaclass.

Our example for presenting metaprofiles is a *model review profile* (cf. Fig. 6). The goal of this profile is to allow for annotating the results of a systematic examination of a model. Since every model irrespectively of its metamodel can be subject to a review, this profile is suitable for every DSML. For simplicity, we just introduce three stereotypes in the review profile, namely Approved, Rework, and Declined, which shall be applicable to every kind of element in every DSML. Therefore, these three stereotypes extend the class EClass and are marked as meta-stereotypes (indicated by «*meta-stereotype*» in Fig. 6). By this, the applicability of these stereotypes is checked by comparing the meta-metatypes of model elements with the metaclasses extended by the stereotypes. As a result, the metaprofile in our example is applicable to every element in every DSML.

In the example shown in Fig. 6, we depicted the Object Diagram of two separate applications of the same metaprofile to two models conforming to different metamodels. In the first Object Diagram, an `Event` and one `LogicalConnector` within an Event-driven Process Chain (EPC) model have been annotated with the meta-stereotype «*Approve*» and «*Rework*», respectively. This is possible because both instances in the EPC model are an instance of a metaclass which is again an instance of `EClass`. The same metaprofile can also be applied to any other modeling language. Of course, also UML itself is supported by EMF Profiles. Therefore, the model review profile may also be applied to, for example, a UML Use Case Diagram (cf. Fig. 6). In this figure, the stereotype «*Approve*» has been assigned to the `UseCase` named "Order Goods" and the stereotype «*Declined*» is applied to the `Includes` relationship.

3.3   Summary

Both techniques for enabling the reuse of profiles for several DSMLs have their advantages and disadvantages depending on the intended use case. Meta profiles are immediately applicable to all DSMLs without further user intervention. However, with meta profiles no means for restricting the use of such profiles for concrete DSMLs exist. If this is required, generic profiles are the better choice. When specifying generic profiles, explicit conditions may be used to control a profile's usage for concrete DSMLs. On the downside, this can only be done with additional efforts for specifying such conditions in the generic profile and creating manual bindings from generic profiles to concrete DSMLs.

4   A Tour on EMF Profiles

In this section, we present our prototypical implementation of EMF Profiles which is realized as Eclipse plug-in on top of the Eclipse Modeling Framework and Graphical Modeling Framework[4] (GMF). Please note that we refrained from modifying any artifact residing in EMF or GMF. EMF Profiles only uses well-defined extension points provided by these frameworks for realizing profile support within the EMF ecosystem. For a screencast of EMF Profiles, we kindly refer to our project homepage[5].

Profile Definition. To define a profile, modelers may apply either the tree editor automatically generated from the Profile Metamodel or our graphical EMF Profiles Editor which is realized with GMF (cf. Fig. 7 for a screenshot). The graphical notation used in this editor takes its cue from the UML Profiles syntax. With these editors, modelers may easily create stereotypes containing tagged values and set up inheritance relationships between stereotypes and extension relationships to metaclasses of arbitrary DSML's metamodels. Metaclasses may be imported by a custom popup menu entries when right-clicking the canvas of the editor and are visualized using the graphical notation from Ecore.

---

[4] http://www.eclipse.org/gmf
[5] http://www.modelversioning.org/emf-profiles

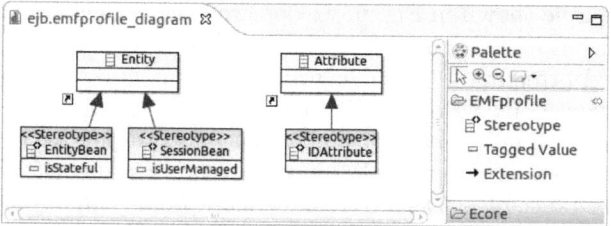

Fig. 7. EJB Profile Defined with Graphical EMF Profiles Editor

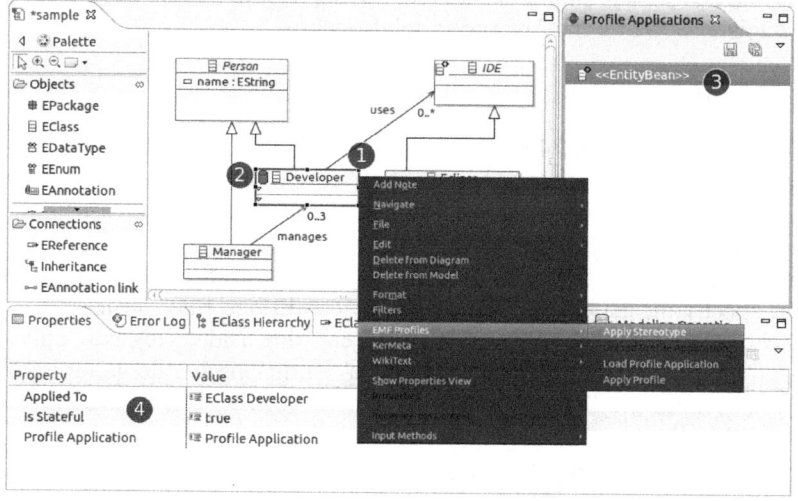

Fig. 8. Screenshot of Applied EJB Profile to an Ecore Diagram

Profile Application. Defined profiles may also be applied using any EMF-generated tree-based editor or any GMF-based diagramm editor. The screenshot depicted in Fig. 8, shows the afore presented EJB profile applied to an example Ecore diagram. To apply profiles, our plugin contributes a popup menu entry (cf. Fig. 8 (1)) which appears whenever a model element is right-clicked. By this menu, users may apply defined profiles (i.e., creating new profile application) or import already existing profile applications. Once a profile application is created or imported, stereotypes may be applied using the same popup menu. When a stereotype is applied, the defined stereotype icon is attached to the model element (cf. Fig. 8 (2)). For this purpose we used the GMF Decoration Service, which allows to annotate any existing shapes by adding an image at a pre-defined location. Furthermore, we created a Profile Applications view, which shows all applied stereotypes of the currently selected model element (cf. Fig. 8 (3)). The currently selected model element is retrieved using the ISelectionProvider interface which is implemented by every EMF or GMF-based editor. For assigning the tagged values of an applied stereotype, we leverage the PropertyView (cf. Fig. 8 (4)) which generically derives all defined tagged values from the loaded

profile's metamodel. The separate file resource which contains the profile applications is added to the EditingDomain of the modeling editor. Hence, as soon
as the model is saved, all profile applications are saved as well. Finally, profile applications can be unloaded and reloaded at any time without loosing the
application information.

5   Related Work

One alternative to profiles as an annotation mechanism is to use weaving models
(e.g., by using Modelink[6] or the Atlas Model Weaver[7] [6]). Model weaving enables to compose different separated models, and thus, could be used to compose
a core model with a concern-specific information model in a non-invasive manner. However, although weaving models are a powerful mechanism, annotating
models with weaving models is counter-intuitive. Since this is not the intended
purpose of weaving models, users cannot annotate models using their familiar
environment such as a diagramming editor which graphically visualizes the core
model. Current approaches only allow to create weaving models with specific
tree-based editors in which there is no different visualization of the core model
and the annotated information. Not least because of this, weaving models may
quickly become very complex and challenging to manage.

Recently, Kolovos et al. presented an approach called *Model Decorations* [8]
tackling a very similar goal as EMF Profiles. Kolovos et al. proposed to attach
(or "decorate") the additional information in terms of text fragments in GMF's
diagram notes. To extract or inject the decorations from or into a model, hand-
crafted model transformations are employed which translate the text fragments
in the notes into a separate model and vice versa. Although their approach is
very related to ours, there also are major differences. First, for enabling the
decoration of a model, an extractor and injector transformation has to be manually developed which is not necessary with EMF Profiles. Second, since Kolovos
et al. exploit GMF notes, only decorating GMF-based diagrams is possible. In
contrast to our approach, models for which no GMF editor is available cannot
be annotated. Third, the annotations are encoded in a textual format within
the GMF notes. Consequently, typos or errors in these textual annotations cannot be automatically identified and reported while they are created by the user.
Furthermore, users must be familiar with the textual syntax as well as the decoration's target metamodel (to which the extractor translates the decorations)
to correctly annotate a model. In EMF Profiles, stereotypes may only be applied
if they are actually applicable according to the profile definition and editing the
tagged values is guided by a form-based property sheet. Consequently, invalid
stereotype applications and tagged values can be largely avoided.

EMF Facet[8], a spin-off of the MoDisco subproject [3] of Eclipse, is another
approach for non-intrusive extensions of Ecore-based metamodels. In particular,

---

[6] http://www.eclipse.org/gmt/epsilon/doc/modelink
[7] http://www.eclipse.org/gmt/amw
[8] http://www.eclipse.org/modeling/emft/facet

EMF Facet allows to define additional derived classes and features which are computed from already existing model elements by model queries expressed, e.g., in Java or OCL. Compared to EMF Profiles, EMF Facet targets on complementary extension direction, namely the dynamic extension of models with additional *transient information* derived from queries. In contrast, EMF Profiles allow to add new (not only derived) information and is able to persist this additional information in separate files. Nevertheless, the combination of both complementary approaches seems to be a subject for future work. For example, this would allow to automatically extend or complete models based on EMF Facet queries and persist this information with EMF Profiles.

The concept of meta-packages has been proposed in [5] for the lightweight extension of the structural modeling language XCore which is based on packages, classes, and attributes. New modeling concepts are defined by extending the base elements of XCore and can be instantly used in the standard XCore editor. Compared to meta-packages, EMF Profiles are more generic, because not only one modeling language may be extended, but any Ecore-based modeling language.

6   Conclusions and Future Work

In this paper, we adapted the notion of UML Profiles to the realm of DSMLs residing in the Eclipse Modeling Framework. Using our prototype EMF Profiles, DSMLs may be easily extended in a non-invasive manner by defining profiles in the same way as done in UML tools. Moreover, we introduced two novel mechanisms, namely *Generic Profiles* and *Meta Profiles*, for reusing defined profiles with several DSMLs. Although, the presented approach has been presented based on EMF, the general procedure is also applicable for other metamodeling frameworks which comprise a similar metalevel architecture as EMF. Furthermore, the presented metalevel lifting strategies may also be adopted for other scenarios in which model elements on M_1 need to be instantiated.

We successfully applied EMF Profiles for instance in the context of our model versioning system AMOR[9]. In AMOR we created and applied a *change profile* for annotating changes performed on models. Moreover, we also used EMF Profiles for marking conflicts caused by concurrent changes of the same model artifact using a *conflict profile*. Both profiles have been defined as *meta profiles* to build change detection and conflict detection components which are generically applicable, i.e., independent of the used modeling languages.

In the future, we plan to elaborate on more sophisticated restriction mechanisms to allow constraining the application of stereotypes (e.g. with OCL conditions) and composing several independent profiles which are not mutually complementary in one profile application as proposed by [11]. A consistent mix of several profiles requires a mechanism to specify conditions constraining applicability across more than one profile. For instance, one may need to specify that a stereotype of profile A may only be applied after a stereotype of profile B, holding a specific tagged value, has been applied. Next, we plan to derive an

---

[9] http://www.modelversioning.org

easy-to-use API for programmatically creating, modifying, and accessing profile applications. Finally, we aim at integrating EMF Profiles into the EMF Facet project to combine their complementary features. By this, a synergy of the extension mechanism of EMF Profiles for additional persisted information and of EMF Facet's for derived information can be accomplished.

References

1. Atkinson, C., Kühne, T.: The Essence of Multilevel Metamodeling. In: Gogolla, M., Kobryn, C. (eds.) UML 2001. LNCS, vol. 2185, pp. 19–33. Springer, Heidelberg (2001)
2. Atkinson, C., Kühne, T.: A Tour of Language Customization Concepts. Advances in Computers 70, 105–161 (2007)
3. Bruneliere, H., Cabot, J., Jouault, F., Madiot, F.: MoDisco: a generic and extensible framework for model driven reverse engineering. In: Automated Software Engineering (ASE 2010), pp. 173–174. ACM Press, New York (2010)
4. Chen, P.P.-S.: The Entity-Relationship Model—Toward a Unified View of Data. ACM Transactions on Database Systems 1, 9–36 (1976)
5. Clark, T., Evans, A., Sammut, P., Willans, J.: Applied Metamodelling, A Foundation for Language Driven Development (2004), http://www.ceteva.com
6. Del Fabro, M.D., Bézivin, J., Jouault, F., Breton, E., Gueltas, G.: AMW: a generic model weaver. In: Journe sur l' Ingnierie Dirige par les Modles, IDM 2005 (2005)
7. Kelly, S., Tolvanen, J.-P.: Domain-Specific Modeling: Enabling Full Code Generation. Wiley-IEEE Computer Society Press (2008) (2008)
8. Kolovos, D.S., Rose, L.M., Drivalos Matragkas, N., Paige, R.F., Polack, F.A.C., Fernandes, K.J.: Constructing and Navigating Non-invasive Model Decorations. In: Tratt, L., Gogolla, M. (eds.) ICMT 2010. LNCS, vol. 6142, pp. 138–152. Springer, Heidelberg (2010)
9. Kühne, T.: Matters of (meta-) modeling. Software and Systems Modeling 5, 369–385 (2006)
10. Musser, D., Stepanov, A.: Generic Programming. In: Gianni, P. (ed.) ISSAC 1988. LNCS, vol. 358, pp. 13–25. Springer, Heidelberg (1989)
11. Noyrit, F., Gérard, S., Terrier, F., Selic, B.: Consistent Modeling Using Multiple UML Profiles. In: Petriu, D.C., Rouquette, N., Haugen, Ø. (eds.) MODELS 2010. LNCS, vol. 6394, pp. 392–406. Springer, Heidelberg (2010)
12. Object Management Group (OMG): Meta Object Facility, Version 2.0 (2006), http://www.omg.org/spec/MOF/2.0/PDF/
13. Object Management Group (OMG): Unified Modeling Language Infrastructure Specification, Version 2.1.2 (2007), http://www.omg.org/spec/UML/2.1.2/Infrastructure/PDF
14. Selic, B.: A Systematic Approach to Domain-Specific Language Design Using UML. In: Int. Symposium on Object-Oriented Real-Time Distributed Computing, pp. 2–9. IEEE Computer Society Press, Los Alamitos (2007)

Domain-Specific Profiling

Alexandre Bergel[1], Oscar Nierstrasz[2], Lukas Renggli[1], and Jorge Ressia[2]

[1] PLEIAD Lab, Department of Computer Science (DCC),
University of Chile
`pleiad.dcc.uchile.cl`

[2] Software Composition Group, University of Bern, Switzerland
`scg.unibe.ch`

Abstract. Domain-specific languages and models are increasingly used within general-purpose host languages. While traditional profiling tools perform well on host language code itself, they often fail to provide meaningful results if the developers start to build and use abstractions on top of the host language. In this paper we motivate the need for dedicated profiling tools with three different case studies. Furthermore, we present an infrastructure that enables developers to quickly prototype new profilers for their domain-specific languages and models.

1 Introduction

Recent advances in domain-specific languages and models reveal a drastic change in the way software is being built. The software engineering community has seen a rapid emergence of domain-specific tools, ranging from tools to easily build domain-specific languages [18], to transform models [17], to check source code [11], and to integrate development tools [13].

While research on domain-specific languages has made consistent progress in language specification [5], implementation [4], evolution [6] and verification [8], little has been done to support profiling. We consider profiling to be the activity of recording and analyzing program execution. Profiling is essential for analyzing transient run-time data that otherwise would be difficult to harvest and compare. Code profilers commonly employ execution sampling as the way to obtain dynamic run-time information. Unfortunately, information extracted by regularly sampling the call stack cannot be meaningfully used to profile a high-level domain built on top of the standard language infrastructure. Specialized domains need specialized profilers.

Let us consider the example of the Mondrian visualization engine (details follow in Section 2.1). Mondrian models visualizations as graphs, *i.e.*, in terms of nodes and edges. One of the important performance issues we recently faced is the refresh frequency: nodes and edges were unnecessarily refreshed too often. Standard code profilers did not help us to localize the source of the problem since they are just able to report the share of time the CPU spends in the method `displayOn:` of the classes `MONode` and `MOEdge`. The problem was finally resolved by developing a custom profiler that could identify which nodes and

---

J. Bishop and A. Vallecillo (Eds.): TOOLS 2011, LNCS 6705, pp. 68–82, 2011.

edges were indeed refreshed too often. This domain-specific profiler was able to exploit knowledge of Mondrian's domain concepts to gather and present the needed information.

We argue that there is a need for a general approach to easily develop specialized profilers for domain-specific languages and tools. A general approach must offer means to (i) *specify* the domain concepts of interest, (ii) *capture* the relevant information from the run-time execution, and (iii) *present* the results to the developer.

In this paper we introduce MetaSpy, an event-based approach for domain-specific profiling. With MetaSpy, a developer specifies the events of interest for a given domain. A profiler captures domain information either by subscribing to existing application events, or by using a reflective layer to transparently inject event emitters into the domain code. The collected events are presented using graph-based visualizations.

The contributions of this paper are: (1) the identification of the need for domain-specific profilers, (2) the presentation of three real-world case-studies where domain-specific profilers helped to significantly improve performance and correctness of domain-specific code, and (3) the presentation of an infrastructure for prototyping domain-specific profilers.

Outline. The remainder of this paper is structured as follows: Section 2 illustrates the problems of using a general-purpose profiler on code that is built on top of a domain-specific language. Section 3 introduces our approach to domain-specific profiling. Section 4 demonstrates how our approach solves the requirements of domain-specific profilers with three use cases. Section 5 presents our infrastructure to implement domain-specific profilers. Section 6 presents an analysis on the performance impact of MetaSpy. Section 7 summarizes the paper and discusses future work.

2   Shortcomings of Standard Profilers

Current application profilers are useful to gather runtime data (*e.g.,* method invocations, method coverage, call trees, code coverage, memory consumption) from the static code model offered by the programming language (*e.g.,* packages, classes, methods, statements). This is an effective approach when the low-level source code has to be profiled.

However, traditional profilers are far less useful for a domain different than the code model. In modern software there is a significant gap between the model offered by the execution platform and the model of the actually running application. The proliferation of meta-models and domain-specific languages brings new abstractions that map to the underlying execution platform in non-trivial ways. Traditional profiling tools fail to display relevant information in the presence of such abstractions.

2.1 Difficulty of Profiling a Specific Domain

This section illustrates two shortcomings of traditional profiling techniques when applied to a specific domain.

CPU time profiling

Mondrian [10] is an open and agile visualization engine. Mondrian describes a visualization using a graph of (possibly nested) nodes and edges. In June 2010 a serious performance issue was raised[1]. Tracking down the cause of the poor performance was not trivial. We first used a standard sample-based profiler.

Execution sampling approximates the time spent in an application's methods by periodically stopping a program and recording the current set of methods under executions. Such a profiling technique is relatively accurate since it has little impact on the overall execution. This sampling technique is used by almost all mainstream profilers, such as JProfiler, YourKit, xprof [7], and hprof.

MessageTally, the standard sampling-based profiler in Pharo Smalltalk[2], textually describes the execution in terms of CPU consumption and invocation for each method of Mondrian:

```
54.8% {11501ms} MOCanvas>>drawOn:
  54.8% {11501ms} MORoot(MONode)>>displayOn:
    30.9% {6485ms} MONode>>displayOn:
      | 18.1% {3799ms} MOEdge>>displayOn:
      ...
      | 8.4% {1763ms} MOEdge>>displayOn:
      |   | 8.0% {1679ms} MOStraightLineShape>>display:on:
      |   | 2.6% {546ms} FormCanvas>>line:to:width:color:
      ...
    23.4% {4911ms} MOEdge>>displayOn:
    ...
```

We can observe that the virtual machine spent about 54% of its time in the method displayOn: defined in the class MORoot. A root is the unique non-nested node that contains all the nodes of the edges of the visualization. This general profiling information says that rendering nodes and edges consumes a great share of the CPU time, but it does not help in pinpointing which nodes and edges are responsible for the time spent. Not all graphical elements equally consume resources.

Traditional execution sampling profilers center their result on the frames of the execution stack and completely ignore the identity of the object that received the method call and its arguments. As a consequence, it is hard to track down which objects cause the slowdown. For the example above, the traditional profiler says that we spent 30.9% in MONode>>displayOn: without saying which nodes were actually refreshed too often.

---

[1] http://forum.world.st/Mondrian-is-slow-next-step-tc2257050.html#a2261116
[2] http://www.pharo-project.org/

Coverage

PetitParser is a parsing framework combining ideas from scannerless parsing, parser combinators, parsing expression grammars and packrat parsers to model grammars and parsers as objects that can be reconfigured dynamically [12].

A number of grammars have been implemented with PetitParser, including Java, Smalltalk, XML and SQL. It would be useful to establish how much of the grammar is actually exercised by a set of test files to identify untested productions. The `if` statement parsing rule is defined as follows[3]:

```
PPJavaSyntax>>ifStatement
   ^ ('if' asParser token , conditionalExpression , statement) ,
     ('else' asParser token , statement) optional
```

Coverage tools assess the coverage of the application source code by listing the methods involved in an execution. Some tools can even detect the coverage inside methods. Let us consider a Java grammar in PetitParser which is defined in 210 host language methods. These methods build a graph of objects describing the grammar. Traditional coverage tools focus on the source code artifacts instead of domain-specific data. In the example this means that all methods are covered to build the grammar, but some parts of the resulting graph are not used. This is why we are unable to analyze the parsing and production coverage of this grammar with traditional tools.

2.2 Requirements for Domain-Specific Profilers

The two examples given above are representative. They illustrate the gap between a particular domain and the source code model. We argue that to efficiently profile an arbitrary domain, the following requirements need to be fulfilled:

– *Specifying the domain.* Being able to effectively designate the objects relevant for the profiling is essential. Since we are concerned with what makes up a visualization in Mondrian, we are interested in the different nodes and the invocation of the `displayOn:` methods, rather than focusing on the implementation classes. Grammars in PetitParser are represented as an executable graph of primitive parser objects, each with its own execution behavior.
– *Capturing domain related events.* Relevant events generated by the domain have to be monitored and recorded to be analyzed during or after the execution. An event represents a particular change or action triggered by the domain being profiled. Whereas the class `MOGraphElement` and its subclasses

---

[3] Readers unfamiliar with the syntax of Smalltalk might want to read the code examples aloud and interpret them as normal sentences: An invocation to a method named `method:with:`, using two arguments looks like: `receiver method: arg1 with: arg2`. Other syntactic elements of Smalltalk are: the dot to separate statements: `statement1. statement2`; square brackets to denote code blocks or anonymous functions: `[ statements ]`; and single quotes to delimit strings: `'a string'`. The caret `^` returns the result of the following expression.

total more than 263 methods, only fewer than 10 methods are related to displaying and computing shape dimensions.

– *Effectively and concisely presenting the necessary information.* The information collected by traditional profilers is textual and targets method invocation. A method that invokes another will be located below it and indented. Moreover, each method frame represented has a class name and a method name, which completely ignores the identity of the object and arguments that are part of the call. Collected information has to be presented in such a way as to bring the important metrics and domain object composition into the foreground.

Common code profilers employ execution sampling as the way to cheaply obtain dynamic information. Unfortunately, information extracted when regularly sampling the method call stack cannot be used to profile a domain other than the source code model.

3   MetaSpy in a Nutshell

In this section we will present MetaSpy, a framework to easily build domain-specific profilers. The key idea behind MetaSpy is to provide domain-specific events that can later be used by different profilers with different objectives.

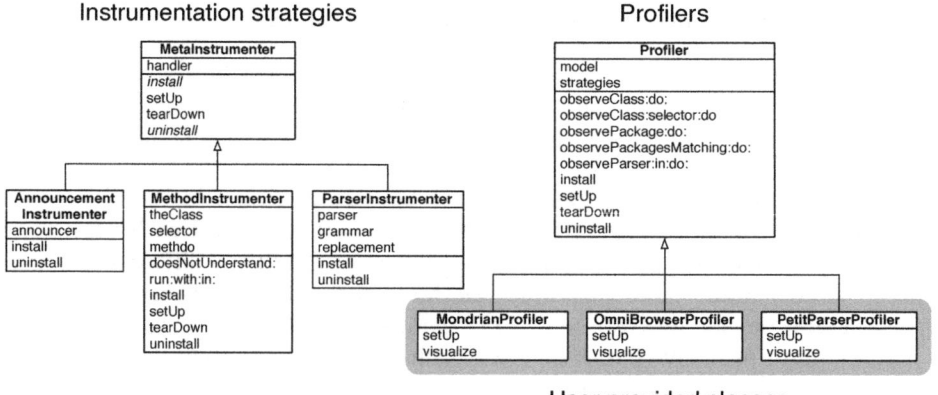

Fig. 1. The architecture of the MetaSpy profiler framework

Figure 1 shows a class diagram of MetaSpy. There are two main abstractions: the instrumentation strategies and the domain-specific profilers.

An instrumentation strategy is responsible for adapting a domain-specific model and triggering specific actions in the profiler when certain events occur. A profiler models a domain-specific profiling requirement by composing multiple instrumentation strategies.

Some instrumentation strategies work by registering to existing events of the application domain. Other instrumentation strategies intercept the system by meta-programming, *i.e.,* conventional instrumentation. Installing an instrumentation strategy activates it and its associated events, while uninstalling deactivates them.

Some of the instrumentation strategies provided by MetaSpy are:

– *Announcement Instrumenter* dispatches events satisfying a particular condition from the announcement framework to the external profiler.
– *Method Instrumenter* triggers an event whenever a specific method is invoked on any instance of a specified class.
– *Object Instrumenter* triggers an event whenever a specific method is invoked on a particular object. This is called object-specific profiling.
– *Parser Instrumenter* triggers an event whenever a specific grammar production is activated. This is a very specific instrumentation strategy only working with PetitParser productions.

Other dedicated instrumentation strategies can be implemented by adhering to the same interface.

Profilers are responsible for modeling the domain-specific behavior to profile the main abstractions in each domain. The abstract `Profiler` class models the behavior of a general profiler. Subclasses are instantiated with a domain-specific model and implement the set-up and tear-down of one or more instrumentation strategies into the model. Furthermore, they define how and what data is collected when the instrumented model is exercised. To actually instrument the model and start collecting events the method `install` is used. Similarly, to remove all instrumentation from the model, `uninstall` is used. Both methods dispatch the requests to the respective instrumentation strategies using the current model.

Each profiler is responsible for presenting the collected data in the method `open`. Depending on the nature of the data, this method typically contains a Mondrian [10] or Glamour [3] script, or a combination of both. Mondrian is a visualization engine to depict graphs of objects in configurable ways. Glamour is a browser framework to script user interfaces for exploratory data discovery.

Next, we will show real-world examples of domain-specific profilers.

4 Validation

In this section we will analyze three case studies from three different domains. We will show how MetaSpy is useful for expressing the different profiling requirements in terms of events. We will also demonstrate how MetaSpy fulfills the domain-specific profiling requirements, namely specifying, capturing and presenting domain-specific information.

For each case study we show the complete code for specifying and capturing events. We do not show the code for visualizing the results, which typically consists of 20–50 lines of Mondrian or Glamour scripts.

4.1   Case Study: Displaying Invocations

A Mondrian visualization may comprise a great number of graphical elements. A refresh of the visualization is triggered by the operating system, resulting from user actions such as a mouse movement or a keystroke. Refreshing the Mondrian canvas iterates over all the nodes and edges and triggers a new rendering. Elements that are outside the window or for which their nesting node has an active bitmap in the cache should not be rendered.

A graphical element is rendered when the method `display:on:` is invoked. Monitoring when these invocations occur is key to having a global view of what should be refreshed.

Capturing the events

The MetaSpy framework is instantiated to create the `MondrianProfiler` profiler.

```
Profiler subclass: #MondrianProfiler
  instanceVariableNames: 'actualCounter previousCounter'
```

`MondrianProfiler` defines two instance variables to monitor the evolution of the number of emitted events: `actualCounter` keeps track of the current number of triggered events per event type, and `previousCounter` the number of event types that were recorded before the previous visualization step.

```
MondrianProfiler>>initialize
  super initialize.
  actualCounter := IdentityDictionary new.
  previousCounter := IdentityDictionary new
```

The installation and instrumentation of Mondrian by MetaSpy is realized by the `setUp` method:

```
MondrianProfiler>>setUp
  self model root allNodes do: [ :node |
    self
      observeObject: node
      selector: #displayOn:
      do: [ :receiver :selector :arguments |
        actualCounter
          at: receiver
          put: ((actualCounter at: receiver ifAbsent: [ 0 ]) + 1) ] ]
```

All the nodes obtained from the root of the model object are "observed" by the framework. At each invocation of the `displayOn:` method, the block given as parameter to `do:` is executed with the object receiver on which `displayOn:` is invoked, the selector name and the argument. This block updates the number of displays for each node of the visualization.

Specifying the domain

The instrumentation described in the `setUp` method is only applied to the model specified in the profiler. This model is an object which models the domain to be profiled, in this case a Mondrian visualization. The instrumentation is only applied to all nodes in this visualization. Only when these nodes receive the the message `displayOn:` will increment the actual counter. This object-specific behavior is possible due to the use of a reflection framework called Bifröst [14].

Presenting the results

The profiling of Mondrian is visualized using Mondrian itself. The `visualizeOn:` method generates the visualization given in Figure 2.

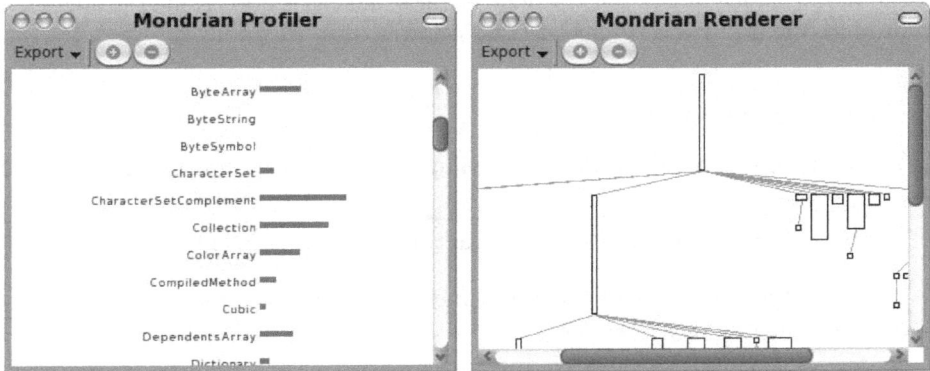

Fig. 2. Profiling (left) the System Complexity visualization (right)

One important point of `visualizeOn:` is to regularly update the visualization to be able to see the evolution of the domain events over time. The profiler is uninstalled when the profiler Mondrian visualization is closed.

Figure 2 gives a screenshot of a visualization and the profiler. The right-hand side is an example of the *System Complexity* visualization [9] of the collection class hierarchy in Pharo. The left-hand side shows the profiler applied to the visualization. The horizontal bar indicates the number of times the corresponding node has been displayed.

The profiling monitors each node of the profiled visualization. Each node is associated to a progress bar that widens upon node refresh. The profiled visualization remains interactive. Clicking and drag-and-dropping nodes refreshes the visualization, thus increasing the progress bar of the corresponding nodes. This profile helps identifying unnecessary rendering. We identified a situation in which nodes were refreshing without receiving user actions. This was perceived by the user with a sluggish rendering. Edges were constantly refreshed, even without being apparent. This problem is addressed in version 2.30 of Mondrian.

4.2   Case Study: Events in OmniBrowser

OmniBrowser [2] is a framework to define and compose new browsers, *i.e.,* graphical list-oriented tools to navigate and edit elements from an arbitrary domain. In the OmniBrowser framework, a browser is described by a domain model specifying the domain elements that can be navigated and edited, and a metagraph specifying the navigation between these domain elements. Nodes in the metagraph describe states the browser is in, while edges express navigation possibilities between those states. The OmniBrowser framework then dynamically composes widgets such as list menus and text panes to build an interactive browser that follows the navigation described in the metagraph.

OmniBrowser uses announcements for modeling the interaction events of the user with the IDE. A very common problem is to have certain announcements be triggered too many times for certain scenarios. This behavior impacts negatively the performance of the IDE. Moreover, in some cases odd display problems are produced which are very hard to track down.

Capturing the events

To profile this domain-specific case we implemented the class OmniBrowserProfiler:

```
Profiler subclass: #OmniBrowserProfiler
  instanceVariableNames: 'actualCounter previousCounter'
```

The instrumentation in the setUp method counts how many times each announcement was triggered.

```
OmniBrowserProfiler>>setUp
  self
    observeAnnouncer: self model announcer
    do: [ :ann |
      actualCounter
        at: ann class
        put: (actualCounter at: ann class ifAbsent: [ 0 ]) + 1 ]
```

Specifying the domain

We specify the entities we are interested in profiling by defining the model in the profiler. For example, we could define OBSystemBrowser browsing a specific class. All OmniBrowser instances have an internal collaborator named *announcer* which is responsible for the signaling of announcements. This is the object used by the profiler to catch the announcement events.

Presenting the results

A Mondrian visualization was implemented to list the type and the number of announcements triggered (Figure 3).

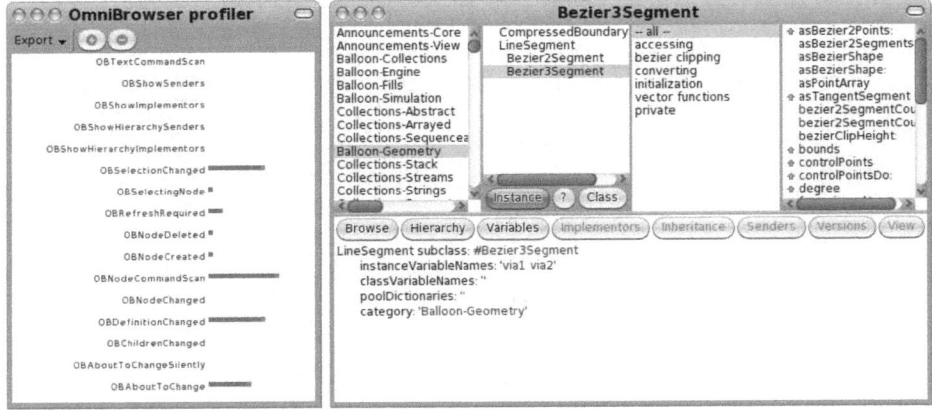

Fig. 3. Profiling (left) an OmniBrowser instance (right)

4.3   Case Study: Parsing framework with PetitParser

Rigorous test suites try to ensure that each part of the grammar is covered by tests and is well-specified according to the respective language standards. Validating that each production of the grammar is covered by the tests is a difficult activity. As mentioned previously, the traditional tools of the host language work at the method and statement level and thus cannot produce meaningful results in the context of PetitParser where the grammar is modeled as a graph of objects.

Capturing the events

With MetaSpy we can implement the grammar coverage with a few lines of code. The instrumentation happens at the level of the primitive parser objects. The method `observeParser:in:` wraps the parser object with a handler block that is called for each activation of the parser.

```
1  PetitParserProfiler>>setUp
2    self model allParsers do: [ :parser |
3      self observeParser: parser in: self grammar do: [
4        counter
5          at: parser
6          put: (counter at: parser ifAbsent: [ 0 ]) + 1 ] ]
```

Line 2 iterates over all primitive parser objects in the grammar. Line 3 attaches the event handler on Lines 4–6 to each parser in the model. The handler then counts the activations of each parser object when we run the test suite of the grammar.

Specifying the domain

The domain in this case is an instance of the grammar that we want to analyze. Such a grammar may be defined using hundreds of interconnected parser objects.

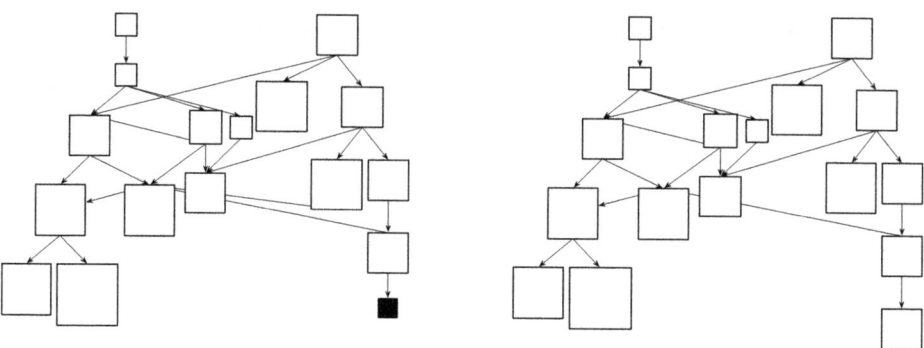

Fig. 4. Visualization of the production coverage of an XML grammar with uncovered productions highlighted in black (left); and the same XML grammar with updated test coverage and complete production coverage (right). The size of the nodes is proportional to the number of activations when running the test suite on the grammar.

Presenting the results

This provides us with the necessary information to display the grammar coverage in a visualization such as that shown in Figure 4.

5   Implementing Instrumentation Strategies

MetaSpy has two ways of implementing an instrumentation strategies: listening to pre-existing event-based systems, or using the meta-level programming techniques of the host language to define a meta-event the strategy is interested in.

Let us consider the class `AnnouncementInstrumenter`, whose responsibility is to observe the generation of specific announcements.

```
AnnouncementInstrumenter>>install
  self announcer
    on: Announcement
    send: #value:
    to: self handler
```

The `install` method installs an instrumentation strategy object on the domain specified in the `install` method. In this snippet of code we can see that the strategy is hooked into the announcement system by evaluating the strategy's handler when an announcement is triggered.

However, not all profiling activities can rely on a preexisting mechanism for registering to events. In some cases, a profiler may be hooked into the base code using an existing event mechanism, for example the OmniBrowser profiler. In other cases, extending the base code with an appropriate event mechanism is simply too expensive. Because of this, we need to rely on the meta-programming facilities of the host language. These facilities are not always uniform and require ad hoc code to hook in behavior. To avoid this drawback we decided to use a framework that provides uniform meta-programming abstractions. Bifröst [14] offers a model of fined-grained unanticipated dynamic structural and behavioral adaptation. Instead of providing reflective capabilities as an external mechanism, Bifröst integrates them deeply into the environment. Bifröst is a reflective system based on explicit meta-objects to improve meta-level engineering.

Bifröst has been designed as an evolution of partial behavioral reflection for Smalltalk [15], which in turn was conceived as an extension of the Reflex model [16]. Bifröst's meta-objects provide a structural view and a behavioral view. In the context of MetaSpy we were mainly interested in behavioral reifications. A behavioral meta-object reifying message sends was used for the message send instrumenter. A Message Received event is also provided by the behavioral meta-object. State read and write are also supported thus MetaSpy can profile these dynamic events. Bifröst meta-objects when attached to a single object are object-specific in nature, thus fulfilling an important domain-specific profiler design requirement.

Let us consider the Message Received Instrumenter, whose responsibility is to instrument when a specific object receives a specific message.

```
MessageReceivedInstrumenter>>install
  self observerMetaObject bind: self object
```

```
MessageReceivedInstrumenter>>setUp
  profilingMetaObject := BehaviorMetaObject new
    when: self selector
    isReceivedDo: self handler
```

The method `install` binds a meta-object to the object to be observed. The method `setUp` initializes the profiling meta-object with a behavioral meta-object. This meta-object evaluates the handler when a specific message is received by the profiled object. This mechanism is termed *object-specific instrumentation*.

Object-specific instrumentation is not trivial to achieve in class-based languages like Smalltalk and Java. Classes are deeply rooted in the language interpreter or virtual machine and performance is tweaked to rely heavily on these constructs. Moreover, most languages provide a good level of structural reflection to deal with structural elements like classes, method, statements, *etc*. Most languages, however, do not provide a standard mechanism to reflect on the dynamic abstractions of the language. There are typically no abstractions to intercept meta-events such as a message send, a message receive, a state read, *etc*.

In our implementation, the profiled application, the profiler, and the visualization engine are all written in the same language, Pharo, and run on the same virtual machine. Nothing in our approach prevent from decoupling these components and having them written in a different language or running remotely. This is actually what often happen with the profilers and debuggers running on the Java virtual machine (*e.g.*, Java debugging interface[4]).

---

[4] http://download.oracle.com/javase/1.5.0/docs/guide/jpda/jvmdi-spec.html

6   Micro-Benchmark

Profiling always impacts the performance of the application being analyzed. We have performed a micro-benchmark to assess the maximal performance impact of MetaSpy. We assume that the behavior required to fulfill the profiling requirements is constant to any instrumentation strategy.

We analyze the impact of MetaSpy on both profiling uses cases. All benchmarks were performed on an Apple MacBook Pro, 2.8 GHz Intel Core i7 in Pharo 1.1.1 with the jitted Cog VM.

Registering instrumentation strategies to a preexisting event-based system depends heavily on the the system used and how it is used.

Using meta-level programming techniques on a runtime system can have a significant performance impact. Consider a benchmark in which a test method is being invoked one million times from within a loop. We measure the execution time of the benchmark with Bifröst reifying the 10^6 method activations of the test method. This shows that in the reflective case the code runs about 35 times slower than in the reified one. However, for a real-world application with only few reifications the performance impact is significantly lower. Bifröst's meta-objects provide a way of adapting selected objects thus allowing reflection to be applied within a fine-grained scope only. This provides a natural way of controlling the performance impact of reflective changes.

Let us consider the Mondrian use case presented in Section 2.1. The main source of performance degradation is from the execution of the method `displayOn:` and thus whenever a node gets redisplayed. We developed a benchmark where the user interaction with the Mondrian easel is simulated to avoid human delay pollution in the exercise. In this benchmark we redraw one thousand times the nodes in the Mondrian visualization. This implies that the method `displayOn:` is called extensively. The results showed that the profiler-oriented instrumentation produces on average a 20% performance impact. The user of this Mondrian visualization can hardly detect the delay in the drawing process. Note that our implementation has not been aggressively optimized. It has been shown [1] that combining instrumentation and sampling profiling leaded to accurate profiles (93–98% overlap with a perfect profile) with low overhead (3–6%). The profilers we presented in this paper are likely to benefit from such instrumentation sampling.

7   Conclusions and Future Work

Our contributions are the following:

1. We demonstrated the need for domain-specific profilers. We argued that traditional profilers are concerned with source code only and are inadequate for profiling domain-specific concerns. We demonstrated this drawback with two use cases.
2. We formulated the requirements domain-specific profilers must fulfill: specifying the domain, capturing domain related events and presenting the necessary information.

3. We presented MetaSpy, a framework for defining domain-specific profilers. We also presented three real-world case-studies showing how MetaSpy fulfills the domain-specific profiler requirements.

As future work we plan to:

- Provide ready-made and pluggable visualizations that can be used by new domain-specific profilers. We plan to use Glamour to build these visualizations.
- Apply MetaSpy in the context of large meta-models, such as the FAMIX meta-model in Moose and the Magritte meta-model in Pier.
- Provide additional ready-made event types that enhance the expressibility of new profilers.
- Profiler scoping is of key importance to obtain adequate information. We plan to enhance the scoping mechanism to be able to dynamically attach events to groups of objects.

Acknowledgments

We gratefully acknowledge the financial support of the Swiss National Science Foundation for the project "Synchronizing Models and Code" (SNF Project No. 200020-131827, Oct. 2010 – Sept. 2012). We also like to thank Toon Verwaest for his feedback on earlier drafts of this paper.

References

1. Arnold, M., Ryder, B.G.: A framework for reducing the cost of instrumented code. In: Proceedings of the ACM SIGPLAN 2001 conference on Programming language design and implementation, PLDI 2001, pp. 168–179. ACM, New York (2001)
2. Bergel, A., Ducasse, S., Putney, C., Wuyts, R.: Creating sophisticated development tools with OmniBrowser. Journal of Computer Languages, Systems and Structures 34(2-3), 109–129 (2008)
3. Bunge, P.: Scripting Browsers with Glamour. Master's thesis, University of Bern (April 2009)
4. Cuadrado, J.S., Molina, J.G.: A model-based approach to families of embedded domain specific languages. IEEE Transactions on Software Engineering 99(1) (2009)
5. van, A., Klint, P., Deursen, J.V.: Domain-specific languages: An annotated bibliography. ACM SIGPLAN Notices 35(6), 26–36 (2000)
6. Freeman, S., Pryce, N.: Evolving an embedded domain-specific language in Java. In: OOPSLA 2006: Companion to the 21st Symposium on Object-Oriented Programming Systems, Languages, and Applications, pp. 855–865. ACM Press, Portland (2006)
7. Gupta, A., Hwu, W.-M.W.: Xprof: profiling the execution of X Window programs. In: Proceedings of the 1992 ACM SIGMETRICS Joint International Conference on Measurement and Modeling Of Computer Systems, SIGMETRICS 1992/PERFORMANCE 1992, pp. 253–254. ACM, New York (1992)

8. Kabanov, J., Raudjärv, R.: Embedded typesafe domain specific languages for Java. In: PPPJ'08: Proceedings of the 6th International Symposium on Principles and Practice of Programming in Java, pp. 189–197. ACM Press, Modena (2008)

9. Lanza, M., Ducasse, S.: Polymetric views—a lightweight visual approach to reverse engineering. Transactions on Software Engineering (TSE) 29(9), 782–795 (2003)

10. Meyer, M., Gîrba, T., Lungu, M.: Mondrian: An agile visualization framework. In: ACM Symposium on Software Visualization (SoftVis 2006), pp. 135–144. ACM Press, New York (2006)

11. Renggli, L., Ducasse, S., Gîrba, T., Nierstrasz, O.: Domain-specific program checking. In: Vitek, J. (ed.) TOOLS 2010. LNCS, vol. 6141, pp. 213–232. Springer, Heidelberg (2010)

12. Renggli, L., Ducasse, S., Gîrba, T., Nierstrasz, O.: Practical dynamic grammars for dynamic languages. In: 4th Workshop on Dynamic Languages and Applications (DYLA 2010), Malaga, Spain (June 2010)

13. Renggli, L., Gîrba, T., Nierstrasz, O.: Embedding languages without breaking tools. In: D'Hondt, T. (ed.) ECOOP 2010. LNCS, vol. 6183, pp. 380–404. Springer, Heidelberg (2010)

14. Ressia, J., Renggli, L., Gîrba, T., Nierstrasz, O.: Run-time evolution through explicit meta-objects. In: Proceedings of the 5th Workshop on Models@run.time at the ACM/IEEE 13th International Conference on Model Driven Engineering Languages and Systems (MODELS 2010), pp. 37–48 (October 2010)

15. Röthlisberger, D., Denker, M., Tanter, É.: Unanticipated partial behavioral reflection: Adapting applications at runtime. Journal of Computer Languages, Systems and Structures 34(2-3), 46–65 (2008)

16. Tanter, É., Noyé, J., Caromel, D., Cointe, P.: Partial behavioral reflection: Spatial and temporal selection of reification. In: Proceedings of OOPSLA 2003, ACM SIGPLAN Notices, pp. 27–46 (2003)

17. Tisi, M., Cabot, J., Jouault, F.: Improving higher-order transformations support in ATL. In: Tratt, L., Gogolla, M. (eds.) ICMT 2010. LNCS, vol. 6142, pp. 215–229. Springer, Heidelberg (2010)

18. Visser, E.: Program transformation with stratego/XT. In: Lengauer, C., Batory, D., Blum, A., Vetta, A. (eds.) Domain-Specific Program Generation. LNCS, vol. 3016, pp. 216–238. Springer, Heidelberg (2004)

Metamodel Dependencies for Executable Models

Carlos Rodríguez, Mario Sánchez, and Jorge Villalobos

Universidad de los Andes
Bogotá, Colombia
{ce.rodriguez390,mar-san1,jvillalo}@uniandes.edu.co

Abstract. Cumbia is our platform to develop applications based on multiple, coordinated executable models which can be described using different languages. The coordination of models is achieved by describing how their elements should interact, and mapping those descriptions into low level coordination primitives. Moreover, the description of the coordination is described externally: it does not have an impact either on the metamodels or on the models, and this results in lower coupling and increased flexibility. This approach, which is appropriate when the metamodels are highly independent, has limitations when it comes to describing dependencies that are inherent to the concerns. In those cases, it makes sense to incorporate those dependencies into the metamodels descriptions. The goal of this paper is thus to discuss two alternative ways to establish those dependencies, and illustrate their usage, benefits, and drawbacks in a concrete example.

Keywords: Metamodel relations, Model relations, Executable models, Model composition, Cumbia.

1 Introduction

Cumbia is a platform to develop applications based on model driven engineering (MDE) and using multiple *concern specific languages*. For each language supported in Cumbia, a metamodel has to be defined whose goals are to describe the abstract syntax and the semantics of the language. This is achieved by using metamodels based on *open objects* [1].

Open Objects are an abstraction that we developed to describe all the elements that belong in a Cumbia metamodel, and therefore all the elements of a concern specific language. Open objects are composed by three elements: an entity, a state machine associated with the entity, and a set of actions. *Entities* are plain old Java objects with properties and methods. *State machines* are abstractions of the associated entity life cycle and stay in sync with the entity state. State machines are formed by states and transitions, and each of the latter has to be marked with the type of the events that can trigger it. *Actions* represent behavior associated with the transitions of the state machine.

The execution of a set of open objects is coordinated by means of event passing and by means of method invocations. Open objects generate events in two situations: when methods of the entity are executed, or when the state machine

J. Bishop and A. Vallecillo (Eds.): TOOLS 2011, LNCS 6705, pp. 83–98, 2011.
© Springer-Verlag Berlin Heidelberg 2011

follows a transition and switches its current state. Events are distributed among open objects, and they are locally processed. The state machine of each open object that received an event is updated based on the type of the event, and in turn this generates more events. Furthermore, actions, implemented as Java classes and associated to transitions, are executed when these transitions occur. The coordination based on method invocation is more straightforward: any open object can invoke methods of another one at any given moment, and these invocations can be found in methods implementations, or in actions associated to the state machine [1].

Open objects are used to describe and structure the elements that belong in a metamodel. Afterwards, models conformant to these metamodels are executed by a component called Cumbia Kernel. This kernel, which is an engine to execute open objects' based models, is generic and is reused for every Cumbia based application and language. In fact, the essence of this kernel is managing event distribution and processing, which includes updating the state machines, but does so independently of the languages or metamodels used.

A common issue in the design of modeling languages is to balance their expressiveness and generality, and their size and complexity. If a language is very expressive and general, then it is likely to be big or complex, and thus difficult to implement, to support, and to use. On the other hand, if the language is small or simple, then it is likely to be less expressive and thus insufficient to solve certain problems. The Small DSLs approach addresses this by grouping multiple languages that are very expressive but that have a relatively small scope [2]. This approach is followed in Cumbia, where we can have multiple and complementary concern specific languages. By doing so, each language can be designed to focus on a particular concern, and focus on offering very expressive constructs for it. From a technical point of view, this is achieved by offering means to coordinate the execution of models, regardless of the languages used to describe each one of them.

Previously, we have explored two different mechanisms to describe the coordination of the models. In [3], we presented the means to describe the coordination at the model level, and externally to the models themselves. This description is used, at run time, to synchronize the execution of the models. The second mechanism to describe coordination does so at a higher level of abstraction (the metamodel level) and externally to the metamodels themselves [4]. This is done via a language called M2CL, which describes the relations that can be established between elements from different metamodels. This second strategy is built on top of the elements provided by the first one, and both of them have in common that they maintain the independence of the metamodels or the languages. They are always oblivious one of the other, and as a result, they can be easily replaced, removed, or modified. Also, new languages and concerns can be added as they become necessary.

Nevertheless, these two types of mechanisms are not always adequate. There are cases where some concerns have strong dependencies towards other concerns, which may or may not be known. To address this, metamodels should be designed from the beginning to be composed with those other metamodels. Therefore, in those cases it is desirable to include inter-metamodel dependencies, and include those within the metamodels' definitions. That implies higher coupling and lower flexibility, but it reflects better the dependencies between the concerns.

The goal of this paper is to present two strategies that we implemented in Cumbia to describe relationships between metamodels. The first one of these strategies is based on the definition of explicit dependencies between concrete metamodels. The second one, is based on the description of contracts for entities of the metamodels, and deferring the specification of the concrete bindings. These strategies are useful in different cases, and provide different degrees of flexibility. Furthermore, this paper illustrates the usage of these strategies with a concrete application: a simulator that uses four domain specific languages to describe complementary aspects of a traffic simulation scenario.

This paper is structured as follows: in section 2 we introduce the traffic simulation application, and we describe the concerns and languages involved in it. While doing so, we also introduce some additional background on the Cumbia platform. Then, in section 3, we present the strategies proposed to establish and maintain relations between metamodels. Finally, sections 4 and 5 present related work and conclude the paper.

2   An Application for Traffic Simulation

In this section we describe a traffic simulation tool based on the Cumbia platform. There are several reasons that make this an interesting application to illustrate Cumbia. In the first place, this is an application intended to be used by domain experts (traffic experts), and it would thus be desirable to offer high level, domain specific languages for the definition of simulation scenarios. Secondly, each simulation scenario needs to include many details, which can be of different natures. Therefore, it makes sense to modularize scenario definitions, for instance by separating concerns. This decision makes it possible to have concern specific languages and facilitates the reuse of scenarios. Finally, the concerns that we can identify for a traffic simulation application are not totally crosscutting: there are relations and interactions between them, and we can even identify a few elements that appear in multiple concerns.

For the traffic simulation that we are about to present, we have identified the four concerns shown in figure 1. For each one of these, we have defined a concern specific language, and built the elements to run models described using those languages. Furthermore, we have analyzed the interactions between these concerns, and we have created the artifacts to coordinate their execution. The rest of this section presents more details about each concern, about their implementation on top of Cumbia, and about the coordination of their execution.

2.1   Crossroads Structure

This is the central concern in the scenario, and it describes roads, lanes and routes for cars in the simulation to travel. This concern also handles the location

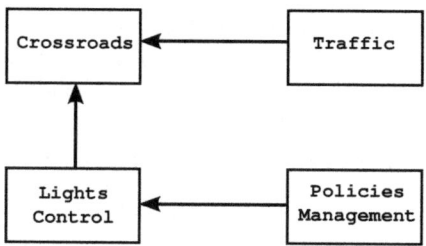

Fig. 1. Concerns and relations in the traffic simulation scenario

and state of pedestrian and traffic lights. The Crossroads concern is limited to describing structural aspects of the simulation: without further inputs from other concerns, a simulation of this concern would be static.

We have designed a graphical notation to describe crossroads models, and implemented an editor for domain experts to use. Besides serving to create diagrams like the one shown in figure 2, this editor also hides the complexity of the XML-based syntax that Cumbia uses to describe models.

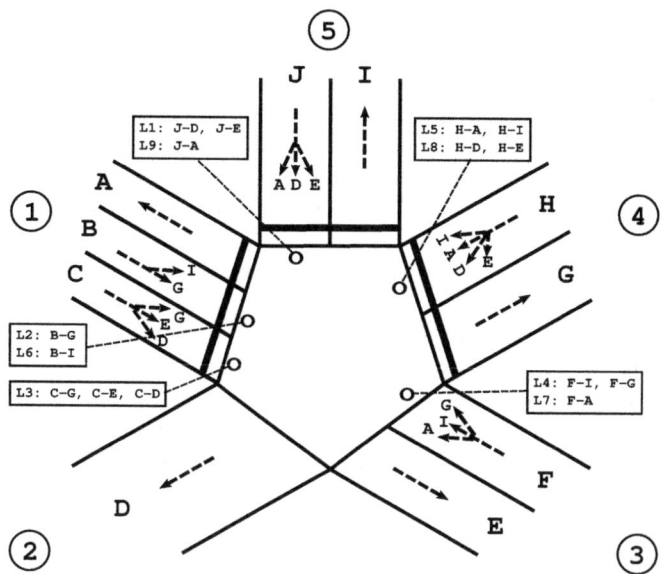

Fig. 2. Crossroads diagram

The diagram in figure 2 presents five *roads*, labeled from *1* to *5*. Each road contains at least one *lane*. For example, road *3* has two lanes, named *E* and *F*. The arrows drawn over the lanes indicates the orientation of the lane and also represent the available *routes*. For example, cars traveling on lane *F* can continue to lanes *A*, *I* or *G*, but not *H*.

This syntax also describes *pedestrian lights* and *traffic lights*. The former are represented by solid lines drawn over the roads. Figure 2 shows three pedestrian lights, located on roads *1*, *4* and *5*. Traffic lights are more complex than pedestrian lights because it is necessary to specify which routes they control. These lights are represented by small circles located in front of the lanes, connected to boxes that provide additional information about one or several traffic lights and the routes they control. In our example we place two traffic lights, *L1* and *L9*, in front of lane *J*. Traffic light *L1* controls the cars coming from lane *J* that are going to take lanes *D* and *E*, while *L9* controls the cars coming from lane *J* that are going to take lane *A*.

2.2 Lights Control

During the simulation, *policies* control the traffic lights, determining when each one has to show its green light. Each policy is defined as a sequence of *states*, and each state has a set of traffic lights that are supposed to show green when the state is active. A policy also indicates for how long each state has to be active and their order of activation. The language designed for this concern is textual, as shown in the following snippet:

```
Policy Normal
    St1 := {L2,L3,L5};
    St2 := {L1,L9,L4};
    St3 := {L7};
    St4 := {L8};
    St5 := {L2,L6,L3};
    Sequence {(St1,100) (St2,80) (St3,20) (St4,20) (St5,20)};
```

In this description, a policy called *Normal* is defined. The policy has five states, *St1* to *St5*. The sequence indicates that the first state is *St1* and has to be activated for 100 seconds. During those 100 seconds, only the lights L2, L3, and L5 in a simulation scenario have to show a green light. The last state of the sequence is *St5* and it has to be activated for 20 seconds. Afterwards, the cycle has to restart by reactivating state *St1*.

2.3 Policies Management

After defining the policies available to control the traffic lights in the simulation, it is necessary to specify the conditions to apply each policy. For this application, we use a simple mechanism which associates policies to time intervals in a day. The language to describe this is illustrated in the next snippet:

```
TimeBased ("6:30 - 9:00") => RushHour
TimeBased ("9:01 - 16:29") => Normal
TimeBased ("16:30 - 20:30") => RushHour
```

The example presents three time intervals and the policies that have to be applied for each one. During rush hours (6:30 to 9:00 and 16:30 to 20:30) the *RushHour* policy is applied. From 9:01 to 16:29 the *Normal* policy controls the traffic lights. This language can be extended to include new types of conditions besides time-based, with minimal impact to the rest of the concerns.

2.4   Traffic Generation

The previous concerns would not be interesting without simulated cars traveling the routes and being controlled by traffic lights. In our simulator, the traffic is modeled using probability distributions of car arrivals to the routes and lanes of a crossroads model. The language developed to model traffic is textual and is illustrated in the following example:

```
Route "B-G"
    Poisson 3
Route "C-G"
    Poisson 4
    Poisson 7
```

This snippet shows that routes are represented by a source lane and a target lane. The snippet also shows that it is possible to assign multiple probability distributions to a single route.

2.5   Implementing the Concerns in Cumbia

To build the traffic simulator on top of Cumbia, for each of the previously described concerns, a metamodel had to be created. Figure 3 shows the structure of the four metamodels, but because of space restrictions we cannot present in detail each one of them. Nevertheless, it has to be highlighted that each element in those metamodels is an open object, and that each metamodel reflects the abstract syntax of one of the concern specific languages previously shown. Given this context, creating a simulation scenario involves the creation of four models, each one conformant to one of the metamodels.

From the descriptions of the concerns, it should be clear that they have several points of contact. Therefore, to execute a complete simulation scenario it is not enough to independently execute the four models that compose it: they have to be executed in a coordinated way and information has to be shared between them. For instance, the element **Generator** in the Traffic model has an indirect responsibility in creating **Cars** in the Crossroads model.

This kind of coordination is achieved by means of CCL, M2CL, and M1CL (see figure 4) [4]. *CCL* (Cumbia Coordination Language) is a low level language that provides primitives, based on event passing and methods invocations, to describe how to coordinate model instances. CCL is useful to describe coordination between model instances, but does not offer mechanisms to describe coordination at higher levels, i.e, between metamodels and models. To solve this we developed a language called *M2CL*, that serves to encapsulate coordination rules between metamodel elements (M2 level). The entities that encapsulate this information are called *composites*, and they include the structural and behavioral aspects of the coordination. Finally, there is *M1CL*, the language to describe instances of those composites, which depend on the selection of elements from particular models. With the information available in the M2CL and M1CL descriptions, CCL code is generated automatically and is used, at run time, to ensure the coordination of the model instances.

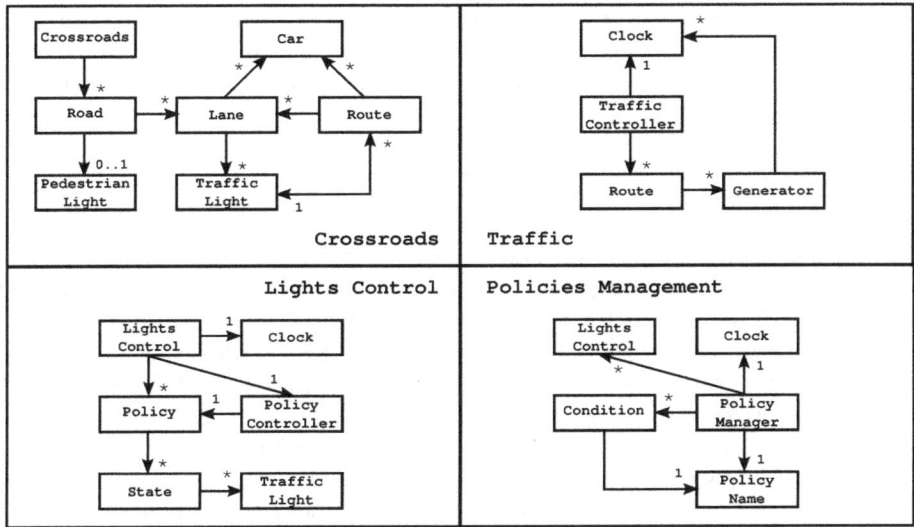

Fig. 3. Metamodels created for the traffic simulation scenario

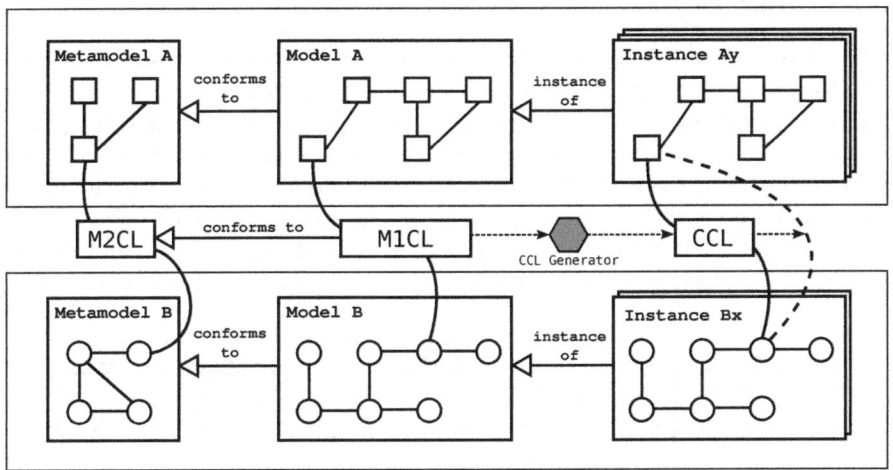

Fig. 4. Coordinating the execution with external descriptions

This coordination mechanism describes the coordination rules and restrictions externally to the coordinated elements themselves. This means that neither model definitions, nor metamodel definitions are impacted by the presence of coordination. As a result, the coupling between languages and metamodels is low, and languages can be replaced or modified with relative ease.

The downside of this approach is that the strict dependencies between the metamodels are not materialized. For example, with the means available it is not possible to say that the Lights Control element in the Lights Control model should be *the same* Lights Control element in the Policies Management model.

Instead, we are forced to first duplicate the elements in the two metamodels, and then to keep their instances in sync while executing. To solve these issues, the next section presents new composition and coordination concepts that we are introducing into Cumbia.

3   Dependencies between Metamodels

The mechanism currently offered by Cumbia to establish relations between meta-models, models and model instances does not properly support the representation of strict dependencies between Cumbia metamodels. To address this, we now propose a set of extensions to Cumbia that have an impact on the way open objects and metamodels are defined, as well as on M2CL, M1CL, and CCL. We have categorized these extensions according to the kind of dependencies that they aim to support: on the one hand, we have *direct dependencies*, which have the highest impact on coupling and flexibility; on the other hand, we have *behavioral dependencies*, which are not as rigid and do not eliminate all the flexibility that we gain from the usage of externalized coordination descriptions.

3.1   Direct Dependencies

The first mechanism we propose is to enable the specification of explicit dependencies between metamodels. This means that we are enabling the usage of elements in metamodels where they were not initially defined. Besides impacting the definition of the metamodels where these elements are used, this also has an impact on the definition of models, and on model instances (see figure 5). In the original open objects model, the elements used in a model definition had to be completely defined in the metamodel used to describe the model. With this extension, it is no longer necessary to duplicate open objects across metamodels.

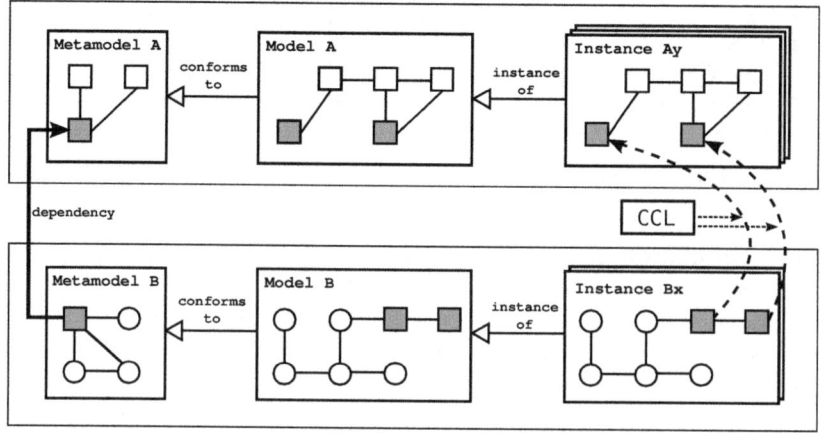

Fig. 5. Direct dependencies in two metamodels

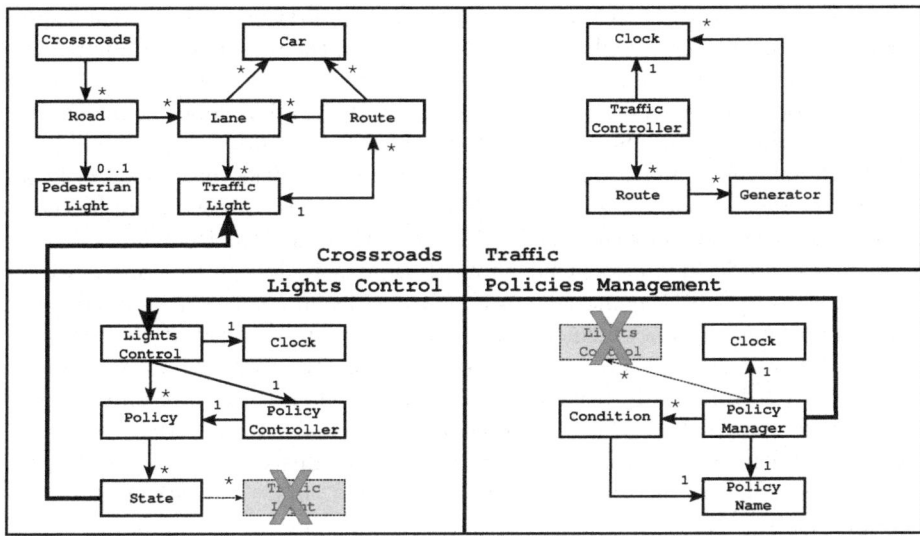

Fig. 6. Direct dependencies between metamodels in the traffic simulation scenario

Figure 6 shows how the metamodels in the traffic simulator can be redefined using direct dependencies, in order to better convey the dependencies that exist between them. In particular, we are defining two direct dependencies. The first one states that the element **Traffic Light** in the Lights Control metamodel is now going to be the element **Traffic Light** in the Crossroads metamodel. The second one states that the element **Lights Control** of the Policies Management metamodel is going to be the element **Lights Control** of the Lights Control metamodel. We are now going to show how the first dependency affects the metamodels and models definition.

```
<metamodel name="LightsControl" version="1.1">
  <dependencies>
    <metamodel-dependency name="crossroads" version="1.1"
      metamodel="Crossroads" />
  </dependencies>

  <external-type with="crossroads" externalTypeName="TrafficLight"
        typeName="Traffic Light"/>
  ...
</metamodel>
```

Prog. 1. Metamodel definition: direct dependency description

In the first place, we have to modify the definition of the metamodel. Program 1 shows the relevant parts of the metamodel description that define that a type in a given metamodel is defined in another metamodel. For this, a general dependency towards the Crossroads metamodel is first defined, and then specific dependencies are described. This is achieved with the tag `external-type`, which creates a local reference to the type defined in the other metamodel. In the sample case, we declare an external type called `Traffic Light`, which depends on the element with the same name in the Crossroads metamodel.

Models conformant to metamodels with dependencies must explicitly state which models satisfy which dependencies. They also have to explicitly "import" the necessary elements defined in the other models. Program 2 is a fragment of a model definition that shows how this is done in a sample scenario. The description of the model starts with a declaration of a dependency towards another model, which satisfies a dependency declared at the metamodel level. Then, the structure of the model explicitly states which elements are going to be "imported" from the other model. For this, it is only necessary to specify in which model the element sought is located, and its name. The Cumbia platform is now capable of verifying the consistency of those "imports", with respect to the types of the elements and the structure of the metamodels.

```
<definition metamodel="LightsControl" version="1.1"
            modelName="LightsSample">

  <dependencies>
    <model-dependency name="crSample"
      model="CrossroadsSample"
      mmDependencyName="crossroads"/>
  </dependencies>

  <model-structure>
    <elements>
      <external-element externalName="tl1" dependency="crSample" />
      ...
    </elements>
    ...
  </model-structure>
</definition>
```

Prog. 2. Model definition: direct dependencies usage

The final step is to use CCL to properly establish the references between elements in the model instances. Program 3 shows how this is achieved, using the new instruction `fixReference`. The usage of this instruction used in the sample CCL program can be translated as follows: "In the instance *Linstance* of the LightsSample model, resolve the declared dependency *crSample* using the elements found in the instance *c_instance* of the CrossroadsSample model". Given these directions, the Cumbia Weaver (the component that executes CCL programs) is capable of replacing placeholder elements in the instance of the LightsSample model with references to elements in concrete instances of the CrossroadsSample model.

```
assembly {
  load (LightsControl:LightsSample l_model , Crossroads:CrossroadsSample
       c_model);

  on:Init {
    c_instance = new c_model;
    l_instance = new l_model;
    fixReference(l_instance , "crSample", c_instance);
  }
}
```

Prog. 3. CCL: resolving direct dependencies at model instance level

3.2   Behavioral Dependencies

Defining dependencies directly and explicitly in the metamodel and model definitions is a simple and effective approach, but it results in high coupling. To alleviate this, we propose an alternative which replaces explicit dependencies with dependencies based on behavioral contracts. By doing so, it will still be possible to have dependencies between metamodels, but they will not be completely known beforehand. This new strategy involves extensions to the metamodel specification language, to M2CL, to M1CL, and to CCL. Figure 7 shows the elements involved in this strategy.

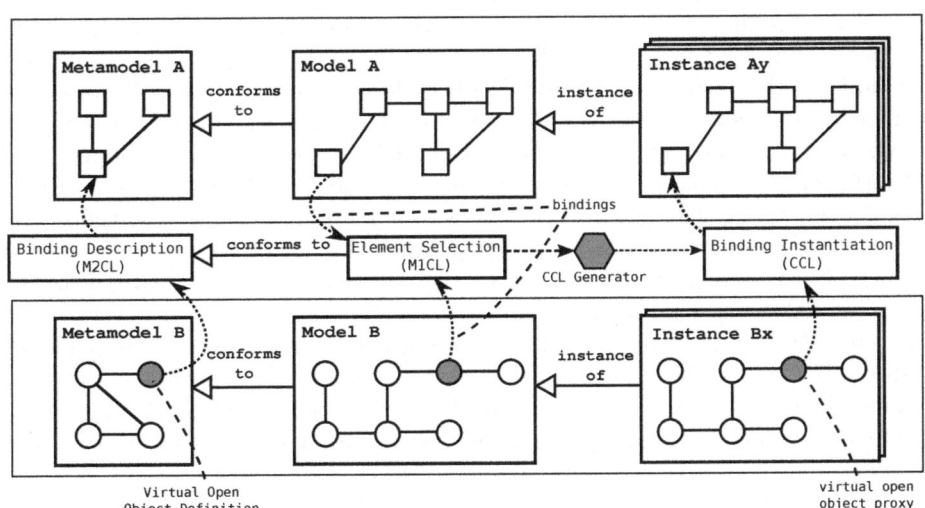

Fig. 7. Behavioral dependencies using virtual open objects

To describe behavioral contracts and dependencies in metamodel definitions, we introduced a new type of open object called *virtual open object*. Virtual open objects have some similarities to normal open objects [1]: they have a state machine, they generate events, and they have a public interface that announces the set of methods understood by each open object. However, virtual open objects are not executable, because they do not implement the methods declared on the interface, and because they cannot autonomously generate events. In the rest of the section we will revise the case study used in section 3.1, but we will use behavioral dependencies instead of direct ones. Program 4 presents the definition of a virtual open object called `TrafficLight` in the Lights Control metamodel.

```
<metamodel name="LightsControl" version="1.0">

  <state-machine-reference name="tlight" file="light.xml" />

  <virtual-type name="TrafficLight"
    interface="simulator.lights.ITrafficLight"
      state-machine-name="light">
      <event name="becameGreen"/>
      <event name="becameRed"/>
  </virtual-type>
</metamodel>
```

Prog. 4. Metamodel definition: virtual open objects defined

To execute an instance of a model conforming to a metamodel that includes virtual open objects, it is necessary to bind the virtual open objects with regular open objects. This means that, at run time, each virtual open object needs to be bound to a concrete open object.

These bindings have to be defined at the model level, using M1CL. Furthermore, at the metamodel level it is necessary to characterize the types of valid bindings. This is achieved in M2CL, using descriptions similar to the one shown in program 5. In that snippet, we have established that instances of the virtual type added to the Lights Control metamodel can be bound to instances of the `TrafficLight` type in the Crossroads metamodel. Furthermore, we had to describe a mapping between the two types: this mapping relates 1) methods in the interface of the virtual open object with methods implemented in the concrete open object; 2) and events emitted by the concrete open object with events that the virtual open object should emit.

Once the types of bindings have been defined using M2CL, it is possible to use M1CL to establish concrete bindings between model elements. Program 6 shows how this is done: an instance of the binding type is defined, and it specifies which pair of elements are going to be bound together. Note that exactly one of these elements has to be a virtual open object.

Finally, to create the concrete bindings between elements in model instances, some CCL code is required. This code is generated from the M2CL and the M1CL descriptions and in particular from the mapping defined for events and methods. Program 7 shows a fragment of the code generated in the sample case studied. It illustrates the new instructions added to CCL, namely `bindEvent` and `bindMethod`. Using the former, an instance of a virtual open object, which operates as a proxy, is configured to re-emit certain events produced by the concrete element. The latter instruction serves to configure which methods of the concrete element to invoke when a method is invoked in the virtual element.

```
binding TrafficLightBinding
  use Crossroads.TrafficLight cLight
  use LightsControl.TrafficLight vLight

  bind cLight:isOn to vLight:becameGreen
  bind cLight:isOff to vLight:becameRed

  bind vLight.reset to cLight.setOff
end
```

Prog. 5. M2CL: definition of a binding

```
TrafficLightBinding L2_to_Ll2
  cLight : CrossroadsModel.L2
  vLight : LightsControlModel.L2
end
```

Prog. 6. M1CL: binding of elements in models

4   Related Work

Meta case tools, such as MetaEdit+[5], GME[6], the Eclipse GMF[1], or the Microsoft DSL Tools[2] have been used to define and use DSMLs in industrial settings [7,8,9]. These tools are based on metamodeling, and one of their main strengths is the capability of automatically generating the tools that the DSMLsâĂŹ users require (editors). Up to this point, we have not used any of these tools to describe Cumbia models. Instead, we have developed ad-hoc editors for each of our DSMLs. However, we plan on using one of the available open tools with Cumbia soon.

Because of the importance of establishing and maintaining relationships between modelsâĂŹ elements, there are many proposals to manage these relationships. In [10], BrÃd'uer and Lochmann identify four of those strategies. The first strategy is based on model weaving, such as in the Motorola WEAVR [11] and in AMW [12,13]. A second strategy is based on model mappings and model-to-model transformations, which are also used on [12]. The third strategy is based on named-based references between model elements, and it is used in SMART [9] and NAOMI [14]. SmartEMF [15] is a tool to represent, check, and maintain constraints in multimodels that use these kinds of references. The Cumbia framework can be partially classified in this strategy, although the semantic relationships are stronger than just a name: with open objects, the notion of element type also exists. Finally, the strategy presented in [10] is based on an upper ontology, and on connectors that establish semantic links between languages. This approach also has similarities to Cumbia (the open objects structure can be

---

[1] Eclipse Graphical Modeling Framework, http://www.eclipse.org/modeling/gmf/
[2] Microsoft: Domain-Specific Language Tools, http://msdn.microsoft.com/en-us/library/bb126235(VS.80).aspx

```
load (LightsControl:LightsSample l_model,
      Crossroads:CrossroadsSample c_model);
...
c_instance = new c_model;
l_instance = new l_model;
...
c_L2 = findByName(c_instance,"L2");
l_L2 = findByName(l_instance,"L2");

bindEvent(l_L2, "becameGreen", c_L2, "isOn");
bindEvent(l_L2, "becameRed", c_L2, "isOff");

bindMethod(l_L2, "reset", c_L2, "setOff");
```

Prog. 7. CCL: binding of methods and events

likened to an upper ontology), but, since it is much more general, it is not executable, i.e. for each upper ontology an implementation has to be created.

Executability is the primer goal of some modeling frameworks, although the meaning of the term execution, and the reasons to achieve execution, vary from tool to tool. According to [16], executing a model involves the computation of a sequence of states in the model, in response to input data. This definition is consistent with their overall reason for using models, which is to define, validate, simulate, and generate the code of a system. Although it is less formal, Ptolemy II [17] follows a similar perspective on execution, and, in particular, it aims to generate code for embedded systems. In NAOMI [14], model execution has a slightly different meaning and intent: NAOMIs models are executed by taking some inputs from a repository, running the models to obtain outputs, and writing the outputs back into the repository. The execution of NAOMIs multimodels is achieved by executing each model while following an execution plan based on model dependencies.

5   Conclusions

In this paper we have presented two strategies to define dependencies between metamodels. The first one, which we call direct dependencies, results in highly coupled metamodels. In spite of the negative effect on flexibility, this strategy is useful because of its simplicity and because it removes the need to duplicate elements or coordinate several elements between several metamodels. Furthermore, this approach enables the static validation of dependencies, while metamodels are designed, instead of doing it dynamically when models are executed.

To reduce the coupling introduced with the first strategy, we proposed a second one that introduces a level of indirection in the definition of the dependencies. This indirection materializes in the definition of contracts which specify the name of methods and events used to bound elements. This strategy depends on external information available outside the metamodels and models to resolve the dependencies at run time, which is provided using M2CL and M1CL.

Moreover, the two strategies proposed do not replace the coordination mechanisms that were already present in Cumbia. They complement them, and they are intended to be used when the characteristics of a domain require a tighter coupling between the metamodels.

The strategies presented in this paper are our first attempt to implement new types of relations between metamodels, models and model instances in the Cumbia platform. Because of that, they have some evident limitations that we expect to remove in the future. For example, currently behavioral dependencies only support the binding of methods that do not receive parameters and one-to-one event mappings. In the future, we expect to remove this kind of limitations by supporting the definition of more complex mappings. In particular, we want to support methods with more detailed signatures, and also complex events mapping.

References

1. Sánchez, M., Villalobos, J., Romero, D.: A state machine based coordination model applied to workflow applications. Avances en Sistemas e Informática 6(1), 35–44 (2009)
2. Warmer, J.B., Kleppe, A.G.: Building a flexible software factory using partial domain specific models. In: Sixth OOPSLA Workshop on Domain-Specific Modeling (DSM 2006), pp. 15–22. University of Jyvaskyla, Jyvaskyla (2006)
3. Sánchez, M., Jiménez, C., Villalobos, J., Deridder, D.: Extensibility in model-based business process engines. In: Oriol, M., Meyer, B. (eds.) TOOLS EUROPE 2009. LNBIP, vol. 33, pp. 157–174. Springer, Heidelberg (2009)
4. Rodríguez, C., Sánchez, M., Villalobos, J.: Executable Model Composition - A Multilevel Approach. In: Proceedings of the 26th Symposium On Applied Computing, TaiChung, Taiwan, pp. 875–882 (March 2011)
5. Tolvanen, J.-P., Rossi, M.: MetaEdit+: defining and using domain-specific modeling languages and code generators. In: Companion of the 18th Annual ACM SIGPLAN Conference on Object-oriented Programming, Systems, Languages, and Applications. OOPSLA 2003, pp. 92–93. ACM Press, New York (2003)
6. Davis, J.: GME: the generic modeling environment. In: Companion of the 18th Annual ACM SIGPLAN Conference on Object-oriented Programming, Systems, Languages, and Applications. OOPSLA 2003, pp. 82–83. ACM Press, New York (2003)
7. Ledeczi, A., Bakay, A., Maroti, M., Volgyesi, P., Nordstrom, G., Sprinkle, J., Karsai, G.: Composing domain-specific design environments. COMPUTER 34, 44–51 (2001)
8. Luoma, J., Kelly, S., Tolvanen, J.-p.: Defining domain-specific modeling languages: Collected experiences. In: Proceedings of the 4th OOPSLA Workshop on Domain-Specific Modeling, DSM04 (2004)
9. Warmer, J.B., Kleppe, A.G.: Building a flexible software factory using partial domain specific models. In: Sixth OOPSLA Workshop on Domain-Specific Modeling (DSM 2006), pp. 15–22. University of Jyvaskyla, Jyvaskyla (2006)
10. Bräuer, M., Lochmann, H.: Towards semantic integration of multiple domain-specific languages using ontological foundations. In: Proceedings of 4th International Workshop on (Software) Language Engineering (ATEM 2007) co-located with MoDELS (2007)

11. Cottenier, T., Van Den Berg, A., Elrad, T.: The motorola weavr: Model weaving in a large industrial context. In: Proceedings of the International Conference on Aspect Oriented Software Development, Industry Track (2006)
12. Bézivin, J., Jouault, F., Kurtev, I., Valduriez, P.: Model-based DSL frameworks. In: OOPSLA 2006: Companion to the 21st ACM SIGPLAN Conference on Object-oriented Programming Systems, Languages, and Applications, pp. 602–616. ACM Press, New York (2006)
13. Del Fabro, M.D., Bézivin, J., Jouault, F., Breton, E.: Amw: A generic model weaver. In: Proceedings of the 1ere Journée sur l'Ingénierie Dirigée par les Modèles, IDM 2005 (2005)
14. Denton, T., Jones, E., Srinivasan, S., Owens, K., Buskens, R.W.: NAOMI – an experimental platform for multi–modeling. In: Busch, C., Ober, I., Bruel, J.-M., Uhl, A., Völter, M. (eds.) MODELS 2008. LNCS, vol. 5301, pp. 143–157. Springer, Heidelberg (2008), http://dx.doi.org/10.1007/978-3-540-87875-9_10
15. Hessellund, A., Busch, C., Wąsowski, A.: Guided development with multiple domain-specific languages. In: Engels, G., Opdyke, B., Schmidt, D.C., Weil, F. (eds.) MODELS 2007. LNCS, vol. 4735, pp. 46–60. Springer, Heidelberg (2007)
16. Hardebolle, C., Boulanger, F., Marcadet, D., Vidal-Naquet, G.: A generic execution framework for models of computation. In: MOMPES 2007: Proceedings of the Fourth International Workshop on Model-Based Methodologies for Pervasive and Embedded Software, pp. 45–54. IEEE Computer Society, Washington DC, USA (2007)
17. Brooks, C., Hong Cheng, C., Feng, T.H., Lee, E.A., Hanxleden, R.V.: Model engineering using multimodeling. In: 1st International Workshop on Model Co-Evolution and Consistency Management, MCCM 2008 (2008)

KlaperSuite: An Integrated Model-Driven Environment for Reliability and Performance Analysis of Component-Based Systems

Andrea Ciancone[1], Antonio Filieri[1], Mauro Luigi Drago[1], Raffaela Mirandola[1], and Vincenzo Grassi[2]

[1] Politecnico di Milano, Piazza Leonardo Da Vinci 32, 20133 Milano, Italy
`andrea.ciancone@mail.polimi.it`, {`filieri,drago,mirandola`}`@elet.polimi.it`
[2] Università di Roma "Tor Vergata", Viale del Politecnico 1, 00133 Roma, Italy
`vgrassi@info.uniroma2.it`

Abstract. Automatic prediction tools play a key role in enabling the application of non-functional requirements analysis to selection and assembly of components for Component-Based Systems, reducing the need for strong mathematical skills to software designers. Exploiting the paradigm of Model Driven Engineering (MDE), it is possible to automate transformations from design models to analytical models, enabling for formal property verification. MDE is the core paradigm of KlaperSuite presented in this paper, which exploits the KLAPER pivot language to fill the gap between Design and Analysis of Component-Based Systems for reliability and performance properties. KlaperSuite is a family of tools empowering designers with the ability to capture and analyze QoS views of their systems by building a one-click bridge towards a number of established verification instruments.

1 Introduction

Discovering late during the development process that a software system does not meet certain non-functional requirements can be harmful. The impact of changes — if applied when a complete implementation of a system exists — on development costs and on failure risks may be non negligible. Indeed, it has been already pointed out that anticipating the analysis of non-functional properties — such as performance and reliability — at design time can mitigate these issues [1,2,3]. The work we present in this paper goes in this direction, by supporting early analysis of non-functional attributes for software systems built with a Component-Based (CB) development paradigm.

Component-based software systems are essentially assemblies of preexisting, independently developed components. The focus of the development process shifts from custom design and implementation to selection, composition and coordination [4,5]. In a component based setting, analysis must be carried out before assembling and this can lead to early discovery potential problems related

J. Bishop and A. Vallecillo (Eds.): TOOLS 2011, LNCS 6705, pp. 99–114, 2011.

to non-functional attributes. Which components are selected, how they are composed, and how they are coordinated should in turn depend on the results of analyses, as pointed out by Crnkovic in [4].

However, existing techniques for non-functional analysis rely on very specific performance-related formalisms — such as Queueing Networks (QNs), Petri Nets (PNs), or Markovian models — but software systems are rarely represented in these terms. Designers, who usually lack sufficient experience in performance engineering, prefer *design-oriented* formalisms such as UML [6] which reflect more the modeling intent. Although both design-oriented models and performance-related models carry the same pieces of information required for the analysis of non-functional properties, the way such information is captured, i.e., the syntax, makes the difference from a user perspective.

To cope with this mismatch between representations, tools have been recently proposed in literature. The idea is leverage Model Driven Engineering (MDE) [7] techniques to automatically derive, by means of *model transformations*, performance models from design-oriented models of the system (augmented with additional information related to the non-functional attributes of interest). Existing analysis methodologies [2,8,9,10] may be in turn applied as is.

However, defining this kind of transformations could be quite difficult. The large semantic gap between the source and the target meta-models of the transformation, the heterogeneous design notations that could be used by different component providers, and the different target analysis formalisms are all examples of barriers for transformations development. The usage of intermediate modeling languages, which capture relevant information for QoS analyses, has been proposed to mitigate these problems. Intermediate languages in fact bridge design-oriented and analysis-oriented notations, and help in distilling the information needed by performance analysis tools [11,12,9]. Instead of directly transforming design models to performance models, a two-step transformation from the source model to the intermediate model, and from the intermediate model to the target model is proposed.

In this paper we describe KlaperSuite, an integrated environment for the performance and reliability analysis leveraging KLAPER (Kernel LAnguage for PErformance and Reliability analysis) [11]. KLAPER is an intermediate language supporting the generation of stochastic models, to predict performance and reliability, from design-level models of component-based software systems. Transformations from design models to analytical models are completely automated in a one-click way. Designers are indeed empowered with the ability to analyze their systems, with established verification instruments, in a seamless and integrated environment.

The remainder of this paper is organized as follows. Section 2 outlines the KLAPER language and its main characteristics. In section 3 we present the different types of analysis included in KlaperSuite, spanning from reliability, to performance, and to generation of simulation prototypes. Sections 5 and 6 describe existing literature related to our work and future research directions, respectively.

2   KLAPER

In this section we first present the key points of our MDE-based approach to the generation of a performance/reliability model for a CB system (Section 2.1). Then we present the meta-model of the intermediate language that we use to support this approach (Section 2.2).

2.1   The Basic Methodology

The central element of our framework is the usage of KLAPER [11] whose goal is to split the complex task of deriving an analysis model (e.g. a queueing network) from a high level design model (expressed using UML or other component-oriented notations) into two separate and presumably simpler tasks:

- extracting from the design model only the information that is relevant for the analysis of some QoS attribute and expressing it in terms of the key concepts provided by the intermediate language;
- generating an analysis model based on the information expressed in the intermediate language.

These two tasks may be solved independently of each other. Moreover, as a positive side effect of this two-step approach, we mitigate the *"n-by-m"* problem of translating n heterogeneous design notations (that could be used by different component providers) into m analysis notations (that support different kinds of analysis), reducing it to a less complex task of defining $n + m$ transformations: n from different design notations to the intermediate language, and m from it to different analysis notations.

The KLAPER goal is to capture in a lightweight and compact model only the relevant information for the stochastic performance and reliability analysis of CB systems, while abstracting away irrelevant details.

To integrate this kernel language into an MDE framework, leveraging the current state of the art in the field of model transformation methodologies, KLAPER is defined as a Meta-Object Facility (MOF) meta-model [13]. According to MOF, a (meta)model is basically a constrained directed labeled graph, and a meta-model defines the syntactic and semantic rules to build legal models.

Hence, we can use the MOF facilities to devise transformations to/from KLAPER models, provided that a MOF meta-model exists for the corresponding source/target model. According to the MDE perspective, these transformations can be defined as a set of rules that map elements of the source meta-model onto elements of the target meta-model.

2.2   The KLAPER Meta-Model

Figure 1 shows the structure of the KLAPER meta-model[11]. To support the distillation from the design models of a CB system of the relevant information for stochastic performance/reliability analysis, KLAPER is built around an abstract representation of such a system, modeled (including the underlying platform) as an assembly of interacting *Resources*. Each Resource offers (and possibly requires) one or more *Services*. A KLAPER Resource is thus an abstract modeling concept that can be used to represent both software components and physical resources like processors and communication links.

A *scheduling policy* and a *multiplicity* (number of concurrent requests that can be served in parallel) can be associated with a resource to possibly model access control policies for the services offered by that resource[11]. Each service offered by a resource is characterized by its *formal parameters* that can be instantiated with actual values by other resources requiring that service. We point out that both the formal parameters and their corresponding actual parameters are intended to represent a suitable abstraction (for the analysis purposes) of the real service parameters. For example, a real list parameter for some list processing software component could be abstractly represented as an integer valued random variable, where the integer value represents the list size, and its probability distribution provides information about the likelihood of different sizes in a given analysis scenario. We explicitly introduce service parameters to better support compositional and parametric analysis [11].

To bring performance/reliability related information within such an abstract model, each activity in the system is modeled as the execution of a *Step* that may take time to be completed, and/or may fail before its completion: the *internalExecTime*, *internalFailTime* and *internalFailProb* attributes of each step may be used to give a probabilistic characterization of these aspects of a step execution.

Steps are grouped in *Behaviors* (directed graphs of nodes) that may be associated either with the Services offered by Resources (reactive behavior), or with a *Workload* modeling the demand injected into the system by external entities like the system users (proactive behavior). *Control steps* can be used to regulate the flow of control from step to step, according to a probabilistic setting.

A *ServiceCall* step is a special kind of Step that models the relationship between required and offered services. Each ServiceCall specifies the name of the requested service and the type of resource that should provide it.

The relationship between a ServiceCall and the actual recipient of the call is represented separately by means of instances of the *Binding* metaclass. This allows a clear separation between the models of the components (by means of Resources/Services) and the model of their composition. In fact a set of bindings can be regarded as a self-contained specification of an assembly. Similarly, since the service call concept is also used at the KLAPER level to model the access of software components to platform level services, a suitable set of bindings can model as well the deployment of the application components on the underlying platform.

Finally, we point out that the performance/reliability attributes associated with a behavior step concern only the *internal* characteristics of the behavior; they do not take into account possible delays or failures caused by the use of other required services, that are needed to complete that step. In this respect, we remark that when we build a KLAPER model (first task outlined above) our goal is mainly "descriptive". The Bindings included in the model help to identify which external services may cause additional delays or failure possibilities. How to properly mix this "external" information with the internal information to get an overall picture of the service performance or reliability must be solved during the generation and solution of an analysis model derived from a KLAPER model.

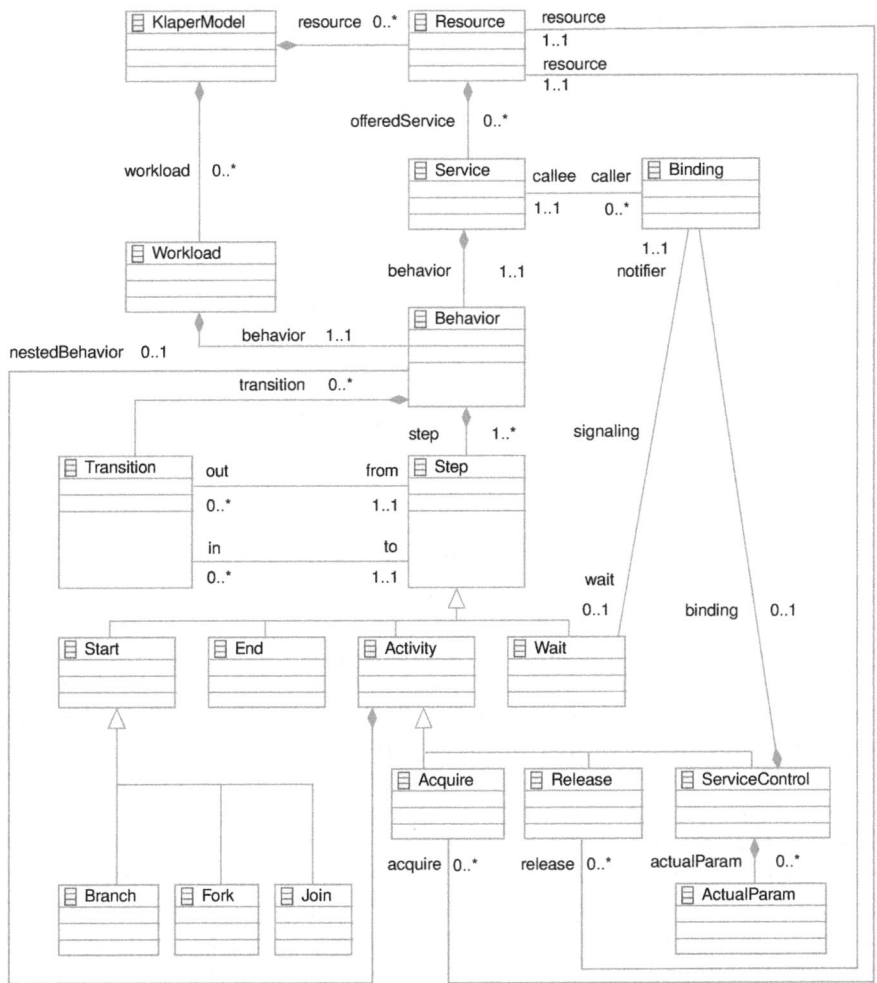

Fig. 1. The KLAPER MOF meta-model

3   The KlaperSuite Analysis Tools

The main purpose of the KLAPER-based analysis is to provide a set of tools that support early verification of non-functional requirements. Such an analysis,

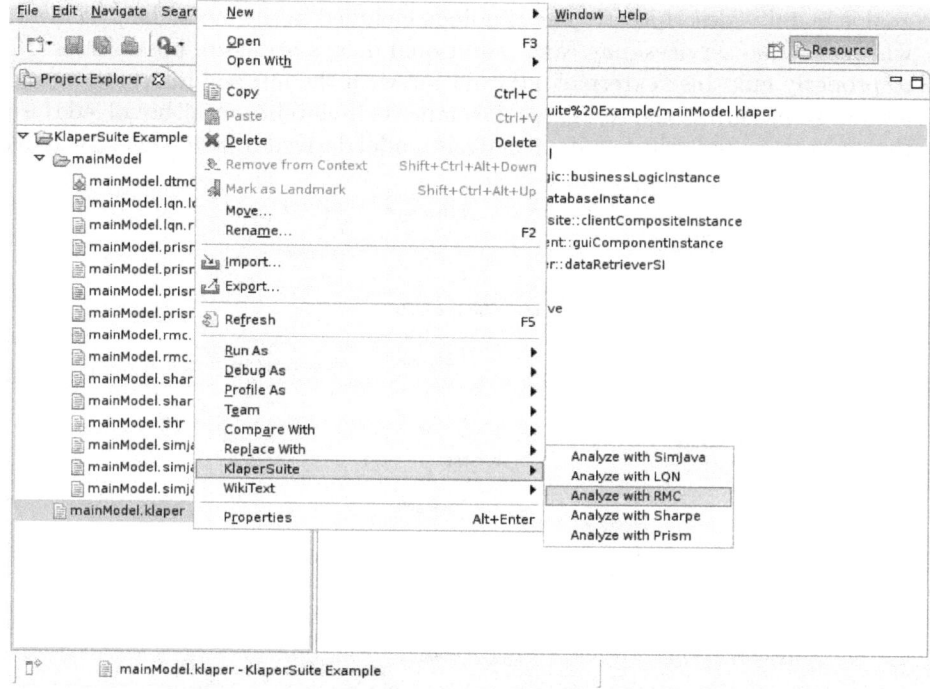

Fig. 2. Menu for the launches of the KlaperSuite tools

applied at early stages of design, allows identifying possible issues while the development team has the largest decision scope.

KlaperSuite aims at providing a family of KLAPER-based tools which can execute a number of analysis tasks on KLAPER models. All the tools in the KlaperSuite are fully automated and require at most a few configuration parameters to be set. The entire environment is integrated in the Eclipse IDE [14], in order to provide a unified interface and a familiar environment for both academic and industrial developers.

Most of the tools are able to automatically transform KLAPER models into appropriate inputs for each of the external tools involved in the analysis process, and then capture analysis results and store them in text files, which are human readable. It is then easy to extend the suite by adding specific parsers in order to put back results into any computer readable form.

The KlaperSuite's purpose is to fill the gap from KLAPER to non-functional verification tools. A consolidated development process may possibly benefit from the implementation of automatic model transformations from already established design metamodels to KLAPER. This single time investment can enable designers to take advantage of the entire family of analysis tools.

Analysis plugins can also store intermediate files (i.e. third parties tools input files) that can be further analyzed for different purposes or by external experts.

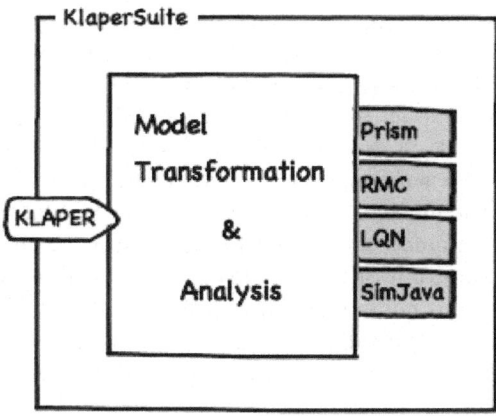

Fig. 3. High level view of KlaperSuite

Download instructions for the KlaperSuite can be found at `http://home.dei.`
`polimi.it/filieri/tools2011`. In the same location is also available an example workspace, which has not been described in this paper because of the lack of space. A snapshot of the KlaperSuite is shown in Fig. 2

In the following of this section we present the set of verification features currently supported by KlaperSuite and illustrated in Fig. 3. They will be grouped in three subsets depending on the purpose of their inclusion. More specifically, Section 3.1 will present analysis features concerning reliability estimation, Section 3.2 concerns performance prediction, while Section 3.3 will present a simulation-based analysis tool which provides verification of both reliability and performance properties, as well as a lightweight prototype of the system to be.

3.1 Reliability

Reliability is the first non functional aspect we focus on. There are a number of tools that allow the evaluation of various facets of reliability [15]. A KLAPER model can be automatically mapped in a Markov Chain, that is a stochastic characterization of the system under design able to capture various information affecting software reliability.

Reliability is one of the so-called *user-centered* property [16], in the sense that the reliability of a system strictly depends on its usage. While a failure probability is associated with each system component, the actual usage determines which parts of the systems are more stressed by clients and thus can have an higher perceived impact. The usage profile of a system is embedded in two parts of a KLAPER model, namely *workload* and *branch annotations*. Workload is directly related to the intended usage of the system by its clients, that is, which functionalities they invoke. Branch probabilities are instead more related to the distribution of inputs inserted by the clients.

PRISM Model-Checking. Mapping a KLAPER model into a corresponding *Discrete Time Markov Chain* (DTMC) is straightforward. A DTMC can be roughly seen as finite state-transition automata where each state s_i has a certain probability p_{ij} to reach state s_j. As for Probability theory, for each state s_i it holds that $\sum_j p_{ij} = 1$. States of a DTMC are used to represent relevant states of the execution of a software system. For example a state may represent an internal action or the invocation of a service. In DTMC-based reliability analysis, it is common to enhance the model of the system with a set of states that represents meta-condition of the execution, that is, they do not correspond to neither internal actions nor external invocations, but rather to failures or success. These *meta-states* are typically related to permanent conditions of the system, and thus their counterpart in the domain of DTMCs are *absorbing states*. Any state s_i such that $p_{ii} = 1$ is said to be absorbing, with the immediate meaning that state s_i, once reached, cannot be left.

Reliability can be defined as the probability of reaching any absorbing state corresponding to a success condition from the state corresponding to the execution's start. But a designer may be interested also in more complex properties related to reliability, such as the probability that the system fails given that it reached a certain execution state, or that a certain kind of failure arises. In order to specify those properties, given a DTMC model of the system under design, it is possible to use special purpose logic languages, such as PCTL [17] and its extension, PCTL* [18]. Such logics allow the formal description of a set of paths through a DTMC. Then a Probabilistic Model-Checker is able to compute the probability for the execution to follow exactly those paths.

For example, assuming that there is a single absorbing success state s_s, we are interested in considering all the possible paths which will eventually reach s_s. Such a path property can be easily formalized in PCTL(*) as $\diamond s = s_s$, which literally means that eventually ($\diamond$) the current state of execution (s) will be equal to the success state (s_s). The eventually operator assumes that the execution of the system always begin from its defined initial state (which corresponds to a *start* step of a KLAPER workflow) and that can reach s_s in any finite number of state transitions.

This preamble is to justify the idea to include in our suite a transformation toward a DTMC+PCTL* model. In order to be able to exploit available model checkers, transformation must finally provide input files for one of them. The two mostly established are PRISM [19,20] and MRMC [21]. The former exploits symbolic manipulation of PCTL properties in order to verify them on a compact representation of the state space; so it might be beneficial in case of complex formulae. The latter uses an explicit state-space representation that makes it possibly require more memory, but makes the verification quite fast, at least for simple formulae such as reachability. The reader interested in more details about Probabilistic Model Checking could refer to [22].

KlaperSuite is able to automatically transform a KLAPER model into a PRISM input, that is, a DTMC and a PCTL represented in PRISM's textual syntax. Our tool is able to extract the global reliability and to put it in a text file. But the produced PRISM models are completely consistent with all the information in the KLAPER source, and can thus be further analyzed by means of the other PRISM's advanced features [20], viable also through its graphical interfaces. Also PRISM can itself convert models and properties in MRMC's syntax, thus enabling a second way of analysis.

The transformation from KLAPER to PRISM is realized in two steps. The first is a model-to-model transformation from KLAPER to an intermediate meta-model which reproduce the structure of a PRISM model. This transformation is implemented in QVT-Operational, the imperative model-to-model transformation language standardized by the OMG [23]. The second step is a model-to-text transformation implemented in Xpand2 [24], that generates the textual representation of the PRISM model to be analyzed. Both QVTO and Xpand2 are natively supported by Eclipse.

The most critical issue in analyzing KLAPER models for reliability through PRISM is that KLAPER model supports the specification of (possibly recursive) function calls. Such a feature is not naturally captured by Discrete Time Markov Chains, which are instead successfully adopted in many research works [25]. The reason is that software's control flow is hard to be flattened in a finite sequence of function calls without loosing precision (remember that highly reliable software may require estimation's precision up to 10^{-7}). In order to properly analyze our models through PRISM, we need to enhance DTMC models with some Process Algebra constructs in order to stochastically simulate function calls. This formalization allows PRISM to obtain results with arbitrary accuracy. By default KlaperSuite requires results with maximum error magnitude of 10^{-12}. This value can be increased or decreased at will.

The problem with the combination of DTMCs and Process Algebra lies in the exponential state-space explosion. Hence even small KLAPER models can lead to untreatable PRISM analyses, in presence of recursive invocations. This issue introduce the need for a more efficient way to deal with recursiveness, namely Recursive Markov Chains, that will be presented in the next section.

Recursive Markov Chains. A Recursive Markov Chain can be seen as a collection of finite-state Markov Chains with the ability to invoke each other, possibly in a recursive way. They have been introduced in [26] and come with a strong mathematical support. RMCs can be analyzed (by means of equation systems) in a very efficient way in order to evaluate reachability properties. Reliability, intended as the probability of successfully accomplish the assigned task, as well as the probability of failure given that the execution has reached a certain execution state, can be formalized as reachability properties, as well as a number of other interesting requirements.

Also, by construction KLAPER behaviors are *1-exit* control flows, that is they only have a single *end* step. This allow us to verify any reachability property in P-time. In practice RMC analysis of KLAPER models has been successfully applied in the european project Q-Impress [27] and proved to be really efficient on real-world industrial models.

The first step of the transformation from KLAPER to RMC is the same model-to-model transformation used for the PRISM based analysis. From the intermediate PRISM-tailored model, KlaperSuite extrapolates a system of equations that is directly solved by our Java implementation, without any need for external tools.

Reliability estimation is then reported in the result file, while an extensive log file contains a textual representation of the equations system and the complete solution, that is, the probability, from each modeled execution state to reach the successful completion of the execution.

With respect to PRISM, RMC-based analysis can handle very large models with recursive invocations. On the other hand it does only support verification of reachability properties over Markov chains. The accuracy of results is arbitrary also for RMC analysis and set by default to 10^{-12}.

3.2 Performance

Early evaluation of performance can be obtained by either analytical modeling or simulation. In this Section we focus on modeling, while in Section 3.3 we will briefly discuss simulation facilities of the KlaperSuite.

The two most basic, though general-purpose, measurable properties for performance are response-time and throughput. One of the most widely accepted mathematical models to estimate those properties are Layered Queuing Networks (LQNs) [9,28]. LQNs introduce new modeling concepts to represent software systems. Systems are represented as a layered hierarchy of LQN tasks (each one corresponding to a KLAPER *Resource*) which interact, and generate demands for underlying physical resources. Each task may offer different kinds of services, called *entries*. An entry corresponds to a KLAPER service and can be described either as a *phase* or as an *activity*. Phases allow for description of simple sequential behaviors; activities allow for description of more complex behaviors, e.g., with control structures such as forks, joins, and loops.

An LQN model can be analyzed by means of special purpose mathematical softwares. In the KlaperSuite we make use of the LQN Solver from Carleton University[1]. In order to produce input files for that solver we designed a two step model transformation. The first step is a QVTO model-to-model transformation from KLAPER to an intermediate meta-model which is an abstract representation of the analytical model. Then, the abstract representation is transformed into an input file for the LQN solver by means of an Xpand model-to-text transformation.

The obtained LQN models can then be solved. Examples of the kind of analysis results that can be derived applying the LQN solver to the obtained LQN model are task utilization, throughput and response time. Different configurations can be easily analyzed by a simple change in the LQN parameters. The analysis of the obtained performance results can help in the identification of critical components, such as bottlenecks, which can prevent the fulfillment of performance requirements.

---

[1] http://www.layeredqueues.org

3.3   Simulation

The simulation engine of the KlaperSuite was initially designed with the only purpose to validate the previous analysis tools, but can be used to simulate any KLAPER model, tough it was not designed to deal with scalability issues.

The simulator is based on the SimJava library for the simulation of discrete event systems[2]. Upon SimJava, KlaperSuite builds a lightweight prototype of the system in which each service is simulated through a SimJava Entity. Each entity runs in its own thread and is connected to the others by *ports* which allow communications consisting of sending and receiving events. Communications among entities are defined consistently with the corresponding KLAPER behavior to be simulated. A central control thread monitors the execution of the prototype and records execution times and failure occurrences of each Entity, as they are inferred from the trace of events. The control thread's log is then analyzed in order to derive statistical estimation for performance and reliability properties.

In order to produce the Java code of the prototype another two steps model transformation is in place. The first step transforms the KLAPER model into an intermediate meta-model corresponding to the structure of the prototype[3] and is implemented in QVTO. The second step is a model-to-text transformation implemented in Xpand which generates the Java code.

The previous tools have been validated through simulation [29]. Notice that for intrinsic reasons simulation is computationally expensive with respect to mathematical analysis to verify the set of reliability and performance properties discussed in this paper. Nevertheless, the use of an established tool such as SimJava allows for further enhancement of the Java prototypes, that can, for example, be instrumented with a larger set of monitors or with special purpose features.

4   Tools Integration Status

Table 1 shows the current development status of the KlaperSuite. Some of the tools have been developed in the past as standalone and their integration is still ongoing. All the single tools are hosted on Sourceforge[4].

5   Related Work

In the last years, it has been widely recognized the need of including early quality prediction in the software development process. In particular, there has been an increasing interest in model transformation methodologies for the generation of analysis-oriented target models (including performance and reliability models) starting from design-oriented source models, possibly augmented with suitable

---

[2] http://www.dcs.ed.ac.uk/home/hase/simjava/
[3] The meta-model can be found in the Sourceforge repository.
[4] http://sourceforge.net/projects/klaper/

Table 1. Tools integration status

Tool	Purpose	Features	Integration Status
Klaper2Prism	Reliability	− System mapped to DTMC model. − Reliability properties expressed in PCTL*. − Efficient on complex formulae. − Does not scale on recursive service invocations.	Fully integrated
Klaper2RMC	Reliability	− System mapped to RMC model. − State reachability properties only. − Efficient for recursive service invocations. − Highly scalable on large systems.	Fully integrated
Klaper2LQN	Performance	− System mapped to LQN model. − Response time, throughput, state residence time. − Does not scale on large systems	Still standalone
Klaper2 SimJava	Simulation	− System mapped to SimJava application. − Reliability and performance estimation. − Extensible via SimJava features.	Partially integrated

annotations. Several proposals have been presented concerning the direct generation of performance analysis models. Each of these proposals focuses on a particular type of source design-oriented model and a particular type of target analysis-oriented model, with the former including, for example, UML, Message Sequence Chart, Use Case Maps, formal or ADL languages and the latter including Petri nets, queueing networks, layered queueing network, stochastic process algebras, Markov processes (see [2,3]. To have an overview the topic, see for example the WOSP conference series [10].

The gap between design-oriented models and analysis-oriented ones is often long. Nevertheless, most of the proposals we are aware of start from UML models with proper annotations, and *directly* generate reliability models such as fault trees, state diagrams, Markov processes, hazard analysis techniques and Bayesian models. (e.g. [30,31]). Another tool specialized to the prediction of QoS is Palladio tool suite [8]. It provides its own meta-model called PCM (Palladio Component Model), able to describe component-based software architecture with support for parametric QoS contacts[8]. Currently, it allows to design

PCM models with its own graphical editor and analyze them for performance and reliability via simulation.

A different way to deal with transformation complexity is to pass through an intermediate model (the "kernel") by pruning the information from the design model that is not needed to execute the desired analyses, but still retaining needed one.

Among the transformation approaches that make use of intermediate models, Petriu et al. [32] proposed the CSM (Core Scenario Model). CSM is a MOF compliant kernel metamodel, specifically related to performance analysis. Transformation from UML to CSM and from it to different performance models are provided. PUMA [9] adopts CSM as intermediate language to predict performance via layered queueing networks, an analysis model that extends queueing networks and stochastic Petri nets. Gu et al. [12] proposed, in a similar way, their own intermediate metamodel to transform UML model with performance annotations to performance modeling formalisms.

With respect to the kernel languages of [12,9,32], KLAPER is intended to serve also for reliability and, possibly trade-off analysis between performance and reliability. KLAPER and is specifically targeted to component-based systems. It has been applied for the analysis of performance and reliability using queuing networks and Markov models [11] and experienced with the CoCoME case study [33,34]. Extensions of KLAPER has also been proposed to analyze self-adaptive [35] and reactive [36] systems. In these works the KLAPER models have been designed manually, without using any automated transformation tool.

Recently, KLAPER has been used within the European project Q-ImPrESS [27]. Q-ImPrESS aims at building a framework for service orientation of critical systems. The framework provides a tool suite for the modeling and the prediction of QoS. Q-ImPreSS models can be manually created and extracted from software source code thought reverse engineering tools. Once, the model is completed, several tools are exploitable for the analysis of reliability, performance, and maintainability. Such a framework is deeply founded on model transformations, which allow to automatically fill the gap between design and analysis models. In Q-ImPreSS, KLAPER facilities have been exploited for the construction of the reliability features in the Q-ImPrESS tool chain, and validated on industrial cases.

With respect to previous works, we presented in this paper KlaperSuite a fully automated and integrated environment including a family of tools empowering designers with the ability to capture and analyze the performance and reliability figures of their systems. The possibility of using different verification tools together with a simulation-based analysis tool could make KlaperSuite a valuable instrument for predicting the software qualities during the development process.

6   Conclusions

In this paper we presented KlaperSuite, an integrated environment for performance and reliability analysis leveraging KLAPER intermediate language.

KlaperSuite allows the automatic generation of stochastic models to verify and predict performance and reliability properties of component-based software systems. Analyses can be applied on high level design models, in order to provide support for early properties evaluation. By using this tool, designers are empowered with the ability to analyze their systems, with established verification instruments, in a seamless and integrated environment.

As future extension of the KlaperSuite, we are planning to implement model transformations from higher level design models (first of all UML) to KLAPER. In this way KlaperSuite will be easier to integrate in established development cycles. On a longer perspective, we also plan to explore the possibility of extracting KLAPER model directly from annotated code, which will encourage the use of analytical models by programmers.

Finally, only part of the tools have been evaluate on real industrial models inside the Q-Impress project. We are currently working on the experimentation of this environment on different testbeds, to assess its effectiveness through a more comprehensive set of real experiments.

Acknowledgments

The authors would like to thank all the persons who have worked on the tools belonging to KlaperSuite, in particular Federico Carbonetti and Enrico Randazzo who implemented LQN and SimJava transformations. The work has been partially supported by the EU project Q-ImPrESS (FP7 215013).

References

1. Smith, C.U., Williams, L.G.: Performance and Scalability of Distributed Software Architectures: an SPE Approach. Addison-Wesley, Reading (2002)
2. Balsamo, S., DiMarco, A., Inverardi, P., Simeoni, M.: Model-based performance prediction in software development: A survey. IEEE Transactions on Software Engineering 30(5), 295–310 (2004)
3. Koziolek, H.: Performance evaluation of component-based software systems: A survey. Perform. Eval. 67(8), 634–658 (2010)
4. Crnkovic, I.: Building Reliable Component-Based Software Systems. Artech House, Inc., Norwood (2002)
5. Szyperski, C.: Component Software: Beyond Object-Oriented Programming. Addison-Wesley Longman Publishing Co., Inc., Boston (2002)
6. Object Management Group: UML 2.0 superstructure specification (2002)
7. Atkinson, C., Kühne, T.: Model-driven development: A metamodeling foundation. IEEE Softw. 20(5), 36–41 (2003)
8. Becker, S., Koziolek, H., Reussner, R.: The palladio component model for model-driven performance prediction. Journal of Systems and Software 82(1), 3–22 (2009)
9. Woodside, M., Petriu, D.C., Petriu, D.B., Shen, H., Israr, T., Merseguer, J.: Performance by unified model analysis (puma). In: WOSP 2005: Proceedings of the 5th International Workshop on Software and Performance, pp. 1–12. ACM Press, New York (2005)

10. Wosp: Proceedings of the international workshop on software and performance (1998-2010)
11. Grassi, V., Mirandola, R., Sabetta, A.: Filling the gap between design and performance/reliability models of component-based systems: A model-driven approach. J. Syst. Softw. 80(4), 528–558 (2007)
12. Gu, G.P., Petriu, D.C.: From uml to lqn by xml algebra-based model transformations. In: WOSP 2005: Proceedings of the 5th International Workshop on Software and Performance, pp. 99–110. ACM Press, New York (2005)
13. Object Management Group: MOF version 2.0, ptc/04-10-15 (2004)
14. Foundation, T.E.: Project website (2010), http://www.eclipse.org
15. Horgan, J., Mathur, A.: Software testing and reliability. The Handbook of Software Reliability Engineering, 531–565 (1996)
16. Cheung, R.C.: A user-oriented software reliability model. IEEE Trans. Softw. Eng. 6(2), 118–125 (1980)
17. Hansson, H., Jonsson, B.: A logic for reasoning about time and reliability. Formal Aspects of Computing 6, 512–535 (1994)
18. Reynolds, M.: An axiomatization of pctl*. Information and Computation 201(1), 72–119 (2005)
19. Hinton, A., Kwiatkowska, M., Norman, G., Parker, D.: PRISM: A tool for automatic verification of probabilistic systems. In: Hermanns, H. (ed.) TACAS 2006. LNCS, vol. 3920, pp. 441–444. Springer, Heidelberg (2006)
20. Kwiatkowska, M., Norman, G., Parker, D.: Prism 2.0: a tool for probabilistic model checking. In: Proceedings First International Conference on the Quantitative Evaluation of Systems, QEST 2004, pp. 322–323 (2004)
21. Katoen, J.-P., Khattri, M., Zapreevt, I.S.: A markov reward model checker. In: Second International Conference on the Quantitative Evaluation of Systems, pp. 243–244 (2005)
22. Baier, C., Katoen, J., et al.: Principles of model checking (2008)
23. Group, O.M.: Qvt 1.0 specification (2008), http://www.omg.org/spec/QVT/1.0/
24. Efftinge, S., Kadura, C.: Xpand language reference (2006)
25. Goseva-Popstojanova, K., Trivedi, K.S.: Architecture-based approach to reliability assessment of software systems. Performance Evaluation 45(2-3), 179 (2001)
26. Etessami, K., Yannakakis, M.: Recursive markov chains, stochastic grammars, and monotone systems of nonlinear equations. In: Diekert, V., Durand, B. (eds.) STACS 2005. LNCS, vol. 3404, pp. 340–352. Springer, Heidelberg (2005)
27. Consortium, Q.I.: Project website (2010), http://www.q-impress.eu
28. Rolia, J.A., Sevcik, K.C.: The method of layers. IEEE Transactions on Software Engineering 21(8), 689–700 (1995)
29. Randazzo, E.: A Model-Based Approach to Performance and Reliability Prediction. PhD thesis, Universitá degli Studi di Roma - Tor Vergata (2010)
30. Immonen, A., Niemelä, E.: Survey of reliability and availability prediction methods from the viewpoint of software architecture. Software and System Modeling 7(1), 49–65 (2008)
31. Bernardi, S., Merseguer, J., Petriu, D.C.: Adding dependability analysis capabilities to the MARTE profile. In: Busch, C., Ober, I., Bruel, J.-M., Uhl, A., Völter, M. (eds.) MODELS 2008. LNCS, vol. 5301, pp. 736–750. Springer, Heidelberg (2008)
32. Petriu, D.B., Woodside, C.M.: An intermediate metamodel with scenarios and resources for generating performance models from uml designs. Software and System Modeling 6(2), 163–184 (2007)

33. Herold, S., Klus, H., Welsch, Y., Deiters, C., Rausch, A., Reussner, R., Krogmann, K., Koziolek, H., Mirandola, R., Hummel, B., Meisinger, M., Pfaller, C.: CoCoME - the common component modeling example. In: Rausch, A., Reussner, R., Mirandola, R., Plášil, F. (eds.) The Common Component Modeling Example. LNCS, vol. 5153, pp. 16–53. Springer, Heidelberg (2008)
34. Grassi, V., Mirandola, R., Randazzo, E., Sabetta, A.: KLAPER: An intermediate language for model-driven predictive analysis of performance and reliability. In: Rausch, A., Reussner, R., Mirandola, R., Plášil, F. (eds.) The Common Component Modeling Example. LNCS, vol. 5153, pp. 327–356. Springer, Heidelberg (2008)
35. Grassi, V., Mirandola, R., Randazzo, E.: Model-driven assessment of qoS-aware self-adaptation. In: Cheng, B.H.C., de Lemos, R., Giese, H., Inverardi, P., Magee, J. (eds.) Software Engineering for Self-Adaptive Systems. LNCS, vol. 5525, pp. 201–222. Springer, Heidelberg (2009)
36. Perez-Palacin, D., Mirandola, R., Merseguer, J., Grassi, V.: Qos-based model driven assessment of adaptive reactive systems. In: Proceedings of the 2010 Third International Conference on Software Testing, Verification, and Validation Workshops,ICSTW 2010, pp. 299–308. IEEE Computer Society Press, Washington, DC, USA (2010)

Unifying Subjectivity

Daniel Langone, Jorge Ressia, and Oscar Nierstrasz

Software Composition Group, University of Bern, Switzerland
http://scg.unibe.ch/

Abstract. Subjective behavior is essential for applications that must adapt their behavior to changing circumstances. Many different solutions have been proposed in the past, based, for example, on perspectives, roles, contextual layers, and "force trees". Although these approaches are somehow equally expressive, each imposes a particular world view which may not be appropriate for all applications. We propose a unification of these approaches, called Subjectopia, which makes explicit the underlying abstractions needed to support subjective behavior, namely *subjects*, *contextual elements* and *decision strategies*. We demonstrate how Subjectopia subsumes existing approaches, provides a more general foundation for modeling subjective behavior, and offers a means to alter subjective behavior in a running system.

1   Introduction

We, as humans, generally strive to be objective, that is we try to behave in a unique and consistent way, independent of personal feelings or external influences. In practice, however, we are often required to behave *subjectively*, that is, we must adapt our behavior depending on circumstances.

In fact, real world entities are subjective. We have learned, for example, in the 20th century that physical measurements are relative to the frame of reference used by the observer. As a consequence, real-world problem domains that we model in software applications are also subjective. The various elements that collaborate to achieve a common goal may need to adapt their behavior when specific events or conditions are met.

Object-oriented languages follow the *objective* approach. An object behaves always the same way when receiving the same stimulus. To faithfully model the real-world domains we need mechanisms to model subjectivity. We can characterize the key approaches that have previously been proposed as follows:

Perspectives. Smith and Ungar proposed adding multiple *perspectives* to an object, where each perspective implements different behavior for that object [12]. When an object sends a message through a perspective the receiver behaves differently depending on this perspective. Therefore, an object behaves subjectively depending on the perspective through which other objects see it.

Roles. Kristensen introduced the concept of *roles* to model subjective behavior [6]. People behave differently depending on the role they are playing. For

J. Bishop and A. Vallecillo (Eds.): TOOLS 2011, LNCS 6705, pp. 115–130, 2011.

example, the same person may behave differently as a father, an employee or a shopper. A role is attached to an object to specify additional or modified behavior. Kristensen explicitly models *subjects* — objects with roles — whose behavior depends on the role they are playing for the sender of a message.

COP. *Context-oriented programming* (COP) was introduced by Costanza *et al.* [1]. The behavior of an object is split into layers that define the object's subjective behavior. Layers can be activated and deactivated to represent the actual contextual state. When a message is sent, the active context determines the behavior of the object receiving the message.

SMB. Darderes and Prieto proposed *subjective message behavior* [2]. The different behaviors for a message are split into a set of independent methods and combined with a tree-based decision mechanism, called a *force tree*.

Although formally the approaches are equivalent in expressive power, they are not equally suitable in all circumstances. Each of these approaches imposes a particular modeling paradigm which may be appropriate for certain problem domains, but not for others. Consider the use case where a user wants to send an email using a mobile device [2]. If the network is available the email should be sent immediately, otherwise the email should be saved and sent when possible. Modeling the network with either roles or perspectives does not make sense. This subjective problem is not about roles of networks or emails, or about perspectives through which they may be seen, but rather about whether the network is available in the current context. Whereas COP or SMB might be more appropriate for modeling subjectivity in this domain, perspectives or roles would be more suitable to model behavior that varies with respect to the sender of a message.

Furthermore, the responsibility of determining which subjective behavior should be selected may lie varyingly with the sender of a message, the receiver, or even the context. For example, in the perspective- and role-based approaches it is the sender of the message which determines the perspective or role to be used. Consider communicating with a person who might be at work or on holidays, thus triggering completely different responses. In such a case it would make more sense for the receiver and not the sender to determine the subjective behavior.

Our approach. To alleviate the problem of having a fixed subjectivity model, we propose a framework, called Subjectopia, which unifies and generalizes the earlier approaches. Subjectopia reifies three key abstractions that are only implicit in the other approaches. A *subject* is an object that behaves subjectively. Any object may be turned into a subject. Subjective behavior is modeled by a *decision strategy*. A decision strategy determines the appropriate subjective behavior based on the value of a set of *contextual elements*. Decision strategies can be configured to model roles, perspectives, force trees or layers, thus subsuming the earlier approaches. Furthermore, they can be dynamically adapted at runtime, which is important for adapting long-lived software systems.

section 2 presents a review of previous approaches to modeling subjective behavior. In section 3 we explain how Subjectopia models the subjective behavior of objects and discuss our implementation. section 4 validates our approach by showing the drawbacks of previous approaches in solving subjective problems and demonstrates how Subjectopia circumvents these shortcomings. In section 5 we summarize the paper and discuss future work.

2   State of the Art

Subject-oriented programming was first introduced by Harrison and Ossher [4]. They advocated the use of subjective views to model variation, thus avoiding the proliferation of inheritance relations. Up to that point subjective behavior was modeled in an *ad hoc* fashion using idioms such as self-delegation and multiple dispatch. Various researchers subsequently proposed dedicated approaches to model subjective behavior in a more disciplined way. We briefly survey the key approaches and discuss their limitations.

2.1   Perspectives

Smith and Ungar [12] proposed to model subjective behavior through a set of possible views of an object. These views are called *perspectives* and are composed of zero or more hierarchically ordered *layers*. Each layer is composed of pieces modeling one behavior for one message and one object. For the approach to be deterministic a layer should never have two or more pieces corresponding to the same message and one object. An object sending a message selects the perspective through which it views the subject. Smith and Ungar developed a prototype called *US* on top of the *Self* [14] programming system.

The approach forces the developer to translate a given problem in terms of perspectives, which may not always suit the problem domain. Consider again the use case in which a user wants to send an email using a mobile device [2]. (If the network is available the email should be sent immediately, otherwise the email should be saved and sent when possible.) Network availability is a property of the current context of the user, not a "perspective" through which sending of email can be viewed.

A further difficulty is that the object initiating an interaction is responsible for selecting the current perspective. By contrast, in this use case it would be more appropriate for the mobile device to decide how to behave.

A general problem of this approach is that there is no way to overrule the process that decides the subjective behavior to be executed for a method. This decision is hardcoded in the internals of the approach.

2.2   Roles

Kristensen [6] stressed the importance of roles in the subjective behavior of entities: *"we think and express ourselves in term of roles"* when dealing with the real world. The notion of a role can be deduced from psychology as a set of connected behaviors, rights and obligations as conceptualized by actors in a social situation.

A role object is attached to a regular object, called an *intrinsic object*, and adds, removes or redefines the latter's original behavior. An intrinsic object together with its role is called a *subject*. Roles have no responsibilities of their own, *i.e.*, they only have meaning when attached to an intrinsic object. The *is-part-of* relationship of the role to its intrinsic object refers to the location of *part objects* introduced by Madsen and Møller-Pedersen [10]. An object sending a message selects the role through which it knows the subject. There are implementations of role-based programming relying on BETA [7] and Smalltalk [7].

Role-based programming forces the developer to model domain entities as playing various roles. Let us consider the group programming example [12] of a system for registering changes on source code of an object-oriented application. In the original implementation changes were modeled as perspectives, allowing us to have different views of the source-code. However, modeling changes as roles does not reflect reality. The source code does not play a particular role but rather is viewed differently by different developers.

As with perspectives, it is the sender of a message that decides which role the subject plays in an interaction. Scenarios in which the subjective behavior should be selected by the subject cannot be modeled directly.

2.3   Context-Oriented Programming

Context-Oriented Programming (COP) refers to programming language mechanisms and techniques that support dynamic adaptation to context [5]. COP was first introduced by Costanza and Hirschfeld [1]. The behavior of an object in COP is split into several layers (not to be confused with the layers introduced by perspectives). Each layer models the behavior associated to a particular context. Every definition not explicitly placed in a user-defined layer belongs to a default root layer. When an object receives a message, its behavior depends on the active layer, representing the current context.

ContextL [5] extends CommonLisp with layers and PyContext [9] does the same for Python. Implementations also exist for Java, JavaScript, Smalltalk and Scheme[1].

With COP the developer is required to model subjective behavior in terms of contextual layers. Consider again the use case where a user wants to send an email using a mobile device [2]. If the receiver of the email is in the same room as the sender then the email is sent with high priority. The mail deliverer is responsible for delivering the emails with a given priority. With layers, we will have two implementations for the send mail responsibility, one with high priority and the other without. The default layer activation of COP, using explicit layer activation, does not allow us to faithfully model this problem domain. We require a mechanism from the sender to activate the appropriate layer before sending the message. Thus a perspective approach would model this problem better.

---

[1] http://www.swa.hpi.uni-potsdam.de/cop/implementations/index.html

2.4 Subjective Message Behavior

Darderes and Prieto [2] proposed to represent subjective behavior by modeling the forces that might influence an object to behave subjectively. There are four types of *forces*: (i) the *sender force* is the object sending the message, (ii) the *self force* is the receiver of the message, *i.e.*, the subject, (iii) the *collaborator force* is any object collaborating with the subject, and (iv) the *acquaintance force* is any other object influencing the message.

Subjective Message Behavior proposes to split all possible behaviors for one message into a set of behaviors. The decision process is realized by a dispatch mechanism called a *force-tree*, consisting of *determinant nodes*, each consisting of a condition to be fulfilled and corresponding behavior. The *method determinant node* models one possible behavior for a given message of the object. The *force determinant node* models a boolean condition based on one force to decide which determinant has to be evaluated next. When an object receives a message, the root determinant of the force tree corresponding to that message is evaluated. The force tree has to be complete, acyclic and free of simultaneously active determinants in order for its evaluation to result in a unique possible behavior for a given message in a particular invocation context. Leaf nodes should always be *method determinant*.

Subjective Message Behavior requires the developer to model subjective behavior using a force tree, which may be overly complex for certain domains: Consider again the group programming example [12] of a system for registering changes to source code of an object-oriented application. Perspectives naturally model the behavior of a developer who wants to see his version of the source code. Casting this use case in terms of forces and force trees introduces unnecessary complexity.

3   Modeling Subjective Behavior

In this section we introduce Subjectopia[2] Both Subjectopia and the examples presented in this paper are implemented in Pharo Smalltalk[3]. Objects with subjective behavior are explicitly modeled as *subjects*, emphasizing the difference to common objects. A subject needs to select its correct behavior from a set of possible behaviors. We use *decision strategies* to explicitly model the way subjective decisions are taken. Finally, *contextual elements* model context-dependent information, which can influence the behavior of a subject. Our model allows us to change the subjective behavior of a subject by changing its decision strategy. Decision strategies and contextual elements allow us to model perspectives, roles, context-oriented programming, subjective message behavior and other subjectivity models. Hence, Subjectopia does not force the developer to use a fixed modeling paradigm.

---

[2] http://scg.unibe.ch/research/subjectopia/
[3] http://www.pharo-project.org/

To explain the Subjectopia model we use the bank account example from the perspective approach [12]. The use case consists of users transferring money through bank accounts. The user object sends the message `transfer:to:` to its bank account indicating as arguments the amount of money and the bank account the money should be transferred to. The bank account object changes its balance by the amount of money transferred and sends the message `addAndRecord:` to the bank account receiving the money. However, a user should not be able to directly send the message `addAndRecord:` to a bank account to guarantee that only bank accounts can trigger a transfer and maintain the balance invariant of the banking application. As a consequence the message `addAndRecord:` has two different behaviors for a bank account, depending on whether a user or a bank account object sends the message.

The following subsections introduce the concepts of *subject, decision strategy* and *contextual element* and describe how they can be used to model the example

3.1   Subjects

A *subject* is an object that behaves differently under different contextual circumstances. A subject may be fully subjective or only present subjective behavior for certain responsibilities. To transform a regular object into a subject we send the message `becomeSubject` to the object. For example, we can tell the bank account object `aBankAccount` to become a subject:

```
aBankAccount becomeSubject.
```

The transformation of `aBankAccount` into a subject adds the necessary behavior to enable it to behave subjectively for certain messages. The bank account object can also directly inherit from Subject, which will have the same effect. The bank account subject will only change its balance if the sender of the message `addAndRecord:` is a bank account. We therefore define the message `addAndRecord:` in the `aBankAccount` subject as being subjective:

```
aBankAccount register: aDecisionStrategy for: #addAndRecord:.
```

The original behavior of the `aBankAccount` subject for the message `addAndRecord:` is replaced by a decision strategy which models the subjective decision process. Modeling subjects explicitly has the advantage that the subjective parts of an application can be detected and thus reflected upon accordingly. Otherwise, this information would be encoded in the application source code and we would have to use *ad hoc* mechanisms to detect the subjects.

3.2   Decision Strategies

A decision strategy models the process of deciding how a subject has to behave when it receives a specific message. Because we use explicit decision strategies

---

[3] Readers unfamiliar with the syntax of Smalltalk might want to read the code examples aloud and interpret them as normal sentences: An invocation to a method named `method:with:`, using two arguments looks like: `receiver method: arg1 with: arg2`.

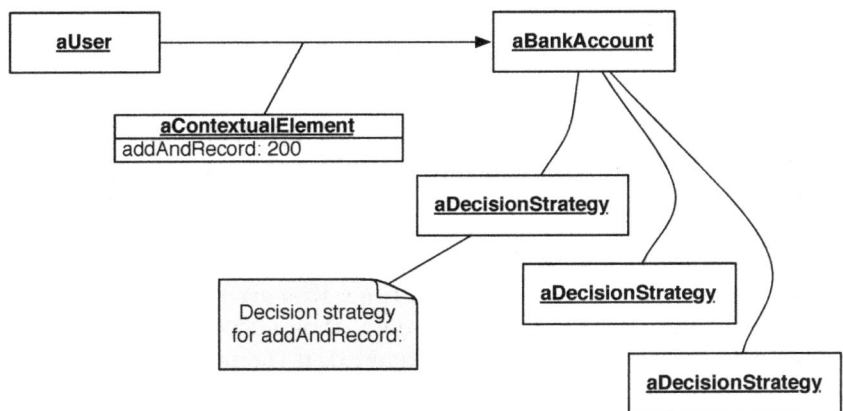

Fig. 1. The object `aUser` sends message `addAndRecord:` with argument 200 to `aBankAccount`. The subject performs a lookup and finds the subjective method. The method evaluates the decision strategy selecting the appropriate behavior for the current context.

we can define our own or reuse existing decision models such as those that express perspectives, roles, context-oriented programming or subjective message behavior. We can also directly implement behavior in a decision strategy.

Figure 1 shows the process of the subject `aBankAccount` receiving the message `addAndRecord:` from `aUser`. The subject performs a traditional method-lookup. Since `addAndRecord:` was defined as a subjective method, the method's behavior is adapted to evaluate the decision strategy:

```
aBankAccount>>addAndRecord: aNumber
   | message |
   message := self generateCommunicationInformation.
   ^(self findDecisionStrategyFor: #addAndRecord: evaluate: message)
```

The subjective method uses two steps to make the subject behave subjectively. The first step consists in the subject creating a contextual element representing the meta-information of the message. In Figure 1 this message object contains the following information:

- The message selector `#addAndRecord:`
- The argument 200.
- The sender of the message, the `aUser` object.
- The receiver of the message, the `aBankAccount` subject.

The second step consists in evaluating the decision strategy with the contextual information provided by the message object. The decision strategy determines which information provided by the message object is used. The evaluation of a decision strategy may be resolved as:

- Delegating to another decision strategy for further evaluation, allowing us to model decision hierarchies.

- Executing behavior, if the decision strategy directly models behavior.
- Sending a message to the subject, if we model all possible behaviors in the subject.

In Figure 1 the user object aUser wants to change the balance of the bank account aBankAccount, increasing it by 200 Fr. The decision strategy examines the message object and denies the request to change the balance because the sender is a user object.

Decision strategies can be replaced, in case the paradigm for modeling subjective behavior needs to be adapted over time. It is even possible to use multiple decision strategies within a single subject, thus allowing, say, role-based and perspective-based approaches to be combined, if the problem domain demands it.

3.3   Contextual Elements

Contextual elements model information available to a decision strategy for selecting subjective behavior. We have already seen the example above where a message object reifies the meta-information of a communication, to be used by the decision strategy.

Other examples of contextual elements are perspectives, roles or context layers. These abstractions are contextual objects that can affect the decision strategy depending on the subjective model we are in. We can also directly implement behavior in a contextual element, for example to simulate roles. A contextual element can be passed to a decision strategy in two ways: either the decision strategy has direct access or it is sent together with the message.

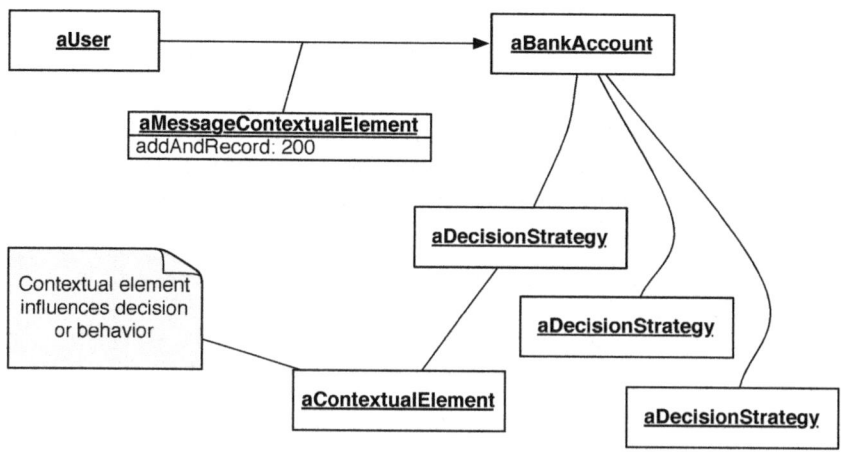

Fig. 2. Two ways of using contextual elements

Figure 2 describes the process of how a decision strategy uses a contextual element to model subjective behavior. We can use contextual elements to model the bank account using perspectives. Bank account subjects send the message `addAndRecord:` through the perspective, modeled as `aMessageContextualElement`. Since `addAndRecord:` was defined as a subjective method, the method behavior is adapted to allow the use of contextual elements:

```
aBankAccount>>addAndRecord: aNumber through: aContextualElement
    | message |
    message := self generateCommunicationInformation.
    ^(self findDecisionStrategyFor: #addAndRecord: evaluate: message
    with: aContextualElement)
```

Because the decision strategy is modeled explicitly we can change the way the decision is taken. For example we can let the decision strategy automatically determine, using the message object, which perspective has to be used. In this way we do not have to send the contextual element together with the message. In Figure 2 this corresponds to the green contextual element, modeling the perspective, which is directly accessed by the decision strategy.

Sometimes we need composed contextual elements, for example when modeling perspectives. One contextual element models one layer of the perspective. The layers as contextual elements are hierarchically composed to one perspective. The evaluation order of the composed contextual elements is determined by the decision strategy.

3.4   Implementation

The proof-of-concept implementation of Subjectopia is written in Smalltalk, due to its advanced support for run-time reflection. At present, a subject must directly inherit from the class `Subject` to be able register subjective behavior. We transform existing objects to subjects by sending the message `becomeSubject` which adds the necessary behavior to the object receiving the message.

Each subject has a special decision strategy, called *decision meta-object*, which maps subjective message names to decision strategies. Registering a subjective method by sending `register:for:` to the subject consists of two steps. First, it creates an entry in the decision meta-object with the message as key and the decision strategy as value. Second, it adapts the behavior of the registered method. Instead of performing the original behavior, the method collaborates with the subject's decision meta-object to evaluate the corresponding decision strategy.

For example, to model subjective behavior on the bank account subject for the message `addAndRecord:` we send the message `register: aDecisionStrategy for: #addAndRecord:`. First, the subject creates an entry with key `addAndRecord:` and value `aDecisionStrategy` in its decision meta-object. Second, the subject generates the following method automatically:

```
aBankAccount>>addAndRecord: aNumber
```

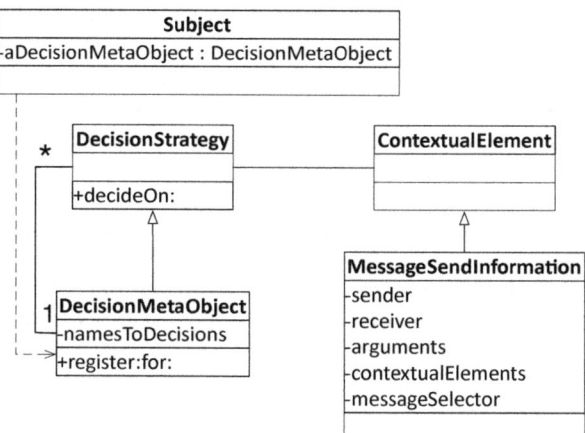

Fig. 3. Class diagram of Subjectopia

```
^self findDecisionStrategyFor: #addAndRecord: evaluate: thisContext
```

The object `thisContext` represents the communication context, which is automatically generated in Smalltalk. If an object sends the message `addAndRecord:` to a bank account subject, it evaluates the decision strategy corresponding to the message `addAndRecord:`.

Prior to the evaluation of the decision strategy, the subject generates an object representing the meta-information of the message with the help of the `thisContext` object. Next, the subject sends the message `decideOn:` to the decision strategy with the meta-information object as argument, which triggers the evaluation. Currently Subjectopia models decision strategies for perspectives, roles and subjective message behavior.

Subjectopia allows the sender of any subjective message to add `through:` to send a contextual element together with it. Since we are in the context of Smalltalk we solved this by overriding `doesNotUnderstand:` in the `Subject` class. The `doesNotUnderstand:` method will look for the decision strategy corresponding to the message without `through:`. Then it evaluates the decision strategy sending the contextual element together with the message send information. It is possible to implement a solution in other languages as well, even if it requires modifications to the virtual machine or the compiler.

Consider an object that sends the message `addAndRecord: 200 through:` `aBankAccountPerspective` to a bank account subject. Since this message is not defined for the subject the `doesNotUnderstand:` method of the class `Subject` will be evaluated. The subject performs a decision lookup to get the decision strategy for the message `addAndRecord:` from the decision meta-object. The contextual element `aBankAccountPerspective` will be included in the object representing the meta-information of the message. The decision strategy can take the contextual element `aBankAccountPerspective` into consideration available through the meta-information object.

4 Validation

Subjectopia does not force the developer to use a fixed subjectivity model. Because we can choose among different subjectivity models we can model where the subjective decision is taken, whether it is the sender or receiver of the message. In this section we demonstrate this flexibility through four use cases. Two of them were used by previous approaches as examples of subjective behavior. The other two use cases are subjectivity requirements taken from the *Moose* platform for software and data analysis[4].

4.1 Mobile Mail Application

Let us consider the mobile mail application introduced by Darderes and Prieto [2]. The use case is about having users sending emails from their mobile device. A user can only send emails from his own device. The user collaborates with a mail deliverer which can only send the email if the the device is connected to a network. Otherwise, the mail deliverer retains the email until a connection is established.

The mail deliverer behaves subjectively for the message `deliver: aMail`, as users may only send emails from their own device. The original implementation models the subjective behavior for the message `deliver:` as a force tree associated to the mail deliverer. Our implementation follows the original approach since Subjectopia can model subjective message behavior.

Modeling the `deliver:` message's subjective behavior with perspectives delegates the decision to the sender. However, in reality the user does not choose through which perspective he sees the mail deliverer, but the mail deliverer chooses how to react to the message depending on the context. Modeling this problem domain with perspectives is not natural.

Perspectives are not suitable to model the mail deliverer problem due to the sender-oriented context definition. However, since Subjectopia models the decision taking process explicitly, we can modify it. We can make the mail deliverer responsible for deciding through which perspectives other objects send their messages. The mail deliverer has two perspectives: *delivery* and *deny delivery*, which model the acceptance and denial of the mails being sent by users.

4.2 Group Programming

The group programming application is introduced by Smith and Ungar to explain perspectives [12]. In this use case a system keeps track of all the changes to the source code of an object-oriented application. We can either see the changes performed by a single developer or the merged changes of several developers.

For this particular example we consider objects to be containers of methods. When a developer needs to see an object's method source code he collaborates with its `MethodContainer`. A `MethodContainer` models a container for the

---

[4] http://www.moosetechnology.org. A ready-made image with Subjectopia and Moose can be found at: http://scg.unibe.ch/research/subjectopia/

source code of one object. To obtain the textual representation for a particular method the developers send the message `getSourceCodeFor: aMethodName` to the `MethodContainer`. The `MethodContainer` reacts subjectively to the message `getSourceCodeFor:` depending on the contextual view of the developer. To model the different views of the object we use perspectives thus we install a perspective decision strategy for the message `getSourceCodeFor:`. A single perspective defines the changes that a developer performs to the system. The changes of the source code for a particular method are modeled as contextual elements which represent layers. The perspectives are modeled as composed contextual elements which are sent by the developer together with the message `getSourceCodeFor:`. The textual representation of the source code is different depending on the chosen perspective.

The group programming use case can be modeled by using a perspective decision strategy with Subjectopia. Other approaches are not well suited for naturally solving this problem domain. For example, Subjective Message Behavior would model changes to the source code as forces. This is not natural because forces influence the behavior of objects and we need to have multiple views on an object. Additionally, force trees are not supposed to change, *i.e.*, add or remove determinants, at runtime. If we want to have dynamic force trees we need to check after each change that the force tree is still complete, acyclic, free of simultaneously active determinants and that all leaf nodes are method determinants.

4.3   Subjective Behavior Regarding Types of Objects in Moose

Moose is a platform for software and data analysis providing facilities to model, query, visualize and interact with data [3,11]. For analyzing software systems, Moose represents the source code in a model described by the FAMIX languages-independent meta-model [13]. For example, the model of the software system consists of entities representing various software artifacts such as methods (through instances of `FAMIXMethod`) or classes (through instances of `FAMIXClass`).

Each type of entity offers a set of dedicated analysis actions. For example, a `FAMIXClass` offers the possibility of visualizing its internal structure, and a `FAMIXMethod` presents the ability of browsing the source code. These actions are renderable as a contextual menu.

A group of entities is modeled through a `MooseGroup`, and is also an entity. Like any other entity, groups can support specific actions as well. For example, a group of `FAMIXClass` can be visualized using a System Complexity View [8], a visualization that highlights the number of attributes, methods and lines of code of classes within a class hierarchy.

We want to solve the problem of offering different behavior depending on the type of the collected entities. As an example we take the subjective behavior for the System Complexity View. When a `MooseGroup` receives the message `viewSystemComplexity` it should only display the contained entities that are of the type `FAMIXClass`. Thus, ideally, we should offer the possibility of viewing the system complexity only if all contained entities are classes.

Our solution models a `MooseGroup` as a subject that behaves subjectively when receiving of the message `viewSystemComplexity`. We separately model the decision, called *decideAvailableActions*, and the behavior, called *systemComplexity*, as decision strategies. The *decideAvailableActions* strategy determines whether the `MooseGroup` has a behavior for `viewSystemComplexity` or not. If a `MooseGroup` contains only `FamixClass` entities, the *decideAvailableActions* strategy attaches the *systemComplexity* strategy. Each time the list of entities is manipulated the decision strategy *decideAvailableActions* recalculates subjectively which actions are available.

Up until now, subjective behavior in Moose is currently realized by subclassing `MooseGroup` (see Figure 4). For example a group of classes is of type `FAMIXClassGroup`, while a group of methods is of type `FAMIXMethodGroup`. Therefore, changes in the list of entities can result in a change of the runtime type of the group. The decision which type to choose for a given group is currently implicit and it is based on names. For example, we cannot easily introduce a decision of defining actions for a mixed group containing both classes and methods.

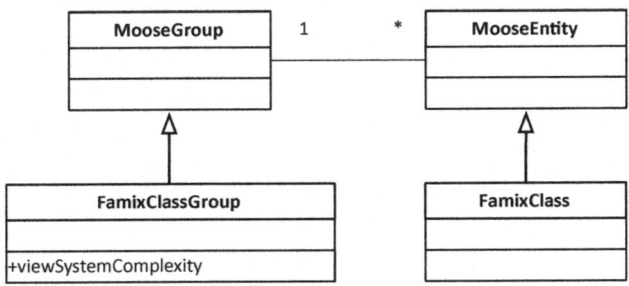

Fig. 4. Current class hierarchy of Moose elements

Using our approach, we extend `MooseGroup` to implement subjective behavior, without depending on the class hierarchy. We simply change the *decideAvailableActions* strategy to decide the new case and model the new behavior as a decision strategy.

Moose is a large system with many extensions defined on top. Thus, any change to the core should limit the impact on the other parts. This would imply significant effort with other subjectivity approaches. For example, using COP would have implied to translate a large part of the system to layers which entails a considerable engineering effort. The subjective behavior is influenced by the elements contained in the `MooseGroup`, thus we would need to define an activation protocol for the layers. Splitting the contextual behavior of `MooseGroup` into several layers also implies a high effort because of the shared behavior between the different kinds of groups.

4.4   Subjective Behavior Depending on the Moose Environment

Moose provides a generic graphical user interface to interact with the model of the software system. In Figure 5 the `MooseGroup` entities of the model are listed. A right click on a group opens the contextual menu listing the possible actions. For example a group of `FamixClass` entities shows the action *Visualize → System complexity*. By selecting a menu entry a message is sent to the selected group. For example, selecting *Visualize → System complexity* sends the message `viewSystemComplexity` to the selected `FAMIXClassGroup`.

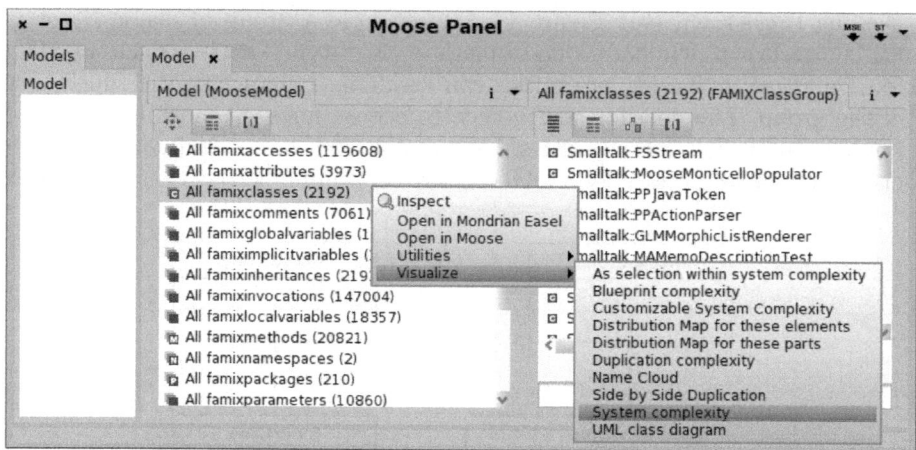

Fig. 5. User interface provided by Moose. Selecting the entry `System Complexity` results in sending the message `viewSystemComplexity` to the selected group of classes.

The problem is that some visualizations may require contextual information not retrievable from the objects and subjects involved in the communication. Let us consider that we select a group of classes and that we want to view them as highlighted on the overall system complexity. This can be achieved by sending the message `viewAsSelectionOnSystemComplexity` to the group. This behavior also requires *all* other `FamixClass` entities of the model to create this visualization. However, in different analysis contexts we want to see only a subset of all classes as a basis for the visualization. Thus, the simple action of `viewAsSelectionOnSystemComplexity` requires both the receiving group and the reference group. Moose currently uses model-wise global variables to store this information. The problem is that each new instance of the graphical user interface of Moose can override the value of that global variable and this results in unwanted side effects.

Our solution uses contextual elements to model the additional, context-sensitive information. The context influencing the behavior of the selected `FamixClass` group is *all* `FamixClass` entities of that model. Therefore, each model creates and maintains its own set of contextual elements holding *all* of its `FamixClass` entities for each user interface. We use a decision strategy modeling

the behavior for the message `viewAsSelectionOnSystemComplexity`. The decision
strategy has access to the contextual elements of its model, *i.e.*, all `FamixClass` entities of the model. The decision strategy determines, using the meta-information
of the message, which interface has sent the message and accordingly uses that
contextual element.

With the Subjectopia approach we can model context-dependent behavior
while other approaches cannot. For example, using roles would not suit this
problem domain, as roles model different behaviors and not a way of reflecting
on the context. The Moose groups behave subjectively depending on contextual
information which is not included in the default message object. Roles also assume that the sender determines through which role it knows the `MooseGroup`,
whereas it is the `MooseGroup` that determines its roles.

5   Conclusion

In this paper we have presented Subjectopia, a unified approach to modeling
subjectivity. Specifically, our contributions are the following:

1. We surveyed prior work and identified a lack of generality when modeling
   different problem domains.
2. We presented a novel approach to subjectivity that explicitly models subjects, decision strategies and contextual elements. The reification of these abstractions avoids the need to impose on the developer a particular paradigm
   for modeling subjective behavior.
3. We developed a fully working prototype of the Subjectopia system and presented the implementation of non-trivial subjective use cases.
4. We demonstrated that our approach can model all other existing subjective
   approaches as well as new, customized strategies. Moreover, we showed that
   other approaches cannot model all use cases while our approach can adapt
   and represent them all.

Introducing subjective behavior in legacy applications might have a considerable impact on the overall behavior of the application. Being able to scope the
subjective changes to specific objects helps in controlling this impact. We plan
to analyze reflection frameworks to allow Subjectopia to perform object-specific
subjective adaptations.

Acknowledgments

We gratefully acknowledge the financial support of the Swiss National Science
Foundation for the project "Synchronizing Models and Code" (SNF Project No.
200020-131827, Oct. 2010 – Sept. 2012). We thank Tudor Gîrba for providing
the Moose case studies which greatly helped in the development of Subjectopia.
We thank Tudor Gîrba, Lukas Renggli and Fabrizio Perin for their feedback on
earlier drafts of this paper. We also thank CHOOSE, the special interest group
for Object-Oriented Systems and Environments of the Swiss Informatics Society,
for its financial contribution to the presentation of this paper.

References

1. Costanza, P., Hirschfeld, R.: Language constructs for context-oriented programming: An overview of ContextL. In: Proceedings of the Dynamic Languages Symposium (DLS) 2005, co-organized with OOPSLA 2005, pp. 1–10. ACM, New York (2005)
2. Darderes, B., Prieto, M.: Subjective behavior: a general dynamic method dispatch. In: OOPSLA Workshop on Revival of Dynamic Languages (October 2004)
3. Gîrba, T.: The Moose Book. Self Published (2010), http://www.themoosebook.org/book
4. Harrison, W., Ossher, H.: Subject-oriented programming (a critique of pure objects). In: Proceedings OOPSLA 1993, ACM SIGPLAN Notices, vol. 28, pp. 411–428 (October 1993)
5. Hirschfeld, R., Costanza, P., Nierstrasz, O.: Context-oriented programming. Journal of Object Technology 7(3) (March 2008)
6. Kristensen, B.B.: Object-oriented modeling with roles. In: Murphy, J., Stone, B. (eds.) Proceedings of the 2nd International Conference on Object-Oriented Information Systems, pp. 57–71. Springer, Heidelberg (1995)
7. Kristensen, B.B.: Osterbye, K.: Roles: Conceptual abstraction theory & practical language issues. In: Special Issue of Theory and Practice of Object Systems (TAPOS) on Subjectivity in Object-Oriented Systems. pp. 143–160 (1996)
8. Lanza, M., Ducasse, S.: Polymetric views—a lightweight visual approach to reverse engineering. Transactions on Software Engineering (TSE) 29(9), 782–795 (2003)
9. von Löwis, M., Denker, M., Nierstrasz, O.: Context-oriented programming: Beyond layers. In: Proceedings of the 2007 International Conference on Dynamic Languages (ICDL 2007). pp. 143–156. ACM Digital Library (2007)
10. Madsen, O.L., Møller-Pedersen, B.: Part objects and their location. In: Proceedings of the Seventh International Conference on Technology of object-oriented languages and systems. pp. 283–297. Prentice Hall International (UK) Ltd., Hertfordshire (1992)
11. Nierstrasz, O., Ducasse, S., Gîrba, T.: The story of Moose: an agile reengineering environment. In: Proceedings of the European Software Engineering Conference (ESEC/FSE 2005), pp. 1–10. ACM Press, New York (2005) (invited paper)
12. Smith, R.B., Ungar, D.: A simple and unifying approach to subjective objects. TAPOS special issue on Subjectivity in Object-Oriented Systems 2(3), 161–178 (1996)
13. Tichelaar, S., Ducasse, S., Demeyer, S., Nierstrasz, O.: A meta-model for language-independent refactoring. In: Proceedings of International Symposium on Principles of Software Evolution (ISPSE 2000), pp. 157–167. IEEE Computer Society Press, Los Alamitos (2000)
14. Ungar, D., Smith, R.B.: Self: The power of simplicity. In: Proceedings OOPSLA 1987, ACM SIGPLAN Notices. vol. 22, pp. 227–242 (December 1987)

An Overview of ALIA4J

An Execution Model for Advanced-Dispatching Languages

Christoph Bockisch[1], Andreas Sewe[2], Mira Mezini[2], and Mehmet Akşit[1]

[1] Software Engineering group, University of Twente, The Netherlands
{c.m.bockisch,aksit}@cs.utwente.nl
[2] Software Technology group, Technische Universität Darmstadt, Germany
{sewe,mezini}@st.cs.tu-darmstadt.de

Abstract. New programming languages that allow to reduce the complexity of software solutions are frequently developed, often as extensions of existing languages. Many implementations thus resort to transforming the extension's source code to the imperative intermediate representation of the parent language. But approaches like compiler frameworks only allow for re-use of code transformations for syntactically-related languages; they do not allow for re-use across language families. In this paper, we present the ALIA4J approach to bring such re-use to language families with advanced dispatching mechanisms like pointcut-advice or predicate dispatching. ALIA4J introduces a meta-model of dispatching as a rich, extensible intermediate language. By implementing language constructs from four languages as refinements of this meta-model, we show that a significant amount of them can be re-used across language families. Another building block of ALIA4J is a framework for execution environments that automatically derives an execution model of the program's dispatching from representations in our intermediate language. This model enables different execution strategies for dispatching; we have validated this by implementing three execution environments whose strategies range from interpretation to optimizing code generation.

1 Introduction

A recent IBM whitepaper [23] identifies complexity as the most relevant factor in the software development process: A reduction of complexity is directly proportional to an improvement of the overall process. Accidental complexity, i.e., complexity not inherent to the problem solved by a program, is mainly caused by the inability to accurately represent the conceptual solution in a given programming language. Thus, research in programming languages produces many new languages with mechanisms to structure a program in a way more suitable to conceptual solutions. The key technique here is *abstraction* where one concrete program module does not refer to another explicitly, but only abstractly specifies the functionality or data to be used. The relevance of abstraction can be seen in the continuous progress in the history of programming language research [24],

J. Bishop and A. Vallecillo (Eds.): TOOLS 2011, LNCS 6705, pp. 131–146, 2011.
© Springer-Verlag Berlin Heidelberg 2011

resulting in advanced abstraction mechanisms like multiple [10] and predicate dispatching [15], pointcut-advice[1] [20], or context-oriented programming [18].

Many new languages employing these mechanisms are extensions of Java: MultiJava [11], JPred [21], AspectJ [19], CaesarJ [2], Compose*/Java [12], ContextJ [18], etc. Some of these are further extended by others; thus, languages and their extensions can be arranged in a genealogical tree, with languages of different paradigms being siblings, as exemplified below for a few languages.

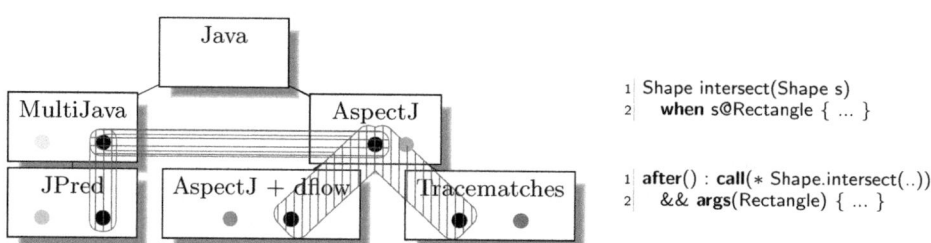

Language constructs provided by the individual languages are presented as dots in different shades of gray in the figure. The black dot represents a concept shared by all languages except Java, e.g., resolution of abstractions based of argument values. Vertical and horizontal overlap of the languages with regard to this construct is highlighted by the rounded boxes, hatched vertically and horizontally, respectively. But as the two listings to the right show, languages like JPred (top) and AspectJ (bottom) express the same concept using different notations: a predicate (s@Rectangle) respectively a pointcut designator (args(Rectangle)).

Dispatching is the mechanism that resolves abstractions and binds concrete functionality to their usage, e.g., when invoking Shape.intersect above. Abstractions commonly found in programming languages influence the resolution of method calls and field accesses. In the following, we use the term *dispatch site* uniformly to refer to sites of both method calls and field accesses in a program. A common example of dispatching is receiver-type polymorphism: Whenever a virtual method is invoked, the runtime environment chooses from among different functionalities (i.e., the overriding methods) and transfers control to the one alternative applicable in the current program state (i.e., corresponding to the dynamic receiver type). We call languages that go beyond classic receiver-type polymorphism *advanced-dispatching languages*, as they compose functionality in different, more powerful ways (e.g., before/after advice) and can act on additional runtime state (e.g., argument values/types).

The implementation of a programming language typically consists of two parts, a *front-end* and a *back-end*, which are decoupled by means of an intermediate language. The front-end processes source code and emits a code representation conforming to the intermediate language. The back-end either

---

[1] A particular flavor of aspect-oriented programming (AOP).

executes this *intermediate representation* (IR) directly or further compiles it into a machine-executable form. Typically, implementations of new languages build on the back-ends of established languages; thus, their front-ends have to emit IR in an intermediate language tailored to a different source language. For the aforementioned source languages, e.g., only the parent (Java) provides its own intermediate language (Java bytecode).

The resulting *semantic gap* between source and intermediate language, i.e., the inability of the intermediate language to express the new mechanisms directly, requires transforming the high-level language concepts to low-level imperative code. Compiler frameworks support this task by means of code transformations [22,14,3]. They only support re-use along the *vertical* dimension as they require a language to be a syntactic extension of another in order to re-use its implementation; *horizontal* re-use is not possible. While code transformations defined on the common intermediate language are shared among all language extensions, they cannot exploit knowledge about source language constructs, which is lost during the transformation to the common intermediate language.

In this paper, we present the ALIA4J approach[2] for implementing advanced-dispatching languages. It offers a meta-model consisting of just a small number of well-defined, language-independent abstractions commonly found in advanced-dispatching languages. This meta-model can act as an intermediate language, thereby closing the semantic gap that currently exists between these source languages and their parent's intermediate language. Furthermore, re-using the implementation of horizontally overlapping constructs becomes viable.

For executing code defined in the intermediate language, we provide several back-ends, including platform-independent ones. These back-ends instantiate a framework that can automatically derive an execution model from the advanced-dispatch's intermediate representation. As the execution model retains the IR's declarative nature, the back-end is free to chose from different *execution strategies*, ranging from interpretation to optimizing code generation.

The goal of ALIA4J is to ease the burden of programming-language implementation resting upon both researchers of new abstraction concepts and designers of domain-specific languages. It should be emphasized that our approach is concerned with the *execution* semantics of the different languages. They may differ greatly in the way language (sub-)constructs are used or combined. Based on this, the languages can make different guarantees on the program behavior or perform different semantic checks. For example, in the case of predicate dispatching, a compiler ensures that there is always exactly one applicable predicate method at runtime. Performing syntactic and semantic checks is the responsibility of a language's compiler and not covered by our approach.

The contributions of this work are threefold:

1. We introduce advanced-dispatching as an execution model.
2. We provide a meta-model for advanced dispatching. Its generality is shown by refining it with (sub-)constructs of the languages AspectJ, Compose*,

---

[2] See http://www.alia4j.org/.

CaesarJ, JPred, ConSpec, and several domain-specific languages; the overlap in refinements used by these languages shows their re-usability.

3. For executing the advanced-dispatch IR, we provide a framework that does not impose any particular execution strategy on the back-end and demonstrate this freedom of choice by providing three back-ends based on different execution strategies: STEAMLOOM^ALIA, SiRIn, and NOIRIn.

In the following section, we discuss approaches related to ours and their limitations. The ALIA4J approach, including the meta-model and the framework, is fully presented in Sect. 3 and evaluated in Sect. 4. Section 4.1 describes how to map existing and new languages to our approach, thus demonstrating re-usability of meta-model refinements. Section 4.2 outlines the different framework instantiations, proving the independence of our execution model from a back-end's execution strategy. Finally, Sect. 5 concludes and discusses future work.

2   Related Work

Several approaches provide abstractions in the intermediate language that are closer to the source-language constructs of aspect-oriented, context-oriented, or similar languages than established intermediate languages. The immediate goals of these approaches range from improving performance to providing a precise operational semantics of the intermediate language. Nevertheless, they also facilitate horizontal re-use of the implementation of the constructs added to the intermediate language. But as the granularity of the added abstractions is very coarse, many re-use opportunities are still missed. Furthermore, intermediate languages and the definition of their semantics are tied to a specific execution strategy in all cases; this hinders moving to back-ends with different strategies.

The *Nu* project [13] extends Java bytecode with two instructions supporting aspect-oriented programming: *bind* and *remove*. By means of these primitives, dynamic deployment and undeployment of aspects can be realized. The bind instruction expects two arguments: a *Pattern* object selecting relevant code locations by means of their syntactic and lexical properties and a *Delegate* object specifying a method to execute as advice. It returns a *BindHandle*, which then may be passed as argument to the *remove* primitive to undo a specific binding. Nu requires an imperative definition of Delegates and other concepts like the execution order of aspects; it only supports access to a limited set of context values. Nu's two primitives are implemented on top of the HotSpot Java virtual machine, which has been modified to accept the extended IR.

The *Reflex* project [27] provides behavioral reflection implemented through dynamic bytecode instrumentation. *Hooksets* are expressions over properties of structural abstractions of the code, like classes or methods. *Links* associate hooksets and *metaobjects* which are Java classes that may be implicitly instantiated. A link specifies which method of the metaobject is to be called and is configured by link attributes. While some attributes are first-class entities in Reflex, this model is not very fine-grained. As a consequence, their implementation cannot be re-used in the implementation of language (sub-)constructs that *partially* map to existing activation conditions or parameterizations. Parameters as well as scopes cannot be user-defined and extending the available parameters and scopes requires a modification of the Reflex framework.

Schippers et al. [25] present a delegation-based execution model for the *Multi-Dimensional Separation of Concerns* (delMDSOC). They define primitive operations in their execution model and provide an operational semantics that allows formal reasoning about language constructs. The model's expressiveness is shown by realizing Java-like, AspectJ-like, and context-oriented languages in it. The delMDSOC model is not declarative in the definition of dynamic behavior; instead, language constructs are represented by imperative and often program-specific code. A declarative model of context exposure is missing.

The *Java Aspect Metamodel Interpreter* (JAMI) [17] defines a meta-model to capture the semantics of features in aspect-oriented languages. Due to JAMI's interpreter approach, meta-model refinements must resort to using reflection and optimizing code generation cannot be realized.

3   The ALIA4J Architecture

In this section, we present the *Advanced-dispatching Language-Implementation Architecture for Java* (ALIA4J) that facilitates both vertical and horizontal re-use of implementations of all language (sub-)constructs governing dispatch. Predecessors of ALIA4J have been the subject of earlier work [8,5]. ALIA4J has two main components: The *Language-Independent Advanced-dispatching Meta-model* (LIAM), a common meta-model for expressing advanced-dispatch declarations as well as relations between them, and the *Framework for Implementing Advanced-dispatching Languages* (FIAL), a framework for execution environments that handle LIAM-based advanced-dispatch intermediate representations.

3.1   Components of ALIA4J

Figure 1 shows the architecture of our proposed approach. It is centered around LIAM, a meta-model of primitive concepts participating in advanced dispatch. When implementing a new language following the ALIA4J approach, the building blocks of the language's semantics must be concretized by either re-using existing meta-model refinements, implementing new refinements, or a mixture of both; this yields a language-specific LIAM refinement. When compiling a program in the new language, the compiler needs to separate the advanced dispatch declarations from those parts directly expressible in Java. From the former, a program-specific advanced-dispatch IR conforming to the refined, language-specific meta-model is created; the latter are turned directly into Java bytecode.

When executing a program, the FIAL framework (top right) derives an execution model for each dispatch site—i.e., for each method call, field read or write—from the program-specific advanced-dispatching IR. To this end, FIAL processes the IR but only refers to it in terms of the language-independent LIAM entities; thus, FIAL and its instantiations are de-coupled from the given source language.

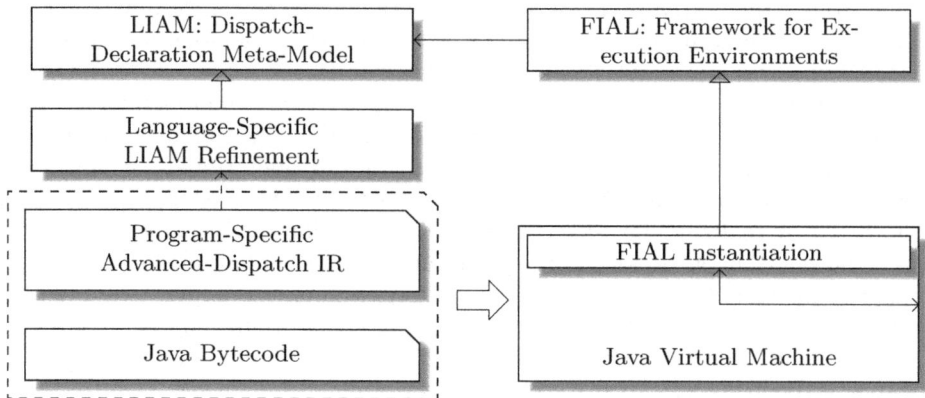

Fig. 1. Overview of an ALIA4J-based language implementation

Since our targeted languages are based on the Java platform, we expect that FIAL is instantiated as a plug-in or extension for an existing Java virtual machine (bottom right). By interacting with this JVM, the FIAL instantiation implements dispatch as mandated by the provided execution model, e.g., by interpretation or different code generation approaches (cf. Sect. 4.2). FIAL itself handles services like dynamic class loading and dynamic deployment, i.e., to add or remove intermediate representations of advanced-dispatch at runtime. FIAL instantiations only need to implement a few well-defined interfaces and LIAM refinements are not at all concerned with these services' implementation.

FIAL offers four generic services required by any execution environment supporting LIAM-based advanced-dispatch IR:

1. FIAL assists in deploying and undeploying such IR at runtime.
2. It handles dynamic class loading in the presence of dispatch IR already deployed.
3. It can trigger an *importer* component which transforms advanced dispatch declarations from the source language to the intermediate representation.
4. From the currently deployed advanced-dispatch IR it derives an execution model for each dispatch site in the executed program.

To derive a dispatch site's execution model, FIAL partially evaluates the LIAM-based IR and constructs the *dispatch function* for the dispatch site combining all individually declared dispatch predicates. In the ALIA4J approach, the result of a dispatch function can be composed of multiple actions; it is a Boolean function $f : \mathbb{B}^n \rightarrow \mathbb{B}^m$ that characterizes which of the m actions should be executed when the dispatch site is reached, depending on the evaluation of n predicates. A detailed discussion of the construction of dispatch functions [26], and of partially evaluating LIAM-based IR and resolving relations between dispatch declarations [7, Sect. 5] is found elsewhere.

3.2   The Meta-Model of Advanced Dispatching

Figure 2 shows a UML class diagram of LIAM's meta-entities for the declaration of advanced dispatch, termed an *Attachment*, and relations between such declarations. An Attachment specifies which *functionality* should execute (*Action*) at which *join points*[3] (*Specialization*) and *when* it should execute relative to the join point (*Schedule Info*), i.e., before, after, or around. The Specialization entity is divided into entities specifying static (*Pattern*) and dynamic (*Predicate*) properties of selected join points as well as a list of values (*Context*) which must be exposed to the Action at selected join points. Hereby, a Pattern specifies syntactic and lexical properties of instructions executing at a join point. These instructions are generally connected to a member, e.g., the target method for an invocation. Patterns are composed of multiple sub-patterns matching on the different elements of the member's signature like the name or parameter types [4]. A Predicate is a Boolean expression of *Atomic Predicate* entities modeling conditions on a join point's dynamic state.

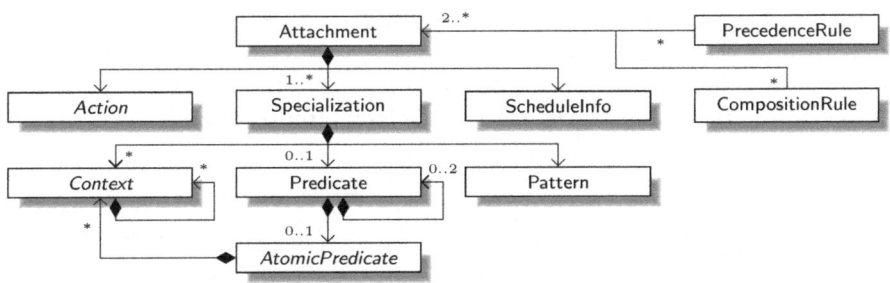

Fig. 2. Entities of the Language-Independent Advanced-dispatching Meta-Model

As Fig. 2 shows, it is not only a Specialization that can refer to a Context to specify that this context value is exposed to an Action; Atomic Predicate and Context itself can also refer to Contexts. This means that the evaluation of Atomic Predicates and Contexts, respectively, depends on the exposure of further context values.[4] For example, a refinement of Context that realizes the reflective **thisJoinPoint** keyword of AspectJ declares its dependency on the individual context values that it composes, like argument values passed to the join point and whether the join point is a method call or field access.

Relations between Attachments are defined in terms of *Precedence Rules* and *Composition Rules*. Both kinds of rules govern the execution of Actions jointly applicable at the same join point. The former rules specify a partial order among the Actions and the latter rules specify which Actions must or must not be executed together. In all cases, a relation between Attachments carries over to the Actions contributed by the Attachments. The entities printed in italics in Fig. 2,

---

[3] The term, borrowed from AOP, refers to a specific execution of a dispatch site.

[4] Circular dependencies must be ruled out by the front-end.

i.e., Action, Atomic Predicate and Context, can be refined with the specific sub-constructs of a language being implemented in the ALIA4J approach. All other entities represent logical groupings of the refinable entities. They are fixed and used by FIAL to partially evaluate LIAM-based IR.

The listing below shows an AspectJ aspect with one pointcut-advice. This aspect will be compiled to a class with the name A and a method, say before_0(), containing the body of the **before** advice. The aspect's instantiation strategy is to create a singleton instance of A and always invoke the method thereon.

```
1  aspect A issingleton() {
2    before() : call(* *.m(..)) { /* advice body */ }
3  }
```

Figure 3 shows the LIAM-based IR for the pointcut-advice in this example. This example is minimalistic on purpose and does not use all of LIAM's features; section 4.1 discusses creating our IR from advanced-dispatch declarations in different languages, including AspectJ, in detail. At the moment, just note that AspectJ pointcuts are expressed by Specializations in LIAM. But Specializations also have additional purposes, for instance, they refer to a Context entity that realizes the aspect's instantiation strategy. In the example, PerTupleContext realizes the **issingleton** strategy. The Action maps to the advice functionality and the Schedule Info maps to the keyword **before, after** or **around**.

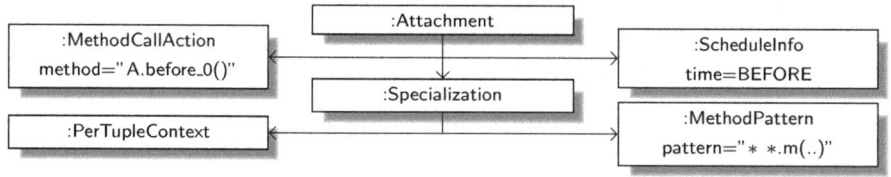

Fig. 3. Example of a LIAM-based advanced-dispatching IR

3.3 FIAL and LIAM in Practice

The execution model of FIAL gives rise to both default compilation and interpretation strategies for dispatch sites. Either can be pursued by a FIAL instantiation. This facilitates a modular implementation of a LIAM entity's semantics in terms of a plain Java method, referred to as the entity's "compute" method.

When using the default code generation, the execution model is traversed depth-first until a LIAM entity is reached that does not depend on another one. For such a leaf, code is generated to invoke the "compute" method. In case of, e.g., a Context, this "compute" method returns the modeled value, which can then be passed to the "compute" method of the entity depending on the Context, and so forth. Glue code is generated to ensure the correct evaluation of the dispatch function, depending on the result values of the Atomic Predicates.

A variation to this default compilation strategy is to delegate bytecode generation to the LIAM entity itself rather than just generating a call to its "compute" method. Because the bytecode-generation method is called individually for each dispatch site, its static context can be considered and the bytecode can be tailored to each site. Both strategies can be mixed freely; a LIAM entity must simply implement a "compute" method or one that directly emits Java bytecode.

As an example of a LIAM entity, consider the JoinPointKindContext presented below. It represents a string value describing the kind of the join point, accessible via **thisJoinPoint**.getKind() in AspectJ. The entity passes a signature Context to its super-constructor (line 3), thus stating that it depends on this Context, which returns the signature of the member associated with the current join point. As a consequence, a signature object is passed to the method getObjectValue,[5] the "compute" method, whenever the JoinPointKindContext is to be evaluated. In the example, this method picks one of the constant values defined in the JoinPoint class from the AspectJ runtime library appropriate to the signature (lines 6 ff.).

```
1 public class JoinPointKindContext extends Context {
2   public JoinPointKindContext() {
3     super(Collections.singletonList(ContextFactory.findOrCreateSignatureContext()));
4   }
5   public Object getObjectValue(Object liamSignature) { // "compute" method
6     if (liamSignature instanceof FieldReadSignature)
7       return JoinPoint.FIELD_GET;
8     else ...
9 } }
```

An alternative implementation declaring BytecodeSupport (line 1) is presented below. Its method emitting bytecode for a specific dispatch site (lines 5–10) inspects the signature of the associated member (line 6) and simply emits an instruction fetching the appropriate constant (line 7 ff.). Because the generated bytecode does not contain conditional control flow, it is more efficient than the "compute" method. No required Contexts have to be declared (line 3) as evaluation of this Context now does not depend on the signature Context.

```
1 public class JoinPointKindContext extends Context implements BytecodeSupport {
2   public JoinPointKindContext() {
3     super(Collections.<Context>emptySet());
4   }
5   public void build(BytecodeBuilder builder, GenericFunction site) {
6     if (site.getSignature() instanceof FieldReadSignature)
7       builder.appendGetstatic(JOIN_POINT_CLASS, "FIELD_GET",
8         TypeDescriptorConstants.STRING_CLASS);
9     else ...
10 } }
```

---

[5] The name, parameters and return type of a "compute" method must follow naming conventions that are ruled by methods not shown in this example.

The generation of bytecode for a LIAM entity may also depend on the actual execution strategy of the back-end. Therefore, ALIA4J uses Abstract Factories to create LIAM entities. A FIAL-based execution environment can override the factory methods for those entities for which back-end-specific bytecode can be generated; this is completely transparent to the front-end.

4 Evaluation

We evaluate the ALIA4J approach on two levels: First, we investigate LIAM's ability to realize new as well as existing languages and the degree of re-use facilitated by our approach. Second, we show the independence of both FIAL and our execution model of a concrete environment's execution strategy.

4.1 Evaluation of LIAM

To validate our approach, we have refined LIAM with the concrete language sub-constructs found in several languages. In the following, we will briefly discuss these refinements. For a full discussion of AspectJ, CaesarJ, Compose*, JPred, MultiJava, and ConSpec as well as the necessary LIAM refinements, we refer to our electronic appendix.[6] For the languages AspectJ and ConSpec we provide importers that automatically map source code to program-specific LIAM models.

AspectJ. The AspectJ compiler creates a class for each aspect, with a virtual method for each advice. The aspect's instantiation strategy, defined in the "per-clause", specifies whether a new instance of this class must be created at a join point or an existing instance is to be used. In either case, the virtual methods compiled from the advice are invoked on this instance. When mapped to LIAM, an aspect's instantiation strategy is represented by a Context: The **pertarget**, **perthis** and **issingleton** strategies are mapped to a PerTupleContext, which associates a tuple of input values with a lazily created instance of the aspect class; for the former two a 1-ary tuple containing a CalleeContext or a CallerContext is used, for the latter a 0-ary tuple. The **percflow** and **percflowbelow** strategies are mapped to a PerCFlowContext and PerCFlowBelowContext, respectively. Each Specialization refers to the Context representing the instantiation strategy as its first exposed Context. All pointcuts defined in an aspect are replaced by their conjunction with the pointcut by which the aspect's per-clause is parameterized.

For each pointcut-advice pair in the aspect body, one Attachment is created, its Action being a MethodCallAction that refers to the method the compiler created for the advice. The Schedule Info trivially mirrors the keyword **before**, **after**, or **around**. Each pointcut is mapped to a set of Specializations. The mapping of individual pointcut designators to LIAM is best illustrated by a representative example: The **args** pointcut designator can be parameterized by an identifier corresponding to a pointcut parameter. This imposes a dynamic constraint on an argument's type and exposes the argument's value to the advice. The restriction is mapped to an InstanceofPredicate with an associated ArgumentContext. For the value exposition, an ArgumentContext is associated with the Specialization.

---

[6] See http://www.alia4j.org/alia4j-languages/mappings.

When precedence is defined between aspects in terms of **declare precedence**, for each pair of Attachments from the referred aspects one Precedence Rule is created. Named pointcuts, abstract aspects and pointcuts, and inter-type *member* declarations [16] can also be realized with the ALIA4J approach, but we omit their discussion for the sake of brevity. Inter-type declarations that modify the type hierarchy (**declare parents**) or emit errors and warnings during compilation (**declare error**, **declare warning**) are naturally out of scope for ALIA4J.

CaesarJ. While CaesarJ's pointcut-advice language features are the same as AspectJ's, a CaesarJ class can also be deployed and undeployed dynamically using **deploy**, **undeploy**, or a dedicated API. In this case, the program specifies an actual instance of the class which is to be deployed, i.e., an ObjectConstantContext parameterized with this object is used as the first context of all Specializations. Dynamic deployment also can add a scope, i.e., the class's pointcut-advice may be active only within in a single thread or while a specified object is executing. This scope is modeled as an Atomic Predicate and the Predicates of all Specializations are replaced by a conjunction with this Atomic Predicate.

Compose*. In Compose*, filter modules are superimposed (deployed) on so-called *inner* objects and contain filters that react upon methods invoked either on (**inputfilters**) or by (**outputfilters**) the inner object. Data fields in a filter module can be defined, e.g., as **internals** that have a distinct value for each inner object.

For each of a module's filters, consisting of filter type, condition part, matching part, and substitution part, an Attachment is created. Hereby, the filter type and the substitution part are together mapped to an Action, the former determining the kind of Action and the latter its parameterization. Filter types like the **Exception** filter are predefined and are mapped to dedicated Action entities. Filter types provide a specification of their effects: Whether they are active in the calling or returning flow is captured by a Schedule Info entity; whether the message flow continues after the Action or whether subsequent filters are skipped is captured by Composition Rules. Conditions are implemented as methods in Compose* and represented by LIAM's MethodPredicate. Access to internal data fields is represented as PerTupleContext configured with a 1-ary tuple exposing the CalleeContext, when accessed from an input filter, or the CallerContext, when accessed from an output filter.

Filter modules have to be explicitly superimposed; the corresponding Attachments are not deployed by default. Superimposition acts on a set of classes on whose instances a filter module is to be superimposed. This is modeled by a conjunction of the affected Attachments' Predicates with an ExactTypePredicate Atomic Predicates (configured with either CalleeContext or CallerContext for input and output filters, respectively). Further constraints between filter modules specified in Compose* can be represented using LIAM's Precedence Rules and Composition Rules.

JPred. In JPred, methods may have a predicate in a **when** clause. A class can contain multiple methods with the same name and formal parameters but with different **when** clauses. When the method is invoked, the implementation with the most specific, satisfied predicate is executed; an implementation whose predicate implies the predicate of another implementation overrides it. Methods defined in a super-class are also overridden. The JPred compiler statically checks that for each method-call site exactly one implementation will be applicable.

For all these predicate methods, the compiler generates a plain Java method with a unique name. For each predicate method an Attachment is created with a MethodCallAction configured to execute this method. The Pattern of the Attachment selects invocations of the method according to the predicate-method name and the Predicate corresponds to the predicate specified by the **when** clause. As only a single predicate method must ever be executed, even if multiple predicates may be satisfied, the overriding relations are mapped to Composition Rules.

ConSpec. Unlike the above languages, ConSpec [1] is not a general-purpose language but used only to express security policies. Regardless, it shares a number of characteristics with aspect-oriented languages: Its notion of events and guards is akin to AOP's pointcuts whereas its notion of updates is akin to advice, the key difference being a constrained set of possible actions; updates can only affect a limited set of state variables in limited ways. These state variables can moreover exist in several scopes, which allows them to be associated with particular objects (**OBJECT**) or persisted across program runs (**MULTISESSION**). In either case, LIAM can express scopes using an appropriate PerTupleContext; in the latter case, e.g., the lazily created instance is initialized with the persisted state.

New, Domain-Specific Languages. The ALIA4J approach was used in the course "Advanced Programming Concepts" (2009/10) taught at the University of Twente to illustrate the execution semantics of advanced-dispatching languages and to perform practical assignments. During this course, groups of two or three students developed prototypes of domain-specific languages (DSLs), covering domains as diverse as (1) the declarative definition of debugging activities, (2) annotation-defined method-level transactions, (3) asynchronous Future-based inter-thread communication, (4) runtime model checking, (5) authentication and authorization, and (6) the automatic enforcement of the Decorator design pattern. All language prototypes except the sixth could be implemented by re-using the already existing LIAM entity implementations. This shows that our approach is well suited for the implementation of domain-specific languages.

Summary and Lessons Learned. Table 1 shows the different concrete entities we implemented while mapping the languages AspectJ, CaesarJ, JPred, Multi-Java, Compose*, and ConSpec to LIAM, as well as their usage in the different language mappings. CaesarJ shares the column with AspectJ, as the pointcut-advice part of the language largely overlap with AspectJ; JPred and MultiJava share a column because the former subsumes the latter.

Table 1. Usage of LIAM entities in different languages. ✓: non-trivial entity directly used in language mapping; ✓*: trivial context adapting interface of value; (✓): non-trivial entity used indirectly.

Context	AspectJ/ CaesarJ	Com-pose*	JPred/ MultiJava	Con-Spec
Argument	✓	✓	✓	✓
Callee	✓	✓	✓	✓
Caller	✓	✓		
Result	✓	✓		✓
Arguments	✓	✓		
DebugInfo	✓			
Signature	✓	✓		
PerTuple	✓	✓		✓
PerCFlow	✓			
PerCFlowBelow	✓			
ObjectConstant	✓		✓	
AspectJSignature	✓*			
JoinPointKind	✓*			
SourceLocation	✓*			
ThisJoinPoint	✓*			
Thread	✓ (CaesarJ)			
Constant			✓	✓
Field			✓	✓
ArrayElement			✓	✓
BinaryOperation			✓	✓
UnaryOperation			✓	✓
MethodResult	✓	✓	✓	
ReifiedMessage	✓*			

Pattern	AspectJ/ CaesarJ	Com-pose*	JPred/ MultiJava	Con-Spec
Method	✓	✓	✓	✓
Constructor	✓		✓	✓
StaticInit.	✓			
FieldRead	✓			
FieldWrite	✓			
AtomicPredicate				
Instanceof	✓	✓	✓	
Method	✓	✓	✓	✓
ExactType	✓	✓	✓	
CFlow	✓			
CFlowBelow	✓			
Bin.Relation		✓	✓	✓
Action				
FieldRead	(✓)	(✓)	(✓)	(✓)
FieldWrite	(✓)	(✓)	(✓)	(✓)
MethodCall	✓	✓	✓	✓
CFlowEnter	✓			
CFlowExit	✓			
NoOp			✓	✓
Throw			✓	✓

4.2 Evaluation of FIAL

We have developed various FIAL-based back-ends (STEAMLOOM^ALIA, SiRIn, and NOIRIn) using different execution strategies reaching from interpretation over bytecode generation to direct generation of machine code. Experiments have shown that native machine-code generation for LIAM entities of simple language concepts does not improve performance significantly. Thus, we will not discuss the implementation of STEAMLOOM^ALIA and its use of modularly implemented machine-code generation strategies here. Nevertheless, this support is useful for more complex VM-integrated optimizations, e.g., for **cflow** [6].

SiRIn. SiRIn, the Site-based Reference Implementation, wraps every dispatch site into a special method and generates bytecode for these "reified" dispatch sites using the ASM bytecode engineering library.[7] Each wrapper method

---

[7] See http://asm.ow2.org/

contains code derived from the dispatch function. SiRIn may duplicate code if several leaf nodes share an Action. This code-splitting approach opens up new optimization opportunities for the JVM's just-in-time compiler. SiRIn itself is a Java 6 agent; it does not require a native component and is thus fully portable.

NOIRIn. NOIRIn, the Non-Optimizing Interpreter-based Reference Implementation, refrains from code generation and interprets the execution model produced by FIAL. Based on NOIRIn, implementing generic IDE support for debugging FIAL's execution models is straight-forward [28,9]. Because NOIRIn does not generate bytecode for dispatch sites, it can only handle LIAM entities which implement a "compute" method. This is not a restriction because it can be expected that for each LIAM refinement a "compute" method is implemented at first, eventually supplanted by an optimizing bytecode generation. Like SiRIn, NOIRIn integrates with any standard Java 6 VM.

Integration Testing. We provide an extensive suite of integration tests, which use the FIAL framework to define and deploy LIAM-based dispatch representations, execute an affected dispatch site, and verify the correct execution. The suite is independent of any concrete FIAL instantiation and, thus, also acts as compatibility test. It contains one JUnit test case per provided LIAM entity and several test cases for FIAL's services like dynamic deployment or ordering actions at shared join points. Each test case contains up to 512 tests using the tested entity or service in different ways and executing dispatch sites with different characteristics. Nearly all of the 4,045 tests are systematically generated to cover all relevant variations of dispatch sites: execution in a static or virtual context; dispatch of a method call, field read or write; etc.

5   Conclusions and Future Work

In this paper, we have presented the ALIA4J approach to implementing language extensions. Phrasing them in terms of advanced-dispatching enables us to implement numerous languages, ranging from AspectJ to new, domain-specific languages, using just a few core abstractions. With a fine-grained intermediate representation close to the source-level abstractions, re-using the implementation of language sub-constructs is possible even across language families.

The re-use of implementation facilitated by ALIA4J allows programming-language researchers and designers of domain-specific languages to focus on their immediate task: developing source languages for solving certain problems. Already established language sub-constructs do not have to be implemented anew. ALIA4J's back-end-independent execution model and the possibility to modularly implement bytecode generation for language constructs make optimizations developed in back-ends immediately available to all languages implemented with our approach using the affected construct. We believe that this can improve the quality of language prototypes, but this is subject to future studies.

Language extensions developed using ALIA4J all build on the same language-independent meta-model: LIAM. This gives rise to the possibility of combining, e.g., AspectJ and JPred within a single program without unwanted interferences caused by low-level code transformations. But such a detailed study of the high-level interactions of different language implementations has yet to be done.

We also plan to re-implement several past research results uniformly within the ALIA4J approach. An optimized implementation of control-flow-based Atomic Predicates [6] in STEAMLOOM^ALIA, e.g., will benefit everyone using this platform-dependent back-end. As the LIAM-based intermediate representation is independent of a specific execution strategy, the same code is still executable on a less optimizing but platform-independent back-end. We also plan to map additional languages to our approach to further strengthen our claim of its generality.

Research is currently going on in developing new optimizations of language sub-constructs and making them available through the interface of LIAM. Furthermore, we are investigating extensions to LIAM and FIAL to make them more suitable to support tasks like debugging or profiling advanced-dispatching programs [9,28]. Other research focuses on optimizing the generic service implementations in FIAL like the evaluation of Patterns [4], which will benefit all FIAL-based back-ends and thus all languages implemented in our approach.

Acknowledgements

We would like to thank everyone who has contributed to ALIA4J in the past few years (in alphabetical order): Matthew Arnold, Remko Bijker, Tom Dinkelaker, Sebastian Eifert, Sarah Ereth, Pascal Flach, Michael Haupt, Michael Hausl, Jannik Jochem, Sebastian Kanthak, Michael Krebs, Andre Loker, Markus Maus, Suraj Mukhi, Heiko Paulheim, Nico Rottstädt, Christian Rüdiger, Jan Sinschek, Kai Stroh, Zied Trabelsi, Nathan Wasser, Haihan Yin, and Martin Zandberg. We would also like to thank Eric Bodden and Jan Sinschek for their comments on earlier drafts of this paper. This work was supported by CASED (www.cased.de).

References

1. Aktug, I., Naliuka, K.: ConSpec: A formal language for policy specification. In: Proceedings of REM (2008)
2. Aracic, I., Gasiunas, V., Mezini, M., Ostermann, K.: Overview of CaesarJ. In: Coding Theory 1988. LNCS, vol. 388, pp. 135–173. Springer, Heidelberg (2006)
3. Avgustinov, P., Christensen, A.S., Hendren, L., Kuzins, S., Lhoták, J., Lhoták, O., de Moor, O., Sereni, D., Sittampalam, G., Tibble, J.: abc: An extensible aspectJ compiler. In: Rashid, A., Aksit, M. (eds.) Transactions on Aspect-Oriented Software Development I. LNCS, vol. 3880, pp. 293–334. Springer, Heidelberg (2006)
4. Bijker, R., Bockisch, C., Sewe, A.: Optimizing the evaluation of patterns in pointcuts. In: Proceedings of VMIL (2010)
5. Bockisch, C.: An Efficient and Flexible Implementation of Aspect-Oriented Languages. PhD thesis, Technische Universität Darmstadt (2009)
6. Bockisch, C., Kanthak, S., Haupt, M., Arnold, M., Mezini, M.: Efficient control flow quantification. In: Proceedings of OOPSLA (2006)

7. Bockisch, C., Malakuti, S., Aksit, M., Katz, S.: Making aspects natural: Events and composition. In: Proceedings of AOSD (2011)
8. Bockisch, C., Mezini, M.: A flexible architecture for pointcut-advice language implementations. In: Proceedings of VMIL (2007)
9. Bockisch, C., Sewe, A.: Generic IDE support for dispatch-based composition. In: Proceedings of Composition (2010)
10. Chambers, C.: Object-oriented multi-methods in Cecil. In: ECOOP 1992. LNCS, vol. 615, Springer, Heidelberg (1992)
11. Clifton, C., Millstein, T., Leavens, G.T., Chambers, C.: MultiJava: Design rationale, compiler implementation, and applications. ACM TOPLAS 28(3) (2006)
12. A. de Roo, M. Hendriks, W. Havinga, P. Dürr, and L. Bergmans. Compose*: a language- and platform-independent aspect compiler for composition filters. In: Proceedings of WASDeTT (2008)
13. Dyer, R., Rajan, H.: Supporting dynamic aspect-oriented features. ACM TOSEM 20(2) (2010)
14. Ekman, T., Hedin, G.: The JastAdd extensible Java compiler. In: Proceedings of OOPSLA (2007)
15. Ernst, M., Kaplan, C., Chambers, C.: Predicate dispatching: A unified theory of dispatch. In: Proceedings of ECOOP (1998)
16. Flach, P.: Implementierung von AspectJ-Intertypdeklarationen. Bachelor's Thesis, Technische Universität Darmstadt (2008) (in German)
17. Havinga, W., Aksit, M.: Prototyping and composing aspect languages. In: Ryan, M. (ed.) ECOOP 2008. LNCS, vol. 5142, pp. 180–206. Springer, Heidelberg (2008)
18. Hirschfeld, R., Costanza, P., Nierstrasz, O.: Context-oriented programming. Journal of Object Technology 7(3) (2008)
19. Kiczales, G., Hilsdale, E., Hugunin, J., Kersten, M., Palm, J., Griswold, W.G.: An overview of aspectJ. In: Lee, S.H. (ed.) ECOOP 2001. LNCS, vol. 2072, p. 327. Springer, Heidelberg (2001)
20. Masuhara, H., Kiczales, G.: Modeling crosscutting in aspect-oriented mechanisms. In: Proceedings of ECOOP (2003)
21. Millstein, T., Frost, C., Ryder, J., Warth, A.: Expressive and modular predicate dispatch for Java. ACM TOPLAS 31(2), 1–54 (2009)
22. Nystrom, N., Clarkson, M.R., Myers, A.C.: Polyglot: An extensible compiler framework for java. In: Hedin, G. (ed.) CC 2003. LNCS, vol. 2622, pp. 138–152. Springer, Heidelberg (2003)
23. Royce, W.: Improving software economics-top 10 principles of achieving agility at scale. White paper, IBM Rational (May 2009)
24. Ryder, B.G., Soffa, M.L., Burnett, M.: The impact of software engineering research on modern progamming languages. ACM TOSEM 14 (2005)
25. Schippers, H., Janssens, D., Haupt, M., Hirschfeld, R.: Delegation-based semantics for modularizing crosscutting concerns. In: Proceedings of OOPSLA (2008)
26. Sewe, A., Bockisch, C., Mezini, M.: Redundancy-free residual dispatch. In: Proceedings of FOAL (2008)
27. Tanter, É.: An extensible kernel language for AOP. In: Proceedings of the Workshop on Open and Dynamic Aspect Languages (2006)
28. Yin, H., Bockisch, C.: Developing a generic debugger for advanced-dispatching languages. In: Proceedings of WASDeTT (2010)

A Heuristic Approach for Computing Effects

Phillip Heidegger and Peter Thiemann

University of Freiburg, Germany

Abstract. The effect of an operation on an object network can be described by the access paths along which the function reads or writes object properties. Abstracted to access path permissions, the effect can serve as part of the operation's documentation, augmenting a type signature or a contract for the operation. Statically determining such an effect is a challenging problem, in particular in a dynamic language which represents objects by hash tables like the current breed of scripting languages.

In this work, we propose an analysis that computes access permissions describing the effect of an operation from a set of access paths obtained by running the program. The main ingredient of the analysis is a novel heuristic to abstract a set of access paths to a concise access permission.

Our analysis is implemented as part of JSConTest, a testing framework for JavaScript. It has been applied to a range of examples with encouraging results.

1 Introduction

For a program in an untyped scripting language like JavaScript, maintenance and understanding can be a nightmare. Given a function or method, it is often not clear which types of arguments are required to make the function work as expected and which types of values are returned. A first step towards understanding such an operation is thus to find a type signature for it.

However, a type signature only describes the functional behavior of an operation, but its side effects are equally important. In most object-oriented languages side effects are limited thanks to data encapsulation. The situation is different in a scripting language like JavaScript: Objects lack any kind of encapsulation, so that an operation can arbitrarily explore and modify the object graph starting from any object in scope.

The goal of this work is thus to provide a concise description of the way that an operation accesses and modifies the object graph. This information can be vital for program understanding and program maintenance.

Our approach is to describe the effect of an operation on the object graph by the set of access paths along which the function and its callees read or write object properties. These paths can start from any object accessible to the operation, that is, it either has to be passed as an argument or it must be bound to a global variable. Reads and writes in objects that are created within the operation do not matter for the effect as they are not observable from the outside.

J. Bishop and A. Vallecillo (Eds.): TOOLS 2011, LNCS 6705, pp. 147–162, 2011.

As the set of access paths is potentially infinite, it cannot usefully serve as a high-level description of an operation's effect. Instead, we approximate sets of access paths by concise access path permissions. Such a permission can be attached to any variable in scope and can thus become part of the operation's documentation in addition to a type signature or a contract. Permissions are easy to understand because they are structured like file paths with wildcards.

In a statically typed language, it would be feasible to compute the effect of an operation statically. In a scripting language with dynamic types and where objects also serve as hash tables and arrays, computing an access permission statically would be much harder, if possible at all, because the description of a permission may depend on particular values like strings and indexes. A manual effect annotation is, of course, possible, but too time consuming.

The main contribution of this work is a heuristic analysis that learns access path permissions from access paths sampled from running JavaScript programs. This information can be used to enhance type-signature-based contracts as proposed in our previous work [1]. Because a static analysis of the effects is not feasible, we perform a dynamic analysis which collects access paths during runs of the program. The heuristic extracts concise access path permissions from the collected path sets. The extraction procedure is user configurable so that the results can be refined interactively.

Our analysis is implemented and available as part of JSConTest,[1] a testing framework for JavaScript. It has been applied to a range of examples with encouraging results.

2   Testing Effects

Previous work of the authors [1] proposes a contract framework for JavaScript. It permits the specification of contracts which are similar to type signatures and provides the facilities to perform contract monitoring as well as contract-based testing. This contract system is value-oriented in the sense that a contract specifies restrictions on the values that are passed to a method and returned from it. However, a value-oriented contract misses an important facet of the semantics of a method because a type signature does not specify its side effects.

Subsequent work [2] extends the contract language with access permissions that restrict the side effects that a method is allowed to perform. An access permission explicitly states the set of paths (sequences of property accesses) that a method may access from the objects in scope. Being able to state such permissions is important in a language like JavaScript, where a side effect is often the raison d'être of an operation. For such an operation, a value-oriented contract is insufficient as the following example code shows:

```
function redirectTo (url) {
    window.location = url;
}
```

The type signature /*c (string) → undefined */ fully describes the functional behavior of redirectTo: its argument should be a string and it returns the value **undefined** as there is no explicit return statement. However, the interesting information about the function is that it changes the location property of the window object, which has the further effect of redirecting the web browser to a new page. To specify this effect, our extended contract language enables us to add an *access permission* to the above contract:

... **with** [window.location]

This access permission lets the function access and modify the location property of window but denies access to any other object. Contract monitoring for the thus extended contract enforces the permission at run time. For example, if the function's implementation above were replaced by

```
function redirectTo (url) {
    window.location = url;
    myhistory.push (url);
}
```

while keeping the same type signature and access permission, then monitoring would report a contract violation as soon as the function accesses myhistory.

The paper further reports two case studies to validate the significance of access permission contracts. The results demonstrate that contracts with effects can detect 6-13% more programming errors than contracts without effects.

While these results are encouraging, their preparation is tedious. Functional contracts are mostly straightforward to write and can be finalized in a few iterations of testing with the framework, but careful manual scrutiny is required to come up with concise and useful effect annotations. The main problem is the dynamic nature of JavaScript, which permits non-obvious control flows (e.g., callback functions or method invocation through several levels of prototypes) as well as non-obvious data accesses when object properties are addressed using the array notation as in obj[prop]. Furthermore, from an interprocedural perspective, it is not straightforwardly possible to compose effect annotations of callees to the effect annotation of the caller.

For these reasons, we propose to record all access paths by running test cases on the program after constructing the type-signature contracts. These access paths are generated by our framework by setting all effect annotations to $\emptyset$ and recording all access violations. From the collected access paths, we compute a set of access permissions by abstracting the recorded paths to a restricted regular expression.

This abstraction is guided by a heuristic because there is no easy way to define a best abstraction of a finite language to a regular expression. As each finite language is regular, there is always a (potentially huge) regular expression specifying the language of observed access paths exactly. On the other hand, every language is contained in the regular language .*. As both extremes are useless, the goal of the heuristic is to find a regular language that includes the observed access paths but which also includes further likely access paths exhibited by the same program.

Fig. 1. Syntax of access paths and access permissions

$p \in Prop$	property names	$P \subseteq Prop$	set of property names
$\pi ::= \varepsilon \mid p.\pi$	access paths	$b ::= \varepsilon \mid P.b \mid P*.b$	path permissions
$\gamma ::= \mathbf{R} \mid \mathbf{W}$	access classifiers	$a ::= \emptyset \mid b \mid a + a$	access permissions
$\kappa ::= \gamma(\pi)$	classified access path	$? = Prop,$ $\quad @ = \emptyset \subseteq Prop$	

For that reason, our inference algorithm is based on the intuition[2] that objects have an fixed structure a few levels of properties deep, followed by a traversal of a recursive structure (repeated list or tree links), and ending in objects with fixed structure. Thus, we have chosen a particular result template for an access permission. The inferred permissions are either concrete paths of small lengths or they start with a few concrete path elements, followed by an arbitrary sequence of path elements, and then finish with a few concrete path elements. The number of concrete initial and final path elements are parameters of the algorithm, which can be modified by the user to interactively find a satisfactory permission. The underlying algorithm guarantees the soundness of the resulting permission.

The arbitrary list of path elements in the middle can be further refined to enumerate the properties that can be repeated.

3   Inference Algorithm

This section first formally defines the syntax and semantics of access paths and access permissions and states some of their properties. Then, it describes the three phases of the inferences algorithm: trie building, extraction of access permissions, and simplification. Finally, it considers some special cases which are covered by the implementation, but which are not reflected in the formal development.

3.1   Access Paths and Access Permissions

Fig. 1 defines the syntax of access paths and access permissions. An access path is a sequence of property names. It is classified with an access classifier γ as either a read path or a write path yielding a classified access path κ.

A path permission extends an access path by admitting a set P of properties in each step. A component in a path permission may also be $P*$ to match any sequence of property names in P. An access permission is either empty, a path permission, or the union of two access permissions. We abbreviate the path component $? *$ to $*$.

While the definitions of path permissions and access paths inductively add path elements only to the left ends, we also decompose permissions and paths

---

[2] Which is supported by our examples, but not yet empirically validated.

Fig. 2. Matching access permissions

$$\mathbf{W}(\varepsilon) \prec \varepsilon \qquad \mathbf{R}(\varepsilon) \prec b \qquad \frac{\gamma(\pi) \prec b \qquad p \in P}{\gamma(p.\pi) \prec P.b} \qquad \frac{\gamma(\pi) \prec b}{\gamma(\pi) \prec P*.b}$$

$$\frac{\gamma(\pi) \prec P*.b \qquad p \in P}{\gamma(p.\pi) \prec P*.b} \qquad \frac{\kappa \prec a_1}{\kappa \prec a_1 + a_2} \qquad \frac{\kappa \prec a_2}{\kappa \prec a_1 + a_2} \qquad \frac{(\forall \kappa \in K)\ \kappa \prec a}{K \prec a}$$

---

from the right as in $\pi = \pi'.p$ or even consider the infix "." as concatenation operator as in the permission $\pi. * .\pi'$. We write $|\pi|$ for the length of a path and say that π' *is a prefix of* π if $\pi = \pi'.\pi''$, for some π''. Dually, π' *is a suffix of* π if $\pi = \pi''.\pi'$, for some π''. A set of paths Π is prefix-closed (suffix-closed) if $\pi \in \Pi$ implies that $\pi' \in \Pi$, for each prefix (suffix) of π.

We define the semantics of access permissions using the inference rules in Fig. 2. Let K be a set of classified access paths. A classified access path κ (or a set K of those) matches an access permission a, if the judgment $\kappa \prec a$ ($K \prec a$) is derivable from the inference rules. Property names in the permission must be matched exactly in the path, whereas $*$ components in the permission match any sequence of property names. The component @ matches no property. When the path is exhausted ($\pi = \varepsilon$), matching distinguishes read and write paths. While a read path is accepted with any remaining permission, a write path requires the permission to be exhausted, too. With this convention, a permission ending in @ specifies a set of read paths without giving write permission. In summary, write accesses $\mathbf{W}(\pi)$ must be matched entirely by a path permission whereas read accesses $\mathbf{R}(\pi)$ just need to be extensible to a full match. Hence, the set of read access paths is closed under prefixes.

Lemma 1. *1. If $\mathbf{R}(\pi.p) \prec a$, then $\mathbf{R}(\pi) \prec a$.*
2. If $\mathbf{W}(\pi.p) \prec a$, then $\mathbf{R}(\pi) \prec a$.
3. $\mathbf{W}(\pi) \not\prec b.@$.

3.2   Algorithm

The task of the access path inference algorithm is thus to map a set of classified access paths to a set of reasonable path permissions. This task is akin to the problem of learning a (regular) language from a set of positive examples.[3] The problem of this task is that there is no best solution. For example, there are always two trivial path permissions that match a given classified path set:

Lemma 2. *Let $K = \{\gamma_i(\pi_i) \mid i \in I\}$.*

1. Let $b_i = \pi_i$ considered as a path permission. Then $K \prec \sum_i b_i$.
2. $K \prec *$.

---

[3] A negative example would be an impossible access path.

Fig. 3. Example trie

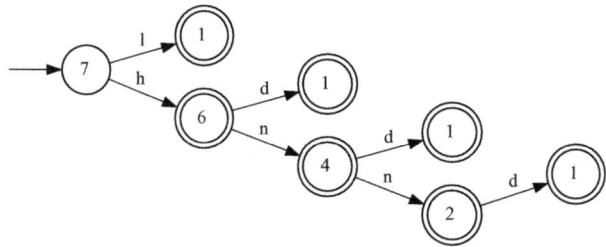

For that reason, we have devised an algorithm based on a heuristic that computes reasonable results for a range of interesting examples.

Our algorithm has three phases. The first phase collects access paths in a trie data structure. This data structure enables efficient operations during the second phase. The second phase extracts access permissions from the trie. The third phase simplifies the resulting access permissions. The first two phases keep read and write paths separate because there are subtle differences in their handling due to the prefix closure of read accesses.

Building the Trie. For our purposes, a trie [3] is a rooted, directed graph where each node is labeled with an integer and each edge is labeled with a property name. The trie $T(\Pi)$ represents a set of access paths Π as follows. The root node r is labeled with the number of paths $|\Pi|$. For each property p, let $p \backslash \Pi = \{\pi \mid p.\pi \in \Pi\}$ be the set of path tails of paths that start with p. If $p \backslash \Pi$ is non-empty, then the trie for Π includes $T(p \backslash \Pi)$ where there is an edge from r to the root node of $T(p \backslash \Pi)$.

For example, the path set $\Pi_{list} = \{l, h, h.d, h.n, h.n.d, h.n.n, h.n.n.d\}$ is represented by the trie in Fig. 3. The trie can also be considered a finite automaton recognizing the set Π with final states indicated by the double circles in the figure.

Extracting Access Permissions. The goal of the extraction algorithm is to create access permissions of one of the forms π or $\pi.P*.\pi'$ where $P \subseteq Prop$ and π' may be empty. The initial component π is determined by computing a set of "interesting" prefixes from a set of paths Π, where π is a prefix of Π if there exists some $\pi' \in \Pi$ such that π is a prefix of π'.

Given two integers $l \geq 0$ and $d \geq 1$, we consider a path as (l, d)-interesting with respect to a path set Π if it is a prefix of Π and it is either shorter than the *base length* l or it has a *branching degree* less than or equal to d above length l. Here, the branching degree of a path $\mathrm{BDeg}_\Pi(\pi)$ is the number of properties q such that $\pi.q$ is a prefix of some path in Π. The (l, d)-interesting prefixes of Π are formalized by $\mathrm{Prefixes}_{l,d}(\Pi)$, which is simple to compute from $T(\Pi)$.

$$\mathrm{BDeg}_{\varPi}(\pi) \quad = |\{q \mid (\exists \pi') \; \pi.q.\pi' \in \varPi\}|$$
$$\mathrm{Prefixes}_{l,d}(\varPi) = \{\, p_1 \ldots p_n \mid$$
$$(\exists \pi) \; p_1 \ldots p_n.\pi \in \varPi,$$
$$(\forall j \in \{l, \ldots, n-1\}) \; \mathrm{BDeg}_{\varPi}(p_1 \ldots p_j) \le d\}$$

To continue the example from the preceding subsection,

$$\mathrm{Prefixes}_{0,1}(\varPi_{list}) = \{\varepsilon\}$$
$$\mathrm{Prefixes}_{1,1}(\varPi_{list}) = \{\varepsilon, l, h\}$$
$$\mathrm{Prefixes}_{2,1}(\varPi_{list}) = \{\varepsilon, l, h, h.d, h.n\}$$
$$\mathrm{Prefixes}_{0,2}(\varPi_{list}) = \{\varepsilon, l, h, h.d, h.n, h.n.d, h.n.n, h.n.n.d\}$$
$$= \mathrm{Prefixes}_{k,2}(\varPi_{list}) \qquad (\forall k)$$

At this point, we distinguish the treatment of read paths from the treatment of write paths. As read paths are closed under taking the prefix, we may compute the prefix reduct by removing all paths that are proper prefixes of other paths.

$$\mathrm{Reduct}(\varPi) = \{\pi \in \varPi \mid (\forall \pi') \; |\pi'| > 0 \Rightarrow \pi.\pi' \notin \varPi\}$$

Continuing the example further:

$$\mathrm{Reduct}(\mathrm{Prefixes}_{0,1}(\varPi_{list})) = \{\varepsilon\}$$
$$\mathrm{Reduct}(\mathrm{Prefixes}_{1,1}(\varPi_{list})) = \{l, h\}$$
$$\mathrm{Reduct}(\mathrm{Prefixes}_{2,1}(\varPi_{list})) = \{l, h.d, h.n\}$$
$$\mathrm{Reduct}(\mathrm{Prefixes}_{0,2}(\varPi_{list})) = \{l, h.d, h.n.d, h.n.n.d\}$$

For write paths, a more conservative reduction must be applied. Only those proper prefixes can be removed that are not members of the underlying original set. Let $\varPi$ be a set of prefixes of $\varPi_0$.

$$\mathrm{ReductW}(\varPi, \varPi_0) = \mathrm{Reduct}(\varPi) \cup (\varPi \cap \varPi_0)$$

Given an interesting prefix π of path set $\varPi$, we now construct the left quotient of $\varPi$ with respect to π, i.e., the set of suffixes

$$\pi \backslash \varPi = \{\pi' \mid \pi.\pi' \in \varPi\}$$

Technically, we construct this set in time linear in the length of π by returning the subtrie of the trie $T(\varPi)$ obtained by following the path π.

If we continue the example with $\mathrm{Reduct}(\mathrm{Prefixes}_{1,1}(\varPi_{list})) = \{l, h\}$, we obtain the following sets of suffixes:

$$l \backslash \varPi_{list} = \{\varepsilon\}$$
$$h \backslash \varPi_{list} = \{\varepsilon, d, n, n.d, n.n, n.n.d\}$$

For each of these sets, we now consider the set of interesting suffixes, where "interesting" is defined in the same way as for prefixes. Technically, we just reverse all path suffixes and apply the interesting-prefixes algorithm. That is,

$$\mathrm{Suffixes}_{l,d}(\varSigma) = \overleftarrow{\mathrm{Prefixes}_{l,d}(\overleftarrow{\varSigma})}$$

Fig. 4. Reversed suffix trie

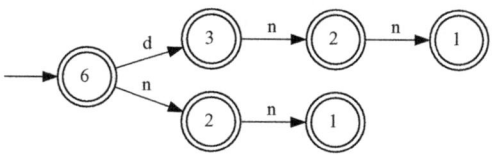

where $\overleftarrow{\Sigma} = \{\overleftarrow{\pi} \mid \pi \in \Sigma\}$ and $\overleftarrow{\pi}$ is the reverse of a path π.

Going back to the example, Fig. 4 shows the trie containing the reversed suffixes of $h\backslash\Pi_{list}$. From this trie, it is easy to see that the $(0, 1)$-interesting suffixes of $h\backslash\Pi_{list}$ are $\{\varepsilon, d, n\}$, whereas there is only one respective suffix of $l\backslash\Pi_{list}$, namely ε.

The final step of the algorithm considers for each pair of interesting prefix and interesting suffix the remaining part in the middle. The *right quotients* of the suffix language yield exactly this remaining part. The right quotient Π/π of a language with respect to a path π is defined dually to the left quotient by

$$\Pi/\pi = \{\pi' \mid \pi'.\pi \in \Pi\}$$

To abstract the resulting middle language, we restrict the algorithm to two choices. Either ε, if the middle language is $\{\varepsilon\}$, or $P*$ in all other cases.

In the example, we need to consider four cases, with the computation shown left and the resulting access permission shown in the right column:

$$
\begin{aligned}
(l\backslash\Pi_{list})/\varepsilon &= \{\varepsilon\} & &\mapsto l \\
(h\backslash\Pi_{list})/\varepsilon &= h\backslash\Pi_{list} & &\mapsto h.\{n, d\} * \\
(h\backslash\Pi_{list})/d &= \{\varepsilon, n, n.n\} & &\mapsto h.n * .d \\
(h\backslash\Pi_{list})/n &= \{\varepsilon, n\} & &\mapsto h.n * .n
\end{aligned}
$$

This result is not entirely satisfactory because $h.\{n, d\} *$ clearly subsumes $h.n * .d$ and $h.n * .n$, but the latter two permissions are more informative and thus preferable. Unfortunately, even together, they do not cover the access path h, which is only covered by $h. *$.

The source of the problem is that the set $\{\varepsilon, d, n\}$ is suffix-closed. For prefixes, we apply the prefix reduction because the semantics of access paths is prefix-closed. However, we cannot just apply suffix reduction as the example shows: If the suffix (in this case ε) is actually an element of the underlying set $h\backslash\Pi_{list}$, then dropping the suffix would be incorrect.

The solution is to treat the suffixes which would be removed by suffix reduction but which are elements of the underlying set specially and drop the rest. The special treatment is simple: we just declare their middle language to be $\{\varepsilon\}$. With this treatment (specified in function BUILDPERMISSIONS in Fig. 5), the case $(h\backslash\Pi_{list})$ with suffix ε yields the access permission h. The function has to be called for each interesting prefix with the corresponding suffix language (function PERMISSIONSFROMPATHSET).

Fig. 5. Building access permissions

function BUILDPERMISSIONS(π, Σ, sl, sd)
   ▷ π is a prefix, Σ corresponding suffix language, sl, sd suffix length and degree
   $R \leftarrow \emptyset$ ▷ result set of access permissions
   $\Sigma_0 \leftarrow \text{Suffixes}_{sl,sd}(\Sigma)$ ▷ set of interesting suffixes of Σ
   for all $\sigma \in \Sigma_0$ do
      if σ is proper suffix of an element of Σ_0 then
         if $\sigma \in \Sigma$ then
            $R = R + \pi.\sigma$
      else
         if $\Sigma/\sigma = \{\varepsilon\}$ then   ▷ middle language is empty
            $R = R + \pi.\sigma$
         else
            $R = R + \pi.P{*}.\sigma$ ▷ P is set of properties in Σ/σ
   return R

function PERMISSIONSFROMPATHSET(Π_0, Π, sl, sd)
   ▷ Π_0 set of prefixes of Π, sampled set of paths, sl, sd suffix length and degree
   $R \leftarrow \emptyset$ ▷ result set of access permissions
   for all $\pi \in \Pi_0$ do
      $R = R + \text{BUILDPERMISSIONS}(\pi, \pi\backslash\Pi, sl, sd)$
   return R

The final result of this phase applied to the running example is the set of access permissions $\{l, h, h.n{*}.d, h.n{*}.n\}$.

Simplifying Access Permissions. The result of the previous phase is not as concise as it could be. It may still generate redundant access permissions. Consider the result of the example $\{l, h, h.{*}.d, h.{*}.n\}$. As this set only contains read permissions, which are closed under prefix, it follows that permissions h is subsumed by $h.{*}.d$ and $h.{*}.n$, so that the result is equivalent to (the simpler set) $\{l, h.{*}.d, h.{*}.n\}$.

To perform this simplification, we first define a subsumption relation $\subseteq$ on path permissions.

$$\vdash \varepsilon \subseteq b \qquad \frac{\vdash b \subseteq P'{*}.b' \quad P \subseteq P'}{\vdash P.b \subseteq P'{*}.b'} \qquad \frac{\vdash P.b \subseteq b'}{\vdash P.b \subseteq P'{*}.b'}$$

$$\frac{\vdash b \subseteq b' \quad P \subseteq P'}{\vdash P{*}.b \subseteq P'{*}.b'}$$

This relation is sound in the sense that it reflects the semantic subset relation on sets of accepted access paths.

Lemma 3. *If $\mathbf{R}(\pi) \prec b$ and $\vdash b \subseteq b'$, then $\mathbf{R}(\pi) \prec b'$.*

Given this relation, simplification just removes all read path permissions that are subsumed by other (read or write) path permissions as specified in Fig. 6.

Fig. 6. Simplification

---

function SIMPLIFY(R, W) ▷ sets of path permissions, R for reading, W for writing
    while $(\exists b, b')\ b \in R \wedge (b' \in R \wedge b \neq b' \vee b' \in W) \wedge\ \vdash b \subseteq b'$ **do**
       $R \leftarrow R - b$
    return (R,W)

Fig. 7. Overall algorithm

---

function MAIN$(\Pi^r, \Pi^w, pl = 1, pd = 1, sl = 0, sd = 1)$
                                                  ▷ Π^r read paths, Π^w write paths
                         ▷ pl, pd prefix length and degree, sl, sd suffix length and degree
$\Pi^r_0 \leftarrow \text{Prefixes}_{pl,pd}(\Pi^r)$ ▷ interesting prefixes of Π^r
$\Pi^w_0 \leftarrow \text{Prefixes}_{pl,pd}(\Pi^w)$ ▷ interesting prefixes of Π^w
$R \leftarrow \text{PERMISSIONSFROMPATHSET}(\text{Reduct}(\Pi^r_0), \Pi^r, sl, sd)$
$W \leftarrow \text{PERMISSIONSFROMPATHSET}(\text{ReductW}(\Pi^w_0), \Pi^w, sl, sd)$
$(R, W) \leftarrow \text{SIMPLIFY}(R, W)$
return $R.@ + W$

In the example, clearly $\vdash h \subseteq h.n{*}.d$, so that h can be removed from the read path permissions.

Putting it Together. Fig. 7 summarizes the overall algorithm as explained up to this point. The parameters that determine the length and degree for the computation of interesting prefixes and suffixes have default values that yield good results in our experiments. In addition, our implementation makes them accessible through the user interface for experimentation, on a global as well as on a per-function basis.

3.3 Special Cases

There are two special cases of property accesses that lead to extremely high branching degrees. The first case is that an object is used as an array. The symptom of this case is the presence of accesses to numeric properties. Our implementation assumes that arrays contain homogeneous data and collapses all numeric property names to a single *pseudo property name* ♯. This collapsing already happens when the trie is constructed from the access paths.

Similarly, an object might be used as a hash table. This use leads to the same high branching degrees as array accesses, but cannot be reliably detected at trie construction time. Instead, the implementation makes a pre-pass over the trie that detects nodes with a high number of successors (e.g., set with the parameter HIGH_DEGREE which defaults to 20), merges these subtries, and relabels the remaining edge to the merged successor trie with a wildcard pseudo property name ?.

As the rest of the algorithm does not depend on the actual form of the property names, the introduction of these pseudo property names is inconsequential.

3.4 Soundness

To establish the soundness of the algorithm, we need to prove that each element of the original path set is matched by the extracted access permission. The first phase, building the trie, is trivially sound. The third simplification phase is sound by Lemma 3. It remains to consider the second phase. We only examine the case for read paths with write paths handled similarly.

Suppose $\pi \in \Pi$, the initial set of access paths. As $\Pi_0 = \text{Reduct}(\text{Prefixes}_{l,d}(\Pi))$ is prefix free, there are two possibilities. Either, there is exactly one element $\pi_0 \in \Pi_0$ such that π_0 is a prefix of π, or there is at least one element $\pi' \in \Pi_0$ such that π is a prefix of π'.

In the second case, π' will be prefix of an access path $\pi'.b$ with $\pi \prec \pi'.b$.

In the first case, it remains to show that π_0 is extended to an access path that matches $\pi = \pi_0.\pi_1$. Let Σ_0 be the set of interesting suffixes of $\Sigma = \pi_0 \backslash \Pi$. By construction, $\pi_1 \in \Sigma$. We need to show that there is an element $\sigma \in \Sigma_0$ where either $\pi_1 = \sigma$ or $\pi_1 \prec *.\sigma$.

For a contradiction, suppose that neither is the case and let σ be the maximal suffix of π_1 in Σ_0 (such σ must exist). If σ is a proper suffix of an element of Σ_0 and $\sigma \in \Sigma$, then $\sigma = \pi_1$, a contradiction. If $\Sigma/\sigma = \{\varepsilon\}$, then $\sigma = \pi_1$, a contradiction. If $\Sigma/\sigma \neq \{\varepsilon\}$, then $\pi_1 \prec *.\sigma$, a contradiction.

Hence, all cases are matched.

4 Implementation

Our effect inference algorithm is implemented as part of the JSConTest system for contract-based testing of JavaScript programs. JSConTest supports a typical workflow for unit testing, which starts with augmenting the unit under test with a specification of the tests that should be performed. Then JSConTest generates the test cases from the contracts and produces a test report from the outcomes. The test report either contains concrete evidence that some part of the desired behavior of the unit under test is incorrect or, if all tests pass, it increases the confidence that the unit under test behaves according to its specification.

Figure 8 illustrates this workflow. First, the tester specifies the desired properties of the program under test by annotating functions with contracts. The resulting annotated source file (Fig. 8, annotated linked−list.js) is passed to the JSConTest compiler. The compiler generates an instrumented version of the program (instr. linked−list.js). To test a JavaScript program inside a browser, a HTML file is needed to start the JSConTest framework and include the necessary files. The result of execution is a test report that documents which of the contracts are fulfilled by the unit under test. Depending on the parameters passed to the JSConTest compiler, the instrumented code does not only report contract violations, but also collects run-time data, for instance, what properties are accessed during test execution. As the JSConTest run-time framework is event-driven, it is possible to extend it to execute arbitrary algorithms on the collected data and thus create comprehensive test reports instead of just reporting raw data to the user.

Fig. 8. Overview over JSConTest

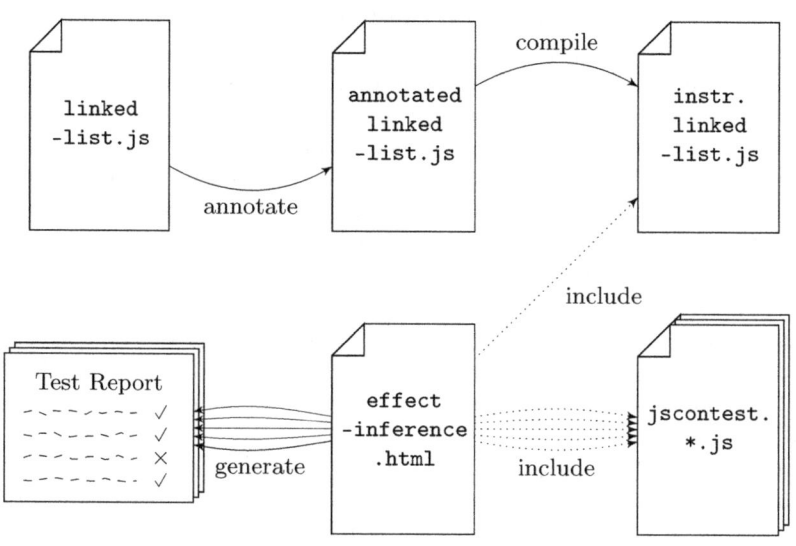

In this work we make use of this feature and let the JSConTest compiler generate code that reports all property accesses and invokes a handler for doing effect inference. As the effect inference is an interactive process, which depends on a number of interactively modifiable parameters, the test report is not just a static page with the test results, but a dynamic interface that interacts with the inference algorithm.

5 Evaluation

To evaluate the inference algorithm, we applied it to a few examples and compared the computed access permissions with manually constructed permissions.

The first example is a small third-party library (200 LOC) which implements a singly-linked list data structure.[4] Its interface comprises one constructor for list nodes and six methods to operate on the list: add, remove, find, indexOf, size, and toString.

The first step towards effect inference is to come up with contracts for each of the functions. The result is a source file annotated as in this code snippet:

```
1  /*c js:ll.(top) → undefined */
2  function add(data) { ... }
3  /*c js:ll.(top) → top */
4  function item(index) { ... }
5  /*c js:ll.(top) → top */
6  function remove(index) { ... }
```

---

[4] https://github.com/nzakas/computer-science-in-javascript

In these contracts, js:ll describes the receiver object, the parenthesized phrase the types of the arguments, and the phrase following the → the result type. In particular, js:ll refers to JavaScript function that generates and checks a certain kind of lists, top stands for any value, and undefined is the undefined value, which is returned when no return value is given.

The JSConTest compiler picks up the contracts in the special comments, generates code for assertions derived from the contracts, and creates a test suite for checking the contracts. This setup enables the tester to test the input/output behavior of all functions using directed random testing as explained in our previous work [1].

In the current version of JSConTest it is furthermore possible to infer the effects of the functions as follows. To obtain a first impression what properties are accessed by the different functions, it is sufficient to add the empty effect to the contract as in the contract /*c js:ll.(top) → undefined **with** [] */ for the add function. This augmented contract states that the function with this contract is not allowed to change anything in the heap that already exists before invocation of the function. Extending the remaining functions' contracts in the same way and applying the JSConTest compiler again results in instrumented code that monitors all property accesses.

When the compiled code executes in a browser, it collects, as a side effect, thousands of property accesses which violate the empty effect annotation. From this raw data, our effect inference computes concise access permissions. The syntax of these permissions is inspired by the syntax of file paths. For example, the computed effect for add is

$$\text{this.\_head, this.\_head.next*, this.\_length}$$

which means that add only accesses objects via its this pointer, it reads and writes the _head and _length properties, and it reads and writes a next property that is reachable via _head followed by a sequence of next properties as indicated by next*. All three path permissions are write permissions that implicitly permit reading all prefixes of any path leading to a permitted write.

The computed effect for remove is also interesting:

$$\text{this.\_head.next*.data.@, this.\_head.next*, this.\_length}$$

The function remove deletes a given value from the list. To this end, it compares this value with all data properties reachable via _head and a sequence of (all next) properties, as indicates with the first access path. Its ending in @ indicates a read-only path. Furthermore, remove changes next pointers and modifies the _length property of this.

Full details of this example are available on the project homepage of JSConTest.[5] It presents the outcomes of four examples complete with the annotated source code, the instrumented source code, and a web page to execute the example locally.

---

[5] http://proglang.informatik.uni-freiburg.de/jscontest/

On the webpage, there is another similar example implementing binary search trees. For these two examples the algorithm infers a precise effect annotation.

As a larger example, which is also detailed on the webpage, we consider the Richards benchmark from the Google V8 benchmark suite. After annotating its source code with contracts as outlined above, the effect inference algorithm automatically obtains informative results albeit less precise than the manually determined effects that we used in our previous work [2]. This example uncovered a number of new points for our inference algorithm, in particular, that special treatment for arrays and objects used as hash tables is required (see Sec. 3.3). This treatment is also covered in a micro benchmark in the webpage.

6   Related Work

Effect analysis in programming languages has some history already. Initial efforts by Gifford and Lucassen [4] perform a mere side-effect analysis which captures allocation as well as reading from and writing to variables. Subsequent work extends this approach to effects on memory regions which abstract sets of heap-allocated objects [5,6]. Such an effect describes reading, writing, and allocation in terms of regions. An important goal in these works is automatic effect inference [7], because regions and effects are deemed as analysis results in a phase of a compiler.

Path related properties are also investigated by Deutsch [8], but with the main goal of analyzing aliasing. His framework is based on abstract interpretation and offers unique abstract domains that provide very precise approximations of path properties.

In object-oriented languages, the focus of work on regions and effects is much more on documentation and controlling the scope of effects than on uncovering optimization opportunities. Greenhouse and Boyland [9] transpose effects to objects. One particular point of their effect system is that it preserves data abstraction by not mentioning the particular field names that are involved in an effect, but by instead declaring effect regions that encompass groups of fields (even across classes) and by being able to have abstract regions. In contract, our work is geared towards the scripting language JavaScript, which provides no data abstraction facilities and where the actual paths are important documentation of an operation that aids program understanding.

Skalka [10] also considers effects of object-oriented programs, but his effects are traces of operations. The goal of his is to prove that all traces generated by a program are safe with respect to some policy. Data access is not an issue in this work.

The learning algorithm in Sec. 3.2 abstracts a set of access paths to a set of access permissions, which are modeled after file paths with wildcards. The more general problem is learning a language from positive examples, which has been shown to be impossible, as soon as a class of languages contains all of the finite languages and at least one infinite language [11,12]. Clearly, the class of regular languages qualifies. Better results can be achieved by restricting the view to "simple examples" [13] or to more restricted kinds of languages [14].

Transformation of JavaScript programs is a well-studied topic in work on enforcing and analyzing security properties. For example, Maffeis and coworkers [15] achieve isolation properties between mashed-up scripts using filters, rewriting, and wrapping. Chugh and coworkers [16] present (among others) a dynamic information flow analysis based on wholesale rewriting. Yu and coworkers [17] perform rewriting guided by a security policy. BrowserShield [18] relies on similar techniques to attain safety. As detailed in our submitted work [2], extensive rewriting has a significant performance impact and gives rise to subtle semantic problems. These problems are shared among all transformation-based tools.

7 Conclusion

The current version of JSConTest induces access path permissions from sample test runs. In many cases, the resulting permissions are as good as manually determined ones. In the few remaining cases, interactive tweaking of the parameters is required to obtain good results. Thus, effect inference appears to be a useful tool to analyze JavaScript programs and enhance their contracts with effect information.

Effect inference or effect learning removes much of the tedium of declaring effect annotations for a given program. However, it is important for then inference to run with tight contracts or/and a test suite with high coverage, since the inference algorithm can only find a accurate effect annotation, if all aspects of the code under test are explored.

Tightness of the contract is required because a loose contract essentially causes the generation of entirely random test cases. It is unlikely that these random test cases discover the access path pattern of a function. For that reason, some of our examples rely on custom contracts that generate random values in the shape expected by the function.

Similarly, if the coverage of a test session is low, then it is likely that some paths through the input data are never traversed. Thus, high coverage increases the probability that all access paths are exercised.

One way to circumvent these restrictions is to observe the program running in the wild and collect and evaluate the resulting trace data. To be most effective and efficient, this approach would require instrumenting a JavaScript engine to collect the required access traces. Our evaluation back end and inference algorithm, however, would remain the same.

References

1. Heidegger, P., Thiemann, P.: Contract-driven testing of javaScript code. In: Vitek, J. (ed.) TOOLS 2010. LNCS, vol. 6141, pp. 154–172. Springer, Heidelberg (2010)
2. Heidegger, P., Bieniusa, A., Thiemann, P.: Access permission contracts. Submitted for publication (2010),
   http://proglang.informatik.uni-freiburg.de/jscontest/
3. Fredkin, E.: Trie memory. Communications of the ACM 3, 490–499 (1960)

4. Gifford, D., Lucassen, J.: Integrating functional and imperative programming. In: Proc. 1986 ACM Conf. on Lisp and Functional Programming, pp. 28–38 (1986)
5. Talpin, J.P., Jouvelot, P.: The type and effect discipline. Information and Computation 111(2), 245–296 (1994)
6. Tofte, M., Talpin, J.P.: Region-based memory management. Information and Computation 132(2), 109–176 (1997)
7. Birkedal, L., Tofte, M.: A constraint-based region inference algorithm. Theoretical Computer Science 58, 299–392 (2001)
8. Deutsch, A.: A storeless model of aliasing and its abstractions using finite representations of right-regular equivalence relations. In: Proc. IEEE International Conference on Computer Languages 1992, pp. 2–13. IEEE, CA (1992)
9. Greenhouse, A., Boyland, J.: An object-oriented effects system. In: Liu, H. (ed.) ECOOP 1999. LNCS, vol. 1628, pp. 205–229. Springer, Heidelberg (1999)
10. Skalka, C.: Trace effects and object orientation. In: Proceedings of the ACM Conference on Principles and Practice of Declarative Programming, Lisbon, Portugal (2005)
11. Gold, E.M.: Language identification in the limit. Information and Control 10(5), 447–474 (1967)
12. Angluin, D.: Inductive inference of formal languages from positive data. Information and Control 45(2), 117–135 (1980)
13. Denis, F.: Learning regular languages from simple positive examples. Machine Learning 44(1/2), 37–66 (2001)
14. Firoiu, L., Oates, T., Cohen, P.R.: Learning a deterministic finite automaton with a recurrent neural network. In: Honavar, V.G., Slutzki, G. (eds.) ICGI 1998. LNCS (LNAI), vol. 1433, pp. 90–101. Springer, Heidelberg (1998)
15. Maffeis, S., Mitchell, J.C., Taly, A.: Isolating javaScript with filters, rewriting, and wrappers. In: Backes, M., Ning, P. (eds.) ESORICS 2009. LNCS, vol. 5789, pp. 505–522. Springer, Heidelberg (2009)
16. Chugh, R., Meister, J.A., Jhala, R., Lerner, S.: Staged information flow for JavaScript. In: Proc. 2009 ACM Conf. PLDI, pp. 50–62. ACM Press, Ireland (2009)
17. Yu, D., Chander, A., Islam, N., Serikov, I.: JavaScript instrumentation for browser security. In: Felleisen, M. (ed.) Proc. 34th ACM Symp. POPL, pp. 237–249. ACM Press, France (2007)
18. Reis, C., Dunagan, J., Wang, H.J., Dubrovsky, O., Esmeir, S.: BrowserShield: Vulnerability-driven filtering of dynamic HTML. ACM Trans. Web 1(3), 11 (2007)

Systems Evolution and Software Reuse in Object-Oriented Programming and Aspect-Oriented Programming

Adam Przybyłek

University of Gdansk
Piaskowa 9, 81-824 Sopot, Poland
adam@univ.gda.pl

Abstract. Every new programming technique makes claims that software engineers want to hear. Such is the case with aspect-oriented programming (AOP). This paper describes a quasi-controlled experiment which compares the evolution of two functionally equivalent programs, developed in two different paradigms. The aim of the study is to explore the claims that software developed with aspect-oriented languages is easier to maintain and reuse than this developed with object-oriented languages. We have found no evidence to support these claims.

Keywords: AOP, maintainability, reusability, separation of concerns.

1 Introduction

Object-oriented programming (OOP) aims to support software maintenance and reuse by introducing concepts like abstraction, encapsulation, aggregation, inheritance and polymorphism. However, years of experience have revealed that this support is not enough. Whenever a crosscutting concern needs to be changed, a developer has to make a lot of effort to localize the code that implements it. This may possibly require him to inspect many different modules, since the code may be scattered across several of them.

An essential problem with traditional programming paradigms is the tyranny of the dominant decomposition [36]. No matter how well a software system is decomposed into modules, there will always be concerns (typically non-functional ones) whose code cuts across the chosen decomposition [25]. The implementation of these crosscutting concerns will spread across different modules, which has a negative impact on maintainability and reusability.

The need to achieve better separation of concerns (SoC) gave rise to aspect-oriented programming (AOP) [19]. The idea behind AOP was to implement secondary concerns as separate modules, called aspects. AOP has been proven to be effective in lexically separating different concerns of the system [33]. However, the influence of AOP on other quality attributes is still unclear.

J. Bishop and A. Vallecillo (Eds.): TOOLS 2011, LNCS 6705, pp. 163–178, 2011.
© Springer-Verlag Berlin Heidelberg 2011

On the one hand, replacing code that is scattered across many modules by a single aspect can potentially reduce the number of changes during maintenance [27]. In addition, modules may be easier to reuse, since they implement single concerns and do not contain tangled code.

On the other hand, constructs such as pointcuts and advices can make the ripple effects in aspect-oriented (AO) systems far more difficult to control than in OO systems. Current AO languages rely on referencing structural properties of the program such as naming conventions and package structure. These structural properties are used by pointcuts to define intended conceptual properties about the program. The obliviousness property of AspectJ implies that the underlying system does not have to prepare any hooks, or in any way depend on the intention to apply an aspect over it [18]. Thus, maintenance changes that conflict with the assumptions made by pointcuts introduce defects [27]. This phenomenon is called the pointcut fragility problem [20]. It occurs when a pointcut unintentionally captures or misses a given join point as a consequence of seemingly safe modifications to the base code [20], [27]. Kästner et al. [17] reported such silent changes during AO refactoring.

Obliviousness also leads to programs that are unnecessarily hard to understand [14]. Since not all the dependencies between the modules in AO systems are explicit, an AO maintainer has to perform more effort to get a mental model of the source code [35]. Creating a good mental model is crucial to understand the structure of a system before attempting to modify it [24]. Studies of software maintainers have shown that 30% to 50% of their time is spent in the process of understanding the code that they have to maintain [11], [34], [13].

Moreover, incremental modifications and code reuse are not directly supported for the new language features of AspectJ [15]. In particular, concrete aspects cannot be extended, advice cannot be overridden, and concrete pointcuts cannot be overridden. Hanenberg & Unland proposed four rules of thumb [15], which allow one to build reusable and incrementally modifiable aspects. However, enormous complexity is the price that has to be paid for it.

2 Motivations

Many unsupported claims have been made about AOP. Here are a few examples:

- AOP "can be seen as a way to overcome many of the problems related to software evolution" [25].
- AOP "produces code that is simpler and more maintainable, as well as increasing the flexibility, extensibility and re-usability of the separated concerns" [3].
- AO software "is supposed to be easy to maintain, reuse, and evolution" [41].
- AOP leads to "the production of software systems that are easier to maintain and reuse" [33].
- AOP "increases understandability and eases the maintenance burden, because modules tend to be more cohesive and less coupled" [22].

It is commonly acknowledged that designs with low coupling and high cohesion lead to software that is both, more reusable and more maintainable. Table 1 enumerates work that documented these relationships. Since in our previous study [30] we did not find empirical evidence that AOP increases cohesion, but we found that AOP increases coupling, we doubt the claims about the positive impact of AOP on reusability and evolvability. However, we do not intend to reject these claims as invalid with indirect evidences. Therefore, we conduct a quasi-experiment. We assume that the reader has a basic knowledge of AspectJ programming.

Table 1. Impact of coupling and cohesion on reusability and maintainability

	reusability	maintainability
coupling	[5], [16]	[5], [16], [6], [8], [23]
cohesion	[5], [4]	[5], [29]

3   Measurement System

In order to identify the metrics to be collected during the study, we used the G-Q-M (Goal-Question-Metric) approach [2]. G-Q-M defines a measurement system on three levels (Fig. 1) starting with a goal. The goal is refined in questions that break down the issue into quantifiable components. Each question is associated with metrics that, when measured, will provide information to answer the question.

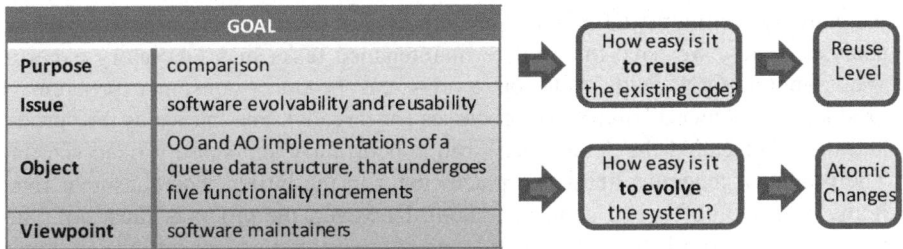

Fig. 1. GQM diagram of the study

Our goal is to compare AO and OO systems with respect to software evolvability and reusability from the viewpoint of the developer. Evolvability and reusability are quality characteristics that we cannot measure directly. Instead, we can perform an experiment that involves maintenance tasks and then we can measure how much effort is required to evolve the system and how much of the existing code can be reused in the consecutive release.

The amount of reuse is usually measured by comparing the number of reused "items" with the total number of "items" [12], where items depend on the granularity chosen, e.g. lines of code (LOC), function, or class. Since we are going to measure code reuse, we have chosen the granularity of LOC, yet we count only these reused lines that are part of the modules reused by applying the composition mechanisms of the underlying programming language. Thus, our reuse level metric is defined as: LOC_of_reused_modules / total_LOC_in_system.

The evolution metric we use is based on previous studies performed by Zhang et al. [40] and Ryder & Tip [32]. In their work, the difficulty of evolvability is defined in terms of atomic changes to the modules in a program. At the core of this approach is the ability to transform source code edits into a set of atomic changes, which captures the semantic differences between two releases of a program. Zhang et al. [40] presented a catalog of atomic changes for AspectJ programs. For the purpose of our study, we have slightly modified their catalog. Firstly, we consider deleting a non-empty element as an atomic change. Secondly, we use the term "module" as a generalization of class, interface, and aspect. Our list of atomic changes is follows: add an empty module, delete a module, add a field, delete a field, add an empty method, delete a method, change body of method, add an empty advice, delete an advice, change an advice body, add a new pointcut, change a pointcut body, delete a pointcut, introduce a new field, delete an introduced field, change an introduced field initializer, introduce a new method, delete an introduced method, change an introduced method body, add a hierarchy declaration, delete a hierarchy declaration, add an aspect precedence, delete an aspect precedence, add a soften exception declaration, delete a soften exception declaration.

4   Empirical Evaluation

The difficulty of performing evolvability and reusability evaluation in AOP is that there are not yet industrial maintenance reports for AO software projects available for analyses. Thus, we have to simulate maintenance tasks in a laboratory experiment. We compare OOP with AOP on a classical producer-consumer problem. In a producer-consumer dilemma two processes (or threads), one known as the "producer" and the other called the "consumer", run concurrently and share a fixed-size buffer. The producer generates items and places them in the buffer. The consumer removes items from the buffer and consumes them. However, the producer must not place an item into the buffer if the buffer is full, and the consumer cannot retrieve an item from the buffer if the buffer is empty. Nor may the two processes access the buffer at the same time to avoid race conditions. If the consumer needs to consume an item that the producer has not yet produced, then the consumer must wait until it is notified that the item has been produced. If the buffer is full, the producer will need to wait until the consumer consumes any item.

We assume to have an implementation of a cyclic queue as shown in Fig. 2a. The put(..) method stores one object in the queue and get() removes the oldest one. The nextToRemove attribute indicates the location of the oldest object. The location of a new object can be computed using nextToRemove, numItems (number of items) and buf.length (queue capacity). We also have an implementation of a producer and a consumer.

The experiment encompasses five maintenance scenarios which deal with the implementation of a new requirement. We have selected them because they naturally involve the modification of modules implementing several concerns.

4.1 Adding a Synchronization Concern

To use Queue in a consumer-producer system an adaptation to a concurrent environment is required. A thread has to be blocked when it tries to put an element into a full buffer or when it tries to get an element from an empty queue. In addition, both put(..) and get() methods have to be executed in mutual exclusion. Thus, they have to be wrapped within synchronization code when using Java (Fig. 2b). Since the code supporting the secondary concern may throw an exception, there is also a technical concern of error handling. The core concern here is associated with adding and removing item from the buffer. The presented implementation tangles the code responsible for the core functionality with the code responsible for handling errors and for cooperating synchronization. Moreover, the implementation of both secondary concerns are scattered through the accessors methods. As a result, the put(Object) and get() methods contain similar fragments of code.

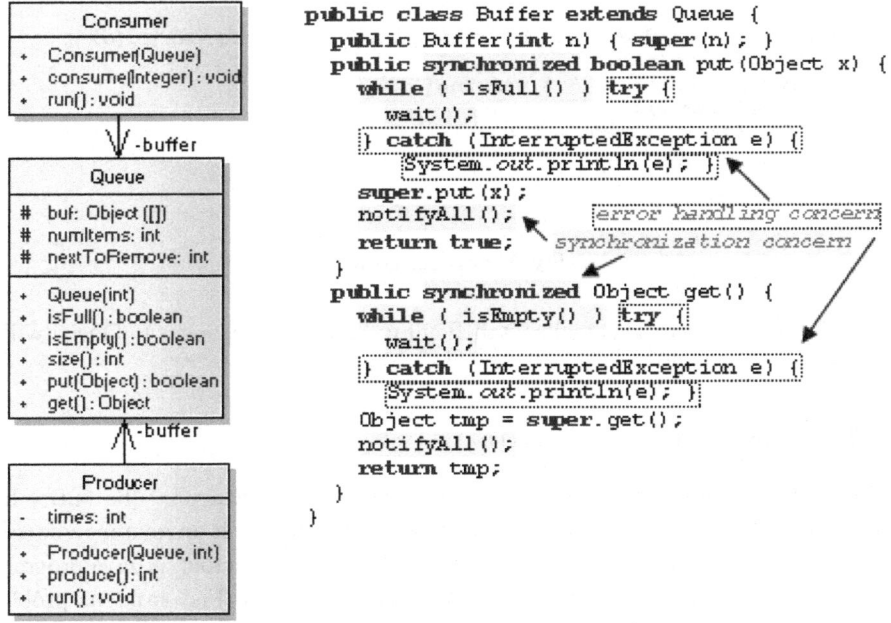

Fig. 2. a) An initial implementation; b) A new class for Stage I

Lexical separation of concerns can be achieved by using AO constructs (Fig. 3). The secondary concerns are implemented in ErrorHandler and SynchronizedQueue. SynchronizedQueue::waiting() is a hook method to introduce an explicit extension point. This joinpoint is used by ErrorHandler to wrap wait() invocation. Despite of lexical separation, SynchronizedQueue is explicitly tied to the Queue class, and so cannot be reused in other contexts. Moreover, Queue is oblivious of

```
public aspect ErrorsHandler {
  protected pointcut waiting():execution(void SynchronizedQueue.waiting());
  void around(): waiting() {
   try{proceed();} catch (InterruptedException e){System.out.println(e);}
  }
  declare soft: InterruptedException:waiting();
}
public aspect SynchronizedQueue pertarget( instantiation() ) {
  protected pointcut instantiation(): target(Queue);
  protected pointcut call_get(): execution( Object Queue.get() );
  protected pointcut call_put(Object x):
    execution( boolean Queue.put(Object) ) && args(x);
  protected void waiting() { wait(); }
  Object around(Queue q): call_get() && target(q){
    synchronized(this) {
      while( q.isEmpty() ) waiting();
      Object tmp = proceed(q);
      notifyAll(); return tmp;
    }
  }
  boolean around(Queue q, Object x): call_put(x) && target(q) {
    synchronized(this) {
      while ( q.isFull() ) waiting();
      proceed(q,x);
      notifyAll(); return true;
    }
  }
}
```

Fig. 3. New aspects for Stage I

SynchronizedQueue. This makes it difficult to know what changes to Queue will lead to undesired behavior.

4.2 Adding a Timestamp Concern

After implementing the buffer a new requirement has occurred – the buffer has to save current time associated with each stored item. Whenever an item is removed, the time how long it was stored should be printed to standard output. A Java programmer may use inheritance and composition as reuse techniques (Fig. 4a). The problem is that three different concerns are tangled within put/get and so these concerns cannot be composed separately. It means that e.g. if a programmer wants a queue with timing he cannot reuse the timing concern from TimeBuffer; he has to reimplement the timing concern in a new class that extends Queue. A slightly better solution seems to be using AOP and implementing the timing as an aspect (Fig. 4b).

Unless explicitly prevented, an aspect can apply to itself and can therefore change its own behavior. To avoid such situations, the instantiation pointcut is guarded by !cflow(within(Timing)). Moreover, the instantiation pointcut in SynchronizedQueue has to be updated. It must be the same as in Timing. This can be done only destructively, because AspectJ does not allow for extending concrete aspects.

```
public class TimeBuffer extends Buffer {
  protected Queue delegateDates;
  public TimeBuffer(int capacity) {
    super(capacity);
    delegateDates = new Queue(capacity);
  }
  public synchronized boolean put(Object x) {
    super.put(x);
    delegateDates.put(new Long(System.currentTimeMillis()));
    return true;
  }
  public synchronized Object get() {
    Object tmp = super.get();
    Long date = (Long) delegateDates.get();
    long curr = System.currentTimeMillis();
    System.out.println(curr - date.longValue());
    return tmp;
  }
}
public privileged aspect Timing pertarget( instant() ) {
  protected Queue delegateDates;

  protected pointcut instant():target(Queue) && !cflow(within(Timing));
  protected pointcut init(Queue q):execution(Queue.new(..)) && target(q);
  protected pointcut execution_get():execution( Object Queue.get() );
  protected pointcut execution_put():execution(boolean Queue.put(Object));

  after(Queue q): init(q) { delegateDates = new Queue(q.buf.length); }
  after(): execution_get() {
    Long date = (Long) delegateDates.get();
    System.out.println(System.currentTimeMillis() - date.longValue());
  }
  after(): execution_put() {
    delegateDates.put(new Long(System.currentTimeMillis())); }
}
```

Fig. 4. a) The TimeBuffer class; b) The Timing aspect

4.3 Adding a Logging Concern

The buffer has to log its size after each transaction. The OO mechanisms like inheritance and overridden allow a programmer for reusing TimeBuffer (Fig. 5a). The only problem is that four concerns are tangled within the LogTimeBuffer class. A module that addresses one concern can generally be used in more contexts than one that combines multiple concerns.

The AO solution is also noninvasive and it reuses the modules from the earlier stages. It just requires defining a new aspect (Fig. 5b). When advice declarations made in different aspects apply to the same join point, then by default the order of their execution is undefined. Thus, the declare precedence statement is used to force timing to happen before logging. The bufferChange pointcut enumerates, by their exact signature, all the methods that need to captured. Such pointcut definition is particularly fragile to accidental join point misses. An evolution of the buffer will require revising the pointcut definition to explicitly add all new accessor methods to it.

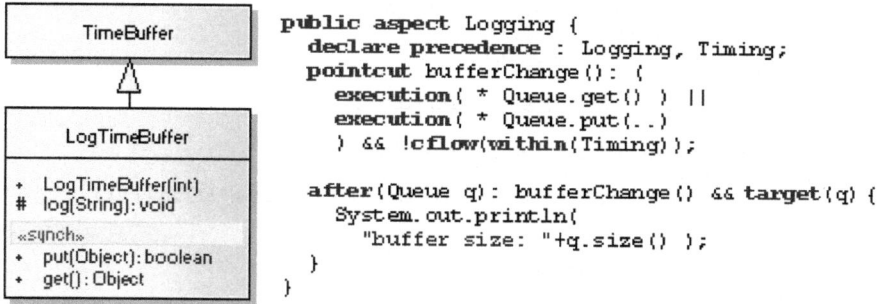

```
public aspect Logging {
    declare precedence : Logging, Timing;
    pointcut bufferChange(): (
        execution( * Queue.get() ) ||
        execution( * Queue.put(..) )
        ) && !cflow(within(Timing));

    after(Queue q): bufferChange() && target(q) {
        System.out.println(
            "buffer size: "+q.size() );
    }
}
```

Fig. 5. a) A new class for Stage III; b) The Logging aspect

4.4 Adding a New Getter

The buffer has to provide a method to get "N" next items. There is no efficient solution of this problem neither using Java nor AspectJ. In both cases, the condition for waiting on an item has to be reinforced by a lock flag. A lock flag is set when some thread initiates the "get N" transaction by getting the first item. The flag is unset after getting the last item. In Java (Fig. 6a), not only does the synchronization concern has to be reimplemented but also logging. The reason is that in LogTimeBuffer logging is tangled together with synchronization, so it cannot be reused separately. The duplicate implementation might be a nightmare for maintenance.

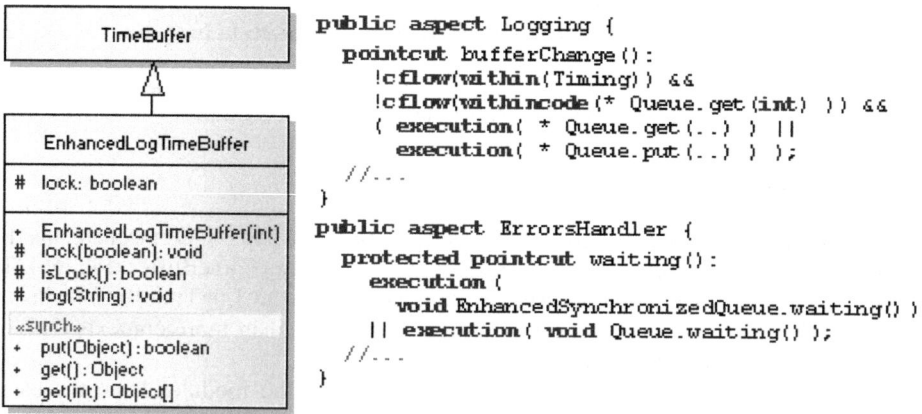

```
public aspect Logging {
    pointcut bufferChange():
        !cflow(within(Timing)) &&
        !cflow(withincode(* Queue.get(int) )) &&
        ( execution( * Queue.get(..) ) ||
          execution( * Queue.put(..) ) );
    //...
}
public aspect ErrorsHandler {
    protected pointcut waiting():
        execution (
            void EnhancedSynchronizedQueue.waiting() )
        || execution( void Queue.waiting() );
    //...
}
```

Fig. 6. a) A new class for Stage IV; b) Modifications in the pointcuts

In AspectJ, although synchronization is implemented in a separate module, it also cannot be reused in any way because an aspect cannot extend another concrete aspect. Thus, all code corresponding to the synchronization concerns has to be reimplemented (Fig. 7). A new method to get N items and locking mechanism are introduced to Queue by means of inter-type declaration.

```
public aspect EnhancedSynchronizedQueue pertarget( instant() ) {
  private boolean Queue.lock = false;
  public void Queue.lock(boolean b) { lock = b; }
  public boolean Queue.isLock() { return lock; }
  public synchronized Object[] Queue.get(int n) {
    while ( isEmpty()||isLock() ) waiting();
    lock(true);
    Object[] tmp = new Object[n];
    for(int i=0; i<n; i++) {
      while ( isEmpty() ) waiting();
      tmp[i] = get();
    }
    lock(false);
    return tmp;
  }
  private void Queue.waiting() { wait(); }
  protected void waiting() { wait(); }
  protected pointcut instant():target(Queue) && !cflow(within(Timing));
  protected pointcut call_get():
    !cflow(withincode(* Queue.get(int) )) && call(Object Queue.get());
  Object around(Queue q):call_get() && target(q) {
    synchronized(this) {
      while(q.isEmpty()||q.isLock()) waiting();
      Object tmp=proceed(q);
      notifyAll(); return tmp;
    }
  }
  declare precedence :
    EnhancedSynchronizedQueue, Logging, Timing;
  //...
}
```

Fig. 7. A new aspect for Stage IV

In addition, destructive changes in the Logging::bufferChange() pointcut are required
(Fig. 6b). Otherwise logs would be reported n times in response to the get(int n)
method, instead of just once after completing the transaction. This is due to that
get(int n) uses get() for retrieving every single item from the buffer. Furthermore, the
ErrorsHandler::waiting() pointcut also needs adjusting to the new decomposition.

4.5 Removing Logging and Timestamp

A programmer needs the enhanced buffer from Stage IV, but without the logging and
timing concerns. In Java, he once again has to reimplement the get(int) method and
much of the synchronization concerns. All to do in the AO version is to remove
Logging and Timing from the compilation list.

5 Lessons Learned

In an AO system, one cannot tell whether an extension to the base code is safe simply
by examining the base program in isolation. All aspects referring to the base program

need to be examined as well. In addition, when writing a pointcut definition a programmer needs global knowledge about the structure of the application. E.g. when implementing the Timing aspect, a programmer has to know that the current implementation of the synchronization concern affects each Queue structure, while the timing concern requires a non-blocking Queue.

Moreover, when a system includes multiple aspects, they can begin to affect each other. At Stage C, we have had to explicitly exclude logging the state of the queue that is used by the Timing aspect. Furthermore, we have observed the problem of managing interactions between aspects that are being composed. When advice declarations made in different aspects affect the same join point, it is important to consider the order in which they execute. Indeed, a wrong execution order can break the program. In our experiment, we have used precedence declarations to force timing to happen before logging and to force both of them to happen within the synchronization block.

In most cases, aspects cannot be made generic, because pointcuts as well as advices encompass information specific to a particular use, such as the classes involved, in the concrete aspect. As a result, aspects are highly dependent on other modules and their reusability is decreased. E.g. at Stage I, the need to explicitly specify the Queue class and the two synchronization conditions means that no part of the SynchronizedQueue aspect can be made generic. In addition, we have confirmed that the reusability of aspects is also hampered in cases where "join points seem to dynamically jump around", depending on the context certain code is called from [3]. Moreover, the variety of pointcut designators makes pointcut expressions cumbersome (see EnhancedSynchronizedQueue::call_get()).

Some advocates of AOP believe that appropriate tools can deal with the problems of AOP we encountered. We think that they should reject AOP at all, since some research [31] "shows" that OOP with a tool support solves the problem of crosscutting concerns:)

6 Empirical Results

Table 2 presents the number of Atomic Changes and Reuse Level for both releases for every stage. The measures were collected manually. Lower values are better for Atomic Changes but worse for Reuse Level. AOP manifests superiority at Stage III and V, while OOP in the rest of the cases. At Stage III we have implemented a logging concern which is one of the flagship examples of AOP usage. At this Stage, the OO version requires significantly more atomic changes and new lines of code than its AO counterpart. At Stage V, the maintenance tasks are focused on detaching some concerns instead of implementing new ones. The AO solution has turned out to be more pluggable.

Table 2. Number of Atomic Changes and Reuse Level per stage

Stage	Atomic Changes		Reuse Level	
	OOP	AOP	OOP	AOP
I. Adding a synchronization concern	7	19	0,71	0,66
II. Adding a timestamp concern	8	19	0,85	0,67
III. Adding a logging concern	9	6	0,88	0,95
IV. Adding a new getter	9	16	0,73	0,58
V. Removing logging and timestamp	5	3	0,74	1,00

7 Threats to Validity

7.1 Construct Validity

Construction threats lie in the way we define our metrics. Evolvability and reusability like other quality factors are difficult to measure. Our dependent variables are based on previous studies performed by Zhang et al. [40], Ryder & Tip [32] and Frakes [12]. It is possible that other metrics will be better fitted for the purpose of our study.

7.2 Internal Validity

Internal validity of our experiment concerns the question whether the effects were caused only by the programming paradigm involved, or by other factors. The experiment has been carried out by the author during his research for the achievement of a Doctor of Philosophy Degree. As the author does not have any interest in favour of one approach or the other, we do not expect it to be a large threat. Nevertheless, other programmers could have chosen the different strategies for implementing secondary concerns.

7.3 External Validity

Synchronization, logging, and timing present the typical characteristics of crosscutting concerns and as such they are likely to be generalizable to other concerns. Unfortunately, the limited number of maintenance tasks and size of the program make impossible the generalization of our results. However, the academic setting allows us to present the whole programs in detail and to put forward some advantages and limitations of AOP.

8 Related Work

Coady & Kiczales [9] compared the evolution of two versions (C and AspectC) of four crosscutting concerns in FreeBSD. They refactored the implementations of the following concerns in v2 code: page daemon activation, prefetching for mapped files, quotas for disk usage, and tracing blocked processes in device drivers. These implementations were then rolled forward into their subsequent incarnations in v3 and v4 respectively. In each case they found that, with tool support, the AO implementation better facilitated independent development and localized change. In three cases, configuration changes mapped directly to modifications to pointcuts and makefile options. In one case, redundancy was significantly reduced. Finally, in one case, the implementation of a system-extension aligned with an aspect was itself better modularized.

Bartsch & Harrison conducted an experiment [1] in which 11 students were asked to carry out maintenance tasks on one of two versions (Java and AspectJ) of an online shopping system. The results did seem to suggest a slight advantage for the subjects using the OO version since in general it took the subjects less time to perform maintenance tasks and it averagely required less line of code to implement a new requirement. However, the results did not show a statistically significant influence of AOP at the 5% level.

Sant'Anna et al. [33] conducted a quasi-controlled experiment to compare the use of OOP and AOP to implement Portalware (about 60 modules and over 1 KLOC). Portalware is a multi-agent system (MAS) that supports the development and management of Internet portals. The experiment team (3 PhD candidates and 1 M.Sc. student) developed two versions of the Portalware system: an AO version and an OO version. Next, the same team simulated seven maintenance/reuse scenarios that are recurrent in large-scale MAS. For each scenario, the difficulty of maintainability and reusability was defined in terms of structural changes to the artifacts in the AO and OO systems. The total lines of code, that were added, changed, or copied to perform the maintenance tasks, equaled 540 for the OO approach and 482 for the AO approach.

Kulesza et al. [21] present a quantitative study that assesses the positive and negative effects of AOP on typical maintenance activities of a Web information system.They compared the AO and OO implementations of a same web-based information system, called HealthWatcher (HW). The main purpose of the HW system is to improve the quality of services provided by the healthcare institution, allowing citizens to register complaints regarding health issues, and the healthcare institution to investigate and take the required actions. In the maintenance phase of their study, they changed both OO and AO architectures of the HW system to address a set of 8 new use cases. The functionalities introduced by these new use cases represent typical operations encountered in the maintenance of information systems. Although they claim that the AO design has exhibited superior reusability through the changes, there is no empirical evidence to support this claim. The collected metrics show only that aspects contributed to: (1) the decrease in the lines of code, number of attributes, and cohesion; (2) the increase in the vocabulary size and lexical separation of crosscutting concerns. They also tried to evaluate coupling, but in our earlier study [30] we argued why their coupling metric is invalid. An additional interesting observation from Kulesza's study [21] is that more modules were needed to be modified in the AO version, because it requires changing both the classes along the layers to implement the use case functionality and the aspects implementing the crosscutting issues.

Munoz et al. [28] showed that aspects offer efficient mechanisms to implement crosscutting concerns, but that aspects can also introduce complex errors in case of evolution. To illustrate these issues, they implemented and then evolved a chat application. They found that it is very hard to reason about the aspects impact on the final application.

Mortensen et al. [26] examined the benefits of refactoring three legacy applications developed by Hewlett-Packard. They followed the evolution of the applications across several revisions. The modifications needed to evolve these systems required changes to fewer software items in the refactored systems when compared to the original. The reduction of the average number of modules and files changed between revisions was 4% and 3% respectively.

Taveira et al. conducted two studies to check if AOP promotes greater reuse of exception handling code than a traditional, OO approach. In the first study [38], they assessed the suitability of AOP to reuse exception handling code within applications. They refactored three medium-size applications implemented originally in Java. Aspects were used to implement the exception handlers. Though AOP promoted a large amount of reuse of error handling code, the overall size of the refactored systems did not decrease due to the code overhead imposed by AspectJ. The number of handlers was sensibly lower in the refactored versions but the amount of error handling code was much higher. In the second study [37], they refactored seven medium-size systems to assess the extent to which AOP promotes inter-application reuse of exception handling code. They found out that reusing error handling across applications is not possible in most of the cases and requires some a priori planning. Only extremely simple handlers could be reused across applications.

The experiment closest to ours is the one conducted by Figueiredo et al. [10] in which they quantitatively and qualitatively assess the positive and negative impacts of AOP on a number of changes applied to MobileMedia. MobileMedia is a software product line for applications with about 3 KLOC that manipulate photo, music, and video on mobile devices. The original release was available in both AspectJ and Java (the Java versions use conditional compilation as the variability mechanism). Then, a group of five post-graduate students was responsible for implementing the successive evolution scenarios of MobileMedia. Each new release was created by modifying the previous release of the respective version. A total of seven change scenarios were incorporated. The scenarios comprised different types of changes involving mandatory, optional, and alternative features, as well as non-functional concerns. Figueiredo et al. found that AOP usually does not cope with the introduction of mandatory features. The AO solution generally introduced more modules and operations. A direct result of more modules and operations is the increase in LOC. Moreover, depending on the evolution scenario, AspectJ pointcuts were more fragile than conditional compilation. In order to compare their and our results, we have derived the simplest form of Reuse Level and Atomic Changes (Table 3) from their measures. Atomic Changes has been limited to counting operations only, while Reuse Level has been calculated as: number_of_reused_LOC / LOC. In general, the measures demonstrate that there is no winner with respect to Reuse Level. The AO solution is significantly better only at Stage VII. With regard to Atomic Changes, the OO implementations are superior for every release.

Table 3. Atomic changes and Reuse Level in MobileMedia

release ▶		II	III	IV	V	VI	VII	VIII
Reuse	OO	0,73	0,86	0,96	0,48	0,75	0,01	0,76
Level	AO	0,62	0,82	0,93	0,55	0,76	0,29	0,74
Atomic	OO	120	68	20	111	88	335	149
Change	AO	150	90	22	134	102	437	175

7 Summary

In 2001 the editors of January/February "MIT Technology Review" announced AOP as a standard in the commercial production of software in the next 15 years. Nowadays, ten years later, AOP is still not widely adopted. We believe that, the transfer of AOP to the mainstream of the software development depends on our ability to find its true benefits and to be aware of its potential pitfalls. In this paper, we have evolved a simple program in order to assess the potential of AOP to improve evolvability and reusability in the presence of crosscutting concerns. Although a definitely conclusion cannot be drawn from only the one discussed experiment, an important outcome has been achieved in that the advocates of AOP have to take a position on our results. By reviewing other research, we have shown that the claims presented in Section 2 are not backed up by any convincing evidence. In our study, the superiority of AOP has been observed only when detaching secondary concerns and when implementing logging, which is a flagship example of AOP usage. OOP has fared better in implementing secondary concerns in three out of four scenarios.

The experience gathered during the maintenance tasks points out that (1) understanding the intricate dependencies existing between the modules of an AO system is an arduous task; (2) aspects are holding too much information (the crosscutting logic and target module information) to fully take advantage of lexical SoC. Thus, it seems that the abstractions that AOP has provided to solve some of the evolution problems with traditional software, actually introduce a series of new evolution problems. This phenomenon has been called the evolution paradox of AOP [39], [28].

References

1. Bartsch, M., Harrison, R.: An exploratory study of the effect of aspect-oriented programming on maintainability. Software Quality Journal 16(1), 23–44 (2008)
2. Basili, V.R., Caldiera, G., Rombach, H.D.: Goal Question Metric Approach. In: Encyclopedia of Software Engineering, pp. 528–532. John Wiley & Sons, Inc., Chichester (1994)
3. Beltagui, F.: Features and Aspects: Exploring feature-oriented and aspect-oriented programming interactions. Technical Report No: COMP-003-2003, Computing Department, Lancaster University (2003)
4. Bieman, J.M., Kang, B.: Cohesion and reuse in an object-oriented system. SIGSOFT Softw. Eng. Notes 20(SI), 259–262 (1995)
5. Bowen, T.P., Post, J.V., Tai, J., Presson, P.E., Schmidt, R.L.: Software Quality Measurement for Distributed Systems. Guidebook for Software Quality Measurement. Technical Report RADC-TR-83-175 vol. 2 (July 1983)

6. Breivold, H.P., Crnkovic, I., Land, R., Larsson, S.: Using Dependency Model to Support Software Architecture Evolution. In: 23rd IEEE/ACM International Conference on Automated Software Engineering, L'Aquila, Italy (2008)
7. Brichau, J., De Meuter, W., De Volder, K.: Jumping Aspects. In: Workshop on Aspects and Dimensions of Concerns at ECOOP 2000, Sophia Antipolis and Cannes, France (2000)
8. Chaumun, M.A., Kabaili, H., Keller, R.K., Lustman, F., Saint-Denis, G.: Design Properties and Object-Oriented Software Changeability. In: 13th Conference on Software Maintenance and Reengineering, Kaiserslautern, Germany (2000)
9. Coady, Y., Kiczales, G.: Back to the future: a retroactive study of aspect evolution in operating system code. In: 2nd Inter. Conf. on Aspect-oriented software development (AOSD 2003), Boston, Massachusetts (2003)
10. Figueiredo et al.: Evolving software product lines with aspects: An empirical study on design stability. In: 30th International Conference on Software Engineering (ICSE 2008), Leipzig, Germany (2008)
11. Fjeldstad, R., Hamlen, W.: Application program maintenance-report to to our respondents. In: Parikh, G., Zvegintzov, N. (eds.) Tutorial on Software Maintenance, pp. 13–27. IEEE Computer Soc. Press, Los Alamitos (1983)
12. Frakes, W.: Software Reuse as Industrial Experiment. American Programmer 6(9), 27–33 (1993)
13. Glass, R.L.: Facts and Fallacies of Software Engineering. Addison-Wesley, Reading (2002)
14. Griswold, W.G., Sullivan, K., Song, Y., Shonle, M., Tewari, N., Cai, Y., Rajan, H.: Modular Software Design with Crosscutting Interfaces. IEEE Software 23(1), 51–60 (2006)
15. Hanenberg, S., Unland, R.: Using and Reusing Aspects in AspectJ. In: Workshop on Advanced Separation of Concerns in Object-Oriented Systems at OOPSLA 2001, Tampa Bay, Florida (2001)
16. Hitz, M., Montazeri, B.: Measuring Coupling and Cohesion in Object-Oriented Systems. In: 3rd International Symposium on Applied Corporate Computing, Monterrey, Mexico (1995)
17. Kästner, C., Apel, S., Batory, D.: A Case Study Implementing Features using AspectJ. In: 11th International Conference of Software Product Line Conference (SPLC 2007), Kyoto, Japan (2007)
18. Katz, S.: Diagnosis of harmful aspects using regression verification. In: Workshop on Foundations of Aspect-Oriented Languages at AOSD 2004, Lancaster, UK (2004)
19. Kiczales, G., Lamping, J., Mendhekar, A., Maeda, C., Cristina Lopes, C., Loingtier, J., Irwin, J.: Aspect-Oriented Programming. In: Aksit, M., Auletta, V. (eds.) ECOOP 1997. LNCS, vol. 1241, pp. 220–242. Springer, Heidelberg (1997)
20. Koppen, C., Störzer, M.: PCDiff: Attacking the fragile pointcut problem. In: European Interactive Workshop on Aspects in Software, Berlin, Germany (2004)
21. Kulesza, U., Sant'Anna, C., Garcia, A., Coelho, R., von Staa, A., Lucena, C.: Quantifying the effects of aspect-oriented programming: A maintenance study. In: 22nd IEEE International Conference on Software Maintenance (ICSM 2006), Dublin, Ireland (2006)
22. Lemos, O.A., Junqueira, D.C., Silva, M.A., Fortes, R.P., Stamey, J.: Using aspect-oriented PHP to implement crosscutting concerns in a collaborative web system. In: 24th Annual ACM International Conference on Design of Communication, Myrtle Beach, South Carolina (2006)
23. MacCormack, A., Rusnak, J., Baldwin, C.: The Impact of Component Modularity on Design Evolution: Evidence from the Software Industry. Harvard Business School Technology & Operations Mgt. Unit Research Paper, vol. 08-038 (2007)

24. Mancoridis, S., Mitchell, B. S., Rorres, C., Chen, Y., Gansner, E.R.: Using Automatic Clustering to Produce High-Level System Organizations of Source Code. In: 6th International Workshop on Program Comprehension (IWPC 1998), Ischia, Italy (1998)
25. Mens, T., Mens, K., Tourwé, T.: Software Evolution and Aspect-Oriented Software Development, a cross-fertilisation. In: ERCIM special issue on Automated Software Engineering, Vienna, Austria (2004)
26. Mortensen, M., Ghosh, S., Bieman, J.: Aspect-Oriented Refactoring of Legacy Applications: An Evaluation. IEEE Trans. Software Engineering 99 (2010)
27. Mortensen, M.: Improving Software Maintainability through Aspectualization. PhD thesis, Department of Computer Science, Colorado State University, CO (2009)
28. Munoz, F., Baudry, B., Barais, O.: Improving maintenance in AOP through an interaction specification framework. In: IEEE Intl. Conf. on Software Maintenance, Beijing, China (2008)
29. Perepletchikov, M., Ryan, C., Frampton, K.: Cohesion Metrics for Predicting Maintainability of Service-Oriented Software. In: 7th International Conference on Quality Software (QSIC 2007), Portland, Oregon (2007)
30. Przybyłek, A.: Where the truth lies: AOP and its impact on software modularity. In: Giannakopoulou, D., Orejas, F. (eds.) FASE 2011. LNCS, vol. 6603, pp. 447–461. Springer, Heidelberg (2011)
31. Robillard, M.P., Weigand-Warr, F.: ConcernMapper: simple view-based separation of scattered concerns. In: Workshop on Eclipse technology eXchange at OOPSLA 2005, San Diego, CA (2005)
32. Ryder, B.G., Tip, F.: Change impact analysis for object-oriented programs. In: 3rd ACM SIGPLAN-SIGSOFT Workshop on Program Analysis for Software Tools and Engineering, Snowbird, Utah (2001)
33. Sant'Anna, C., Garcia, A., Chavez, C., Lucena, C., von Staa, A.: On the Reuse and Maintenance of Aspect-Oriented Software: An Assessment Framework. In: 17th Brazilian Symposium on Software Engineering (SEES 2003), Manaus, Brazil (2003)
34. Standish, T.: An essay on software reuse. IEEE Transactions on Software Engineering 10(5), 494–497 (1984)
35. Storey, M.D., Fracchia, F.D., Müller, H.A.: Cognitive design elements to support the construction of a mental model during software exploration. J. Syst. Softw. 44(3), 171–185 (1999)
36. Tarr, P., Ossher, H., Harrison, W., Sutton, S.M.: N degrees of separation: multi-dimensional separation of concerns. In: 21st International Conference on Software Engineering (ICSE 2009), Los Angeles, California (1999)
37. Taveira, J., Oliveira, H., Castor, F., Soares, S.: On Inter-Application Reuse of Exception Handling Aspects. In: Workshop on Empirical Evaluation of Software Composition Techniques at AOSD 2010, Rennes, France (2010)
38. Taveira, J.C., et al.: Assessing Intra-Application Exception Handling Reuse with Aspects. In: 23rd Brazilian Symposium on Software Engineering (SBES 2009), Fortaleza, Brazil (2009)
39. Tourwé, T., Brichau, J., Gybels, K.: On the Existence of the AOSD-Evolution Paradox. In: AOSD 2003 Workshop on Software-engineering Properties of Languages for Aspect Technologies, Boston, Massachusetts (2003)
40. Zhang, S., Gu, Z., Lin, Y., Zhao, J.: Change impact analysis for AspectJ programs. In: 24th IEEE International Conference on Software Maintenance, Beijing, China (2008)
41. Zhao, J.: Measuring Coupling in Aspect-Oriented Systems. In: 10th International Software Metrics Symposium, Chicago, Illinois (2004)

Lifted Java: A Minimal Calculus for Translation Polymorphism

Matthias Diehn Ingesman and Erik Ernst*

Department of Computer Science, Aarhus University, Denmark
{mdi,eernst}@cs.au.dk

Abstract. To support roles and similar notions involving multiple views on an object, languages like Object Teams and CaesarJ include mechanisms known as lifting and lowering. These mechanisms connect pairs of objects of otherwise unrelated types, and enables programmers to consider such a pair almost as a single object which has both types. In the terminology of Object Teams this is called translation polymorphism. In both Object Teams and CaesarJ the type system of the Java programming language has been extended to support this through the use of advanced language features. However, so far the soundness of translation polymorphism has not been proved.

This paper presents a simple model that extends Featherweight Java with the core operations of translation polymorphism, provides a Coq proof that its type system is sound, and shows that the ambiguity problem associated with the so-called smart lifting mechanism can be eliminated by a very simple semantics for lifting.

Keywords: Formal foundations, language design, lifting/lowering, Translation Polymorphism, type systems

1 Introduction

In this paper we investigate the mechanisms lifting and lowering that provide a means to connect pairs of objects of otherwise unrelated types; mechanisms that have existed since 1998 [15,16,17], but have so far not been proved sound. The Object Teams/Java language (OT/J) [11,9] calls them translation polymorphism [10].

OT/J is an extension of the Java programming language [8] that facilitates non-invasive customisation through addition of code instead of modification. This is done by introducing two new types of classes called *teams* and *roles*. Roles solve many of the same problems as aspects [14,13], i.e. extension of existing code; teams provide the means of controlling which roles are active, along with state that is shared between roles in the team. In other words teams provide the context for families of related roles, and in fact teams implement *family*

* This research was supported by the Danish Council for Independent Research, grant 09-061026.

J. Bishop and A. Vallecillo (Eds.): TOOLS 2011, LNCS 6705, pp. 179–193, 2011.

polymorphism [5]. Furthermore teams can inherit and extend the roles of their super class, a feature known as *virtual classes* [7]. Each role is connected to a regular class, the *base class*, through a special `playedBy` relation, making these two objects seem almost like a single object. The mechanisms *lifting* and *lowering* use the `playedBy` relation and provide the translation between roles and base classes. In situations where a role is expected but a base class is given, lifting translates the base class object into the appropriate role. Similarly if a base class object is expected but a role is given, lowering translates the role into the base class object. In both cases the role and the base are connected via the `playedBy` relation, either through *smart lifting* (OT/J) or through a flexible invariant on the `playedBy` relation (this calculus). In OT/J lifting works across inheritance hierarchies on both the role side and the base side. Smart lifting is an algorithm that lets the run-time system choose the most specific role for a base class. We note that smart-lifting makes it possible to make old code produce errors without modifying it, due to the fact that it tries to always provide the most specific role when lifting. This calculus features a straightforward lifting operation that is always safe. OT/J is defined in terms of its implementation and a language specification document. A soundness proof for the extensions to the Java programming language type system has not been presented so far. For the full details on OT/J see [11].

The main contributions of this paper are: a minimal calculus of translation polymorphism, along with a full soundness proof of this calculus; a resolution of the ambiguity problems of smart lifting through a straightforward semantics for the lifting operation; and a description of a safe language design space for languages with translation polymorphism. The soundness proof is made using the Coq proof assistant [2], on the basis of a Featherweight Java (FJ) [12] soundness proof by De Fraine *et al.* [3].

Excluding comments and empty lines, the modifications to the FJ source code amount to ~550 changed lines of code and ~400 new. To put these numbers into context, the original FJ source code is ~1000 lines of code. The introduction of roles had a large impact in general, while lifting and lowering mainly resulted in an increase in the number of cases for the safety properties.

The concepts described in this paper are not specific to OT/J, and thus no previous knowledge of OT/J is required. However, we use some terminology of OT/J which will be explained as it is introduced. The rest of this paper is structured as follows. In section 2 we describe our choice of features for this calculus, give an example program, and describe the way objects are represented. Section 3 presents the calculus and gives the proof of standard type soundness. Section 4 discusses the semantics of lifting in more detail. In section 5 related and future work is discussed, and in section 6 the paper is concluded.

2   The Model

In this section we first argue why we do not model various features of OT/J. After that an example of a program written in the calculus is provided. The example is used to highlight some problems with the lifting operation that demand careful consideration, and we present our solution to these problems. Finally, because our representation of objects is non-standard, we conclude this section by describing objects.

We ignore all features of OT/J that are not at the core of translation polymorphism. Thus the following features are not part of the model: teams, team activation, call-in bindings, and call-out bindings.

Teams are not in the model because the only part they play in relation to translation polymorphism is to contain roles. Instead of being contained in teams roles are top-level classes. It may seem surprising that our model omits teams, because their semantics are at the core of the semantics of OT/J (just like classes containing cclasses are at the core of CaesarJ). However, we do not need to model the support for virtual classes in order to establish a universe which is sufficiently rich to support a model of lifting and lowering with a semantics that mirrors the behaviour of full-fledged languages. In fact, the connected pairs of roles and base objects in OT/J can simply be modelled as a *cloud* of objects with a label pointing to the currently *active* one. An object in our calculus is then such a cloud, which is just a finite set of objects of which one is an instance of a normal class (the base object), and the remaining objects are instances of role classes: the set of roles which the base class is currently playing. Such an object cloud works as the base object when its label points to the base object, and as a role object when its label points to one of the role objects. Lowering just means changing the label from one of the role objects to the base object, and lifting means changing the label from the base object to one of the roles in the cloud. In case the base object has not yet played the role which is requested in a lifting operation, a fresh instance of that role is created and added to the cloud. This semantics corresponds to a redistribution of the role objects in OT/J, where each team is responsible for storing existing roles of that team in some internal data structure managed by the language run-time. In this way, not modelling teams is in some sense equivalent to restricting OT/J to a single global and always active team, inside which every role is defined. Without teams there is no need for modelling the team activation constructs. As our aim is to stay close to the implementation of translation polymorphism in OT/J, in which a legal base class is not a role of the same team [11], we do not allow roles to be playedBy another role.

Call-in and call-out bindings provide the *Aspect-Oriented Programming* features of OT/J, and are thus unrelated to the core of translation polymorphism. Lifting and lowering do occur inside these bindings, but not in a way that is different from regular method and constructor invocations.

To summarise, translation polymorphism is defined by roles and the operations lifting and lowering. Thus those are the concepts we add to FJ. Roles are restricted in two ways: they cannot be part of an inheritance hierarchy, and they cannot have state. Fields in roles are inessential because roles may still add non-trivial behaviour to a base object by accessing its fields. Moreover, in a calculus that does not support mutable state, role objects with fields would have to initialise their fields to values that could as well be computed when needed. In other words, state could easily be added to roles, but it would be essentially useless unless the calculus were extended with mutable state. This may be an interesting extension in itself, but in line with FJ we claim that a calculus without mutable state is capable of producing a useful analysis of the soundness of an object-oriented language, and that is the approach we have taken here. The main reason for disallowing role inheritance is that it simplifies the calculus, and thus the soundness proof, yet still allows us to model the core semantics of lifting and lowering.

2.1 Example

Let us demonstrate with an example what a program looks like in our calculus, see figure 1. The class `Point` is a regular FJ class that describes a point in the

```
class Point extends Object {
  int x;
  int y;
  Point(int x, int y) { this.x = x; this.y = y; }
}

class Location playedBy Point {
  string getCountry() {
    int x = lower(this).x;
    int y = lower(this).y;
    string country = "DK"; // placeholder for (possibly advanced)
                           // computation converting a point in
                           // the plane to the name of a country
    return country;
  }
}

lift(new Point(3,4), Location).getCountry();
```

Fig. 1. Example

plane. `Location` is a role class that is `playedBy Point`, and provides a view of points in the plane as physical locations on a map of the world. A new instance of `Point` is lifted to a `Location`, which makes it possible to call the method getCountry on that object. getCountry shows how members of the base class are accessed: using the `lower` keyword to retrieve the base class object.

As an example of the difference between our lifting operation and the smart lifting operation of OT/J consider the following situation, where we assume that role inheritance is part of our calculus and that `playedBy` is required to be covariant (as in OT/J): we might have a class `3DPoint` that extends `Point`, and two classes `SpaceLocation` and `SeaLocation` that both extend `Location` and are `playedBy 3DPoint`. In OT/J this could lead to a run-time error due to ambiguity [10], because the smart lifting algorithm would not know whether to lift to `SpaceLocation` or `SeaLocation`, given an instance of `3DPoint` and target role `Location`. In our calculus we avoid this problem because lifting always returns an instance of the requested role.

As mentioned in section 1, smart lifting introduces the possibility of making old code fail without modifying it. This is due to the ambiguity mentioned above; a piece of code that looks safe when viewed in isolation might years later become the source of lifting errors because new code can extend old roles, thereby creating an inheritance hierarchy with similar structure as the previous example. A compile-time warning can be given for the new code, but the old code is not necessarily available so the warning cannot point out which part of the program may fail. This requires a whole program analysis at compile time, which in turn requires that all sources are available. A lifting operation in the old code is now possibly passed a base class object from the new code that makes the lifting operation fail at run-time.

As we have removed the ambiguity of lifting this problem does not exist in our calculus. In general it is always safe to return a role R that is a subtype of the statically required role R_1, as long as R is a super type of the role R_{n-1} after which the hierarchy fans out. This is illustrated in figure 2. For $R_{n,1}$ and $R_{n,2}$, an "ambiguous lifting" error must be raised at run-time unless a choice can be made based on a separate user-defined priority system or something similar.

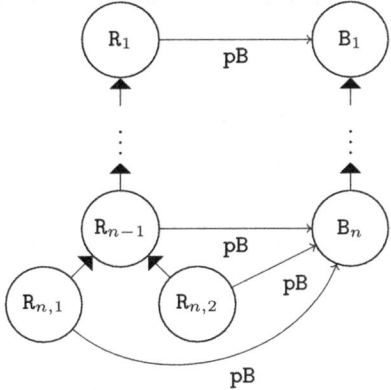

Fig. 2. When a lifting operation lifting to R_1 is given a base class object of type B_n it is always safe to return a role object between R_1 and R_{n-1} (inclusive)

2.2 Objects

This calculus uses objects with more structure than what is common among calculi in the FJ family. As mentioned, what we think of as an object is represented by a cloud of objects. In this section we explain in more detail what requirements this cloud must satisfy, and why.

These requirements are in fact influenced by the possible semantics of the lifting operation. The lifting operation is capable of delivering a role whose `playedBy` class is a strict supertype of the class of the base object of the cloud. This means that we may obtain a `Location` role from a `3DPoint` object, even though `Location` specifies that it is `playedBy` a `Point`. The obvious alternative would be to insist that the cloud contains only roles that directly specify the class of the base object as its `playedBy` class. However, it is necessary in order to preserve type soundness to allow for a flexible invariant. The two situations are illustrated in Fig. 3.

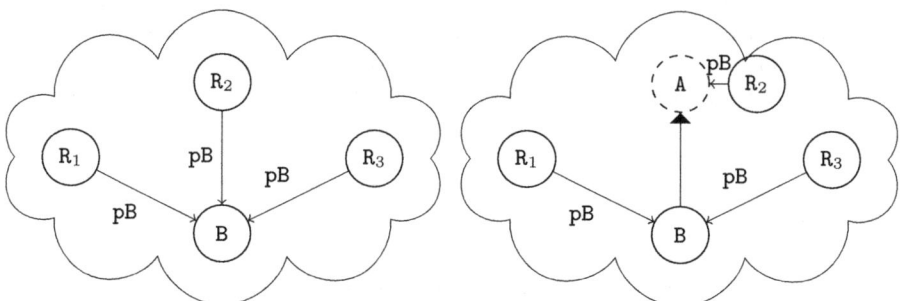

Fig. 3. Left: an object cloud containing only roles directly `playedBy` the base class. Right: an object cloud containing roles `playedBy` super types (`A`) of the base class (`B`).

Assume we have a class `3DPoint` that extends `Point` from the previous example. The wrapper method for the lifting operation, shown in figure 4, illustrates the problem. `makeLocation` might be called with a `p` that is an instance of

```
Location makeLocation(Point p) {
  return lift(p, Location);
}
```

Fig. 4. Example

`3DPoint` at run-time. Thus if lifting is unable to lift to roles `playedBy` super types this might get stuck at run-time. This is obviously also a problem for any full-fledged language which contains our calculus as a sub language, because programs may choose to omit the use of inheritance for roles. Moreover, the use of inheritance will not make the problem go away. Given that FJ is a sub language of Java, our calculus is essentially a sub language of any language that supports translation polymorphism; hence this property applies to them all.

In the `Point` and `Location` example we included a standard `new` expression for the creation of an object. The formal calculus does not include such an expression; instead it directly creates an object cloud containing a base object and a list of roles. It would be easy to define a surface language that includes traditional new expressions and a preprocessing stage that transforms them to cloud creation expressions with an empty role list. In this situation programs would never create clouds with pre-existing roles, they would always come into existence on demand during a lifting operation. However, we note that the actual calculus is safe even without the restriction that all roles are created on demand. We discuss this issue in more detail in section 4.

Before we give the formal definition of the calculus, figure 5 provides the intuitive relation between the base class type hierarchy and the evaluation and typing rules for lifting and lowering.

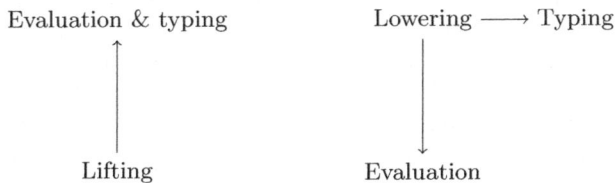

Fig. 5. The relation between the base class hierarchy and lifting/lowering expressions. Lifting both types and evaluates to roles of a super type. Lowering types to the roles' base but evaluates to a subtype of it.

3   Formal Definition of Lifted Java

In this section we present the formal definition of the calculus. Staying in the same style as FJ, we use a sequence notation similar to the one used in the original article on FJ [12], i.e. writing e.g. $\overline{C}$ means $C_1 \ldots C_n$, for some $n \geq 0$. This also applies to binary arguments, such that $\overline{C\,f}$ means $C_1\,f_1 \ldots C_n\,f_n$. We use $\bullet$ to denote the empty list. In the following, the meta variables C and D range over class names; R ranges over role names; G can be both class and role names; f ranges over field names; m ranges over method names; x ranges over variable names; t ranges over terms; v ranges over values; CL ranges over class declarations; RL ranges over role declarations; and M ranges over method declarations.

Section 3.1 describes the syntax, section 3.2 the semantics, and section 3.3 gives the soundness proof of the calculus.

3.1   Syntax

As Lifted Java is an extension of FJ the basic syntax is the same, with the following exceptions: a new class definition for roles has been added, called RL; a new object creation term replaces the standard object creation term to accommodate our objects with more structure; the value is replaced by the new object creation term; and a term for each of the operations lifting and lowering has been added. The complete syntax can be seen in figure 6.

Terms and values

$$t ::= x \mid [\text{new } C(\overline{t}),\ \overline{R},\ C] \mid t.f \mid t.m(\overline{t}) \mid \text{lift}(t,R) \mid \text{lower}(t) \qquad \textit{terms}$$
$$v ::= [\text{new } C(\overline{v}),\ \overline{R},\ G] \qquad \textit{values}$$

Member and top-level declarations

$$CL ::= \text{class } C \text{ extends } D\{\overline{C\ f};\ \overline{M}\} \qquad \textit{classes}$$
$$RL ::= \text{class } R \text{ playedBy } C\ \{\overline{M}\} \qquad \textit{roles}$$
$$M ::= G\ m(\overline{G\ x})\ \{\ \text{return } t;\ \} \qquad \textit{methods}$$

Fig. 6. Syntax

In the new class definition RL the extends relation of regular classes is replaced by the playedBy relation. Using this class definition results in defining a role class that has the class given by the right-hand side of the playedBy relation as its base class. Note that RL does not specify fields, a consequence of the fact that roles cannot have state.

The new object creation term is used to instantiate classes. It is a record that, when fully evaluated, describes an object. From left to right it consists of a base class instance, a list of role instances, and a label set to the class name of the currently active object. As long as roles do not have state, the list of role instances in the tuple can in fact be simplified, and so we replace it by a list of roles. As mentioned in section 2 this tuple can be viewed as a cloud containing a base class and any number of roles floating around it. The list of role names is only used in the evaluation rules for lifting; rules that may also modify the list of role names if the object is lifted into a role not in the list.

The term lift(t, F) lifts the term t to the role F. Similarly the term lower(t) lowers the term t to the base class instance in the object cloud.

For the programmer this syntax amounts to more work compared to that of OT/J. We have chosen this approach in order to prioritise a simple calculus with simple proofs rather than simple programs, as is common when working with calculi. In particular we use explicit lifting and lowering operations; this differs from OT/J where lifting and lowering is typically performed implicitly, with the compiler inserting the appropriate method calls. Thus we assume that the preprocessing step that inserts calls to the lifting and lowering operations has been run. Furthermore, accessing members of a roles' base class does not happen through a base link, but rather by lowering the object first and accessing the field on the resulting object; and lifting an already lifted object to a new role can only be done by lowering the object first.

3.2 Semantics

Apart from the evaluation and typing rules for roles, lifting, and lowering, the small-step semantics of Lifted Java consist of two new auxiliary functions defining the behaviour of the playedBy relation. In the following we will first describe these auxiliary functions, then the evaluation rules, and finally the typing rules. The functions *fields*, *mbody*, *mtype*, and *override*, are the auxiliary functions from FJ; they are standard, so we will omit the formal definition. For the same reason we will omit the congruence rules for method invocation and field access.

Before we proceed we give the definition of the *flexible invariant* on the types of objects in a cloud. As presented in section 2.2 the cloud has the following structure: the base object has a specific type C, and the role objects have role types $R_1 \ldots R_k$ that are playedBy classes $C_1 \ldots C_k$, respectively. The intuitively simplest invariant would then be to require that $C_i = C$ for all i or that C_i is the most specific supertype of C that plays a role which is R_i, but we employ the more flexible invariant where it is just required that C_i is a supertype of C.

Auxiliary functions. The auxiliary functions are defined in figure 7. The rule PLAYEDBY is used to determine whether a role is playedBy a given base class, i.e. *playedBy*(R, C) holds if and only if the playedBy relation in the role definition of R mentions the class name C. Alone this rule is insufficient for a sound approach to translation polymorphism, as discussed in section 2. Thus, we define the rule PLAYEDBYWIDE which is the formal definition of the flexible invariant on the playedBy relation. It is similar to the PLAYEDBY rule except that it takes subtyping into account, i.e. *playedByWide*(R, C) holds if and only if the playedBy relation of R mentions a super type of C.

PLAYEDBY
$$\frac{CT(R) = \text{class R playedBy C } \{\overline{M}\}}{playedBy(R, C)}$$

PLAYEDBYWIDE
$$\frac{C <: B \qquad CT(R) = \text{class R playedBy B } \{\overline{M}\}}{playedByWide(R, C)}$$

Fig. 7. The auxiliary functions for Lifted Java

Evaluation. Figure 8 shows the evaluation rules. The evaluation rules extend those of FJ to include evaluation of the terms lift(t, R) and lower(t). Congruence rules are added for these two terms as well, and the congruence rule for the object creation term is updated.

Lifting of the value v to the role R is split into two rules: one for when R does not occur in the cloud of v (E-LIFT-NEW), and one for when it does (E-LIFT-OLD). In both cases it is required that R is in fact a role and that R is playedBy the currently active class object or a super type of it. Both facts are checked by *playedByWide*. In the first case the role is added to the cloud of v, and the name of the currently active instance is updated to R. In the second case only the name of the currently active instance is updated.

Lowering the value v is taken care of by a single rule, E-LOWER, that only requires that the name of the currently active object of v is a role. It would be straightforward to make it possible to lower a regular class to itself and still maintain soundness, as long as the typing rule for lowering also allows typing of a lower expression where the active object is the base object. However, to maintain a simple calculus we have decided that lowering should not be smarter than lifting.

The congruence rules, EC-LIFT and EC-LOWER, provide the necessary evaluation of the individual arguments to the lifting and lowering terms.

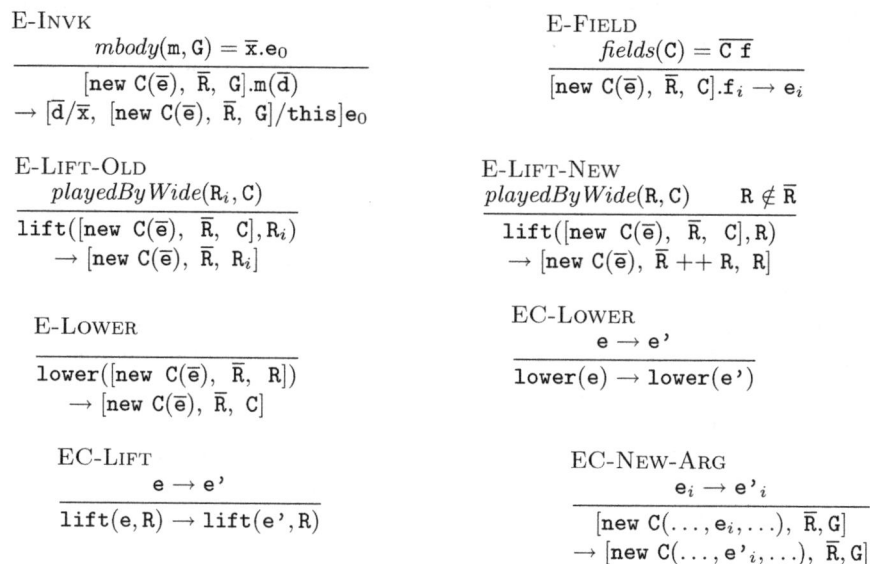

E-INVK

$$mbody(\texttt{m}, \texttt{G}) = \overline{\texttt{x}}.\texttt{e}_0$$

$$[\texttt{new C}(\overline{\texttt{e}}),\ \overline{\texttt{R}},\ \texttt{G}].\texttt{m}(\overline{\texttt{d}})$$
$$\rightarrow [\overline{\texttt{d}}/\overline{\texttt{x}},\ [\texttt{new C}(\overline{\texttt{e}}),\ \overline{\texttt{R}},\ \texttt{G}]/\texttt{this}]\texttt{e}_0$$

E-FIELD

$$fields(\texttt{C}) = \overline{\texttt{C f}}$$

$$[\texttt{new C}(\overline{\texttt{e}}),\ \overline{\texttt{R}},\ \texttt{C}].\texttt{f}_i \rightarrow \texttt{e}_i$$

E-LIFT-OLD

$$playedByWide(\texttt{R}_i, \texttt{C})$$

$$\texttt{lift}([\texttt{new C}(\overline{\texttt{e}}),\ \overline{\texttt{R}},\ \texttt{C}], \texttt{R}_i)$$
$$\rightarrow [\texttt{new C}(\overline{\texttt{e}}),\ \overline{\texttt{R}},\ \texttt{R}_i]$$

E-LIFT-NEW

$$playedByWide(\texttt{R}, \texttt{C}) \qquad \texttt{R} \notin \overline{\texttt{R}}$$

$$\texttt{lift}([\texttt{new C}(\overline{\texttt{e}}),\ \overline{\texttt{R}},\ \texttt{C}], \texttt{R})$$
$$\rightarrow [\texttt{new C}(\overline{\texttt{e}}),\ \overline{\texttt{R}} \texttt{++} \texttt{R},\ \texttt{R}]$$

E-LOWER

$$\texttt{lower}([\texttt{new C}(\overline{\texttt{e}}),\ \overline{\texttt{R}},\ \texttt{R}])$$
$$\rightarrow [\texttt{new C}(\overline{\texttt{e}}),\ \overline{\texttt{R}},\ \texttt{C}]$$

EC-LOWER

$$\texttt{e} \rightarrow \texttt{e'}$$

$$\texttt{lower}(\texttt{e}) \rightarrow \texttt{lower}(\texttt{e'})$$

EC-LIFT

$$\texttt{e} \rightarrow \texttt{e'}$$

$$\texttt{lift}(\texttt{e}, \texttt{R}) \rightarrow \texttt{lift}(\texttt{e'}, \texttt{R})$$

EC-NEW-ARG

$$\texttt{e}_i \rightarrow \texttt{e'}_i$$

$$[\texttt{new C}(\ldots, \texttt{e}_i, \ldots),\ \overline{\texttt{R}}, \texttt{G}]$$
$$\rightarrow [\texttt{new C}(\ldots, \texttt{e'}_i, \ldots),\ \overline{\texttt{R}}, \texttt{G}]$$

Fig. 8. The evaluation rules for Lifted Java

Typing. The typing rules can be seen in figure 9. The FJ typing rules are extended to include well-formedness for roles, typing of the $\texttt{lift}(\texttt{t}, \texttt{R})$ term, and typing of the $\texttt{lower}(\texttt{t})$ term. Furthermore, the typing rule of the new object creation term is updated.

The typing rule for object creation terms, T-NEW, states that the type of an object is always the class corresponding to the active instance. This can be either the base class $\texttt{C}$ or one of the role classes $\texttt{R}_i$ in the cloud. In order for the rule to apply it is required that the arguments to the constructor of the base class have the correct types, and that the currently active instance is either a role $\texttt{playedBy}$ a super type of $\texttt{C}$ or that it is $\texttt{C}$.

The rule T-LIFT is the typing rule for the $\texttt{lift}(\texttt{t}, \texttt{R})$ term. It states that a $\texttt{lift}$ expression has the type of the role lifted to. It is required that the type of the first argument plays the role $\texttt{R}$, or is a subtype of a class that does.

The T-LOWER rule describes the requirements for typing the $\texttt{lower}(\texttt{t})$ term. It states that the $\texttt{lower}$ expression has the type of the base class of the currently active instance, and thus requires that the type of the argument is a role. Like with the evaluation rule for the $\texttt{lower}(\texttt{t})$ term it would be straightforward to allow the term to be typed when the argument has the type of a regular class and still maintain soundness, as long as the evaluation rule is also updated to allow evaluation of a $\texttt{lower}$ expression with a value where the active object is the base object.

The rule for role typing (T-ROLE) is similar to the rule for regular class typing (T-CLASS), except for the fact that there are no fields and no constructor to check. T-METH is the rule for method typing.

T-VAR
$$\overline{\Gamma \vdash \mathtt{x} : \Gamma(\mathtt{x})}$$

T-FIELD
$$\frac{\Gamma \vdash \mathtt{e} : \mathtt{C} \qquad \mathit{fields}(\mathtt{C}) = \overline{\mathtt{C}\ \mathtt{f}}}{\Gamma \vdash \mathtt{e.f}_i : \mathtt{C}_i}$$

T-INVK
$$\frac{\Gamma \vdash \mathtt{e} : \mathtt{C} \qquad \mathit{mtype}(\mathtt{m}, \mathtt{C}) = \overline{\mathtt{D}} \to \mathtt{D} \qquad \Gamma \vdash \overline{\mathtt{e}} : \overline{\mathtt{C}} \qquad \overline{\mathtt{C}} <: \overline{\mathtt{D}}}{\Gamma \vdash \mathtt{e.m}(\overline{\mathtt{e}}) : \mathtt{D}}$$

T-NEW
$$\frac{\mathit{fields}(\mathtt{C}) = \overline{\mathtt{C}\ \mathtt{f}} \qquad \Gamma \vdash \overline{\mathtt{e}} : \overline{\mathtt{D}} \qquad \overline{\mathtt{D}} <: \overline{\mathtt{C}} \qquad \mathit{playedByWide}(\mathtt{G}, \mathtt{C}) \vee \mathtt{G} = \mathtt{C}}{\Gamma \vdash [\mathtt{new}\ \mathtt{C}(\overline{\mathtt{e}}),\ \overline{\mathtt{R}},\ \mathtt{G}] : \mathtt{G}}$$

T-LIFT
$$\frac{\Gamma \vdash \mathtt{e} : \mathtt{C} \qquad \mathit{playedByWide}(\mathtt{R}, \mathtt{C})}{\Gamma \vdash \mathtt{lift}(\mathtt{e}, \mathtt{R}) : \mathtt{R}}$$

T-LOWER
$$\frac{\Gamma \vdash \mathtt{e} : \mathtt{R} \qquad \mathit{playedBy}(\mathtt{R}, \mathtt{C})}{\Gamma \vdash \mathtt{lower}(\mathtt{e}) : \mathtt{C}}$$

T-METH
$$\frac{\mathtt{this} : \mathtt{C} \vdash \mathtt{t}_0 : \mathtt{E}_0 \qquad \mathtt{E}_0 <: \mathtt{C}_0 \qquad CT(\mathtt{C}) = \mathtt{class}\ \mathtt{C}\ \mathtt{extends}\ \mathtt{D}\{\overline{\mathtt{C}\ \mathtt{f}};\ \overline{\mathtt{M}}\} \qquad \mathit{override}(\mathtt{m}, \mathtt{D}, \overline{\mathtt{C}} \to \mathtt{C}_0)}{\mathtt{C}_0\ \mathtt{m}(\overline{\mathtt{C}\ \mathtt{x}})\ \{\ \mathtt{return}\ \mathtt{t}_0;\ \}\ OK\ in\ \mathtt{C}}$$

T-CLASS
$$\frac{\overline{\mathtt{M}}\ OK\ in\ \mathtt{C}}{\mathtt{class}\ \mathtt{C}\ \mathtt{extends}\ \mathtt{D}\{\overline{\mathtt{C}\ \mathtt{f}};\ \overline{\mathtt{M}}\}\ OK}$$

T-ROLE
$$\frac{\overline{\mathtt{M}}\ OK\ in\ \mathtt{R}}{\mathtt{class}\ \mathtt{R}\ \mathtt{playedBy}\ \mathtt{C}\ \{\overline{\mathtt{M}}\}\ OK}$$

Fig. 9. The typing rules for Lifted Java

3.3 Safety Properties

Under the assumption that all defined classes and roles are well-formed, the following safety properties hold for the calculus presented in the previous section:

Theorem 1 (Preservation). *If* $\bullet \vdash \mathtt{e} : \mathtt{T}$ *and* $\mathtt{e} \to \mathtt{e}'$ *then there exists some* $\mathtt{T}'$ *such that* $\bullet \vdash \mathtt{e}' : \mathtt{T}'$ *and* $\mathtt{T}' <: \mathtt{T}$.

Theorem 2 (Progress). *If* $\bullet \vdash \mathtt{e} : \mathtt{T}$ *then* $\mathtt{e}$ *is either a value or* $\mathtt{e} \to \mathtt{e}'$ *for some* $\mathtt{e}'$.

Corollary 1 (Type soundness). *If* $\bullet \vdash \mathtt{e} : \mathtt{T}$ *and* $\mathtt{e} \to^* \mathtt{e}'$ *where* $\mathtt{e}'$ *is a normal form, then* $\mathtt{e}'$ *is a value and* $\bullet \vdash \mathtt{e}' : \mathtt{T}'$, *where* $\mathtt{T}' <: \mathtt{T}$.

Corollary 1 follows easily from the preservation and progress theorems, the proof of which is implemented in the Coq proof assistant, following the pattern introduced in [18]. We invite the reader to download the Coq source code for the proof from [6] for the details.

Note that we have been able to simplify the proofs by assuming empty type environments. The resulting preservation property is still sufficient to prove Corollary 1. Hence, the weaker preservation property is sufficient to show standard type soundness, and consequently the extra work required to show preservation with non-empty environments would be superfluous. This technique was used by De Fraine *et al.* both in their implementation of the *A* Calculus [4] and in the implementation of FJ [3] which we use as a basis.

4   Discussion

In this section we will discuss three things: our choices with regard to the semantics of lifting and lowering; the case of unrestricted roles in object creation expressions as mentioned in section 2.2; and the flexible invariant.

Lifting. In OT/J lifting is smart, i.e. it will produce a role with the dynamically most specific type rather than the statically known type. This can lead to ambiguity, the reason for which is that a base object might be lifted to a role that is extended by two otherwise unrelated roles. If the object cloud of the base object does not already contain a role of the requested type, such a role should now be created. In this situation it is ambiguous which of the two unrelated roles is the most specific, and thus which of them the smart lifting algorithm should select. In OT/J this causes an exception at run-time, and it may happen in a piece of code that was compiled without warnings or errors, possibly long before the two unrelated roles were written.

We have chosen a simpler semantics for lifting whereby the statically known role type is used, and our soundness proof shows that this semantics is sound. However, the difference between our semantics and smart lifting is orthogonal to soundness, because the role chosen at run-time is in any case a subtype of the statically supplied role type, and it is always sound to modify the semantics to yield a more specific value for any given expression. It should be noted that OT/J roles support inheritance, and that the `playedBy` relation enforces covariance (more specific base type means same or more specific role type), whereas our lifting semantics removes the need for subtyping among role types. Hence, our soundness proof shows that all the possible language designs where lifting produces a subtype of the statically known role type are sound. There are many sound ways to remove the ambiguity problem in this language design space: the static approach taken in our calculus; approaches based on taking the most specific type that does not cause ambiguities; or using programmer declared precedence are among the possible choices. It is a main contribution of this work to clarify that this ambiguity problem can be solved by choosing any language design within this language design space.

Lifting and lowering is always explicit in our calculus, using the special functions `lift` and `lower`, whereas they are generally added by the compiler in OT/J. This means more work for programmers using our calculus, but since it would be easy to add calls to these functions to the code in a preprocessing step where needed, there is no need to have implicit lifting and lowering as part of the calculus. In fact the OT/J compiler takes this approach, automatically inserting calls to lifting and lowering methods.

Flexible invariant. An interesting property of our calculus is that it employs a flexible invariant for the types of objects in a cloud, and the soundness proof shows that this is a safe thing to do. We introduced a *widePlayedBy* relation in the calculus in order to express this invariant. The important fact to note is that almost any choice of semantics for the lifting operation from the above-mentioned language design space would require a more or less flexible invariant in the sense defined here.

Objects. From the calculus syntax in section 3.1, it is clear that there is no restriction on the role names that can be in the object cloud of an object creation expression. Programmers could therefore write programs that contain object creation expressions including roles that do not have a *widePlayedBy* relation to the class of the base object, let us call them *junk roles*. Intuitively this creates the problem that the cloud contains roles that are not `playedBy` the given base object, not even via a superclass! Figure 10 illustrates this situation. It may seem dangerous to allow programs to run when some objects contain junk roles, but this is in fact benign. The undeniable argument is that the Coq soundness proof works for a formalisation that allows junk roles to exist; the associated intuition is that these junk roles are unreachable because roles can only come into play when being selected by a lifting operation — this will never happen for a junk role.

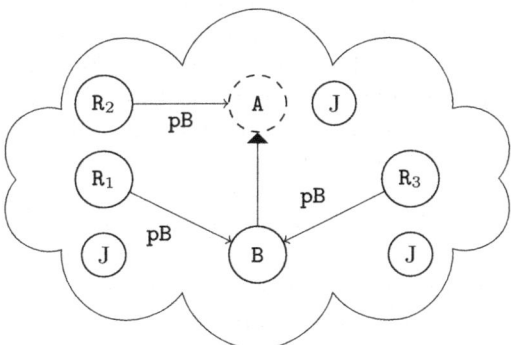

Fig. 10. The cloud as implemented in the model. J marks junk role names.

5   Related and Future Work

The AspectJ language [13] was the first to introduce *Aspect-Oriented Programming* [14] in a general purpose programming language. However, aspects are at the other end of OT/Js features compared to our focus on translation polymorphism, and thus we will not treat them further.

CaesarJ [1] solves the same scenario as OT/J, non-invasive customisation through addition instead of modification. The following are the similarities that are relevant with respect to our work. Like in OT/J, virtual classes and family polymorphism are added to the language. The equivalents to roles and base classes are called *wrappers* and *wrappees*. To translate an object of a wrappee type to an object of a type wrapping it (lifting), a *wrapper constructor* is called with the wrappee object as an argument. The translation from wrapper to wrappee (lowering) is done using an explicit *wrappee* link. We will not go into detail with CaesarJ, but simply note that the model and observations in this paper apply to that language as well.

Adding role inheritance to our calculus would be an interesting direction to explore in the future. For the calculus presented in this paper simplicity is a major feature, because it isolates the core of translation polymorphism. A more elaborate model would be interesting to explore in order to address the problems with ambiguity in smart lifting directly, for instance demonstrating that a certain class of priority mechanisms could enable lifting to produce a most specific role in some sense, and remain free of run-time errors.

6   Conclusion

Translation polymorphism, also known as lifting and lowering, is a language mechanism which enables multiple objects, organised into pairs of base and role objects, to act almost as if they were single objects supporting multiple unrelated interfaces. This paper demonstrates for the first time that the core semantics of translation polymorphism is provably type sound, and that the thorny issues of ambiguity associated with the mechanism known as smart lifting may be eliminated through a very simple choice of semantics for lifting; namely the semantics whereby a base object is lifted to a role via a statically selected base object type. This extends to a smart lifting semantics without ambiguity, because it may be based on the most specific dynamic type of the base object that does not give rise to ambiguity, and in general it outlines a language design space containing many different safe choices. The results in this paper were achieved by means of a very simple formal calculus that models lifting and lowering independently of the advanced features, such as virtual classes and family polymorphism, that are typically present in languages supporting translation polymorphism. The completeness and correctness of the soundness proof of this calculus has been verified mechanically by means of the Coq proof assistant. Consequently, translation polymorphism can now be considered safe.

References

1. Aracic, I., Gasiunas, V., Awasthi, P., Ostermann, K.: An overview of CaesarJ. In: Rashid, A., Aksit, M. (eds.) Transactions on Aspect-Oriented Software Development I. LNCS, vol. 3880, pp. 135–173. Springer, Heidelberg (2006)
2. Bertot, Y., Castéran, P.: Interactive Theorem Proving and Program Development — Coq'Art: The Calculus of Inductive Constructions, Texts in Theoretical Computer Science, vol. XXV. Springer, Heidelberg (2004)
3. De Fraine, B.: Language Facilities for the Deployment of Reusable Aspects. Ph.D. thesis, Vrije Universiteit Brussel (2009),
   http://soft.vub.ac.be/soft/_media/members/brunodefraine/phd.pdf
4. De Fraine, B., Ernst, E., Südholt, M.: Essential AOP: The A calculus. In: D'Hondt, T. (ed.) ECOOP 2010. LNCS, vol. 6183, pp. 101–125. Springer, Heidelberg (2010)

5. Ernst, E.: Family polymorphism. In: Knudsen, J.L. (ed.) ECOOP 2001. LNCS, vol. 2072, pp. 303–326. Springer, Heidelberg (2001)

6. Ernst, E., Ingesman, M.D.: Coq source for Lifted Java (2011), available at http://users-cs.au.dk/mdi/liftedJavaCoq.tar.gz

7. Ernst, E., Ostermann, K., Cook, W.R.: A virtual class calculus. In: Conference record of the 33rd ACM SIGPLAN-SIGACT symposium on Principles of programming languages, POPL 2006, pp. 270–282. ACM, New York (2006)

8. Gosling, J., Joy, B., Steele, G., Bracha, G.: Java(TM) Language Specification, 3rd edn. Addison-Wesley, Reading (2005)

9. Herrmann, S.: A precise model for contextual roles: The programming language Object Teams/Java. Appl. Ontol. 2, 181–207 (2007)

10. Herrmann, S., Hundt, C., Mehner, K.: Translation polymorphism in Object Teams. Tech. rep., Technical University Berlin (2004)

11. Herrmann, S., Hundt, C., Mosconi, M.: OT/J Language Definition, version 1.3 edn. (2010)

12. Igarashi, A., Pierce, B.C., Wadler, P.: Featherweight Java: a minimal core calculus for Java and GJ. ACM Trans. Program. Lang. Syst. 23, 396–450 (2001)

13. Kiczales, G., Hilsdale, E., Hugunin, J., Kersten, M., Palm, J., Griswold, W.G.: An overview of aspectJ. In: Knudsen, J.L. (ed.) ECOOP 2001. LNCS, vol. 2072, pp. 327–353. Springer, Heidelberg (2001)

14. Kiczales, G., Lamping, J., Mendhekar, A., Maeda, C., Lopes, C.V., Loingtier, J.-M., Irwin, J.: Aspect-oriented programming. In: Aksit, M., Matsuoka, S.(eds.) ECOOP 1997. LNCS, vol. 1241, pp. 220–242. Springer, Heidelberg (1997)

15. Mezini, M., Lieberherr, K.: Adaptive plug-and-play components for evolutionary software development. In: Proceedings of the 13th ACM SIGPLAN Conference on Object-oriented Programming, Systems, Languages, and Applications, OOPSLA 1998, pp. 97–116. ACM, New York (1998)

16. Mezini, M., Seiter, L., Lieberherr, K.: Component integration with pluggable composite adapters. In: Software Architectures and Component Technology: The State of the Art in Research and Practice, Kluwer Academic Publishers, Dordrecht (2000)

17. Ostermann, K.: Dynamically composable collaborations with delegation layers. In: Magnusson, B. (ed.) ECOOP 2002. LNCS, vol. 2374, pp. 89–110. Springer, Heidelberg (2002)

18. Wright, A.K., Felleisen, M.: A syntactic approach to type soundness. Inf. Comput. 115, 38–94 (1994)

Location Types for Safe Distributed Object-Oriented Programming*

Yannick Welsch and Jan Schäfer

University of Kaiserslautern, Germany
{welsch,jschaefer}@cs.uni-kl.de

Abstract. In distributed object-oriented systems, objects belong to different *locations*. For example, in Java RMI, objects can be distributed over different JVM instances. Accessing a reference in RMI has crucial different semantics depending on whether the referred object is local or remote. Nevertheless, such references are not statically distinguished by the type system.

This paper presents *location types*, which statically distinguish *far* from *near* references. We present a formal type system for a minimal core language. In addition, we present a type inference system that gives optimal solutions. We implemented location types as a pluggable type system for the ABS language, an object-oriented language with a concurrency model based on *concurrent object groups*. An important contribution of this paper is the combination of the type system with the flexible inference system and a novel integration into an Eclipse-based IDE by presenting the inference results as overlays. This drastically reduces the annotation overhead while providing full static type information to the user. The IDE integration is a general approach of its own and can be applied to many other type system extensions.

1 Introduction

In distributed object-oriented systems, objects belong to different *locations*. A location in this paper is regarded to be an abstract concept, but in practice it may, for example, refer to a physical computation node, some process (like a JVM instance in RMI [19]), or can even be a concept of a programming language. For example, in object-languages with concurrency models based on communicating groups of objects such as E [18], AmbientTalk/2 [24], JCoBox [22], or ABS [15], the location of an object can be considered as the group it belongs to. In these scenarios it often makes a difference whether a reference points to an object at the current location, i.e., the location of the current executing object (in the following called a *near* reference), or to an object at a different location (a *far* reference). For example, in the E programming language [18], a *far* reference can only be used for *eventual sends*, but not for *immediate* method calls. In Java RMI accessing a remote reference may throw a RemoteException, where

---

* This research is funded by the EU project FP7-231620 HATS: Highly Adaptable and Trustworthy Software using Formal Models.

accessing a normal reference cannot throw such an exception. It is thus desirable to be able to statically distinguish these two kinds of references. This is useful for documentation purposes, to reason about the code, and to statically prevent runtime errors.

We present *location types* which statically distinguish far from near references. Location types can be considered as a lightweight form of ownership types [4, 21] with the following two characteristics. The first is that location types only describe a *flat set* of locations instead of a *hierarchy* of ownership contexts. The second is that ownership types typically define the ownership context of an object in a precise way. Location types abstract from these precise locations by only stating whether an object belongs to the current location or some other location. These two simplifications make location types very lightweight and easy to use, while still being expressive enough to guarantee their desired properties. Location types are *not* used to enforce encapsulation, which is the main goal of many ownership type systems.

As with any type system extension, writing down the extended types can become tiresome for programmers. Furthermore, these annotations may clutter up the code and reduce readability, especially when several of such pluggable type systems [2, 9] are used together. This reduces the acceptance of pluggable type systems in practice. The first issue can be solved by automatically inferring the type annotations and inserting them into the code. But this results again in cluttered code with potentially many annotations. Our solution is to leverage the power of an IDE and present the inferred types to the programmer by using unobtrusive *overlays*. They give the programmer full static type information without cluttering the code with annotations nor reducing readability. The overlays can be turned on and off according to the programmer's need. Type annotations are only needed to make the type checking and inference modular, where the degree of modularity just depends on the interfaces where type annotations appear. This way of integrating type inference into the IDE drastically simplifies the usage of the proposed type system and is applicable to similar type system extensions.

Contributions. The three main contributions of this paper are the following. (1) We give the formalization of a type system for location types in a core object-oriented language. (2) We describe a type inference system that gives optimal solutions and helpful error messages. (3) We present an implementation of the type and inference system for the ABS language and show how to integrate such a system into an IDE by using a novel way of visualizing inferred type information.

Outline. The remainder of this paper is structured as follows. In Sect. 2 we give an informal introduction to location types and illustrate their usage by an example. Section 3 presents the formalization of location types for a core object-oriented language and the inference system. In Sect. 4 we explain how we implemented and integrated location types into an IDE, and provide a short evaluation. Section 5 discusses location types in the context of related work. Section 6 concludes.

2   Location Types at Work

Location types statically distinguish *far* from *near* references. To do so, standard types are extended with additional type annotations, namely *location types*. There are three different location types: Near, Far, and Somewhere. Location types are always interpreted *relatively* to the current object. A variable typed as Near means that it may only refer to objects that belong to the *same* location as the current object. Accordingly, a Far typed variable may only refer to objects that belong to a *different* location than the current object. Somewhere is the super-type of Far and Near and means that the referred object may either be Near or Far. Important to note is that only Near precisely describes a certain location. A Far annotation only states that the location of the referred object is *not* Near. This means that a Far typed variable may over time refer to different locations which are not further defined, except that they are not the location of the current object. What a location actually means is irrelevant to the type system. So whether the location of an object refers to a JVM instance or has some other form of object grouping does not matter. It is only important that an object belongs to a unique location for its entire lifetime.

We illustrate the location type system by applying it to a small implementation of a chat application. For the description we use the abstract behavioral specification language (ABS) [15], which we explain hand-in-hand with the example.

ABS is an object-oriented language with a Java-like syntax. It has a concurrency model that is based on so-called concurrent object groups (COGs). COGs can be regarded as the unit of concurrency and distribution in ABS. Every object in ABS belongs to exactly one unique COG for its entire lifetime. This is similar to the Java RMI setting where objects belong to certain JVM instances, which may run distributed on different machines. At creation time of an object it is specified whether the object is created in the current COG (using the standard **new** expression) or is created in a fresh COG (using the **new cog** expression). Communication in ABS between different COGs happen via *asynchronous method calls* which are indicated by an exclamation mark (!). A reference in ABS is *far* when it targets an object of a different COG, otherwise it is a *near* reference. Similar to the E programming language [18], ABS has the restriction that synchronous method calls (indicated by the standard dot notation) are only allowed on near references. Using a far reference for a synchronous method call results in a runtime exception. Our location type system can be used to statically guarantee the absence of these runtime exceptions.

The chat application is a simple IRC-like application, which consists of a single server and multiple clients. For simplicity, there is only a single chat room, so all clients actually broadcast their messages to all other clients. The basic interfaces of the chat application in the ABS language are given in Fig. 1. Note that only

```
interface Server {
   [Near] Session connect(
      [Far] Client c, String name); }
interface Session {
   Unit receive(ClientMsg m);
   Unit close(); }
interface Client {
   Unit connectTo([Far] Server s);
   Unit receive(ServerMsg m); }
```

Fig. 1. The annotated interfaces
of the chat application

Fig. 2. Runtime structure of the chat application

```
1   class ClientImpl(String name) implements Client {
2      [Far] Session session; ...
3      Unit connectTo([Far] Server server) {
4         Fut<[Far] Session> f = server!connect(this, name);
5         session = f.get; } }
```

Fig. 3. Fully annotated implementation of the ClientImpl class

Server, Client, and Session are actually reference types, the types Unit, ClientMsg, and ServerMsg are *data types* and represent immutable data and not objects.

Figure 2 shows a possible runtime structure of the chat application. As the clients and the server run independently of each other, they live in their own COGs. This means that all references between clients and the server are far references. The Session objects that handle the different connections with the clients live in the same COG as the Server object. This means that references between Session and Server are near references. In a typical scenario, the client calls the connect method of the server and passes a reference to itself and a user name as arguments. The server then returns a reference to a Session object, which is used by the client to send messages to the server. The interfaces of Fig. 1 are annotated accordingly, e.g., the connect method of the server returns a reference to a Session object that is Near to the server.

Figure 3 shows the ClientImpl class, an implementation of the Client interface. It has a field session which stores a reference to the Session object which is obtained by the client when it connects to the server. Lines 3-5 show the connectTo method. As specified in the interface, the Server parameter has type Far. In Line 4, the client asynchronously (using the ! operator) calls the connect method of the server. The declared result type of the connect method is [Near] Session (see Fig. 1). The crucial fact is that the type system now has to apply a *viewpoint adaptation* [7]. As the target of the call (server) has location type Far, the return type of connect (which is Near) is adapted to Far. Furthermore, as the call is an asynchronous one, the value is not directly returned, but a future instead (i.e. a placeholder for the value). In Line 5, the client waits for the future to be resolved.

```
1   class ServerImpl implements Server {       10      Unit publish(ServerMsg m) {
2       List<[Near] Session> sessions = Nil;    11          List<[Near] Session> sess =
3       [Near] Session connect(                 12              sessions;
4           [Far] Client c, String name) {      13          while (~isEmpty(sess)) {
5           [Near] Session s =                  14              [Near] Session s = head(sess);
6               new SessionImpl(this, c, name); 15              sess = tail(sess);
7           sessions = Cons(s,sessions);        16              s.send(m);
8           this.publish(Connected(name));      17      } } ...
9           return s; }                         18  }
```

Fig. 4. Fully annotated implementation of the ServerImpl class

Figure 4 shows the ServerImpl class, an implementation of the Server interface. It has an internal field sessions to hold the sessions of the connected clients. List is a polymorphic data type in ABS whose type parameter is instantiated with [Near] Session, which means that it holds a list of near references to Session objects. When a client connects to the server using the connect method, the server creates a new SessionImpl object in its current COG (using the standard **new** expression), which means that it is statically clear that this object is Near. It then stores the reference in its internal list, publishes that a new client has connected, and returns a reference to the session object. In the publish method at Line 16, the send method is synchronously called. As ABS requires that synchronous calls are only done on near objects, the type system guarantees that s always refers to a near object.

3   Formalization

This section presents the formalization of the location type system in a core calculus called LocJ. We first present the abstract syntax of the language and its dynamic semantics. In Sect. 3.1 we introduce the basic type system for location types as-well-as its soundness properties. In Sect. 3.2 we improve the precision of the basic type system by introducing named Far types. In Sect. 3.3 we present the location type inference system.

Notations. We use the overbar notation $\overline{x}$ to denote a list. The empty list is denoted by • and the concatenation of list $\overline{x}$ and $\overline{y}$ is denoted by $\overline{x} \cdot \overline{y}$. Single elements are implicitly treated as lists when needed. $\mathcal{M}[x \mapsto y]$ yields the map $\mathcal{M}$ where the entry with key x is updated with the value y, or, if no such key exists, the entry is added. The empty map is denoted by [] and dom($\mathcal{M}$) and rng($\mathcal{M}$) denote the domain and range of the map $\mathcal{M}$.

Abstract Syntax. LocJ models a core sequential object-oriented Java-like language, formalized in a similar fashion to Welterweight Java [20]. The abstract syntax is shown in Fig. 5. The main difference is that objects in LocJ can be

$$P ::= \overline{C} \qquad\qquad E ::= \text{new } c \text{ in fresh}$$
$$C ::= \text{class } c \ \{ \ \overline{V} \ \overline{M} \ \} \qquad\quad | \ \text{new } c \text{ in } x \ | \ x$$
$$V ::= T \ x \qquad\qquad\qquad | \ x.m(\overline{y}) \ | \ x.f$$
$$M ::= T \ m(\overline{V}) \ \{ \ \overline{V} \ \overline{S} \ \} \quad T ::= c$$
$$S ::= x \leftarrow E \ | \ x.f \leftarrow y$$

$$\zeta ::= \overline{\mathcal{F}}, \mathcal{H} \qquad \text{runtime config.}$$
$$\mathcal{H} ::= \iota \mapsto (l, c, \mathcal{D}) \quad \text{heap}$$
$$\mathcal{F} ::= (\overline{S}, \mathcal{D})^{c,m} \quad \text{stack frame}$$
$$\mathcal{D} ::= x \mapsto v \qquad \text{variable-value map}$$
$$v ::= \iota \ | \ \text{null} \qquad \text{value}$$

Fig. 5. Abstract syntax of LocJ. c ranges over class names, m over method names and x, y, z, f over field and variable names (including this and result)

Fig. 6. Runtime entities of LocJ. ι ranges over object identifiers and l over locations

created at different *locations*. For this, the new-expression has an additional argument, given by the in part, that specifies the target location. The target can either be fresh to create the object in a new (fresh) location, or a variable x to create the object in the same location as the object that is referenced by x[1]. We do not introduce locations as first class citizens as they can be encoded using objects, i.e., objects can be simply used to denote locations. To keep the presentation short, LocJ does not include inheritance and subtyping. However, the formalization can be straightforwardly extended to support these features.

Dynamic Semantics. The dynamic semantics of our language is defined as a small-step operational semantics. The main difference to standard object-oriented languages is that we explicitly model locations to partition the heap. The runtime entities are shown in Fig. 6. Runtime configurations ζ consist of a stack, which is a list of stack frames, and a heap. The heap maps object identifiers to object states $(l, c, \mathcal{D})$, consisting of a location l, a class name c, and a mapping from field names to values $\mathcal{D}$. A stack frame consists of a list of statements and a mapping from local variable names to values. Furthermore the stack frame records with which class c and method m it is associated, which we sometimes omit for brevity.

The reduction rules are shown in Fig. 7. They are of the form $\zeta \rightsquigarrow \zeta'$ and reduce runtime configurations. The rules use the helper functions initO and initF to initialize objects and stack frames. The function $\text{initO}(l, c)$ creates a new heap entry $(l, c, \mathcal{D})$ where $\mathcal{D} = [][\overline{f} \mapsto \overline{\text{null}}]$ and $\overline{f}$ are the field names of class c. Similarly, $\text{initF}(m, c, \iota, \overline{v})$ creates a new stack frame $(\overline{S}, \mathcal{D})^{c,m}$ where $\overline{S}$ are the statements in the method body of method m in class c and $\mathcal{D} = [][\text{this} \mapsto \iota][\text{result} \mapsto \text{null}][\overline{x} \mapsto \overline{v}][\overline{y} \mapsto \overline{\text{null}}]$ and $\overline{x}$ are the variable names of the formal parameters of method m in class c and $\overline{y}$ are the local variable names.

3.1 Basic Location Type System

In this subsection, we present the basic location type system and its soundness properties. To incorporate location types into LocJ programs, we extend types

---

[1] In ABS, **new cog** C() creates a new location (i.e., corresponds to "new c in fresh" in LocJ) whereas **new** C() creates a new object in the same location as the current object (i.e., corresponds to "new c in this" in LocJ).

$$\frac{\iota \notin \mathrm{dom}(\mathcal{H}) \qquad l \text{ is fresh}}{\mathcal{H}' = \mathcal{H}[\iota \mapsto \mathrm{initO}(l,c)] \qquad \mathcal{D}' = \mathcal{D}[x \mapsto \iota]}{(x \leftarrow \mathsf{new}\ c\ \mathsf{in\ fresh} \cdot \overline{S}, \mathcal{D}) \cdot \overline{\mathcal{F}}, \mathcal{H} \rightsquigarrow (\overline{S}, \mathcal{D}') \cdot \overline{\mathcal{F}}, \mathcal{H}'}$$

$$\frac{\mathcal{D}' = \mathcal{D}[x \mapsto \mathcal{D}(y)]}{(x \leftarrow y \cdot \overline{S}, \mathcal{D}) \cdot \overline{\mathcal{F}}, \mathcal{H} \rightsquigarrow (\overline{S}, \mathcal{D}') \cdot \overline{\mathcal{F}}, \mathcal{H}}$$

$$\frac{\iota \notin \mathrm{dom}(\mathcal{H}) \qquad (l, \_, \_) = \mathcal{H}(\mathcal{D}(y))}{\mathcal{H}' = \mathcal{H}[\iota \mapsto \mathrm{initO}(l,c)] \qquad \mathcal{D}' = \mathcal{D}[x \mapsto \iota]}{(x \leftarrow \mathsf{new}\ c\ \mathsf{in}\ y \cdot \overline{S}, \mathcal{D}) \cdot \overline{\mathcal{F}}, \mathcal{H} \rightsquigarrow (\overline{S}, \mathcal{D}') \cdot \overline{\mathcal{F}}, \mathcal{H}'}$$

$$\frac{\mathcal{F} = (x \leftarrow y.m(\overline{z}) \cdot \overline{S}, \mathcal{D})}{(\_,c,\_) = \mathcal{H}(\mathcal{D}(y))}{\mathcal{F}' = \mathrm{initF}(c,m,\mathcal{D}(y),\mathcal{D}(\overline{z}))}{\mathcal{F} \cdot \overline{\mathcal{F}}, \mathcal{H} \rightsquigarrow \mathcal{F}' \cdot \mathcal{F} \cdot \overline{\mathcal{F}}, \mathcal{H}}$$

$$\frac{\iota = \mathcal{D}(x) \qquad (l,c,\mathcal{D}') = \mathcal{H}(\iota)}{\mathcal{D}'' = \mathcal{D}'[f \mapsto \mathcal{D}(y)] \qquad \mathcal{H}' = \mathcal{H}[\iota \mapsto (l,c,\mathcal{D}'')]}{(x.f \leftarrow y \cdot \overline{S}, \mathcal{D}) \cdot \overline{\mathcal{F}}, \mathcal{H} \rightsquigarrow (\overline{S}, \mathcal{D}) \cdot \overline{\mathcal{F}}, \mathcal{H}'}$$

$$\frac{\mathcal{F} = (x \leftarrow y.m(\overline{z}) \cdot \overline{S}, \mathcal{D}')}{\mathcal{D}'' = \mathcal{D}'[x \mapsto \mathcal{D}(\mathsf{result})]}{(\bullet, \mathcal{D}) \cdot \mathcal{F} \cdot \overline{\mathcal{F}}, \mathcal{H} \rightsquigarrow (\overline{S}, \mathcal{D}'') \cdot \overline{\mathcal{F}}, \mathcal{H}}$$

$$\frac{(\_,\_,\mathcal{D}'') = \mathcal{H}(\mathcal{D}(y)) \qquad \mathcal{D}' = \mathcal{D}[x \mapsto \mathcal{D}''(f)]}{(x \leftarrow y.f \cdot \overline{S}, \mathcal{D}) \cdot \overline{\mathcal{F}}, \mathcal{H} \rightsquigarrow (\overline{S}, \mathcal{D}') \cdot \overline{\mathcal{F}}, \mathcal{H}}$$

Fig. 7. Operational semantics of LocJ

$$
\begin{aligned}
T &::= \cdots \mid L\ c &&\text{annotated type}\\
L &::= \mathsf{Near} \mid \mathsf{Far} \mid \mathsf{Somewhere} &&\text{location type}
\end{aligned}
$$

Fig. 8. Basic location types

T with location types L (see Fig. 8), where a location type can either be Near, Far, or Somewhere. We assume that a given program is already well-typed using a standard Java-like type system and we only provide the typing rules for typing the location type extension. The typing rules are shown in Fig. 9. Statements and expressions are typed under a type environment $\overline{V}$, which defines the types of local variables. The typing judgment for expressions is of the form $\overline{V} \vdash e : L$ to denote that expression e has location type L. The helper functions $\mathsf{anno}(c, f)$ and $\mathsf{anno}(c, m, x)$ return the declared location type of field f or variable x of method m in class c and $\mathsf{params}(c, m)$ returns the formal parameter variables of method m in class c.

The crucial parts of the type system are the subtyping $(L <: L')$ and the viewpoint adaptation $(L \triangleright_K L')$ relations which are shown in Fig. 10. The location types Near and Far are both subtypes of Somewhere but are unrelated otherwise. Viewpoint adaption is always applied when a type is used in a different context. There are two different directions $(K \in \{\mathsf{From}, \mathsf{To}\})$ to consider. (1) Adapting a type L *from another viewpoint* L' to the current viewpoint, written as $L \triangleright_{\mathsf{From}} L'$. (2) Adapting a type L from the current viewpoint *to another viewpoint* L', written as $L \triangleright_{\mathsf{To}} L'$.[2] In typing rule WF-FIELDGET we adapt the type of the field *from* the viewpoint of y to the current viewpoint, whereas in rule WF-FIELDSET we adapt the type of y from the current viewpoint to the viewpoint of x.

---

[2] Whereas in other ownership type systems (e.g. [7]), only one direction is considered, we chose to explicitly state the direction in order to achieve a simple and intuitive encoding.

As an example for the viewpoint adaptation, assume a method is called on a Far target and the argument is of type Near. Then the adapted type is Far, because the parameter is Near in relation to the caller, but from the perspective of the callee, it is actually Far in that case. Important is also the case where we pass a Far typed variable x to a Far target. In that case we have to take Somewhere as the adapted type, because it is not statically clear whether the object referred to by x is in a location that is different from the location of the target object.

(WF-P)
$$\frac{P = \overline{C} \qquad \vdash C_i}{\vdash P}$$

(WF-C)
$$\frac{c \vdash M_i}{\vdash \text{class } c \ \{ \ \overline{V} \ \overline{M} \ \}}$$

(WF-NewFresh)
$$\frac{}{\overline{V} \vdash \text{new } c \text{ in fresh} : \text{Far}}$$

(WF-M)
$$\frac{\text{Near } c \text{ this} \cdot T \text{ result} \cdot \overline{V} \cdot \overline{V'} \vdash S_i}{c \vdash T \ m(\overline{V}) \ \{ \ \overline{V'} \ \overline{S} \ \}}$$

(WF-NewSame)
$$\frac{L \ \_ \ x \in \overline{V}}{\overline{V} \vdash \text{new } c \text{ in } x : L}$$

(WF-Var)
$$\frac{L \ \_ \ x \in \overline{V}}{\overline{V} \vdash x : L}$$

(WF-Assign)
$$\frac{\overline{V} \vdash E : L \qquad L' \ \_ \ x \in \overline{V} \qquad L <: L'}{\overline{V} \vdash x \leftarrow E}$$

(WF-FieldGet)
$$\frac{L \ c \ y \in \overline{V} \qquad L' = \text{anno}(c, f)}{\overline{V} \vdash y.f : L' \rhd_{\text{From}} L}$$

(WF-FieldSet)
$$\frac{L \ c \ x \in \overline{V} \qquad L' = \text{anno}(c, f)}{L'' \ \_ \ y \in \overline{V} \qquad (L'' \rhd_{\text{To}} L) <: L'}{\overline{V} \vdash x.f \leftarrow y}$$

(WF-Call)
$$\frac{L \ c \ y \in \overline{V}}{L_i \ \_ \ z_i \in \overline{V} \qquad \overline{x} = \text{params}(c, m)}{(L_i \rhd_{\text{To}} L) <: \text{anno}(c, m, x_i)}{\overline{V} \vdash y.m(\overline{z}) : \text{anno}(c, m, \text{result}) \rhd_{\text{From}} L}$$

Fig. 9. Typing rules of LocJ. Note that indices are implicitly all-quantified

Type Soundness. The location type system guarantees that variables of type Near only reference objects that are in the same location as the current object and that variables of type Far only reference objects that are in a different location to the current object. We formalize this by defining a well-formed runtime configuration. As helper functions, we define the location of a heap entry as $\text{loc}((l, c, \mathcal{D})) = l$ and the dynamically computed location type as $\text{dtype}(l, l') = \text{Near}$ if $l = l'$, and Far otherwise.

Definition 1 (Well-formed runtime configuration). *Let $\zeta = \overline{\mathcal{F}}, \mathcal{H}$ be a runtime configuration. ζ is well-formed iff all heap entries $(l, c, \mathcal{D}) \in \text{rng}(\mathcal{H})$ and all stack frames $\mathcal{F} \in \overline{\mathcal{F}}$ are well-formed under $\mathcal{H}$ and the configuration satisfies all the standard conditions of a class-based language.*

Definition 2 (Well-formed heap entry). *$(l, \_, \mathcal{D})$ is well-formed under $\mathcal{H}$ iff for all f with $\mathcal{D}(f) = \iota$ and $(l', c, \_) = \mathcal{H}(\iota)$, we have $\text{dtype}(l, l') <: \text{anno}(c, f)$.*

Original	$\triangleright_K$	*Viewpoint*	$=$	*Adapted*
L	$\triangleright_K$	Near	$=$	L
Near	$\triangleright_K$	Far	$=$	Far
Far	$\triangleright_K$	Far	$=$	Somewhere
Somewhere	$\triangleright_K$	Far	$=$	Somewhere
L	$\triangleright_K$	Somewhere	$=$	Somewhere

Fig. 10. Subtyping and viewpoint adaptation (where $K \in \{\text{From}, \text{To}\}$). Note that the direction K does not influence basic location types, but is important for our extension in Sect. 3.2

```
1   [Far] Server server = new cog ServerImpl();
2   [Far] Client client1 = new cog ClientImpl("Alice");
3   [Far] Client client2 = new cog ClientImpl("Bob");
4   client1 ! connectTo(server);
5   client2 ! connectTo(server);
```

Fig. 11. The code of the main block of the chat application, annotated with location types

Definition 3 (Well-formed stack frame). $(\overline{S}, \mathcal{D})^{c,m}$ *is well-formed under* $\mathcal{H}$ *iff for all* x *with* $\mathcal{D}(x) = \iota$, *we have* $\text{dtype}(\text{loc}(\mathcal{H}(\mathcal{D}(\text{this}))), \text{loc}(\mathcal{H}(\iota))) <: \text{anno}(c, m, x)$.

Theorem 1 (Preservation for location types). *Let* ζ *be a well-formed runtime configuration. If* $\zeta \rightsquigarrow \zeta'$, *then* ζ' *is well-formed as well.*

Proof. The proof proceeds by a standard case analysis on the reduction rule used and is available in the accompanying report [25]. ∎

3.2   Named Far Location Types

The location type system so far can only distinguish near from far references. The type system knows that a near reference always points to a different location than a far reference. But whether two far references point to the same location or different ones is not statically known. This makes the type system often too weak in practice. As an example, let us consider the *main block*[3] of the ABS chat application in Fig. 11, annotated with location types. The server and both clients are created by using the **new cog** expression. This means that all these objects live in their own, fresh COG and thus they can be typed to Far, because these locations are different to the current COG (the *Main* COG). However, for the method call client1!connectTo(server) to successfully type-check, the formal parameter of the connectTo method would need to be typed as Somewhere because the actual (adapted) parameter type is of type Somewhere (= Far $\triangleright_{\text{To}}$ Far). This issue arises because the type system cannot distinguish that client1 and server point to different locations. The example shows that in its basic form, the location type system often has to conservatively use the Somewhere type to

---

[3] A main block in ABS corresponds to a main method in Java.

remain sound, which in fact means that the type system cannot say anything about the location.

To improve the precision of the location type system we introduce *named* far types:

$$L ::= \cdots \mid \mathsf{Far}(i)$$

A named far type is a far type parametrized with an arbitrary name[4]. Far types with different names represent disjoint sets of far locations and are incompatible to each other. The following typing rule WF-NEWFRESHP is added, which allows new locations to be more precisely described.

(WF-NEWFRESHP)

$$\overline{\overline{V} \vdash \mathsf{new}\ c\ \mathsf{in}\ \mathsf{fresh} : \mathsf{Far}(i)}$$

The subtyping and viewpoint adaptation relations are extended accordingly in Fig. 12. Adapting a $\mathsf{Far}(i)$ to a $\mathsf{Far}(j)$ for $i \neq j$ yields a $\mathsf{Far}(i)$, as they denote different sets of locations. Adapting a $\mathsf{Far}(i)$ to a $\mathsf{Far}(i)$ does not yield Near, however, as two variables with the same $\mathsf{Far}(i)$ type can refer to objects of different locations.

In practice the user does not explicitly provide the names. Instead the inference system automatically infers them when possible. These refined far types are then used to improve the viewpoint adaptation. In the chat example our type system is now able to infer that the server and the client variables actually refer to different far locations. This means that the argument of the connectTo method call can be typed to Far instead of Somewhere.

Our experience with case studies shows that this extension is expressive enough for our purposes (cf. Sect. 4). However, other extensions to improve the expressiveness and precision of the location type system are imaginable, e.g. location type polymorphism similar to owner polymorphism in ownership type systems [4, 3, 17].

Type Soundness. Similar as for Thm. 1, a proof of type soundness for the named far location type system extension is available in the accompanying report [25].

3.3   Location Type Inference

The type system presented in the previous section requires the programmer to annotate all type occurrences with location types. In this subsection we present an inference system for location types. We first present a sound and complete inference system, which makes it possible to use the location type system without writing any type annotations and only use type annotations for achieving modular type checking. The second part then presents an inference system that can deal with type-incorrect programs and that finds not only *some* solution but an *optimal* solution.

---

[4] Note that these are *not* object identifiers.

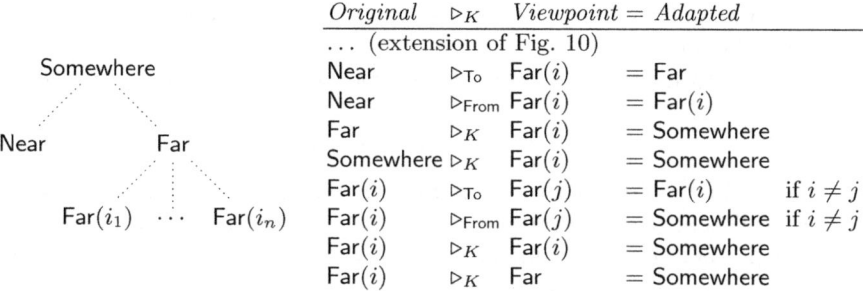

Original	$\triangleright_K$	Viewpoint	= Adapted	
... (extension of Fig. 10)				
Near	$\triangleright_{To}$	Far(i)	= Far	
Near	$\triangleright_{From}$	Far(i)	= Far(i)	
Far	$\triangleright_K$	Far(i)	= Somewhere	
Somewhere	$\triangleright_K$	Far(i)	= Somewhere	
Far(i)	$\triangleright_{To}$	Far(j)	= Far(i)	if $i \neq j$
Far(i)	$\triangleright_{From}$	Far(j)	= Somewhere	if $i \neq j$
Far(i)	$\triangleright_K$	Far(i)	= Somewhere	
Far(i)	$\triangleright_K$	Far	= Somewhere	

Fig. 12. Subtyping and viewpoint adaptation for extended location types

$$
\begin{aligned}
\mathcal{Q} ::=\ & \alpha \triangleright_K \beta = \gamma && \text{adaptation constraint} \\
| & \ \alpha <: \beta && \text{subtype constraint} \\
| & \ \alpha = L \mid \alpha \neq L && \text{constant constraint}
\end{aligned}
$$

Fig. 13. Location type constraints

Sound and Complete Inference. The formal model for inferring location types follows the formalization of other type system extensions [8]. The idea is to introduce location type variables at places in the program where location types occur in our typing rules. Type inference then consists of two steps. First, generating constraints for the location type variables. Second, checking whether a substitution for the location type variables exists such that all constraints are satisfied.

To introduce location type variables into programs we extend the syntax of location types accordingly:

$$ L ::= \cdots \mid \alpha \qquad \text{location type variables (also } \beta, \gamma, \text{ and } \delta) $$

In the following we consider P as a program which is fully annotated with pairwise distinct location type variables. The constraints which are generated by the inference system are shown in Fig. 13. We use the judgment $\vdash P : \overline{\mathcal{Q}}$, defined in Fig. 14, to denote the generation of the constraints $\overline{\mathcal{Q}}$ from program P. Note that additional *fresh* location type variables are introduced during the constraint generation.

Soundness and Completeness. Let σ be a mapping function from location type variables to location types, i.e., α to $\{\text{Near}, \text{Far}, \text{Somewhere}, \text{Far}(i_1), ..., \text{Far}(i_n)\}$. Then $\sigma \models \overline{\mathcal{Q}}$ if the constraints $\overline{\mathcal{Q}}$ are satisfiable under σ. We write σP to denote that all location type variables in P have been replaced by location types according to the substitution function σ.

Conjecture 1 (Soundness and Completeness of the Inference). The inference is sound and complete in the sense that every typing inferred can be successfully type-checked and every typing which type-checks can also be inferred.

$$\frac{P = \overline{C} \qquad \vdash C_i : \overline{\mathcal{Q}}_i}{\vdash P : \overline{\mathcal{Q}}_1 \cdot \ldots \cdot \overline{\mathcal{Q}}_n}$$

$$\frac{\delta \; c \; \mathsf{this} \cdot T \; \mathsf{result} \cdot \overline{V} \cdot \overline{V'} \vdash S_i : \overline{\mathcal{Q}}_i \qquad \delta \text{ is fresh}}{c \vdash T \; m(\overline{V}) \; \{ \; \overline{V'} \; \overline{S} \; \} : \delta = \mathsf{Near} \cdot \overline{\mathcal{Q}}_1 \cdot \ldots \cdot \overline{\mathcal{Q}}_n}$$

$$\frac{c \vdash M_i : \overline{\mathcal{Q}}_i}{\vdash \mathsf{class} \; c \; \{ \; \overline{V} \; \overline{M} \; \} : \overline{\mathcal{Q}}_1 \cdot \ldots \cdot \overline{\mathcal{Q}}_n}$$

$$\frac{\alpha \; c \; x \in \overline{V}}{\beta = \mathsf{anno}(c, f) \qquad \gamma \_ y \in \overline{V} \qquad \delta \text{ is fresh}}{\overline{V} \vdash x.f \leftarrow y : \delta <: \beta \cdot \gamma \triangleright_{\mathsf{To}} \alpha = \delta}$$

$$\frac{\overline{V} \vdash E : \beta, \overline{\mathcal{Q}} \qquad \alpha \_ x \in \overline{V}}{\overline{V} \vdash x \leftarrow E : \beta <: \alpha \cdot \overline{\mathcal{Q}}}$$

$$\frac{\alpha \; c \; y \in \overline{V} \qquad \beta = \mathsf{anno}(c, f) \qquad \gamma \text{ is fresh}}{\overline{V} \vdash y.f : \gamma, \beta \triangleright_{\mathsf{From}} \alpha = \gamma}$$

$$\frac{\delta \text{ is fresh}}{\overline{V} \vdash \mathsf{new} \; c \; \mathsf{in \; fresh} : \delta, \delta \neq \mathsf{Near}}$$

$$\frac{\alpha \; c \; y \in \overline{V} \qquad \alpha_i \_ z_i \in \overline{V} \qquad \overline{x} = \mathsf{params}(c, m)}{\beta_i = \mathsf{anno}(c, m, x_i) \qquad \beta = \mathsf{anno}(c, m, \mathsf{result})}{\mathcal{Q}_i = \alpha_i \triangleright_{\mathsf{To}} \alpha = \gamma_i \cdot \gamma_i <: \beta_i}{\gamma_i \text{ is fresh} \qquad \gamma \text{ is fresh}}{\overline{V} \vdash y.m(\overline{z}) : \gamma, \beta \triangleright_{\mathsf{From}} \alpha = \gamma \cdot \overline{\mathcal{Q}}_1 \cdot \ldots \cdot \overline{\mathcal{Q}}_n}$$

$$\frac{\alpha \_ y \in \overline{V}}{\overline{V} \vdash \mathsf{new} \; c \; \mathsf{in} \; y : \alpha, \bullet} \qquad \frac{\alpha \_ x \in \overline{V}}{\overline{V} \vdash x : \alpha, \bullet}$$

Fig. 14. Constraint generation rules

- *Soundness*: If $\vdash P : \overline{\mathcal{Q}}$ and $_\sigma \vDash \overline{\mathcal{Q}}$, then $\vdash \sigma P$.
- *Completeness*: If $\vdash \sigma P$ for some minimal σ, then $\exists \overline{\mathcal{Q}}$ such that $\vdash P : \overline{\mathcal{Q}}$ and $\exists \sigma'$ such that σ' is an extension of σ and $_\sigma \vDash \overline{\mathcal{Q}}$. Note that σ' is an extension of σ iff $\sigma'(\alpha) = \sigma(\alpha)$ for all $\alpha \in \mathsf{dom}(\sigma)$.

Optimal and Partial Inference. Whereas soundness and completeness is important, it is not sufficient for an inference system to be usable in practice. Two additional properties are required, namely:

1. If multiple inference solutions exist, an *optimal* solution should be taken. This is important, because the user in general wants to have the most precise solution, i.e., with the least amount of Somewhere annotations.
2. If no typable solution can be inferred, at least a partially typable solution should be provided. It is otherwise nearly impossible to use the inference system if one only gets a *"No solution can be found"* result. In addition, this partially typable solution should lead to the least amount of type errors.

To support these two properties, we extend our formal model in the following way. We introduce three constraint categories: *must-have*, *should-have*, and *nice-to-have*. The *must-have* constraints must always be satisfied. These are for example in Fig. 14 the adaptation constraints ($\alpha \triangleright_K \beta = \gamma$) and the constant constraints ($\alpha = L$, $\alpha \neq L$), characterizing the types of subexpressions. They also encompass the constant constraints which result from user annotations (not considered in the formalization of Fig. 14, but present in the implementation). Note that there is always a solution to these constraints in our inference system as they are based on freshly allocated location type variables. The *should-have* constraints, e.g. the subtype constraints ($\alpha <: \beta$) in Fig. 14, should always be satisfied in order to get a valid typing, but can be unsatisfied for partially correct solutions. The *nice-to-have* constraints are those that give us a *nice* (optimal) solution, i.e., with the least amount of Somewhere annotations or with Far types at the places where the precision of Far(i) types is not needed.

Inferring an optimal solution consists of solving the following problem. First, all *must-have* constraints, then the most amount of *should-have* constraints, and finally the most amount of *nice-to-have* constraints should be satisfied. The problem can be encoded as a partially weighted MaxSAT problem by assigning appropriate weights to the constraints. This means that *must-have* constraints are hard clauses (maximum weight) and *should-have* constraints correspond to soft clauses whose weight is greater than the sum of all weighted *nice-to-have* clauses. Solving such a problem can be efficiently done using specialized SAT solvers.

As an example for partial inference, consider the ServerImpl class in Fig. 4. Assume that there are no annotations on the signature and the body of the connect method except for the return type which has been wrongly annotated by the programmer as Far. The inference system then still gives a solution where all constraints are satisfied except one *should-have* constraint, namely s <: result which is generated at the last line of the connect method. The inference system assigns the type Near to variable s because if it were to assign Far to s, more *should-have* constraints would be unsatisfied (i.e. those resulting from lines 5 to 7).

4   Implementation and IDE Integration

We have implemented the type and inference system for location types, including named far location types and optimal and partial inference, as an extension of the ABS compiler suite. The type and inference system is integrated into an Eclipse-based IDE, but can also be used from the command line.

Inference System. The inference system internally uses the Max-SAT solver SAT4J [16] to solve the generated inference constraints. As the inference system may return a solution that is not fully typable, we use the type checker for location types to give user-friendly error messages.

The alias analysis for named Far locations (cf. Sect. 3.2) can be configured to use scopes of different granularity: basic (no alias analysis), method-local, class-local, module-local, and global analysis. This allows the user to choose the best tradeoff between precision and modularity. For the inference, an upper bound on the number of possible named Far(i) locations is needed. This is calculated based on the number of new c in fresh expressions in the current scope.

IDE Integration. ABS features an Eclipse-based IDE[5] for developing ABS projects. The interesting part of the IDE for this paper is that we have incorporated visual overlays which display the location type inference results. For

---

[5] http://tools.hats-project.eu/eclipseplugin/installation.html

each location type there is a small overlay symbol, e.g., N for Near and F for Far, which are shown as superscripts of the type name. For example, a Far Client appears as Client^F. Whenever the user saves a changed program, the inference is triggered and the overlays are updated. They give the user complete location type information of all reference types, without cluttering the code. In addition, the overlays can easily be toggled on or off. It is also possible to write the inference results back as annotations into the source code, with user-specified levels of granularity, e.g., method signatures in interfaces.

Evaluation. We evaluated the location type system by applying it to three case studies. The Trading System (1164 LOC, 150 types to annotate) and Replication System (702 LOC, 62 types to annotate) case studies are ABS programs developed as parts of the case studies in the HATS project. The Chat Application (251 LOC, 55 types to annotate) is an extended version of the one presented in Sect. 2.

The evaluation results are presented in Fig. 15. They show how precise the case studies can be typed and how fast the inference works. We also restricted the alias analysis by various scopes to see the impact on performance and precision. First of all, all case studies can be fully typed using our type system. The chart on the left shows the precision (percentage of near and far annotations) of the type inference. As can be seen, the basic type system already has a good precision ($> 60\%$) in all three case studies. As expected, the precision increased with a broader analysis scope. Using a global aliasing analysis, the inference achieved a precision of 100% in the Chat as well as the Trading System case studies. In the Replication Server case study, the best precision was already achieved with a method-local scope.

The chart on the right shows the performance results of the inference. It shows that the performance of the inference is fast enough for the inference system to be used interactively. It also shows that the performance depends on the chosen scope for the aliasing analysis. Note that the examples where completely unannotated, so that all types had to be inferred. In practice, programs are often partially annotated, which additionally improves the performance of the type inference. Our implementation of the inference focused more on correctness than performance, which means that many improvements in the encoding, and thus in the solving time are still possible.

5 Discussion and Related Work

Location types are a variant of ownership types that concentrate on *flat* ownership contexts. We presented the type system in the context of distributed object-oriented systems, but it can be applied to any context where flat ownership contexts are sufficient. Ownership types [4, 3, 17] and similar type systems [1, 6] typically describe a hierarchical heap structure. On one hand this makes these systems more general than location types, because ownership types could be used for the same purpose as location types; on the other hand this makes

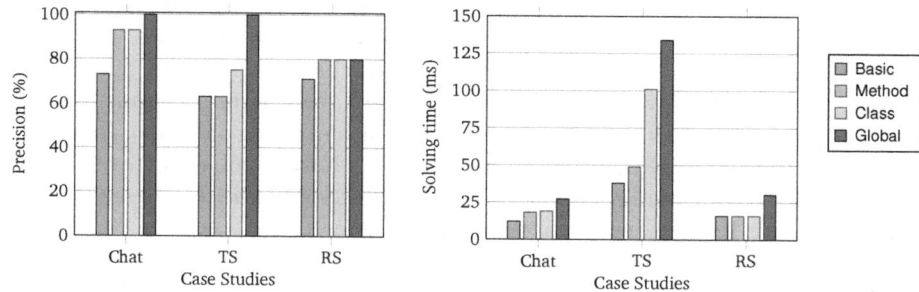

Fig. 15. Precision and solving time of the location type inference for the three case studies, using four different scopes for the aliasing analysis. The measurements where done on a MacBook Pro laptop (Intel Core 2 Duo T7400 2.16GHz CPU, 2GB RAM, Ubuntu 10.04, Sun JDK 1.6.16). We used the `-Xms1024` parameter to avoid garbage collection. As working in an IDE usually consists of an edit-compile-run cycle, we provide the performance results (the mean of 20 complete runs) after warming up the JVM with 5 dry runs. We measured the time that the SAT-solver required for finding a solution using the `System.nanoTime()` method.

these systems more complex. An ownership type system which is close to location types in nature is that by Clarke et al. [5], which applies ownership types to active objects. In their system ownership contexts are also flat, but ownership is used to ensure encapsulation of objects with support for a safe object transfer using unique references and cloning. Haller and Odersky [13] use a capability-based type system to restrict aliasing in concurrent programs and achieve full encapsulation. As these systems are based on encapsulation they do not have the concept of *far* references. Places [12] also partition the heap. However, the set of places is fixed at the time the program is started. Similar, but less expressive than our type system, is Loci [26], which only distinguishes references to be either thread-local or shared. Loci only uses defaults to reduce the annotation overhead. Loci is also realized as an Eclipse plug-in. Regions are also considered in region-based memory management [23], but for another purpose. They give the guarantee that objects inside a region do not refer to objects inside another region to ensure safe deallocation.

Using a Max-SAT solver with weighted constraints was also used in [11] to infer types that prevent data-races and in [8] to find good inference solutions for universe types. A crucial aspect of our work is the integration of type inference results into the IDE by using overlays. To the best of our knowledge there is no comparable approach. A widely used type system extension is the non-null type system [10]. For variations of this type system, there exist built-in inference mechanisms in Eclipse[6] and IntelliJ IDEA[7] as well as additional plug-ins such as [14]. None of these IDE integrations provide type information by using overlays,

---

[6] http://wiki.eclipse.org/JDT_Core/Null_Analysis
[7] http://www.jetbrains.com/idea/webhelp/inferring-nullity.html

but only give warnings in cases of type errors, which makes it difficult for the user to find the root of the problem.

6 Conclusion and Future Work

We have presented a type system for distributed object-oriented programming languages to distinguish near from far references. We applied the type system to the context of the ABS language to guarantee that far references are not used as targets for synchronous method calls. A complete type inference implementation allows the programmer to make use of the type system without making any annotations. The type inference results are visualized as overlay annotations directly in the development environment. Application of the type system to several case studies shows that the type system is expressive enough to type realistic code. The type inference implementation is fast enough to provide inference results within fractions of a second, so that interactive use of the system is possible.

We see two directions for future work. First, the type system could be applied to other settings where the location of an object is important, e.g., Java RMI [19]. Second, it would be interesting to investigate the visual overlay technique for other (pluggable) type systems, e.g., the nullness type system [14].

Acknowledgements. We thank our Master's students Thomas Fischer, Christian Seise, Florian Strauß, and Mathias Weber for implementing most parts of the ABS-Eclipse integration. We also thank Peter Wong for applying the location type system to the Replication System case study, and Arnd Poetzsch-Heffter and Patrick Michel for proof-reading earlier drafts of this paper. Finally, we thank the anonymous reviewers of TOOLS Europe 2011 for their constructive feedback.

References

1. Aldrich, J.: Ownership Domains: Separating Aliasing Policy from Mechanism. In: Vetta, A. (ed.) ECOOP 2004. LNCS, vol. 3086, pp. 1–25. Springer, Heidelberg (2004)
2. Andreae, C., Noble, J., Markstrum, S., Millstein, T.: A framework for implementing pluggable type systems. In: Tarr, P.L., Cook, W.R. (eds.) OOPSLA, pp. 57–74. ACM Press, New York (2006)
3. Boyapati, C., Liskov, B., Shrira, L.: Ownership types for object encapsulation. In: POPL, pp. 213–223. ACM Press, New York (2003)
4. Clarke, D., Potter, J., Noble, J.: Ownership Types for Flexible Alias Protection. In: OOPSLA, pp. 48–64. ACM Press, New York (1998)
5. Clarke, D., Wrigstad, T., Östlund, J., Johnsen, E.B.: Minimal Ownership for Active Objects. In: Ramalingam, G. (ed.) APLAS 2008. LNCS, vol. 5356, pp. 139–154. Springer, Heidelberg (2008)
6. Dietl, W.: Universe Types: Topology, Encapsulation, Genericity, and Tools. PhD thesis. ETH Zurich, Switzerland (2009)

7. Dietl, W., Gairing, M., Müller, P.: Generic Universe Types. In: Bateni, M. (ed.) ECOOP 2007. LNCS, vol. 4609, pp. 28–53. Springer, Heidelberg (2007)
8. Dietl, W., Ernst, M., Müller, P.: Tunable Universe Type Inference. Tech. rep. 659. Department of Computer Science, ETH Zurich (December 2009)
9. Ernst, M.D.: Type Annotations Specification (JSR 308) and The Checker Framework: Custom pluggable types for Java, http://types.cs.washington.edu/jsr308/
10. Fähndrich, M., Leino, K.R.M.: Declaring and checking non-null types in an object-oriented language. In: OOPSLA 2003, pp. 302–312. ACM Press, New York (2003)
11. Flanagan, C., Freund, S.N.: Type inference against races. Sci. Comput. Program. 64, 140–165 (2007)
12. Grothoff, C.: Expressive Type Systems for Object-Oriented Languages. PhD thesis. University of California, Los Angeles (2006)
13. Haller, P., Odersky, M.: Capabilities for Uniqueness and Borrowing. In: D'Hondt, T. (ed.) ECOOP 2010. LNCS, vol. 6183, pp. 354–378. Springer, Heidelberg (2010)
14. Hubert, L., Jensen, T., Pichardie, D.: Semantic Foundations and Inference of Non-null Annotations. In: Barthe, G., de Boer, F.S. (eds.) FMOODS 2008. LNCS, vol. 5051, pp. 132–149. Springer, Heidelberg (2008)
15. Hähnle, R., et al.: Report on the Core ABS Language and Methodology: Part A. Report. The HATS Consortium (March 2010), http://www.hats-project.eu/
16. Le Berre, D., Parrain, A.: The SAT4J library, Release 2.2, System Description. Journal on Satisfiability, Boolean Modeling and Computation 7, 59–64 (2010)
17. Lu, Y.: On Ownership and Accessibility. In: Hu, Q. (ed.) ECOOP 2006. LNCS, vol. 4067, pp. 99–123. Springer, Heidelberg (2006)
18. Miller, M.S., Tribble, E.D., Shapiro, J.S.: Concurrency Among Strangers. In: De Nicola, R., Sangiorgi, D. (eds.) TGC 2005. LNCS, vol. 3705, pp. 195–229. Springer, Heidelberg (2005)
19. Oracle Corporation: Java SE 6 RMI documentation , http://download.oracle.com/javase/6/docs/technotes/guides/rmi/index.html
20. Östlund, J., Wrigstad, T.: Welterweight Java. In: Vitek, J. (ed.) TOOLS 2010. LNCS, vol. 6141, pp. 97–116. Springer, Heidelberg (2010)
21. Potanin, A., Noble, J., Clarke, D., Biddle, R.: Generic Ownership for Generic Java. In: Tarr, P.L., Cook, W.R. (eds.) OOPSLA, ACM Press, New York (2006)
22. Schäfer, J., Poetzsch-Heffter, A.: JCoBox: Generalizing Active Objects to Concurrent Components. In: D'Hondt, T. (ed.) ECOOP 2010. LNCS, vol. 6183, pp. 275–299. Springer, Heidelberg (2010)
23. Tofte, M., Talpin, J.-P.: Region-based Memory Management. Inf. Comput. 2, 109–176 (1997)
24. Van Cutsem, T., Mostinckx, S., Boix, E.G., Dedecker, J., Meuter, W.D.: AmbientTalk: Object-oriented Event-driven Programming in Mobile Ad hoc Networks. In: SCCC, pp. 3–12. IEEE Computer Society Press, Los Alamitos (2007)
25. Welsch, Y., Schäfer, J.: Location Types for Safe Distributed Object-Oriented Programming. Tech. rep. 383/11. University of Kaiserslautern (April 2011)
26. Wrigstad, T., Pizlo, F., Meawad, F., Zhao, L., Vitek, J.: Loci: Simple Thread-Locality for Java. In: Drossopoulou, S. (ed.) ECOOP 2009. LNCS, vol. 5653, pp. 445–469. Springer, Heidelberg (2009)

Static Dominance Inference

Ana Milanova[1] and Jan Vitek[2]

[1] Rensselaer Polytechnic Institute
[2] Purdue University

Abstract. Dominance, the property that all paths to a given object must go through another object, is at the heart of ownership type disciplines. While ownership types have received abundant attention, ownership inference remains an open problem, and crucial questions about the practical impact of ownership remain unanswered. We argue that a static program analysis that infers dominance is a crucial first step to ownership types inference. This paper describes an algorithm for statically computing dominance relations and shows that it can be used as part of an ownership inference algorithm.

1 Introduction

Dominance is at the heart of virtually every ownership discipline [3,2,5], and therefore one would expect dominance inference should be a key part of ownership inference. While there are many ownership disciplines, and there is little question about their benefits, practical adoption is lacking. This is due in part to the lack of software tools that support ownership such as automatic inference and refactoring tools incorporated in IDEs. Dominance inference is the foundation of ownership inference: an algorithm that statically computes dominance relations between objects, allows language designers to prototype ownership inference with respect to different ownership disciplines. Dominance inference has other applications as well. As it subsumes escape analysis, it can be used for lock elimination and deadlock detection [12]. Dominance inference can enable data-centric synchronization [18]. Additionally, dominance inference can be integrated into architecture extraction tools [8], and help enable reasoning about encapsulation properties.

The problem of dominance inference is defined in terms of the notion of *object graph*. Nodes in the graph are objects, and edges capture references between those objects. An edge links object i to object j if i has a field that refers to j, or a local variable in a method invoked on receiver i, refers to j. Fig. 1 shows a program and two object graphs: (1) shows the *concrete object graph* that summarizes the references between objects that arise as the program is evaluated, and (2) shows an *abstract object graph* which is a static approximation of the concrete graph obtained by program analysis. Static analysis entails a loss of precision. In this example, allocation site e is executed twice, resulting in objects e_1 and e_2. A typical static analysis abstraction scheme maps every concrete object to its allocation site, thus e_1 and e_2 map to the same abstract object e.

J. Bishop and A. Vallecillo (Eds.): TOOLS 2011, LNCS 6705, pp. 211–227, 2011.

```
class Main {                                    class Y {
    X x;                                            Contain d;
    Y y;                                            void m() {
    static void main(String[] arg) {                   this.d = new Contain();  [d]
        Main m = new Main();   [m]                      d.put(1,1);
        m.meth();                                   }
    }                                           }
    void meth() {                               class Contain {
        this.x = new X();  [x]                      int[] e;
        x.m();                                      Contain() {
        this.y = new Y();  [y]                          this.e = new int[10];  [e]
        y.m();                                      }
    }                                               void put(int i, int j) { e[i] = j; }
}                                                   Iter iter() {
class X {                                               Iter h = new Iter(e);  [f]
    Contain c;                                          return h;
    void m() {                                  } }
        this.c = new Contain();  [c]            class Iter {
        c.put(0,1);                                 int[] f;
        Iter i = c.iter();                          Iter(int[] f) { this.f = f; }
    }                                           }
}
```

Fig. 1. Concrete (1) and abstract (2) object graphs for the simple program

Every object in the concrete object graph has a *dominance boundary*, defined as the maximal subgraph rooted at that object whose nodes are *dominated* by the object. The problem of dominance inference is stated as follows: given an abstract object graph $\widehat{G}$ and an object i in $\widehat{G}$, find a subgraph with root i that safely approximates the dominance boundary of all concrete objects mapped to i. Dominance inference using *dynamic* analysis has been studied before [11,14,5,19]. The appeal of dynamic inference lies in its simplicity. During program execution a concrete object graph is maintained by the implementation. However, like all dynamic approaches the results are unsound; there is no guarantee that inferred dominance won't be broken by an unseen execution path. Additionally, scalability and performance overheads limit the applicability of dynamic techniques. Surprisingly, static dominance inference has received almost no attention. Traditional dominator algorithms [6] cannot be applied on an abstract object graph as an abstract node corresponds to multiple nodes in the concrete object graph and straight-forward application of dominator algorithms breaks both precision and correctness. Consider Fig. 1. Clearly, d does not dominate e in the abstract graph, thus the results of the dominator algorithm cannot be used to conclude that concrete d dominates e_2. As we shall see, our dominance inference algorithm determines precisely that the abstract dominance boundary of d includes e, and therefore d does dominate e_2.

2 Formal Account of Object Graphs

We explain our algorithm and, later, ownership types, in terms of core Java-like calculus. Throughout the paper we will use the following notation for graphs. A graph G is a pair (N, E) where N is a set of nodes ranged over by variables i, j, k, l and E is a set of directed edges written $i \triangleright j$. We write $G \cup i \triangleright j$ to denote the addition of i and j to N and $i \triangleright j$ to E. We write $i \in G$ and $i \triangleright j \in G$ to test, respectively node and edge membership. For sets (of nodes, edges, etc.) we write $S \mathrel{+{=}} S'$ to denote adding S' to set S and $S \mathrel{-{=}} S'$ for removing S' from S.

2.1 Concrete Semantics

For brevity, we restrict our formal attention to a core calculus in the style of [18] whose syntax appears in Fig. 2. The language models Java with a syntax in A-normal form. Features not strictly necessary were omitted. The semantics operates over configurations of the form $S\ H\ G\ C$ where S is a stack, H is a heap, G is an object graph and C is a creation graph. A stack is a sequence of frames $\langle F\ \mathsf{s} \rangle$ consisting of a mapping F from variables to locations and a statement s. An object $o = \mathsf{C}(\bar{i})$ consists of a class C and values $\bar{i}$ for the object fields. A heap is a mapping from indices, ranged over by meta-variables i, j, k, l, to objects. An object graph G summarizes the references between objects that occur at any time during program execution. A creation graph C records the creator of each object. We write $\bar{i}$ to denote a sequence of indices, $\overline{\tau\ \mathsf{z}}$ for a sequence of local variable declarations, etc. We write 0 to denote the null reference.

Fig. 3 shows the rules of the concrete semantics. Object creation (DNEW) instantiates a new object with all fields set to null and uses a fresh index j to refer to the newly allocated object. The rule adds an edge from i, the receiver of the current frame, to j the newly created object, to G. In addition, it records the edge from i, the creator of j, to j, in creation graph C. Writing to an object field (DWRITE) updates the heap. The value of field f of object $\mathsf{C}(\bar{j'}, j_{\mathsf{f}}, \bar{j''})$ is j_{f}. The rule also adds edge from k to j to G. Reading a field into a local variable (DREAD) has the expected semantics. The summary graph records the read by adding a reference from the receiver (i.e. this) to the value of the field. Invoking a method

$$
\begin{array}{llll}
cd & ::= \mathsf{class}\ \mathsf{C}\ \mathsf{extends}\ \mathsf{D}\ \{\overline{fd}\ \overline{md}\} & \textit{class} \\
fd & ::= \tau\ \mathsf{f} & \textit{field} & \qquad H ::= [\,]\mid H[i \mapsto o] \quad \textit{heap} \\
md & ::= \tau\ \mathsf{m}(\overline{\tau\ \mathsf{x}})\{\overline{\tau\ \mathsf{z}}\ \mathsf{s};\ \mathsf{return}\ \mathsf{y}\} & \textit{method} & \qquad S ::= \epsilon \mid \langle F\ \mathsf{s}\rangle S \quad \textit{stack} \\
\mathsf{s} & ::= \mathsf{s};\mathsf{s}\mid \mathsf{x} = \mathsf{new}\ \tau()\mid \mathsf{x} = \mathsf{y}.\mathsf{f} & \textit{statement} & \qquad F ::= [\,]\mid F[\mathsf{y}\mapsto i] \quad \textit{frame} \\
 & \mid \mathsf{x}.\mathsf{f} = \mathsf{y}\mid \mathsf{x} = \mathsf{y}.\mathsf{m}(\bar{\mathsf{z}}) & & \qquad o ::= \mathsf{C}(\bar{i}) \qquad\qquad \textit{object} \\
\tau & ::= \mathsf{C} & \textit{type} \\
\end{array}
$$

Fig. 2. Syntax

$$\frac{\text{(DNEW)}}{o = \mathsf{C}(\overline{0}) \quad j \; \mathit{fresh} \quad F(\mathsf{this}) = i \quad G' = G \cup i \triangleright j \quad C' = C \cup i \triangleright j}{\langle F \; \mathsf{x} = \mathsf{new} \; \mathsf{C}(); \mathsf{s} \rangle S \; H \; G \; C \quad \rightarrow \quad \langle F[\mathsf{x} \mapsto j] \; \mathsf{s} \rangle S \; H[j \mapsto o] \; G' \; C'}$$

$$\frac{\text{(DWRITE)}}{F(\mathsf{x}) = k \quad H(k) = \mathsf{C}(\overline{j'}, j_{\mathsf{f}}, \overline{j''}) \quad F(\mathsf{y}) = j \quad H' = H[k \mapsto \mathsf{C}(\overline{j'}, j, \overline{j''})] \quad G' = G \cup k \triangleright j}{\langle F \; \mathsf{x.f} = \mathsf{y}; \mathsf{s} \rangle S \; H \; G \; C \quad \rightarrow \quad \langle F \; \mathsf{s} \rangle S \; H' \; G' \; C}$$

$$\frac{\text{(DREAD)}}{F(\mathsf{y}) = i \quad H(i) = \mathsf{C}(\overline{j'}, j_{\mathsf{f}}, \overline{j''}) \quad F(\mathsf{this}) = k \quad G' = G \cup k \triangleright j_{\mathsf{f}}}{\langle F \; \mathsf{x} = \mathsf{y.f}; \mathsf{s} \rangle S \; H \; G \; C \quad \rightarrow \quad \langle F[\mathsf{x} \mapsto j_{\mathsf{f}}] \; \mathsf{s} \rangle S \; H \; G' \; C}$$

$$\frac{\text{(DCALL)}}{F(\mathsf{y}) = k \quad F(\overline{\mathsf{z}}) = \overline{j} \quad H(k) = \mathsf{C}(\ldots) \quad \mathit{mbody}(\mathsf{C.m}) = \overline{\tau_x \; \mathsf{x'}}; \overline{\tau_y \; \mathsf{y'}}; \mathsf{s'}; \mathsf{return} \; \mathsf{y''} \atop F' = [\overline{\mathsf{y'}} \mapsto \overline{0}][\overline{\mathsf{x'}} \mapsto \overline{j}][\mathsf{this} \mapsto k] \quad G' = G \cup \{k \triangleright j \mid j \in \overline{j}\}}{\langle F \; \mathsf{x} = \mathsf{y.m}(\overline{\mathsf{z}}); \mathsf{s} \rangle S \; H \; G \; C \quad \rightarrow \quad \langle F' \; \mathsf{s'}; \mathsf{return} \; \mathsf{y''} \rangle \langle F \; \mathsf{x} = \mathsf{y.m}(\overline{\mathsf{z}}); \mathsf{s} \rangle S \; H \; G' \; C}$$

$$\frac{\text{(DRET)}}{F(\mathsf{this}) = k \quad F'(\mathsf{y}) = j \quad G' = G \cup k \triangleright j}{\langle F' \; \mathsf{return} \; \mathsf{y} \rangle \langle F \; \mathsf{x} = \mathsf{y'.m}(\overline{\mathsf{z}}); \mathsf{s} \rangle S \; H \; G \; C \quad \rightarrow \quad \langle F[\mathsf{x} \mapsto j] \; \mathsf{s} \rangle S \; H \; G' \; C}$$

Fig. 3. Concrete semantics

(DCALL) entails pushing a new frame on the stack with local variables initialized to null and formal parameters set to corresponding actual arguments. Function $\mathit{mbody}(\mathsf{C.m})$ retrieves the formal parameters, local variables and method body of the corresponding method. The summary graph records the edges from the receiver of the call (i.e., $F(\mathsf{y}) = k$) to all arguments.

Lemma 1. *The object graph constructed by the above semantics is a superset of the object graph as defined by Clarke et al. [3].*

2.2 Abstract Semantics

We assume a may points-to analysis [15,7] that computes a safe approximation of the heap $\widehat{H}$ and stack $\widehat{S}$. The abstract semantics computes safe approximations of G and C, denoted $\widehat{G}$ and $\widehat{C}$ respectively. As $\widehat{H}$ and $\widehat{S}$ are conservative approximations, the semantics operates on *sets of abstract objects*. Thus, $\widehat{F}(\mathsf{x})$ evaluates to a set of abstract objects, not to a single object. Similarly, fields of an object in $\widehat{H}$ are sets of references (denoted I). We assume that all allocation sites are labelled with an unique identifier.

$$(\textsc{anew})$$
$$\widehat{G}' = \widehat{G} \cup \{i \triangleright j \mid i \in \widehat{F}(\mathsf{this})\} \quad \widehat{C}' = \widehat{C} \cup \{i \triangleright j \mid i \in \widehat{F}(\mathsf{this})\}$$
$$\overline{\langle \widehat{F} \; \mathsf{x} = \mathsf{new}^j \; \mathsf{C}(); \mathsf{s} \rangle \widehat{S} \; \widehat{H} \; \widehat{G} \; \widehat{C} \;\; \leadsto \;\; \langle \widehat{F} \; \mathsf{s} \rangle \widehat{S} \; \widehat{H} \; \widehat{G}' \; \widehat{C}'}$$

$$(\textsc{awrite})$$
$$\mathit{if} \; \mathsf{x} \neq \mathsf{this} \; \mathit{then} \; \widehat{G}' = \widehat{G} \cup \{k \triangleright j \mid k \in \widehat{F}(\mathsf{x}) \; \mathit{and} \; j \in \widehat{F}(\mathsf{y})\} \; \mathit{else} \; \widehat{G}' = \widehat{G}$$
$$\overline{\langle \widehat{F} \; \mathsf{x.f} = \mathsf{y}; \mathsf{s} \rangle \widehat{S} \; \widehat{H} \; \widehat{G} \; \widehat{C} \;\; \leadsto \;\; \langle \widehat{F} \; \mathsf{s} \rangle \widehat{S} \; \widehat{H} \; \widehat{G}' \; \widehat{C}}$$

$$(\textsc{aread})$$
$$\mathit{if} \; \mathsf{y} = \mathsf{this} \; \mathit{then} \; \widehat{G}' = \widehat{G} \; \mathit{else}$$
$$\widehat{G}' = \widehat{G} \cup \{k \triangleright j \mid k \in \widehat{F}(\mathsf{this}) \; \mathit{and} \; i \in \widehat{F}(\mathsf{y}) \; \mathit{and} \; \widehat{H}(i) = \mathsf{C}(\dots I_{\mathsf{f}} \dots) \; \mathit{and} \; j \in I_{\mathsf{f}}\}$$
$$\overline{\langle \widehat{F} \; \mathsf{x} = \mathsf{y.f}; \mathsf{s} \rangle \widehat{S} \; \widehat{H} \; \widehat{G} \; \widehat{C} \;\; \leadsto \;\; \langle \widehat{F} \; \mathsf{s} \rangle \widehat{S} \; \widehat{H} \; \widehat{G}' \; \widehat{C}}$$

Fig. 4. Abstract Semantics. (Partial).

The abstraction function α is specific to our points-to analysis and is chosen so that $\alpha(i) = i'$ where i' is the index of the allocation site that created i. α acts on G in the obvious way: $\alpha(G) = (N, E)$ where $N = \{\alpha(i) \mid i \in G\}$ and $E = \{\alpha(i) \triangleright \alpha(j) \mid i \triangleright j \in G\}$. As the points-to analysis is safe, the following two conditions hold at every step. The first condition ensures the safety of variables, and the second ensures the safety of fields.

$$F(\mathsf{x}) = i \;\; \Rightarrow \;\; \alpha(i) \in \widehat{F}(\mathsf{x})$$
$$H(i) = \mathsf{C}(\dots k_{\mathsf{f}} \dots) \;\; \Rightarrow \;\; \widehat{H}(\alpha(i)) = \mathsf{C}(\dots I_{\mathsf{f}} \dots) \; \mathit{and} \; \alpha(k_{\mathsf{f}}) \in I_{\mathsf{f}}$$

Fig. 4 shows the rules of the semantics that deal with object creation and field read/write. Rule (ANEW) adds new edges to $\widehat{G}$ and $\widehat{C}$ from every abstract receiver i of current frame $\widehat{F}$, to the abstract object j created at allocation site j. Rule (AWRITE) adds new edges to $\widehat{G}$ from every abstract object k in the points-to set of x to every j in the points-to set of y. The only interesting aspect of this rule is that the edges are added only when $\mathsf{x} \neq \mathsf{this}$. The intuition is that when x is this, the relevant edges are already in $\widehat{G}$ and there is no need to add them again.

Lemma 2. $\widehat{G}$ and $\widehat{C}$ are safe. That is, $\alpha(G) \subseteq \widehat{G}$ and $\alpha(C) \subseteq \widehat{C}$ hold.

3 Dominance Inference Analysis

The dominance inference analysis uses the abstract object and creation graphs as constructed by the above abstract semantics. It takes as input an abstract object i, and computes an abstract dominance boundary, which safely approximates the dominance boundaries of the concrete objects represented by i.

3.1 Flow Triples

Let us consider how object references can be transferred. Assume that i has a reference to j. We say that j flows to k from i if k acquires a reference to j from i. This can happen in one of the following four ways:

1. (DWRITE): Local variable y is assigned to a field of local variable x.
2. (DREAD): The field of local variable y is assigned to local variable x.
3. (DCALL): Local variable z is passed as argument to a method of y.
4. (DRET): The local variable y is returned to the receiver of the parent frame.

In each case, the operation adds an edge to the object graph as a side effect. Consider (DWRITE), x.f = y, and let $F(\mathsf{this}, \mathsf{x}, \mathsf{y}) = i, k, j$. Since y holds j, there has to be an edge $i \triangleright j$ in the object graph. Similarly, as x holds k, and there is an edge $i \triangleright k$ in the graph. After the operation, $k \triangleright j$ is added to the graph. We refer to this pattern as a *flow triple* and denote it $\langle i, k, j \rangle$. Consider Fig. 1. Expression i = c.iter() in method X.m causes the iterator object f to flow to x from c. Before the call, c holds c and h in Contain.iter holds f, and thus, $x \triangleright c$ and $c \triangleright f$. After the call, a new edge, $x \triangleright f$ is added to the graph. The pattern is reflected by flow triple $\langle x, c, f \rangle$.

The analysis records flow triples while processing the rules of the abstract semantics, namely (AWRITE), (AREAD), (ACALL) and (ARET). We set relation $isTriple(\langle i, j, k \rangle)$ to true whenever a flow triple is encountered. For example, for (AWRITE), we set $isTriple(\langle i, k, j \rangle)$ to true for every $i \in \widehat{F}(\mathsf{this})$, $k \in \widehat{F}(\mathsf{x})$ and $j \in \widehat{F}(\mathsf{y})$.

A flow triple captures transfer (i.e., exposure) of an object to another object, and is crucial to our analysis. Consider edge $d \triangleright e$ in the abstract graph in Fig. 1. There is no triple that includes this edge, which means that the concrete e referred by d, namely e_2, is not transferred, and therefore it is not exposed to any object but d; the analysis concludes that at runtime d dominates the concrete e it refers to. On the other hand, edge $c \triangleright e$ is part of triple $\langle c, f, e \rangle$ which captures that c's concrete e, e_1, is exposed to f (i.e., we have $f \triangleright e_1$). Edge $c \triangleright f$ is part of triple $\langle x, c, f \rangle$ and thus f is exposed to x (i.e., $x \triangleright f$). The analysis concludes that c does not dominate its run-time e, because said run-time e is exposed to f, and f in turn is exposed to x (i.e., there is a path $x \triangleright f \triangleright e_1$ that does not go through c).

3.2 Analysis Description

We begin with several definitions. The *root* of a graph, is a node j, such that there is a sequence of edges from j to any node i. We assume that G has root root. A *boundary* of a node i is a graph $B_i \subseteq G$ such that i is a root of B_i. A node j *dominates* node j' in boundary B_i if all paths from i to j' go through j. The *dominance boundary* of i in G is the maximal boundary B_i such that for all nodes $j \in B_i$, i dominates j in G. We denote the dominance boundary of i in G as D_i. $closure(G, i)$ computes the transitive closure of i inductively:

$$G'_0 = \{i \triangleright j \mid i \triangleright j \in G\} \quad \dots \quad G'_n = G'_{n-1} \cup \{j \triangleright k \mid j \in G'_{n-1} \text{ and } j \triangleright k \in G\}$$

Algorithm $computeBoundary(i, \widehat{G}, \widehat{C})$
output $\widehat{B}_i$

[1] $Out = \{j \mid isOutside(i, j)\}$

[2] $In = closure(\widehat{C}, i) - Out$

[3] $W = \{i \rhd j \mid i \rhd j \in \widehat{G} \text{ and } j \in Out\},\ W^+ = W$

[4] **while** $W \neq \emptyset$

[5] $W\ -\!\!= k \rhd j$

[6]   **if** $j \in closure(\widehat{C}, i)$

[7] $In\ -\!\!= closure(\widehat{C}, j)$

[8] $Out\ +\!\!= closure(\widehat{C}, j)$

[9]   **foreach** $k' \in closure(\widehat{C}, j)$

[10]   **foreach** $k'' \rhd k' \in \widehat{C}$ and $k'' \in In$

[11]   **if** $k'' \rhd k' \notin W^+$ **then** $W\ +\!\!= k'' \rhd k',\ W^+\ +\!\!= k'' \rhd k'$

[12]   **foreach** $k' \in \widehat{G}$ s.t. $isTriple(\langle k, j, k' \rangle)$

[13] $In\ -\!\!= k',\ Out\ +\!\!= k'$

[14]   **if** $k \rhd k' \notin W^+$ **then** $W\ +\!\!= k \rhd k',\ W^+\ +\!\!= k \rhd k'$

[15]   **foreach** $k' \in \widehat{G}$ s.t. $isTriple(\langle k, k', j \rangle)$ and $k' \in In$

[16]   **if** $k' \rhd j \notin W^+$ **then** $W\ +\!\!= k' \rhd j,\ W^+\ +\!\!= k' \rhd j$

[17]   **foreach** $k' \in \widehat{G}$ s.t. $isTriple(\langle k', k, j \rangle)$ and $k' \in In$

[18]   **if** $k' \rhd j \notin W^+$ **then** $W\ +\!\!= k' \rhd j,\ W^+\ +\!\!= k' \rhd j$

[19] $\widehat{B}_i = \{j \rhd k \mid j \in In \text{ and } k \in In \text{ and } j \rhd k \in \widehat{G}\}$

Fig. 5. computeBoundary returns $\widehat{B}_i$

The analysis uses $closure(G, i)$ on the abstract creation graph. $closure(\widehat{C}, i) = \widehat{C}'$ returns the creation dependences from i. We overload the notation slightly, and use $closure(\widehat{C}, i)$ to refer to the nodes in $\widehat{C}'$, that is, the objects created by i, directly or transitively.

The analysis uses a predicate *isOutside*:

$$isOutside(i, j) \quad = \quad \exists k \,.\, isTriple(\langle k, i, j \rangle)$$

The predicate captures edges $i \rhd j$ that are part of a triple $\langle k, i, j \rangle$. Such a triple indicates that there are paths from **root** to j through k that do not go through i, and therefore, i does not dominate j.

The analysis is presented in Fig. 5. It takes as input an abstract object i and uses $\widehat{G}$ and $\widehat{C}$. It computes $\widehat{B}_i$, a boundary of i in $\widehat{G}$. The analysis maintains sets of abstract objects *In* and *Out*. Set *In* contains the current overapproximation of the set of objects in every concrete dominance boundary. Set *Out* contains the current underapproximation of the set of objects in the frontier of the dominance boundary. The analysis starts with initial sets *In*, *Out* and tracks flow of objects using *isTriple*. Eventually, all potentially exposed objects are removed from *In*. The nodes remaining in *In* and the edges between them form boundary $\widehat{B}_i$. The correctness of the analysis is stated by the following theorem:

Theorem 1. *Let G be any object graph and i be any object in G. Let B_i' be any boundary of i in G. If $\alpha(B_i') \subseteq \widehat{B}_{\alpha(i)}$ then $B_i' \subseteq D_i$.*

The theorem states that the computed boundary $\widehat{B}_{\alpha(i)}$ safely approximates the dominance boundary of every i. That is, for any concrete boundary B'_i represented by $\widehat{B}_{\alpha(i)}$, B'_i is included in D_i; thus i dominates in G all of the nodes in B'_i. In our running example, $\widehat{B}_d$ is the one-edge graph $d \triangleright e$. The theorem states that concrete edge $d \triangleright e_2$ is in the dominance boundary of d, or in other words, d dominates e_2.

4   Application: Ownership Type Inference

We present one application of the dominance inference analysis: ownership type inference. We choose the owner-as-dominator type system of [3] restricted to one ownership parameter. This restriction simplifies the problem; in future work we plan to investigate empirically the necessity for multiple ownership parameters, as well as extend the current analysis with handling of multiple parameters.

4.1   Type System

The type system of [3] assigns an ownership type $\langle p|p' \rangle$ to each local variable, field and allocation site. The type annotation $\mathsf{C}\langle p|p' \rangle \, \mathsf{x}$ (also written as $p\, \mathsf{C}\langle p' \rangle \, \mathsf{x}$), has the following interpretation: p is the owner of the object i referred to by x, and p' is an ownership parameter passed to that object. p takes one of the following three values: rep, own or p (for brevity, we rename owner to own and

$$(\text{TNEW})$$
$$\frac{E(\mathsf{x}) = \mathsf{C}\, t}{E \vdash \mathsf{x} = \text{new } \mathsf{C}\, t}$$

$$(\text{TWRITE})$$
$$\frac{\mathsf{x} \neq \text{this} \quad E(\mathsf{x}) = \mathsf{C}\, t_x \quad typeof(\mathsf{C.f}) = \mathsf{D}\, t_f \quad E(\mathsf{y}) = \mathsf{D}\, t_y \quad adapt(t_f, t_x) = t_y}{E \vdash \mathsf{x.f} = \mathsf{y}}$$

$$(\text{TWRITETHIS})$$
$$\frac{E(\text{this}) = \mathsf{C}\, t' \quad typeof(\mathsf{C.f}) = \mathsf{D}\, t \quad E(\mathsf{y}) = \mathsf{D}\, t}{E \vdash \text{this.f} = \mathsf{y}}$$

$$(\text{TREAD})$$
$$\frac{\mathsf{y} \neq \text{this} \quad E(\mathsf{y}) = \mathsf{C}\, t_y \quad typeof(\mathsf{C.f}) = \mathsf{D}\, t_f \quad E(\mathsf{x}) = \mathsf{D}\, t_x \quad adapt(t_f, t_y) = t_x}{E \vdash \mathsf{x} = \mathsf{y.f}}$$

$$(\text{TREADTHIS})$$
$$\frac{E(\text{this}) = \mathsf{C}\, t' \quad typeof(\mathsf{C.f}) = \mathsf{D}\, t \quad E(\mathsf{x}) = \mathsf{D}\, t}{E \vdash \mathsf{x} = \text{this.f}}$$

$$(\text{TCALL})$$
$$\frac{E(\mathsf{y}) = \mathsf{C}\, t_y \quad typeof(\mathsf{C.m}) = \overline{\mathsf{D}\, t} \to \mathsf{D}'\, t' \quad \mathsf{y} \neq \text{this} \quad E(\mathsf{x}) = \mathsf{D}'\, t_x \quad E(\overline{\mathsf{z}}) = \overline{\mathsf{D}\, t_z} \quad adapt(\overline{t}, t_y) = \overline{t_z} \quad adapt(t', t_y) = t_x}{E \vdash \mathsf{x} = \mathsf{y.m}(\overline{\mathsf{z}})}$$

$$(\text{TCALLTHIS})$$
$$\frac{E(\text{this}) = \mathsf{C}\, t'' \quad typeof(\mathsf{C.m}) = \overline{\mathsf{D}\, t} \to \mathsf{D}'\, t' \quad E(\mathsf{x}) = \mathsf{D}'\, t' \quad E(\overline{\mathsf{z}}) = \overline{\mathsf{D}\, t}}{E \vdash \mathsf{x} = \text{this.m}(\overline{\mathsf{z}})}$$

Fig. 6. Type rules

omit discussion of norep [3]). rep denotes that object i is owned by this, own denotes that i is owned by the owner of this, and p denotes that i's owner is passed from this as an ownership parameter. p' takes the same values. rep is the most precise value, followed by own, followed by p, or in other words, we have rep $<$ own $<$ p. For this paper we impose the following restriction on ownership types $\langle p|p'\rangle : p \leq p'$. Even though types where $p > p'$ (e.g., $\langle p|rep\rangle$) are allowed in ownership types, the properties of the system entail that if the program type checks with $\langle p|p'\rangle$, where $p > p'$, it will type check with $\langle p'|p'\rangle$ as well. Our analysis naturally restricts the inferred types to the following six ownership types, ordered in order of decreasing precision:

$$\langle rep|rep\rangle < \langle rep|own\rangle < \langle rep|p\rangle < \langle own|own\rangle < \langle own|p\rangle < \langle p|p\rangle$$

Note that the above is an ordering relation over the set of types, not a subtyping relation. The ordering relation is necessary to define an inference algorithm based on fixpoint iteration.

The rules for the ownership type system are given in Fig. 6 (see [3] for additional details). The system assigns types $C\ t$, where C is the class type and t is the ownership type. For brevity, features not strictly necessary are omitted. The viewpoint adaptation function $adapt(t, t')$, gives the view of ownership type t from ownership type t':

$$\begin{aligned}
adapt(\langle own|own\rangle, \langle p|p'\rangle) &= \langle p|p\rangle \\
adapt(\langle own|p\rangle, \langle p|p'\rangle) &= \langle p|p'\rangle \\
adapt(\langle p|p\rangle, \langle p|p'\rangle) &= \langle p'|p'\rangle
\end{aligned}$$

Viewpoint adaptation originates from work on Universe types [4]. As it is explained in [4], the intuition behind $adapt$ is the folowing: if object i sees object j as having ownership type t', and j sees k as having ownership type t, then i sees k as having ownership type t'' where $t'' = adapt(t, t')$ (i.e., t'' is the adapted t from the point of view of t'). In [3] viewpoint adaptation is accomplished through substitution function σ and its inverse ψ; we believe that $adapt$ is more intuitive and have taken the liberty to use $adapt$.

$adapt$ is partially defined: no t that contains rep can be viewed from another type t', which accounts for static visibility.

4.2   Type Inference

Fig. 7 shows the ownership type annotations for our example program as inferred by our analysis. The iterator object at allocation site f receives type $\langle own|own\rangle$ (written in the code as own Iter$\langle own\rangle$). The owner is own which means that the container's owner, x for container c and y for container d, is the owner of the iterator. The ownership parameter passed to the iterator is own as well, but it remains unused, as the analysis infers that the iterator's owner, x or y, owns the corresponding array, e_1 or e_2 respectively. Our prototype reports types for allocation sites and fields. It infers types for local variables as they appear in the intermediate representation but does not map these to Java variables. This

```
class Main {
  rep X<rep> x; rep Y<rep> y;
  static void main(String[] arg) {
    Main m = new Main();    [m]
    m.meth();
  }
  void meth() {
    x = new rep X<rep>();    [x]
    x.m();
    y = new rep Y<rep>();    [y]
    y.m();
  }
}
class X<p> {
  rep Contain<rep> c;
  void m() {
    this.c = new rep Contain<rep>();    [c]
    c.put(0,1);
    Iter i = c.iter();
  }
}
```

```
class Y<p> {
  rep Contain<rep> d;
  void m() {
    this.d = new rep Contain<rep>();    [d]
    d.put(1,1);
  }
}
class Contain<p> {
  own int[] e;
  Contain() { this.e = new own int[10]; }    [e]
  void put(int i, int j) { e[i] = j; }
  Iter iter() {
    Iter h = new own Iter<own>(e);    [f]
    return h;
  }
}
class Iter<p> {
  own int[] f;
  Iter(int[] f) { this.f = f; }
}
```

Fig. 7. Ownership types for simple program

is an engineering issue that we plan to address. We stay faithful to the output of our current prototype and show the types it infers.

We infer an ownership type on every edge of $\widehat{G}$. Subsequently, we join these types to compute types for local variables, fields and allocation sites, and show that the computed types type check in the above type system. Each edge $i {\triangleright} j \in \widehat{G}$ receives an ownership type $T(i {\triangleright} j) = \langle p|p' \rangle$. p is j's owner from the point of view of i: if p is rep, then i is the owner of j; otherwise, if p is own, then the owner of i is also the owner of j, and finally, if p_0 is p, then i's ownership parameter is the owner of j. Analogously, p' is j's ownership parameter from the point of view of i. The problem at hand is a constraint problem. We seek type assignment T on the edges of $\widehat{G}$ such that every flow triple $\langle i, j, k \rangle$ in $\widehat{G}$ is well-typed:

$$isTriple(\langle i, j, k \rangle) \Rightarrow adapt(T(j \triangleright k), T(i \triangleright j)) = T(i \triangleright k)$$

These constraints capture the type constraints in Sec. 4.1. Consider rule (TWRITE) which types x.f = y. In the object graph we have flow triple $\langle i, k, j \rangle$ where this holds i, x holds k and y holds j. t_x is the type of x from the point of view of this, and $T(i \triangleright k)$ is the type of k (x) from the point of view of i (this); t_f is the type of field f from the point of view of an object of class C, and $T(k \triangleright j)$ is the type of j from the point of view of k; finally, t_y is the type of y from the point of view of this and $T(i \triangleright j)$ is the type of j from the point of view of i. Our analysis makes $t_x = T(i \triangleright k)$, $t_f = T(k \triangleright j)$ and $t_y = T(i \triangleright j)$. The well-typedness of flow triple $\langle i, k, j \rangle$ (i.e., $adapt(T(k \triangleright j), T(i \triangleright k)) = T(i \triangleright j)$) guarantees the well-typedness of x.f=y (i.e, $adapt(t_f, t_x) = t_y$).

Clearly, there are many assignments that satisfy the *adapt* constraints. For example, a trivial assignment would assign $\langle p|p \rangle$ to all edges in $\widehat{G}$ except edges $\texttt{root} \triangleright i$, to which it would assign $\langle \mathsf{rep}|\mathsf{rep} \rangle$. This assignment is bad however, as it produces a flat (and useless) ownership tree where $\texttt{root}$ is the owner of all objects. A good assignment would assign a large number of rep types.

A *triple typing* is a triple of types $\langle t_{ij}, t_{jk}, t_{ik} \rangle$. A *well-typed triple typing* is a triple typing that meets the *adapt* constraint: $adapt(t_{jk}, t_{ij}) = t_{ik}$. There are 18 well-typed triple typings: t_{jk} ranges over $\langle \mathsf{own}|\mathsf{own} \rangle$, $\langle \mathsf{own}|p \rangle$ and $\langle p|p \rangle$, and t_{ij} ranges over $\langle \mathsf{rep}|\mathsf{rep} \rangle$, $\langle \mathsf{rep}|\mathsf{own} \rangle$, $\langle \mathsf{rep}|p \rangle$, $\langle \mathsf{own}|\mathsf{own} \rangle$, $\langle \mathsf{own}|p \rangle$, $\langle p|p \rangle$ (recall that *adapt* restricts the values of its first argument to account for static visibility). We define an ordering over the set of well-typed triple typings:

$$
\begin{aligned}
\langle\langle \mathsf{rep}|\mathsf{rep}\rangle, \langle \mathsf{own}|\mathsf{own}\rangle, \langle \mathsf{rep}|\mathsf{rep}\rangle\rangle &< \langle\langle \mathsf{rep}|\mathsf{own}\rangle, \langle \mathsf{own}|\mathsf{own}\rangle, \langle \mathsf{rep}|\mathsf{rep}\rangle\rangle &< \\
\langle\langle \mathsf{rep}|p\rangle, \langle \mathsf{own}|\mathsf{own}\rangle, \langle \mathsf{rep}|\mathsf{rep}\rangle\rangle &< \langle\langle \mathsf{rep}|\mathsf{rep}\rangle, \langle \mathsf{own}|p\rangle, \langle \mathsf{rep}|\mathsf{rep}\rangle\rangle &< \\
\langle\langle \mathsf{rep}|\mathsf{own}\rangle, \langle \mathsf{own}|p\rangle, \langle \mathsf{rep}|\mathsf{own}\rangle\rangle &< \langle\langle \mathsf{rep}|p\rangle, \langle \mathsf{own}|p\rangle, \langle \mathsf{rep}|p\rangle\rangle &< \\
\langle\langle \mathsf{rep}|\mathsf{rep}\rangle, \langle p|p\rangle, \langle \mathsf{rep}|\mathsf{rep}\rangle\rangle &< \langle\langle \mathsf{rep}|\mathsf{own}\rangle, \langle p|p\rangle, \langle \mathsf{own}|\mathsf{own}\rangle\rangle &< \\
\langle\langle \mathsf{rep}|p\rangle, \langle p|p\rangle, \langle p|p\rangle\rangle &< \langle\langle \mathsf{own}|\mathsf{own}\rangle, \langle \mathsf{own}|\mathsf{own}\rangle, \langle \mathsf{own}|\mathsf{own}\rangle\rangle &< \\
\langle\langle \mathsf{own}|p\rangle, \langle \mathsf{own}|\mathsf{own}\rangle, \langle \mathsf{own}|\mathsf{own}\rangle\rangle &< \langle\langle \mathsf{own}|\mathsf{own}\rangle, \langle \mathsf{own}|p\rangle, \langle \mathsf{own}|\mathsf{own}\rangle\rangle &< \\
\langle\langle \mathsf{own}|p\rangle, \langle \mathsf{own}|p\rangle, \langle \mathsf{own}|p\rangle\rangle &< \langle\langle \mathsf{own}|\mathsf{own}\rangle, \langle p|p\rangle, \langle \mathsf{own}|\mathsf{own}\rangle\rangle &< \\
\langle\langle \mathsf{own}|p\rangle, \langle p|p\rangle, \langle p|p\rangle\rangle &< \langle\langle p|p\rangle, \langle \mathsf{own}|\mathsf{own}\rangle, \langle p|p\rangle\rangle &< \\
\langle\langle p|p\rangle, \langle \mathsf{own}|p\rangle, \langle p|p\rangle\rangle &< \langle\langle p|p\rangle, \langle p|p\rangle, \langle p|p\rangle\rangle
\end{aligned}
$$

Triple typings with two rep owners are most precise, followed by triple typings with one rep owner, followed by triple typings with three own owners, etc. The least precise typing is the one where all three edges have type $\langle p|p \rangle$. Function *raiseTriple* takes a flow triple $\langle i, j, k \rangle$ as an argument and returns the smallest (i.e., most precise) typing $\langle t_{ij}, t_{jk}, t_{ik} \rangle$ in the above ordering, such that $T(i \triangleright j) \leq t_{ij}$ and $T(j \triangleright k) \leq t_{jk}$ and $T(i \triangleright k) \leq t_{ik}$. Intuitively, when the analysis encounters a flow triple $\langle i, j, k \rangle$, which is not well-typed, it invokes *raiseTriple* to find the most precise well-typed typing that is larger than the typing on $\langle i, j, k \rangle$. It then raises the types on $\langle i, j, k \rangle$ to $\langle t_{ij}, t_{jk}, t_{ik} \rangle$ to make $\langle i, j, k \rangle$ well-typed. Function *adjTriples* takes an edge $i \triangleright j$ as an argument and returns the set of all flow triples adjacent to this edge: $\{\langle i, j, k \rangle\} \cup \{\langle i, k', j \rangle\} \cup \{\langle k'', i, j \rangle\}$. If an edge changes its type, the change affects all adjacent triples. The analysis is shown in Fig. 8. It uses the dominance analysis from Sec. 3. Procedure *assignEdgeTypes* assigns an initial type to every edge in $\widehat{G}$ as follows: if the edge is in the dominance boundary of its source, then its initial type is $\langle \mathsf{rep}|\mathsf{rep} \rangle$; otherwise, its type is $\langle \mathsf{own}|\mathsf{own} \rangle$ (lines 1-5). Unfortunately, not all flow triples will be well-typed under this initial assignment. The analysis collects the triples that are not well-typed (lines 6-8), and invokes *resolve* (line 9), which repeatedly raises types until it reaches a fixpoint. Procedure *assignTypes* assigns types on locals and fields. For each variable x, it joins the types of the edges in $\widehat{G}$ that correspond to x (line 8); notation $\bigvee$ has the standard lattice-theoretic interpretation as the join of all values — $E(x)$ is assigned the largest $T(i \triangleright j), i \triangleright j \in M$, according to the ordering of ownership types from Sec. 4.1. If one of the edges in M has a type smaller than $E(x)$, the analysis raises its type to $E(x)$ and places its adjacent triples on the conflict list (lines 5-8). The procedure repeats for fields.

procedure $assignEdgeTypes(\widehat{G})$
output T
[1] foreach $i \triangleright j \in \widehat{G}$
[2]   if $i \triangleright j \in \widehat{B}_i$
[3] $T(i \triangleright j) = \langle \mathsf{rep}|\mathsf{rep}\rangle$
[4]   else
[5] $T(i \triangleright j) = \langle \mathsf{own}|\mathsf{own}\rangle$
[6] foreach $\langle i,j,k\rangle$ s.t. $isTriple(\langle i,j,k\rangle)$
[7]   if $adapt(T(j \triangleright k), T(i \triangleright j)) \neq T(i \triangleright k)$
[8] $K += \langle i,j,k\rangle$
[9] $T = resolve(\widehat{G}, K, T)$
[10] return T

procedure $resolve(\widehat{G}, K, T)$
output T
[1] $W = K$
[2] while $W \neq \emptyset$
[3] $W -= \langle i,j,k\rangle$
[4] $\langle t_{ij}, t_{jk}, t_{ik}\rangle = raiseTriple(\langle i,j,k\rangle)$
[5]   if $t_{ij} \neq T(i \triangleright j)$
[6] $T(i \triangleright j) = t_{ij}$
[7] $W += adjTriples(i \triangleright j)$
[8]   if $t_{jk} \neq T(j \triangleright k)$
[9] $T(j \triangleright k) = t_{jk}$
[10] $W += adjTriples(j \triangleright k)$
[11]   if $t_{ik} \neq T(i \triangleright k)$
[12] $T(i \triangleright k) = t_{ik}$
[13] $W += adjTriples(i \triangleright k)$
[14] return T

procedure $assignTypes(\widehat{G}, \widehat{H}, \widehat{S}, T)$
output well-typed E, T
[1] $change = true$
[2] while $change$
[3] $change = false, K = \emptyset$
[4]   foreach class $\mathsf{C} \in$ program P
[5]   foreach method $\mathsf{m} \in \mathsf{C}$
[6]   foreach variable $\mathsf{x} \in \mathsf{m}$
[7] $M = \{i \triangleright j \mid i \triangleright j \in \widehat{G}$ and $i \in \widehat{F}(\mathsf{this_m})$ and $j \in \widehat{F}(\mathsf{x})\}$
[8] $E(\mathsf{x}) = \bigvee_{i \triangleright j \in M} T(i \triangleright j)$
[9]   foreach $i \triangleright j \in M$
[10]   if $E(\mathsf{x}) \neq T(i \triangleright j)$
[11] $T(i \triangleright j) = E(\mathsf{x})$
[12] $change = true$
[13] $K += adjTriples(i \triangleright j)$
[14]   foreach field $\mathsf{f} \in \mathsf{C}$
[15] $M = \{i \triangleright j \mid i \triangleright j \in \widehat{G}$ and $\widehat{H}(i) = \mathsf{C}(...I_f...)$ and $j \in I_f\}$
[16] $E(\mathsf{C.f}) = \bigvee_{i \triangleright j \in M} T(i \triangleright j)$
[17]   foreach $i \triangleright j \in M$
[18]   if $E(\mathsf{C.f}) \neq T(i \triangleright j)$
[19] $T(i \triangleright j) = E(\mathsf{C.f})$
[20] $change = true$
[21] $K += adjTriples(i \triangleright j)$
[22] $T = resolve(\widehat{G}, K, T)$
[23] return E, T

Fig. 8. Type assignment

Theorem 2. *Let E be the type assignment for program P computed by the analysis. P is well-typed in the system from Sec. 4.1.*

Discussion. The above analysis, a fixpoint iteration, can be applied to *any* initial type assignment. An optimistic initial assignment would assign a large number of rep types, and a pessimistic assignment would assign less rep types and more own and p types. An unwise initial assignment would affect scalability, precision or both. If the assignment is overly optimistic, the majority of edges would need to be lowered from rep (since most edges are not rep anyway), and this would likely prohibit scaling the analysis beyond small programs. On the other hand, if the assignment is overly pessimistic, the analysis will converge faster to a fixpoint, but will lose precision. We conjecture that our initial assignment, which makes use of dominance inference, is key to the scalability and precision of ownership type inference. It would immediately filter out edges that cannot be rep; as a result, very few edges would change type (predominantly from $\langle \mathsf{own}|\mathsf{own}\rangle$ to $\langle \mathsf{p}|\mathsf{p}\rangle$), and the analysis would scale well. Also, few edges that can be rep, would not be assigned rep in the initial assignment.

5   Implementation

The object graph analysis, dominance inference analysis and type inference analysis are implemented in Java using Soot 2.2.3 [17] and the Andersen-style points-to analysis provided by Spark [7]. We performed whole-program analysis with the Sun JDK 1.4.1 libraries. All experiments were done on a MacBook Pro with 4GB of RAM. The implementation, which includes Soot and Spark, was run with a max heap size of 1400MB; however, all benchmarks ran within a memory footprint of 800MB. Native methods are handled by utilizing the models provided by Soot. Reflection is handled by specifying the dynamically loaded classes which Spark uses to appropriately resolve reflection calls.

Our benchmark suite is presented in Table 1. It includes 6 software components (from gzip through number) which we have used in previous work and are familiar with. Each component is transformed into a whole program by attaching an artificial main method to complete it which allows whole-program analysis [16]. In addition, the suite includes 12 whole programs: jdepend, javad, JATLite and undo, benchmarks soot and sablecc from the Ashes suite, polyglot, and antlr, bloat, jython, pmd and ps from the DaCapo benchmark suite version beta051009. #Class gives the size of the benchmarks in classes; #Meth gives the size of the benchmarks in methods (user and library) reachable by Spark.

5.1   Results

We report dominance inference results on allocation sites and instance fields of reference type. Multicolumn **Create** in Table 1 shows the number of object creation sites in user classes, excluding String and StringBuffer. Column dom shows the number inferred as dominated by their creating object. Multicolumn **Fields** shows analogous information for instance fields of reference type in user classes, again excluding fields of type String and StringBuffer.

On average, for the 12 large benchmarks, roughly 50% of all creation sites and 30% of all fields were reported as dom. This suggests that *ownership occurs frequently* in real-world object-oriented programs. The high percentage of dom creation sites is not surprising because programs typically create a large number of temporary objects that remain method-local (roughly 30% according to one study [15]). Our analysis captures method-local objects, as well as "object-local" objects (i.e., objects assigned to fields, but remaining in the boundary of their creating "owner" object). These results suggest that the dominance analysis will fare well in another application: escape analysis. Column **Pt** shows the running time for Spark's points-to analysis, **Dom** shows the running time for dominance inference. Except for polyglot, an outlier for all analyses, inference scales well, completing in under 200 seconds.

Additionally, Table 2 shows type inference results for benchmark javad. javad, 4000LOC, was annotated manually and type-checked by a checker built on top of the Checkers framework [13]. Table 2 lists 47 creation sites instead of 48 because one site was static and annotated as norep (see [3]). Interestingly, the additional constraints that ownership types impose on dominance, do not cause dom annotations to become own or p. All but one creation site, and all but one field

Table 1. Information about benchmarks and dominance inference results

Program	Description	Size		Create		Fields		Time	
		#Class	#Meth	#Create	dom	#Field	dom	Pt	Dom
gzip	GZIP IO streams	6	3819	35	31	7	4	25s	2s
zip	ZIP IO streams	6	3844	29	21	10	5	25s	3s
checked	streams/checksums	4	3766	9	8	2	0	96s	2s
collator	text collation	15	3868	40	31	17	9	25s	3s
breaks	iter. over text	13	3822	270	268	7	0	26s	3s
number	number formatting	10	3880	124	119	3	1	25s	4s
jdepend	Quality metrics	17	3962	84	66	29	19	26s	3s
javad	Decompiler	41	3838	48	37	36	19	26s	2s
JATLite	Agent system	45	6279	273	117	142	35	42s	20s
undo	Undo functionality	237	5644	728	313	290	56	50s	31s
soot	Analysis framework	579	6046	703	274	283	64	40s	179s
sablecc	Parser generator	300	7970	1261	865	284	25	49s	34s
polyglot	Compiler	267	7449	1180	278	431	52	141s	365s
antlr	Parser generator	126	5102	596	434	152	38	39s	13s
bloat	Bytecode optimizer	289	6402	1047	453	449	79	41s	95s
jython	Python interpreter	163	5606	520	143	206	41	38s	122s
pmd	Source analyzer	718	8653	374	163	114	46	67s	105s
ps	Postscript engine	200	5396	424	113	19	7	38s	136s

Table 2. Type inference results for benchmark javad

Create							Fields						
rep|rep	rep|own	rep|p	own|own	own|p	p|p	rep|rep	rep|own	rep|p	own|own	own|p	p|p
6	5	24	1	10	1	2	5	11	1	6	11

inferred as dom by dominance inference, stay rep after type inference. We do not report inference results on the other programs, because we have not type checked those programs; we are in the process of integrating the inference analysis with the type checker, which will enable automatic inference and checking.

5.2   Precision

Addressing the issue of precision is highly non-trivial. To the best of our knowledge, there are no large programs annotated with ownership types, that could be used to objectively evaluate an ownership inference analysis. In order to evaluate the precision of our analysis, we performed a study of *absolute precision* [16,8] on a subset of the fields. Specifically, we considered all fields in components gzip through number and all fields in javad. This accounted for 82 fields. Of these, 38 were reported as dom and 44 were reported as not dom.

To evaluate the precision of the dominance inference, we examined every field f that was not reported as dom, and attempted to prove exposure. That is, we attempted to show that there is an execution such that an object j stored in field f of object i is exposed outside of i, or more formally, that i does not dominate j

in the concrete object graph. In *every case*, we were able to prove such exposure. In addition, we examined every dom field. Although the analysis is proven safe and therefore, a dom field must be indeed dominated by its enclosing object, we conducted the detailed examination in order to gain further confidence in the functional correctness of the implementation. In *every case*, the dom field was indeed dominated as expected. Therefore, for this set of 82 fields, the inference analysis achieved very good precision.

6 Related Work

Despite significant effort on ownership types, ownership inference has received much less attention. Work on dynamic ownership inference includes [14,11,5,19]. In their essence, these works take the same approach. They reason about dominance (and hence ownership) on dynamic (i.e., concrete) object graphs by applying well-known dominator algorithms [6] on those graphs. They face challenges such as large concrete object graphs [14,11] and runtime overhead [19], and they are inherently unsafe since inferred dominance (i.e., ownership) holds only on observed runs. Our dominance inference is fundamentally different: it performs deep semantic analysis on the abstract object graph and avoids the problems inherent in dynamic analysis. The empirical investigation suggests that it avoids the usual pitfall of static analysis (i.e., imprecision), and presents a "sweet spot" in the spectrum: an inexpensive but precise analysis. Ma and Foster present Uno [9], a static analysis-based tool for inference of encapsulation properties in Java programs. Among other things, their analysis computes what fields are *owned*. They report 16% of the fields across their benchmarks as owned, while we report (roughly) 30% as owned. The difference can be explained by the difference in the inferred ownership. Uno infers exclusive ownership: that is, an owned object must be accessed only by its owner. Our model is less-restrictive: an owned object can be passed to other owned objects. We inferred exclusive ownership in our framework and we found that 20% of all fields were exclusively owned. This result is close to Uno's 16%. It suggests that objects often flow to other objects, while remaining encapsulated in their owner and therefore, exclusive ownership may not be enough. We observed multiple such cases in our case studies. Aldrich et al. [1] present an ownership type system which includes annotations for uniqueness, ownership, sharing and parameters. They present a type inference analysis and report preliminary results on small programs and Java library classes. Their inference algorithm is conceptually different from ours; it creates several kinds of constraints at the level of the source, namely equality constraints, component constraints and instantiation constraints; subsequently, it uses a worklist-based procedure to resolve the constraints. Our analysis solves one kind of constraints, essentially equality constraints defined with *adapt*; it relies on dominance inference to start at a "good point" in the solution space, which, we conjecture, speeds-up the resolution procedure. It is difficult to judge which analysis is better because the analysis from [1] is never fully described; [1] focuses on the type system and experience with type checking, not on type inference as our work does. Aldrich has pointed out that reasoning about multiple ownership parameters presents significant difficulty. In this sense, we solve a simpler problem, as for this paper we focus on a system with one ownership parameter; we plan to address multiple ownership parameters in future work. Finally, we contrast this work with our own previous work [8] and [10]. This paper presents a substantial extension in that it computes abstract ownership *boundaries*, while [8] reasoned about specific edges in the object graph. The work in [10] presents a preliminary version of the dominance inference analysis.

7 Conclusion

We have presented a novel static dominance inference analysis. One direction of future work is to build a framework for ownership inference. Different inference analyses, each addressing a specific ownership discipline, can be coded easily on top of dominance inference.

References

1. Aldrich, J., Kostadinov, V., Chambers, C.: Alias annotations for program understanding. In: OOPSLA, pp. 311–330 (2002)
2. Boyapati, C., Liskov, B., Shrira, L.: Ownership types for object encapsulation. In: POPL, pp. 213–223 (2003)
3. Clarke, D., Potter, J., Noble, J.: Ownership types for flexible alias protection. In: OOPSLA, pp. 48–64 (1998)
4. Cunningham, D., Dietl, W., Drossopoulou, S., Francalanza, A., Muller, P., Summers, A.: Universe types for topology and encapsulation. In: FMCO (2008)
5. Dietl, W., Müller, P.: Runtime Universe type inference. In: IWACO (2007)
6. Lengauer, T., Tarjan, R.: A fast algorithm for finding dominators in a flowgraph. ACM TOPLAS 1(1), 121–141 (1979)
7. Lhoták, O., Hendren, L.: Scaling java points-to analysis using SPARK. In: Hedin, G. (ed.) CC 2003. LNCS, vol. 2622, pp. 153–169. Springer, Heidelberg (2003)
8. Liu, Y., Milanova, A.: Ownership and immutability inference for UML-based object access control. In: ICSE, pp. 323–332 (2007)
9. Ma, K., Foster, J.: Inferring aliasing and encapsulation properties for Java. In: OOPSLA, pp. 423–440 (2007)
10. Milanova, A.: Static inference of Universe types. In: IWACO (2008)
11. Mitchell, N.: The runtime structure of object ownership. In: Hu, Q. (ed.) ECOOP 2006. LNCS, vol. 4067, pp. 74–98. Springer, Heidelberg (2006)
12. Naik, M., Park, C.-S., Sen, K., Gay, D.: Effective static deadlock detection. In: ICSE, pp. 386–396 (2009)
13. M. Papi, M. Ali, T. Correa Jr., J. Perkins, and M. Ernst. Practical pluggable types for Java. In: ISSTA, pp. 261–272 (2008)
14. Potanin, A., Noble, J., Biddle, R.: Checking ownership and confinement. Concurrency - Practice and Experience 16(7), 671–687 (2004)
15. Rountev, A., Milanova, A., Ryder, B.: Points-to analysis for Java using annotated constraints. In: OOPSLA, pp. 43–55 (2001)

16. Rountev, A., Milanova, A., Ryder, B.G.: Fragment class analysis for testing of polymorphism in Java software. IEEE TSE 30(6), 372–386 (2004)
17. Vallée-Rai, R., Gagnon, E.M., Hendren, L., Lam, P., Pominville, P., Sundaresan, V.: Optimizing java bytecode using the soot framework: Is it feasible? In: Watt, D.A. (ed.) CC 2000. LNCS, vol. 1781, pp. 18–34. Springer, Heidelberg (2000)
18. Vaziri, M., Tip, F., Dolby, J., Hammer, C., Vitek, J.: A type system for data-centric synchronization. In: D'Hondt, T. (ed.) ECOOP 2010. LNCS, vol. 6183, pp. 304–328. Springer, Heidelberg (2010)
19. Vetchev, M., Yahav, E., Yorsh, G.: Phalanx: Parallel checking of expressive heap assertions. In: ISMM, pp. 41–50 (2010)

A Case of Visitor versus Interpreter Pattern

Mark Hills[1,2], Paul Klint[1,2], Tijs van der Storm[1], and Jurgen Vinju[1,2]

[1] Centrum Wiskunde & Informatica, Amsterdam, The Netherlands
[2] INRIA Lille Nord Europe, France

Abstract. We compare the Visitor pattern with the Interpreter pattern, investigating a single case in point for the Java language. We have produced and compared two versions of an interpreter for a programming language. The first version makes use of the Visitor pattern. The second version was obtained by using an automated refactoring to transform uses of the Visitor pattern to uses of the Interpreter pattern. We compare these two nearly equivalent versions on their maintenance characteristics and execution efficiency. Using a tailored experimental research method we can highlight differences and the causes thereof. The contributions of this paper are that it isolates the choice between Visitor and Interpreter in a realistic software project and makes the difference experimentally observable.

1 Introduction

Design patterns [7] provide reusable, named solutions for problems that arise when designing object-oriented systems. While in some cases it is clear which pattern should be used, in others multiple patterns could apply. When this happens, the designer has to carefully weigh the pros and cons ("consequences" [7]) of each option as applied both to the current design and to plans for future evolution of the system.

In this paper we describe one of these choices in the context of an interpreter for the Rascal[1] programming language [13], namely: the choice between structuring an abstract syntax tree-based language interpreter according to either the Visitor or the Interpreter pattern. While it seems clear (Section 3) that either pattern will do from a *functional* point of view, it is unclear what the *non-functional* quality of the interpreter will be in each case. In theory, the Interpreter pattern might have lower method call overhead because it does not involve double dispatch, it should allow easier extension with new language features, and it should be easier to add local state to AST nodes. In theory, the Visitor pattern should allow easier extension with new kinds of operations on AST nodes and should allow better encapsulation of state required by such operations. These and other considerations are exemplified in what has become known as the "expression problem" [18,4]. In this paper we investigate how the assumptions embedded in the expression problem manifest themselves in the context of a concrete case.

Our initial implementation of the Rascal interpreter was fully based on the Visitor design pattern. This choice was motivated mainly by a general argument for modularity, with each function (or algorithm) on the AST hierarchy separated into a single class. To be able to experiment with the decision of whether to use Visitor or Interpreter,

---

[1] http://www.rascal-mpl.org

J. Bishop and A. Vallecillo (Eds.): TOOLS 2011, LNCS 6705, pp. 228–243, 2011.
© Springer-Verlag Berlin Heidelberg 2011

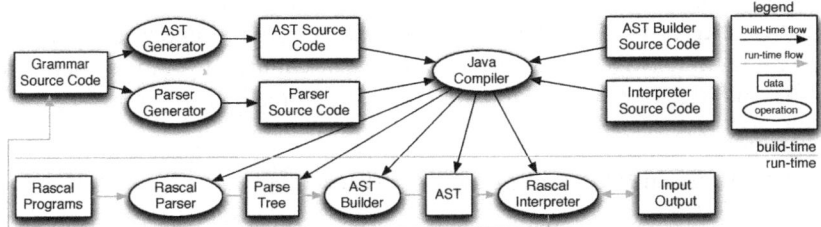

Fig. 1. Simplified build-time and run-time architecture of Rascal

we have used Rascal itself to automate an ad-hoc refactoring transforming the visitor-based design to an interpreter-based design (the details of this refactoring are outside the scope of the current paper, but we do explain the relevance of the *existence* of such an automatic refactoring for our approach). This then allows us to conduct a comparison between two implementations varying only in the choice of design pattern. In this comparison we focus on ease of maintenance and runtime performance. We show the differences between using the Visitor and Interpreter patterns in the Rascal interpreter by analysis of real maintenance scenarios and some initial performance measurements. While the results cannot be directly generalized to other software systems, we expect that other designers of tree-centric object-oriented software—compilers, interpreters, XML processors, etc.—will benefit.

Roadmap. Section 2 describes the Rascal interpreter, including the transformation from the Visitor to the Interpreter pattern, at a level of detail necessary to follow the remainder of the paper. Section 3 then explains the research methods we use to compare the maintainability and performance between the two different versions. Following this, Section 4 and Section 5 then apply these methods to analyze the differences in (respectively) maintainability and performance. Finally, we conclude in Section 6.

2   Design Patterns in the Rascal Interpreter

Rascal is a domain-specific language for meta-programming: to analyze, transform or generate other programs. While it has primitives for parsing, pattern matching, search, template instantiation, etc., it is designed to look like well-known languages such as C and Java. To facilitate integration into Eclipse[2], Rascal is implemented in Java and itself. Figure 1 depicts Rascal's build-time and run-time architecture. Because Rascal source code may contain both context-free grammars and concrete fragments of sentences for these grammars, the run-time and the build-time stages depend on each other.

The interpreter's core is based on classes representing abstract syntax trees (AST) of Rascal programs. These classes implement the Composite pattern (Figure 2) and a part of the Visitor pattern (Figure 3). Each syntactic category is represented by an abstract class, such as `Expression` or `Statement`. These contain one or more nested classes that extend the surrounding class for a particular language construct, such as `If`, `While`

---

[2] http://www.eclipse.org

(both contained in and extending `Statement`), and `Addition` (contained in and extending `Expression`). All AST classes also inherit, directly or indirectly, from `AbstractAST`. AST classes provide access to children by way of getter methods, e.g., `If` and `While` have a `getConditional()` method.

2.1   Creating and Processing Abstract Syntax Trees

Rascal has many AST classes (about 140 abstract classes and 400 concrete classes). To facilitate language evolution the code for these classes, along with the Rascal parser, is generated from the Rascal grammar. The AST code generator also creates a Visitor interface (`IASTVisitor`), containing methods for all the node types in the hierarchy, and a default visitor that returns null for every node type (`NullASTVisitor`). This class prevents us from having to implement a visit method for all AST node

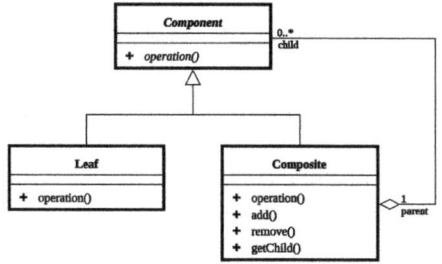

Fig. 2. The Composite Pattern[3]

types, especially useful when certain algorithms focus on a small subset of nodes. Naturally, each AST node implements the `accept(IASTVisitor<T> visitor)` method by calling the appropriate visit method. For example, `Statement.If` contains:

```
public <T> accept(IASTVisitor<T> v) {
    return v.visitStatementIf(this);
}
```

The desire to generate this code played a significant role in initially deciding to use the Visitor pattern. We wanted to avoid having to manually edit generated code. Using the Visitor pattern, all functionality that operates on the AST nodes can be separated from the generated code. When the Rascal grammar changes, the AST hierarchy is regenerated. Many implementations of `IASTVisitor` will contain Java compiler errors and warnings because the signature of visit methods will have changed. This is very

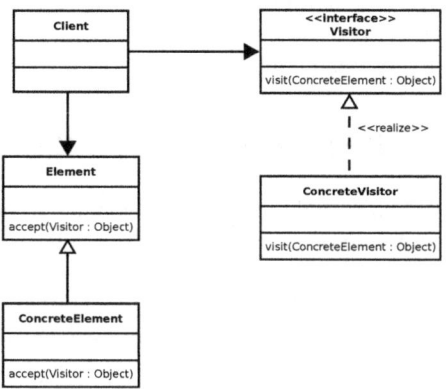

Fig. 3. The Visitor Pattern[4]

helpful for locating the code that needs to be changed due to a language change. Most of the visitor classes actually extend `NullASTVisitor` though, which is why it is

---

[3] Image from `http://en.wikipedia.org/wiki/Composite_pattern`
[4] Image from `http://en.wikipedia.org/wiki/Visitor_pattern`

important that each method they override is tagged with the @Override tag[5]. Note that the class used to construct ASTs at runtime, ASTBuilder, uses reflection to map parse tree nodes into the appropriate AST classes. Hence, this code does not have to change when we change the grammar of the Rascal language.

2.2 A Comparison with the Interpreter Pattern

Considering that our design already employs the Composite pattern, the difference in design complexity between the Visitor and Interpreter patterns is striking (Figure 4). The Composite pattern contains all the elements for the Interpreter pattern (abstract classes that are instantiated by concrete ones)—only an interpret method needs to be added to all relevant classes.

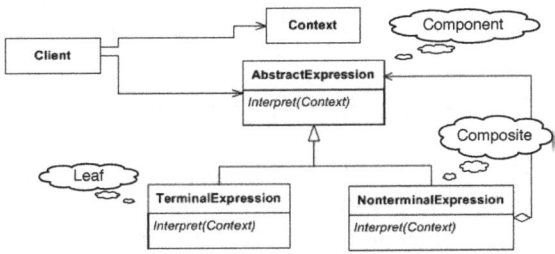

Fig. 4. The Interpreter Pattern with references to Composite (Figure 2).[6]

So rather than having to add new concepts, such as a Visitor interface, the accept method and NullASTVisitor, the Interpreter pattern builds on the existing infrastructure of Composite and reuses it. Also, by adding more interpret methods (varying either the name or the static type) it is possible to reuse the Interpreter design pattern again and again without having to add additional classes. However, as a consequence, understanding each algorithm as a whole is now complicated by the fact that the methods implementing it are scattered over different AST classes. Additionally, there is the risk that methods contributing to different algorithms get tangled because a single AST class may have to manage the combined state required for all implemented algorithms. The experiments discussed in Section 4 help make this tradeoff between separation of concerns and complexity more concrete.

2.3 Refactoring from Visitor to Interpreter using Rascal

We constructed an automated refactoring tool for transforming Visitor classes to Interpreter methods. It is the key to our research method (see Figure 5). However, the details of constructing the refactoring are out of the scope of the current paper. They can instead be found online [11]. The benefits of an automated approach are:

Reproducible target code makes it easy to replay the refactoring during experimentation, while also allowing others to literally replicate the experiment;

Automated analysis checks that semantics are preserved and the transformation is complete (i.e., no visitors are missed during the transformation);

---

[5] If a method is tagged with @Override the Java compiler will warn if it does not override any method anymore.

[6] Image from http://en.wikipedia.org/wiki/Interpreter_pattern, created by Jing Guo Yao and licensed under the Creative Commons Attribution-ShareAlike 3.0 License.

One thing at a time automated refactoring does not suffer from the temptation during a large manual refactoring to make other changes as well, which would confound the analysis and hinder reproducibility.

The tool is implemented using a combination of Rascal and Java. The Java code is used to access features of the Eclipse JDT[7] used for fact extraction, source code cleanup, and refactoring. The Rascal code is used to analyze and aggregate this information, to call JDT refactorings with the right parameters and to generate the new code.

3 Comparing Design Patterns

The research strategy of this paper can be characterized as idiographic [1]: we seek to understand a single phenomenon (i.e. Visitor vs. Interpreter) in a particular context (the implementation of Rascal). The context for our study is further established by fixing the following variables: programming language (Java), application area (programming language interpreter), and the use of the Eclipse IDE. We assume that the AST classes used in the interpreter are implemented using the Composite pattern. Finally, we require all regression tests for the interpreter to run unchanged as we vary the system.

Within this context, the primary free variable is the choice between the patterns we are comparing: Visitor and Interpreter. The two dependent variables we wish to measure are differences in maintainability and runtime performance between two versions of the interpreter that use the two design patterns but are otherwise functionally equivalent. The dependent variables are measured in a number of maintenance scenarios categorized according to ISO 14764 [12]: *perfective* (speed optimization), *corrective* (bug fixes), and *adaptive* (new features).

3.1 Measuring Differences in Runtime Performance

In Section 5 we measure differences in speed between the two versions of the interpreter, as well as showing the improvement in both versions from one of the maintenance scenarios. We use a benchmark of running 4 different Rascal programs, designed as representative workloads. In our experiments runtime performance is measured in wall-clock time, averaged over multiple runs, with an initial run of each test to try to minimize differences from just-in-time compilation during later runs.

3.2 Measuring Differences in Maintainability

Differences in maintainability are less straight-forward to measure. A large number of metrics exist for measuring object-oriented systems [10], including metrics specifically aimed at maintenance. One such metric, "Maintenance Complexity"[8], is defined as an aggregate sum of weighted occurrences of uses of programming language constructs. While this may be used to get an indication of the complexity of maintaining a single method, it is not clear how it could be used to compare the complexity of two systems using different design patterns. In other efforts there have been attempts to quantify

---

[7] Java Development Toolkit; http://www.eclipse.org/jdt
[8] By Mark Miller (unpublished).

differences between systems using design patterns and those without, focusing either on understandability [2], maintenance effort [17], or modularity [8].

Metrics such as the maintainability index (MI) [16,3] and the SIG maintainability model (SMM) [9] also produce numerical results that help predict the long-term maintenance cost. The MI does not allow for cause analysis, while the SMM does. The difference lies in the (ir)reversibility of aggregation formulas. Both metrics produce a system-wide indicator of maintainability independent of the kind of changes that are applied to it. This level of abstraction is useful for managers who wish to track the evolution of a large software system, but is less useful for studying the effect of choosing design patterns. In reality, any object-oriented system is more amenable for certain kinds of changes than others.

Instead of the above metrics, we opt for a metric inspired by the concept of *Evolution Complexity* [5,15] (EC). EC was devised by Mens and Eden to provide a foundation for reasoning about the complexity of changes to software systems. EC is defined as the computational complexity of a meta program that transforms a system to obtain a new version. Each transformation is implied by a shift in requirements. As opposed to the aforementioned system-wide metrics, this provides a means to reason about maintainability, subject to specific evolution scenarios and specific parts of a system.

In the current paper we need a more precise measure that not only measures the effort to transform the system, but also the effort to analyze it before applying any transformations, the cost of which can govern the overall cost of maintenance [14]— one first needs to know where and what to change before actually making any changes. To account for this, we introduce the concept of a *maintenance scenarios*, which then allows us to determine the complexity of maintenance.

Definition 1. *A maintenance scenario S is a description of a required change to a program P that implies a set of changes in its source code. Implicitly, all previous requirements—unless contradicting the current change—need to be conserved.*

Definition 2. *The complexity of maintenance* COM *is the computational complexity of a meta program (M_S) that analyses and transforms the source code of program P to implement a specific maintenance scenario S:*

$$\text{COM}(P, M_S) = \text{COMPUTATIONALCOMPLEXITY}(M_S(P)).$$

This definition implies a detailed subjective model of maintainability that depends on the design of the system, the maintenance scenario, the way the analysis and transformation is executed, and the definition of computational complexity. With so many subjective variables, it is impossible to use it to estimate maintainability of a specific system. Such an absolute complexity metric would be too sensitive to differences in interpretation. Instead, we use it as a *comparative* framework, specifically for comparing two systems that are equal in all but one aspect: the choice between two design patterns.

Figure 5 describes our framework to compare the maintainability of two versions n and m of a given system. Version m has been derived from version n by way of an automated refactoring, i.e. a meta-program that preserves the functional behavior of version n but may change some non-functional characteristics. In our case study, version n is the Rascal interpreter based on the Visitor pattern and version m is the version of the Rascal interpreter based on the Interpreter pattern. The details of this automated

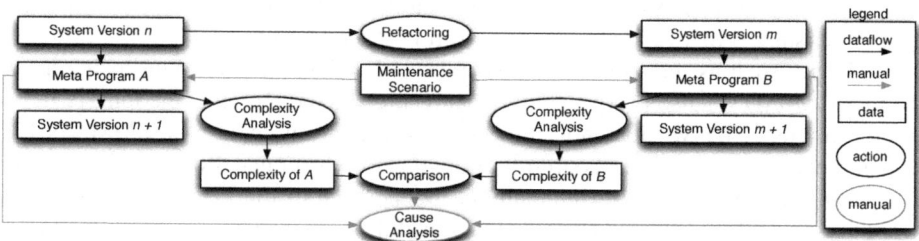

Fig. 5. Comparative framework for observing differences in maintainability

refactoring are not relevant for the present analysis, but it is important to note that it is semantics preserving. The maintainability of both versions is now compared by designing a number of maintenance scenarios and applying them to both versions. For each maintenance scenario we do the following:

- Perform the maintenance scenario manually.
- Create an abstract description of this activity by expressing it as meta-program.
- Compare the computational complexity of the meta-programs needed to carry out the maintenance scenario for versions n and m.

This allows us to objectively calculate the complexity of the scenarios as applied to the two versions while at the same time pinpointing exact causes of the differences.

Results produced by this framework can be replicated by anybody given the source code of the two versions, a precise description of the meta programs and the scenarios, and a precise description of the complexity analysis. In Section 4.1 we define a "virtual machine for maintenance" that provides the foundation for our current comparison.

3.3   Alternative Methods to Measure Maintainability

Our framework tries to abstract from the human programmer that actually carries out the maintenance tasks. This makes it easier to replicate our results. Alternative ways of studying maintenance do focus on human beings, like programmer observation (e.g., [6]) and using models of cognition (e.g., [19]).

Statistical observation of the efficiency of a group of programmers while doing maintenance tasks can be done to summarize the effects of differences between design patterns. However, such an (expensive) study can not explain the causes of these effects, while our method can. The use of cognitive modeling can also shed light on the causes of complexity. With this method one explicitly constructs a representation of the knowledge that a human being is using while analyzing and modifying source code. Complexity measures for such representations exist as well and have been used to study understandability of programming in different kinds of languages [19]. We have not opted for this approach because such detailed cognitive models are difficult to construct well by somebody not well versed in cognitive science (there are many ways to do it), hard to reproduce and therefore hard to validate. Our current method, as inspired by [15], is lightweight and easy to construct by software engineers and easy to replicate.

Table 1. Atomic actions, categorized as (S)earch, (B)rowse or (E)dit actions

Cat	Action	Description	Motivation
(S)	*a*	Save Java file	Collect error messages by running the Java compiler.
(S)	*b*	Get type declaration	Look up a type by name and jump to it.
(S)	*c*	Get type hierarchy	Produces all classes and interfaces that implement or extend a given type.
(B)	*d*	Jump to error	Jump to the source code after having clicked on the error message.
(E)	*e*	Cut or copy a block	This is a basic action to perform removal and movement of consecutive blocks of code. A block is considered to be no longer than a single method.
(E)	*f*	Paste a block	The dual of *e*.
(E)	*g*	Type a block	We abstract from the difficulty of writing consecutive blocks inside method bodies. Typing several method bodies, or parts of method bodies, is counted as several steps, even if the methods are consecutive.
(S)	*h*	Get implementations	Produces all concrete methods that implement a certain abstract/interface method.
(B)	*i*	Jump to declaration	Jumps from a use site or other reference site to a declaration site of any named entity.
(S)	*j*	Find regexp	We abstract from the effort of creating a regular expression. The action produces a list of locations of entities that match the regexp.
(E)	*m*	Generate new class	Make a new class with the given name and superclass, including templates for methods to be implemented.
(E)	*n*	Delete a class	Remove a type and its source file.

4   Maintainability

This section instantiates the comparative framework discussed in Section 3.2 to compare the Visitor-based and Interpreted-based solutions. Section 4.1 defines how we construct and measure the meta-programs representing the scenarios. Section 4.2 then introduces the scenarios that will be measured, while Section 4.3 describes each scenario in detail.

4.1   A Virtual Machine for Maintenance Scenarios

Recall from Section 3.2 that each maintenance scenario is performed manually and then described by an abstract meta-program used to compute the complexity of the scenario. To precisely define these meta-programs we encode them as the language of a "virtual machine" for maintenance scenarios. This VM models the *actions* of a maintenance programmer as she interacts with Eclipse to analyze and transform source code.

The atomic actions (steps) taken by this virtual machine are defined in Table 1. We have Search (S) actions that produce lists of clickable items; Browse (B) actions that involve following links; and Edit (E) actions that change source texts in specific locations. From these atomic actions we may construct meta programs representing the various maintenance scenarios according to the following definition.

Definition 3. *All maintenance programs P have the following syntax*

$$P ::= A \mid PP \mid P^I \mid (P),$$

where A is an atomic action from Table 1, juxtaposition denotes sequential composition, and a superscript (a non-zero positive integer) denotes iteration. We may use brackets to bind iteration to sequences of actions, otherwise iteration binds more strongly than sequence. Parts of a program may be represented by a variable (represented by upper-case letters in italics) and variables may optionally be indexed: A_i represents atomic actions, N_i and M_i represent values in $\mathbb{N}_1$, and P_i represents programs.

Definition 4. *The computational complexity of any maintenance program P is defined recursively as:*

$$\text{Com}(A) = 1, \qquad\qquad \text{Com}(P_0 P_1) = \text{Com}(P_0) + \text{Com}(P_1),$$
$$\text{Com}((P)) = \text{Com}(P), \qquad \text{Com}(P^N) = N \times \text{Com}(P).$$

With these definitions we can now explain each maintenance scenario in detail. The results are summarized in Table 2.

4.2   Maintenance Scenarios

We have picked several maintenance scenarios to cover most categories of maintenance and to be fair to the theoretical (dis)advantages of either design pattern. We skip preventative maintenance, which will appear instead in the discussions below as refactorings that influence the comparison.

S1 (Adaptive). Add $n \geq 2$ new binary expression operators.
S2 (Perfective). Cache the lookup of (possibly) overloaded data-type constructors in expressions to improve efficiency. This can be generalized to caching n static language constructs.
S3 (Adaptive). Change the syntax and semantics of Rascal to allow arbitrary value patterns in function signatures. This new feature allows functions to be extended modularly, which is a big win for analyses and transformations that are constructed for languages that have a modular structure.
S4 (Adaptive). Add an outline feature to the Rascal IDE — a basic IDE feature already supported in IDEs for many different languages.
S5 (Corrective). Fix Bug #1020 — `NullPointerException`[9]

Note that at the time of writing, these are real maintenance scenarios. The interested reader can replay the meta programs below by checking out the Visitor[10] and Interpreter[11] versions of the Rascal interpreter that are used in this paper.

4.3   Results — Maintenance Scenarios

In this section we list all programs for all scenarios. We motivate the actions of each program, analyze the difference in complexity, and point to the possible causes. Table 2

---

[9] http://bugs.meta-environment.org/show_bug.cgi?id=1020
[10] http://svn.rascal-mpl.org/rascal/tags/pre-visitor-migration
[11] http://svn.rascal-mpl.org/rascal/tags/post-visitor-migration

summarizes all the acquired data points. Some scenarios require common preparation for both Visitor and Interpreter. This is discussed for completeness, but not included in the comparison and not represented in Table 2.

Scenario S1 — Add Two New Expression Operators

To prepare, we edit the Rascal grammar to add two new production rules to the definition of `Expression`. Then we generate and compile source code for the AST hierarchy.

For Visitor we find out that no new warnings or errors have arisen. This is due to the fact that all visitors extend `NullASTVisitor`, which is also generated from the grammar. We have to find all visitors now, and use the Show Type Hierarchy feature of Eclipse to find 11 of them (c). We look up the source

code of each visitor to see if expressions are evaluated by it (i^{11}). This is true for just 2 of them, namely the main `Evaluator` and the `DebuggingDecorator`. Both visitors need two extra methods added ($(g^2a)^2$). We run the Java compiler (part of a, above) to ensure we did not make mistakes, obtaining the meta program: $ci^{11}(g^2a)^2$.

For Interpreter we also find out there are no new warnings after AST generation. We now add two concrete sub-classes to the generated sub-classes of

`ast.Expression`(m^2). There appear to be four methods to implement, three of which we clone from `Expression.Add` (selected at random) because they seem to be default implementations ($b(ef^2)^3$). We then adapt the one method (`interpret`) in both classes that we must change ($(ga)^2$). The total meta-program is thus: $m^2b(ef^2)^3(ga)^2$.

A comparison of the complexity (18 vs. 16) shows a minimal difference in favor of Interpreter.

Scenario S1(N) — Add N New Expression Operators

To generalize to N new operators we can replace 2 by N in the two programs for S1 to obtain new programs $ci^{11}(g^Na)^2$ for Visitor and $m^Nb(ef^N)^3(ga)^N$ for Interpreter. Their complexity

breaks even at $N = \frac{5}{2}$. This indicates that after adding 2 operators further additions will be easier in Visitor than in Interpreter. One cause may be the *cloning* of the 3 methods from `Expression.Add`

(See **S1**). It is a seemingly unrelated design flaw. If these methods could be pulled up into `Expression`, the Interpreter program would have no need to clone the other three methods.

Scenario S1'(N) & S1'(N,M) — Pulling Up Methods and Another Generalization

Pulling up the method clones in Interpreter (see S1(N)) leads to a new program for adding N new expression operators, $m^N(ga)^N$. This program has complexity $3n$, which breaks even with Visitor at $N = 14$. Visitor wins in this case, but only after having added 14 operators. The cause is that only 2 out

of 11 of Visitor classes actually need an extra pair of methods. If there would be more visitors to extend however, there would also be more methods to implement per class in the Interpreter version. Abstracting the number of operations on each operator to M (assuming the new ones all need extension,

but 9 of the existing ones do not), we get $ci^{9+M}(g^Na)^M$ for Visitor and $m^N(ga)^{MN}$ for Interpreter. Break-even is when $N = \frac{2M+10}{M+1}$. The constant 10 increases with the number of irrelevant visitors and break even is harder to reach for Visitor while M increases.

In general we can conclude that for **S1** Visitor wins in the long run, although it wins more slowly in situations where there are a large number of visitor classes that do not need to be modified (but still need to be checked). Interpreter has a higher eventual maintenance cost because of the additional classes that need to be created.

Scenario S2 — Cache Constructor Lookup in Expressions

Constructors in Rascal can be defined at the top level of any Rascal module. When a constructor is used in a program, the current module, and all imported modules, are checked for definitions of the constructor. Since these definitions can only be changed when a constructor is (re)defined, it should be possible to improve performance by caching the lookup result, with the cache cleared at each redefinition.

For Visitor we first find the main Evaluator visitor to locate the visit method that represents function and constructor application (i^2). Reading the source code of visitExpressionCall-OrTree we learn that this visit method evaluates the name of the function or constructor to obtain an object of type Result that has a call method. We want to cache this object for future reference if it represents a constructor. In order to do this, a field must be added to the current visitor (we could instead add a field to the underlying AST node class, but since the AST classes are generated this would require changing the generator as

well). This field will reference a hash table that maps the current AST node to the result of the name lookup. We need to add the field (g) and add the two locations in the code that cache and retrieve constructor values (gg). To clear the cache we need to find the method where constructors are declared. We use the outline feature to jump to visitDeclarationData (i) and add some code to clear the entire cache (g). The total program is $i^2 g^3 iga$.

For Interpreter we locate the AST class Expression.CallOrTree and its interpret method (i^2). We add a field to the AST class to store a cached constructor and we surround the lookup with the storage and retrieval code for this cached value (g^3). To clear this field when a module is reloaded, we choose to apply the Listener design pattern [7]. When a constructor is cached a new IConstructorDeclared listener will be registered with the current Evaluator (g), which is passed as a parameter to the interpret method. We now save the

current class (a). The Listener design pattern needs to be completed by adding a container for the listeners, a register method and a clear method to Evaluator. For this we jump to the class and add the field and two methods ($ig^3 a$). Then we find the Declaration.Data class to add the code to call the clear method when a constructor is (re)declared, yielding: $i^2 g^3 gaig^3 aiga$.

In summary, interpreter is harder to maintain. An alternative design choice for Interpreter would be to use a global hash-table, like we did with Visitor. This removes the need for introducing the listener design pattern and thus gives the same complexity. Having a field instead of a hash-table is important for speed though (see Section 5). Alternatively, for Visitor we could have chosen not to use a hash-table but instead add a field to AbstractAST. However, this would break the encapsulation gained through Visitor and, as mentioned above, would require modifying the AST class generator as well.

The following change in requirements (S3) involves non-trivial and non-local changes in the syntax and semantics of the language. Again, we assume the maintainer has full understanding of the concepts and implications for the general architecture of the Rascal interpreter. She does, however, need to locate and check the details of implementing the necessary changes.

Scenario S3 — Allow Patterns in Function Signatures

To prepare, we need to edit the definition of formal parameters in the Rascal grammar. There we replace the use of `Formal` by `Pattern`. The AST hierarchy is regenerated and the Java checker and compiler are executed to produce error messages and warnings. We omit this common prefix in the following discussion.

For Visitor the compiler produces 14 error message, each about a reference to a missing class `Formal`. Uses of `Formal` need to be replaced with `Expression` and imports of `Formal` need to be deleted. This results in a cascade of changes up the call chain starting at these 14 error locations. Using the JDT we adapt each location one-by-one and save each file after each change to produce new error messages. Just the first error leads to dg^5eg. Then we find a nested visitor in `TypeEvaluator` that dispatches over the different kinds of type declarations. We decide to extend it with a type analysis of each pattern kind. There are 15 different kinds of patterns (known from reading the type hierarchy of `Expression`) (cg^{15}). Two more substitutions complete the changes to this file (g^2a).

These were the changes rooted at the first error. We now have 4 of 14 messages left. These happen to point to dead code that can be removed: $(eea)^4$.

Now we add a call to pattern matching. Given we

are modifying function call logic, we first jump to `visitExpressionCallOrTree` in the main `Evaluator` visitor (i^2). We find a call to the `call` method of an abstract class `Result`. All implementation of this method are suspect. We use action h to find all 9 of them. After inspection, 3 of these need additional functionality: `RascalFunction`, `JavaFunction` and `OverloadedFunction`. The others have names related to constructs that are not related to function declarations with formal parameters.

Pattern matching both returns true and binds variables if the match succeeds. We can replace the code that binds actual to formal parameters by pattern matching. We also need to add backtracking logic, and decide to do so with an exception mechanism. If the pattern match fails, the function was not to be called and we throw an (unchecked) exception that can be caught at a choice point in `OverloadedFunction`. The three `call` methods are adjusted to do just that $((ga)^3)$.

The total program for Visitor is $dg^5egcg^{15}g^2a$ $(eea)^4i^2h(ga)^3$.

For interpreter the generation of the AST hierarchy produces 17 error messages. The first is located in `DynamicSemanticsASTFactory` which

refers to a constructor that does not exist anymore (d). The constructor for `Formals.Default` still uses the old form of parameter lists. We fix this first (ig). The next error message is in the `interpret` method of `Formals.Default` that evaluates ASTs of type literals. We jump to it and find a need to substitute `Formal` (iga). This recursive method maps ASTs of type literals to internal type objects. This method will also have to deal with all kinds of patterns now. We add an implementation of it to every kind of pattern. We look up the type hierarchy for `Expression` to identify the 15 classes and add a method to each of them $((iga)^{15})$.

Jumping to the location of the next error, we end up in `JavaBridge`. A number of similar substitutions are needed and an import is removed: $(ig)^3ga$. Then we trace a broken method call to the class `TypeEvaluator` (i). There we find some substitutions (ig^2a). The last 3 errors point to dead code that can be removed, a dead class and a dead import in a class $((igg)^2aniga)$.

Now we may add pattern matching, which is done similarly to the Visitor implementation. We jump to the `Expression.CallOrTree` class to find the semantics of function calling; and use the same strategy we used for Visitor $(ih(ga)^3)$.

The total program for Interpreter is $d(ig)^2a(iga)^{15}(ig)^3$ $gai(ig^2)a(igg)^2anigaih(ga)^3$.

Scenario S3' — S3, but Saving Incrementally for Visitor

The cause of the significant difference in complexity in S3 (43 vs. 83) between the Visitor and Interpreter patterns is clearly the spread of code over the different classes. In Visitor there is much less browsing between classes and saving of classes, leading to almost twice the maintenance complexity for Interpreter.

Note that browsing to a different class that needs editing always costs Interpreter a Browse and a Search action if something needs to be edited (for saving and compiling the file after editing), while Visitor may delay the saving of a file until all is done. It is questionable whether in reality one would delay saving the file after so many edits

in a big visitor class. If we add save actions to the Visitor program after every edit, we get $d(ga)^5egac(ga)^{15} (ga)^2(eea)^4i^2h(ga)^3$, with complexity 70. Visitor still wins, but now it is only 16% cheaper instead of the previous 48%.

Scenario S4 — Add Outline

To prepare, both versions need similar code to register an outline computation with Eclipse.

For Visitor we simply add a new visitor class. This class needs methods for all AST nodes that need to be traversed to find the entries that

appear in the outline view. There are 11 different nodes, yielding $mg^{11}a$.

For Interpreter we add a new virtual method to AbstractAST called outline. It will be overridden by 11 classes. The method needs a parameter

to a TreeModelBuilder interface to construct the outline object that Eclipse will use. So this ties Abstract-AST to an Eclipse interface. The meta program reads $bga(bga)^{11}$.

Visitor clearly wins in this case because of the improved encapsulation of the solution.

The description of Bug #1020 in our Bugzilla database contains the claim that the following Rascal statement produces a NullPointerException due to some issue in a regular expression: switch ("aabb") {case /aa*b$/:println("HIT");}

Scenario S5 — Fix Bug #1020 — NullPointerException

This issue indeed produces stack traces for both versions, and surprisingly the traces are the same. The reason is that a null reference to a result is passed all the way to the top command-line shell.

We trace the flow of this reference down the call chain.

For *Visitor*. The outermost expression is a switch, so we jump to the evaluation of the switch in the method Evaluator.visitStat-

ementSwitch (*bi*). The last statement of this method returns 'null' which needs to be replaced by a 'void' result (*ga*).

The *Interpreter* case has one fewer browse action (*bga*).

4.4 Discussion

On the one hand, even in scenarios where theoretically Interpreter would have better encapsulation (e.g. **S1** and **S2**), Visitor still has a lower cost of maintenance. This is surprising. On the other hand, the scenarios that theoretically suit Visitor better indeed show that it is superior. No counter indicators were found in the context of this realistic case. At least in the context of the Rascal interpreter, our research method consistently produces "Visitor is better".

Table 2. A comparison of all maintenance programs (see Table 1)

S	Visitor	(COM)	Interpreter	(COM)	Vis.>Int.
S1	$ci^{11}(g^2a)^2$	(18)	$m^2b(ef^2)^3(ga)^2$	(16)	yes
S1(N)	$ci^{11}(g^Na)^2$	$(14+2N)$	$m^Nb(ef^N)^3(ga)^N$	$(4+6N)$	if $N \leq 2$
S1'(N,2)	$ci^{11}(g^Na)^2$	$(14+2N)$	$m^N(ga)^N$	$(3N)$	if $N \leq 14$
S1'(N,M)	$ci^{9+M}(g^Na)^M$	$(10+NM+2M)$	$m^N(ga)^{MN}$	$(N+2MN)$	if $N \leq \frac{2M+10}{M+1}$
S2	i^2g^3iga	(8)	$i^2g^3gaig^3aiga$	(14)	no
S3	$dg^5egcg^{15}g^2a(eea)^4i^2h(ga)^3$	(43)	$d(ig)^2a(iga)^{15}(ig)^3gai$ $(ig^2)a(igg)^2anigaih(ga)^3$	(83)	no
S3'	$d(ga)^5egac(ga)^{15}(ga)^2$ $(eea)^4i^2h(ga)^3$	(70)	$d(ig)^2a(iga)^{15}(ig)^3gai$ $(ig^2)a(igg)^2anigaih(ga)^3$	(83)	no
S4	$mg^{11}a$	(13)	$bga(bga)^{11}$	(36)	no
S5	$biga$	(4)	bga	(3)	yes

In terms of *construct validity* one may argue that the COM framework may not measure all relevant aspects of maintenance. The first aspect that is missing is the general understanding that a programmer needs of the particular program, before she can decide what to look for and what to change. We argue that this knowledge is equally needed for Visitor and Interpreter. We do not use COM for predicting maintenance effort, but for comparison. The second aspect is that we did not distinguish whether or not method bodies are hard to understand. Fortunately, in the case of Visitor vs. Interpreter the method bodies are practically equivalent in complexity on both sides.

We do not claim much about *external validity*. The current study is highly focused on the Rascal case. We do expect that if the current study were replicated on different AST processing software written in Java, with different maintenance scenarios, the results would be comparable. This expectation is motivated by the fact that the scenarios above do not refer to any intrinsic details of the syntax and semantics of Rascal.

We have assumed ample use of browsing, searching and editing features of Eclipse. It is unknown what the effect of not having these tools would be on the case of the Rascal interpreter.

Finally, if other quality attributes enter the scene, or other refactorings are applied, our conclusions about maintainability and runtime performance may be invalidated. The dimension of (parallel) collaborative development—as enabled by a modular architecture—might have an unpredictable impact on our results.

In terms of internal validity, we hope to have provided enough detail for the reader to be able to replicate the scenarios and their measurement. If shorter but otherwise plausible meta programs are defined, this might invalidate our analysis. Naturally, our interpretation of the causes of differences is also open to discussion.

5   Efficiency

We now focus on the effect on run-time efficiency of moving from Visitor to Interpreter. The impact is measured using four programs, designed both to highlight different aspects of performance and to represent typical Rascal usage scenarios:

Add finds the sum of the first 1000000 integers using a loop. It isolates the dispatch overhead of the interpreter because the computation is so basic (i.e., does not involve Rascal function calls or complex primitives like transitive closure computation).

Gen consists of running the parser generator (implemented in Rascal) on Rascal's grammar.

Resolve is the name resolution phase of the Rascal type checker, applied to one of the parser generator modules. It exercises a wider range of AST classes then **Gen**.

Lambda is a parser and interpreter for the lambda calculus. The test involves parser generation, parsing and execution of lambda reductions over arithmetic expressions (Church numerals). It highlights the result of caching constructor names.

Each program is run using both the Interpreter and the Visitor versions, before and after applying scenario S2 (cache constructor names).

The results are shown in Table 3. In the **Add** example the Interpreter code is slightly slower, while in the others it is faster by 1.3% (**Gen**), 2.5% (**Resolve**), and 5.8% (**Lambda**). Except perhaps for **Lambda**, this means that the performance difference is not substantial in any of the cases that do not include caching.

Table 3. Interpreter performance figures (4 versions, all times in seconds; tests run on Intel Core2 6420, 2.13 GHz, 2 GB RAM, Fedora linux 2.6.32.21-168.fc12.x86_64)

	Visitor		Interpreter	
	No Caching	Caching	No Caching	Caching
Add	7.55	7.70	7.71	7.52
Gen	275.50	273.65	271.88	243.24
Resolve	35.21	35.67	34.32	32.44
Lambda	610.81	655.19	575.61	567.80

We found this surprising, since one of our assumptions was that we would see a performance improvement based on a reduction in method call overhead. Also, the improvements from an optimization like name lookup caching are far more significant than the improvements from changing from Visitor to Interpreter. While this means that these types of optimizations may be a more fruitful target to pursue, this also means that slow parts in the interpreter may be impacting performance enough that differences between the two patterns are harder to see. Additional performance testing, with a broader suite of test programs, should help to get a clearer idea of the performance differences, especially as additional optimizations are added to the Rascal runtime.

6 Conclusion

We have used quantitative methods to observe the consequences of choosing between the Interpreter design pattern and the Visitor design pattern. The study focused on an AST based interpreter for the Rascal programming language. Surprisingly, for the five realistic maintenance scenarios we have studied, it appears that a solution using the Visitor pattern is more maintainable than a solution using the Interpreter pattern. Only in trivial scenarios is an Interpreter-based solution easier to maintain. Since this contradicts common wisdom regarding the expression problem, it underlines the importance of studying the consequences of choosing design patterns in realistic experiments.

With respect to performance, we have observed no significant differences between unoptimized solutions using the two patterns. Any differences between the two solutions may be easier to see as the Rascal interpreter is further optimized, leaving the call overhead in the Visitor implementation as a larger part of the total execution time. It may also be possible to see more differences as additional performance tests are selected beyond the four given in this paper.

References

1. Benbasat, I., Goldstein, D.K., Mead, M.: The case research strategy in studies of information systems. MIS Q. 11, 369–386 (1987)
2. Chatzigeorgiou, A., Tsantalis, N., Deligiannis, I.S.: An empirical study on students' ability to comprehend design patterns. Computers & Education 51(3), 1007–1016 (2008)
3. Coleman, D., Ash, D., Lowther, B., Oman, P.: Using metrics to evaluate software system maintainability. Computer 27, 44–49 (1994)
4. Cook, W.R.: On understanding data abstraction, revisited. In: Proceedings of OOPSLA 2009, pp. 557–572. ACM Press, New York (2009)
5. Eden, A., Mens, T.: Measuring Software Flexibility. IEE Proceedings—Software 153(3), 113–125 (2006)
6. Fleming, S.D., Kraemer, E., Stirewalt, R.E.K., Dillon, L.K., Xie, S.: Refining Existing Theories of Program Comprehension During Maintenance for Concurrent Software. In: Proceedings of ICPC 2008, pp. 23–32. IEEE, Los Alamitos (2008)
7. Gamma, E., Helm, R., Johnson, R.E., Vlissides, J.: Design Patterns. Elements of Reusable Object-Oriented Software. Addison-Wesley, Reading (1995)
8. Hannemann, J., Kiczales, G.: Design pattern implementation in Java and AspectJ. In: Proceedings of OOPSLA 2002, pp. 161–173. ACM Press, New York (2002)
9. Heitlager, I., Kuipers, T., Visser, J.: A practical model for measuring maintainability. In: Proceedings of QUATIC 2007, pp. 30–39. IEEE, Los Alamitos (2007)
10. Henderson-Sellers, B.: Object-oriented metrics: measures of complexity. Prentice-Hall, Englewood Cliffs (1996)
11. Hills, M.: Rascal Visitor to Interpreter (V2I) Transformation, http://www.cwi.nl/~hills/rascal/V2I.html
12. International Standard, I.: - ISO/IEC 14764 IEEE Std 14764-2006. ISO/IEC 14764:2006 (E) IEEE Std 14764-2006 Revision of IEEE Std 1219-1998), pp. 1–46 (2006)
13. Klint, P., van der Storm, T., Vinju, J.: EASY meta-programming with Rascal. In: Fernandes, J.M., Lämmel, R., Visser, J., Saraiva, J. (eds.) Generative and Transformational Techniques in Software Engineering III. LNCS, vol. 6491, pp. 222–289. Springer, Heidelberg (2011)
14. Littman, D.C., Pinto, J., Letovsky, S., Soloway, E.: Mental models and software maintenance. In: Proceedings of the First Workshop on Empirical Studies of Programmers, pp. 80–98. Ablex Publishing Corp. (1986)
15. Mens, T., Eden, A.H.: On the Evolution Complexity of Design Patterns. In: Proceedings of SETra 2004. ENTCS, vol. 127, pp. 147–163 (2004)
16. Oman, P., Hagemeister, J.: Construction and testing of polynomials predicting software maintainability. J. Syst. Softw. 24, 251–266 (1994)
17. Prechelt, L., Unger, B., Tichy, W.F., Brössler, P., Votta, L.G.: A Controlled Experiment in Maintenance Comparing Design Patterns to Simpler Solutions. IEEE Transactions on Software Engineering 27(12), 1134–1144 (2001)
18. Wadler, P.: The expression problem (November 1998), http://www.daimi.au.dk/~madst/tool/papers/expression.txt (accessed January 2011)
19. Wender, K.F., Schmalhofer, F., Böcker, H.-D. (eds.): Cognition and computer programming. Ablex Publishing Corp. (1995)

Computational REST Meets Erlang

Alessandro Sivieri, Gianpaolo Cugola, and Carlo Ghezzi

Politecnico di Milano
DeepSE Group, Dipartimento di Elettronica e Informazione
Piazza L. da Vinci, 32 Milano, Italy
{sivieri,cugola,ghezzi}@elet.polimi.it

Abstract. Today's applications are developed in a world where the execution context changes continuously. They have to adapt to these changes at run-time if they want to offer their services without interruption. This is particularly critical for distributed Web applications, whose components run on different machines, often managed by different organizations. Designing these programs in an easy and effective way requires choosing the right architectural style and the right run-time platform. The former has to guarantee isolation among components, supporting scalability, reliability, and dynamic changes. The latter has to offer mechanisms to update the applications' code at run-time.

This work builds upon previous research about architectures and run-time platforms. Its contribution is to put together a very promising architectural style – Computational REST – with a language (and run-time environment) designed with dynamic, distributed applications in mind – Erlang. We show how they fit together by developing a new framework, which eases development of highly distributed Web applications capable of operating in dynamic environments. We also provide an initial experimental assessment of the proposed approach.

Keywords: Computational REST, Erlang, OTP, architectural styles, programming languages, mobile code, Internet.

1 Introduction

The technological evolution in networking has changed the way applications are designed and developed: instead of having monolithic programs created for desktop computers running in isolation, more and more often we have large-scale, distributed Web applications, whose components run on many different devices, from personal computers to smartphones, from mainframes to low-power sensors. In the most challenging scenarios, these applications put together components built and administered by different organizations, by invoking the services offered by such components, managing the data that flow among them and using a browser as the front-end.

To further complicate things, these Web applications are usually expected to run for long time without interruption and failures: a challenging goal if we consider that the devices and components they are built upon may change

J. Bishop and A. Vallecillo (Eds.): TOOLS 2011, LNCS 6705, pp. 244–259, 2011.

over time in a way that is often hard to forecast. Software Engineering is asked to address this issue by developing ad-hoc programming frameworks to ease the implementation of largely distributed Web applications capable of handling changes (and failures) in the external services they invoke and in the devices they access and run on, in a smooth and effective way.

Such programming frameworks should integrate an architectural style that guarantees isolation among components, supporting scalability, reliability, and dynamic changes, with a programming language (and run-time support environment) that offers mechanisms for dynamic update of functionalities.

Current research has proposed Computational REST (CREST) [14], as an effective architectural style to build dynamic, Internet-wide distributed applications. CREST extends the REpresentational State Transfer (REST) style [16], changing the focus from *data* to *computations*, while maintaining the REST principles, which guarantee Internet-wide scalability. In a CREST application, each component (called *peer*) is able to exchange computations, in the form of *continuations* or *closures*, with other components, to dynamically install new services on remote components and demand their execution to others. This idea of managing computations as first-class elements comes from the research on mobile code [17], and has proved to be an effective mechanism to easily support dynamic changes for long-running applications.

While CREST is just an architectural style, their authors proposed a prototype programming framework that embeds the CREST principles in Scheme [12], a well-known functional programming language. This choice was motivated by the Scheme capabilities in dealing with continuations, which allow Scheme processes to be easily suspended to be resumed later. On the other hand, Scheme does not offer any native support to building distributed applications, a critical aspect for a framework that has distributed applications as its main target.

Starting from this consideration we decided to see if other languages could better fit the CREST principles. In this we were also motivated by the fact that the original Scheme-based prototype was never made officially public, at least not in a form that allow it to be used in practice for experiments.

In particular, we chose Erlang [5], a functional language that was designed upfront to build long-running distributed applications. Indeed, Erlang and its OTP [5] library natively support distributed programming, offering advanced and easy-to-use mechanisms to remotely spawning components, letting them communicate, and automatically managing failures. In addition, it offers mechanisms to dynamically change the components' code at run-time. These features are embedded in a functional core that supports closures, a fundamental aspect to satisfy the CREST requirements.

The rest of the paper describes the result of our experience. In particular, Section 2 introduces Computational REST and Erlang. Section 3 describes the new Erlang-based CREST framework and the facilities it provides to developers, while Section 4 compares it against the original CREST framework and a pure REST (i.e., Web-based) implementation of the same application, in terms of performance, functionalities offered, and cost to implement them. Finally

Section 5 discusses related work and Section 6 draws some conclusions and suggests possible future work in the area.

2   Background

In this section we briefly introduce the main topic areas upon which our work is based, i.e., the REST and CREST architectural styles and the Erlang language.

2.1   The REST and CREST Styles

Defined by R.T. Fielding (one of the main authors of the HTTP protocol), the REpresentational State Transfer (REST) style provides an *a posteriori* model of the Web, the way Web application operates, and the technical reasons behind the Web success.

Fielding's Ph.D. thesis [16] defines the set of *constraints* that every REST application should satisfy: the structure of the application has to be client-server, communication has to be stateless, caching has to be possible, the interface of servers has to be standard and generic, layering is encouraged, and each single layer has to be independent from the others. An optional constraint suggests using code-on-demand [17] approaches to dynamically extend the client's capabilities.

These constrains are coupled with a set of *foundation principles*:

- the key abstraction of information is a resource, named by a uniform resource identification scheme (e.g., URLs);
- the representation of a resource is a sequence of bytes, plus representation metadata to describe those bytes;
- all interactions are context-free;
- only a few primitive operations are available;
- idempotent operations and representation metadata are encouraged in support of caching;
- the presence of intermediaries is promoted.

While these principles allowed REST to be scalable and supported the current Web dimensions, at the same time not all the Web applications followed these design guidelines; for example, they might require stateful communications or they might create problems to caching devices components.

The main limitation of REST is the generic interface constraint: it improves independence of applications on specific services, because all the components are able to handle any data, but at the same time it hampers the efficiency of communication, since all data must be coded in a standard way to pass through standard, application independent interfaces; something not easy to do especially when there is more than pure "content" to be sent between peers.

The CREST authors identified this and other REST weaknesses in [13] and decided to address them by moving the focus of the communication from *data* to *computations*. If the former is the only subject of an interaction, then a client receiving a message through a generic interface could not be able to interpret it correctly. The REST optional constraint of code-on-demand is too weak to solve the issue, since the same client could not be able to use that code.

The result of this paradigm shift was the Computational REST (CREST) [14] style, which let *peers* exchange *computations* as their primary message, usually implementing them through continuations. These are instances of computations suspended at a certain point and encapsulated in a single entity to be resumed later. They are offered as a basic construct by some languages, usually functional ones like Scheme, which also allow continuations to be serialized and transmitted along a network connection to allow the computation to be resumed on a different node.

Whenever a language does not offer the continuation mechanism, a *closure* can be used instead: it is a function with free variables declared within its scope, and since the extent of these variables is at least as long as the lifetime of the closure, they can be used for saving a state between different calls of the function. Later, in Section 3 we will explain why using this less powerful mechanism instead of continuations does not influence the expressiveness of our framework.

Also notice that in the definitions above we used the term "peer" instead of "client" or "server". This is not by accident, since CREST does not distinguish between clients and servers but rather between *weak peers* that support a minimal subset of the CREST operations and usually operate as initiators of the interaction, and *strong peers* that support the whole set of CREST operations and characteristics and may fully interact with other peers, be they strong or weak.

CREST draws on the REST principles to define a new set of architectural guidelines:

- a resource is a locus of computations, named by a URL;
- the representation of a computation is an expression plus metadata to describe the expression;
- all computations are context-free;
- the presence of intermediaries is promoted;
- only a few primitive operations are always available, but additional per-resource and per-computation operations are also encouraged.

As for the last point, CREST defines two primitive operations: the *spawn* operation requires the creation of a process executing the computation; this process is associated to a unique URL and when this URL is invoked the computation itself is resumed and the results it produces are returned to the caller; thus, new services can be installed in a (strong) peer and then accessed by any client. The *remote* operation installs a computation and resumes it immediately, returning any result to the caller and destroying it when it ends, so that it cannot be accessed again.

In [13,19] the authors further detail the CREST principles:

- any computation has to be included into HTTP operations, so that the new paradigm could be made compatible with the current Internet infrastructure.

To keep up with such compatibility, the authors also distinguish between
machine URLs and human-readable URLs, where the former may contain
the computation itself, while the latter can be used by users;
- computations may produce different results, based on any received parameter, server load or any other factor that changes during time; they can also
  maintain a state between calls, for example for accumulating intermediate
  results;
- computations have to support independency between different calls, and
  avoid data corruption between parallel invocations using synchronization
  mechanisms offered by the languages of choice;
- computations can be composed, creating mashups: a computation may refer to other computations on the same peer or on different peers, and an
  execution snapshot should include the whole state of the computation;
- intermediaries must be transparent to the users;
- peers should be able to distribute computations, to support scaling and lowering latency, also checking temporal intervals between executions of the
  same computation and specifying some sort of expiration date when necessary.

Finally, in [19] a new feature has been introduced: spawned processes should act
as so-called *subpeers*, with their own *spawn* and *remote* capabilities, inheriting
security policies by their ancestors in the process tree, where the root node is
the peer itself. This way a hierarchy of processes is created in a CREST peer,
where each node is limited by its ancestors and limits its successors.

Security concerns. An important issue with architectural styles for distributed
applications is security. Besides traditional security concerns, the CREST adoption of mobile code technologies opens new problems; namely how to secure
the peer against the code it receives and how to secure the code against the
peer in which it is executed [29,30]. The CREST definition recognizes the issue
but provides few details on how to address it. In practice, the current CREST
framework, implemented using a Scheme interpreter running into a Java Virtual Machine, leverages the sandbox mechanism of Java, using an ad-hoc Security Manager that limits the resources accessible to the incoming computations.
Moreover, the authors suggest that the bytecode received by a peer should be
inspected and checked for instruction sets executing commands that are not allowed by the (sub)peer security policy, while self-certifying URLs [23] could be
used for mutual authentication between peers.

2.2   Erlang

Erlang [3,4,5,6] is a programming language originally defined to implement parallel, distributed applications meant to run continuously for long periods[1]. It
provides a set of features that make it a perfect choice for a framework to build
CREST-compliant applications.

[1] The definition of Erlang has been primarily motivated by the requirements of
telecommunications applications within Ericsson.

In particular, its functional language core natively supports *closures*, which – while not offering the full expressive power of continuations – are a step in the right direction to implement the CREST idea of exchanging computations among peers. Moreover, Erlang combines dynamic typing and the use of pattern-matching as the main mechanism to access data and guide the computation, supporting a form of declarative programming that allows programmers to focus on *what* a computation is supposed to do instead of *how* to achieve it. This results in extremely compact code that is easy to develop and maintain. We found these features fundamental to develop a programming framework that has to be open to extensions by application programmers who wish to build their own, CREST-compliant software.

In addition, Erlang enriches its functional core with ad-hoc language constructs to build parallel and distributed applications. In particular, Erlang uses an actor-like concurrency model [22], which allows for easily and naturally organizing every Erlang computation as a (large) set of light processes, automatically mapped by the Erlang runtime into system threads and hardware cores. Since such processes cannot share memory and have to rely on message passing (which is embedded into the language) to communicate, this approach also naturally supports developing distributed applications, another fundamental feature to ease the implementation of our CREST framework.

A further peculiarity of Erlang is the fact that its runtime support system allows application code to be hot-swapped. This mechanism was introduced to support long running applications, like those implemented into telephonic switches, and can be used as a way to change the code of an application at runtime without interrupting it. In particular, if a module function is executed by calling its qualified name, then the runtime guarantees the execution of the last version available of that function; that is, if the module bytecode is updated while the application is running, then each new function invocation will use the last version of the code, while any running instance will continue its execution with the previous one. Notice however that only two versions of a module may live together at the same time: if a third one is added, then the second one becomes the "old" one and the first one is dropped, and each computation using it is automatically killed.

Finally, Erlang provides an extensive, standard library, called the Open Telecom Platform (OTP), which offers predefined modules for process linking and monitoring. By using OTP, supervision trees of processes can be easily constructed so that each supervisor is able to monitor if a process crashes and restart it or propagate the error. OTP also offers several modules, called *behaviors*, which implement the non-functional parts of a generic server so that a developer can focus only on the functional ones. Altogether, these functionalities greatly simplify the development of fault-tolerant applications, and we leveraged them to reduce the effort needed in implementing our CREST framework.

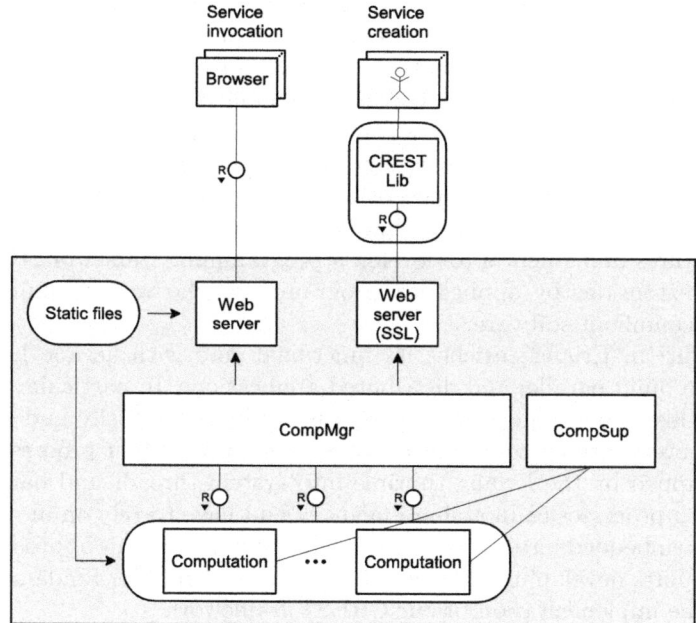

Fig. 1. Server structure

3   CREST-Erlang

In this section we illustrate how the CREST style can be implemented in Erlang. The resulting framework is called CREST-Erlang, as opposed to CREST-Scheme, which denotes the original framework presented in [13]. Figure 1 shows the structure of a CREST peer written in Erlang. At the bottom are the computations running into the peer, which have been installed there by invoking the *spawn* or *remote* CREST primitives. They are managed by an ad-hoc component, the CompMgr, which installs new computations, keeps a list of those running inside the peer, and dispatches incoming invocations.

As we mentioned, one of the main reasons to choose Erlang was the support offered by the language to let (distributed) processes communicate. On the other hand, to be CREST compliant, the communication among peers has to use the HTTP protocol. Accordingly, our peer embeds a Web server, which waits for incoming HTTP requests, unmarshals them, and uses the standard Erlang communication facilities to dispatch them to the CompMgr. More precisely, Figure 1 shows two Web servers, one answers HTTPS requests and is meant to handle *spawn* and *remote* operations, which we choose to securely transfer on top of SSL (more on this later). The other serves standard invocations and static pages, a trivial but required functionality for a Web framework.

As for the adopted protocol we chose, it is worth mentioning here that we decided to send computations using the HTTP POST operation, while the original

CREST approach suggests embedding them into the URL of the *spawn* request. This choice seems more in line with the expected usage of HTTP. Indeed, the POST operation has been designed for those requests that are expected to alter the internal state of the receiving server, and this is the case for the installation of a new service. Moreover, the POST payload may include a large body of data, as it happens in the case of the state of a computation and the associated bytecode.

As shown in Figure 1, our framework also includes the CRESTLib, which provides a set of facilities to invoke local and remote services without having to bother with the underlying communication details. This is used by peer clients, but it can also be used to implement the services themselves, when they have to communicate with other peers.

Finally, to improve fault tolerance each peer is organized in a supervision tree, with a high level supervisor (not shown in figure) in charge of all the fundamental modules including the two Web servers and the CompMgr, and a low level one, the CompSup, to which all the spawned computations are attached. The former is able to monitor and restart each of its children, while the latter, at the current state, just logs any error or exception happening to computations, unlinking them from the CompMgr when this happens.

Listing 1.1. Service template

```
1  my_service (State) ->
2    receive
3      {Pid, [{"par1", P1}, {"par2", P2}, ...]} ->
4        %% Do your job accessing par1, ... parN
5        %% eventually create a new state NewState
6
7        %% If necessary, spawn myself on peer Hostname
8        invoke_spawn (Hostname, ?MODULE,
9                            fun() -> my_service (NewState) end),
10       %% Finish with a tail recursion (or just end this
11       %% computation)
12       my_service (NewState)
13   end.
```

Listing 1.1 shows the template of an Erlang *service* to be spawned or remotely executed on a peer. It receives from the CompMgr the invocation parameters originally coming from the client, uses them to perform its computation, and finishes by invoking itself with the new state calculated during execution, using the typical approach of functional programming based on tail recursion. Lines 8-9 show how the service may spawn a copy of itself (i.e., a copy of the computation) on a different node, if necessary.

Notice that what is transferred to the other peer through the invoke_spawn primitive is the *closure* of the running service, not the *continuation*, as required by CREST. Indeed, as we mentioned in the previous section, this is the only primitive offered by Erlang. On the other hand, the need to transfer computation while it is executing statements in the middle of the service's code is very uncommon. The typical service pattern is the one shown by our template, which transfers the computation just before recursing. If this is the case, transferring the closure obtains the same result as transferring the continuation of the computation.

Technologies involved and details about security. For the Web server part, we analyzed several different platforms developed in the last few years for handling HTTP communications in Erlang. Each has its pros and cons, and in the end we chose *MochiWeb* [1], because of its support to JSON (which we used to effectively serialize parameters and return values passed among peers and clients) and RESTful services, and for its performance.

The MochiWeb library and the OTP modules together provide the main skeleton of our peer: the supervising system, the logging system (not shown in Figure 1), and the two Web servers. This allowed us to focus on developing the functional parts of the framework.

As for security, Erlang does not offer many facilities. Indeed, it was born as a language for handling telephony devices, a domain in which security is usually guaranteed by directly controlling the network itself. Now that Erlang is being used outside its target domain, this weakness has been identified and the first security facilities are being added to the language. On the other hand, we are far from having ad-hoc facilities to manage security in general and the security of mobile code in particular. To address this issue we decided to adopt a strategy based on mutual authentication among peers. This way we bypass the specific problem of protecting the incoming computation from the peer and the peer from the computation, building a trusted network on top of which computations may roam freely. This is clearly a sub-optimal solution, which we plan to overcome in future versions of our prototype.

4   An Assessment of CREST-Erlang vs. CREST-Scheme

In this section we discuss how our CREST framework, based on Erlang, can be compared with the original CREST-Scheme solution. To perform the assessment, we chose to focus on three main dimensions: whether the same functionalities are offered by both, the cost in implementing them, and how they perform.

Functionalities. The original CREST-Scheme framework includes a case study to show the potential of the new approach, namely a shared RSS reader. It includes an AJAX Web site as a front-end, with several widgets to show the news (coming from a given RSS feed URL) using different visualization techniques. Each widget type interacts with a different service (i.e., computation) on a single CREST peer, while different instances of the same widget type (running on different clients) share the same service. This way every client sees the same information about the feeds. A user may duplicate the whole application instance, so that its changes will be separated from the original one.

The drawback of this case study is that every CREST computation resides on the same peer and when new computations are spawned (i.e., when a client duplicates the application's session) they are spawned into the same peer. In other words there is no transmission of computations among peers.

Accordingly, we implemented an additional case study to evaluate our framework: a distributed text mining application. A network of computers, each running a CREST-Erlang peer, share a set of documents to be analyzed. A front-end Web application allows the user to choose the text mining function and the set of peers to use. The former is sent as a spawned computation on the involved peers, which perform their part of the job and return the results back.

Differently from the original one, this case study leverages all the CREST mechanisms: *spawn* and *remote* operations, statefull and stateless computations, and service composition. This allowed us to asses the correctness and ease of use of the new framework.

The only point not covered by our CREST-Erlang framework is the concept of *subpeer*, which has been described by the CREST authors in a subsequent article [19], so it was not included in the current prototype.

Table 1. Line code comparison

Framework	Framework source code	Demo source code
CREST-Scheme	5938	817
CREST-Erlang	2957	768

Implementation effort. To compare the effort in implementing the two framework, and so to indirectly compare the choice of the two languages used, i.e., Scheme vs. Erlang, we counted the lines of code of the main library and of the implemented case studies, not counting the external dependencies. The results are illustrated in Table 1 and show that our code is about a half of the original one. This fact confirms our initial idea that Erlang more easily and naturally supports the CREST mechanisms.

Performance measurement. To compare the two frameworks in terms of performance, we re-built part of the implementation of the original case study, in particular we used the same Web client application (with its graphical widgets) and recreated some of the corresponding CREST services. We also implemented this case study as a standard Web application using MochiWeb alone, to use as a reference. This was possible since the original case study, unless the client duplicates its session, does not exploit any advanced CREST functionality; all computations are installed during system startup, and they are only invoked at the demo.

To actually measure the performance of these three applications, we used a dual core laptop with 4GB of RAM as a server, and we launched several simulated users from a different computer, a 6 core desktop with 8GB of RAM. Notice that

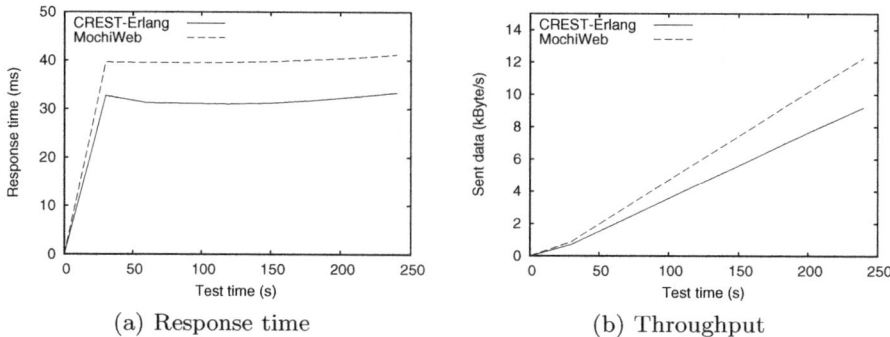

(a) Response time   (b) Throughput

Fig. 2. CREST-Scheme demo

we choose the machine running the clients to be more powerful than the server to be sure the values we measured were not influenced by some limitation on the client side. The two machines are connected by a 100Mbit LAN. The whole test is run by using a client application, written in Erlang, which measures the average response time for each request and the throughput in term of KBytes per second sent to the clients. We used a navigation sample recorded during a browser session through the demo site to simulate the behavior of a standard user. Through our script we simulated the arrival of one of such users every second, each repeating the same session with a delay of one second at the end, for 4 minutes in total.

Figure 2 shows the results we measured in terms of response time and throughput. The CREST-Scheme framework has the worst performances, serving a very low number of pages per second with a response time peaking at more than 30 seconds; Mochiweb performs better than CREST-Erlang in terms of response time, because of the overhead introduced internally by the latter, and it is also able to answer more requests per second in the last minute of the test, because its usage of the server resources is lower than the CREST-Erlang one, especially in terms of CPU usage.

To test the overhead introduced by using the *spawn* and *remote* CREST operations, we compared our prototype against MochiWeb in running a Web application based on a simple CREST service. Each client starts by asking a front-end peer to spawn a new instance of this simple service on a different peer, located on the same machine, and from then on it invokes this new service repeatedly, with one second delay among each invocation; the MochiWeb version has the same service pre-installed, which the client invokes repeatedly as before. As in the previous case, we start one client every second for the 4 minutes of the test. Figure 3 illustrates the results we gathered in terms of response time and throughput. We notice that MochiWeb is able to answer more requests per second, and this explains the higher throughput, while the response time is similar and it remains almost constant while the number of clients increases.

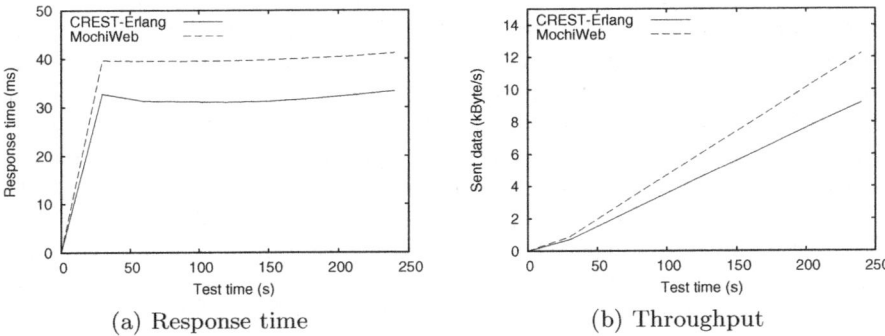

(a) Response time   (b) Throughput

Fig. 3. Test application

5   Related Work

The work we presented here is related with current research on evolvable and dynamically adaptable software architectures and on programming languages supporting dynamic adaptation. Seminal work on the identification of the critical architectural issues concerning run-time evolution is described in [25,28,26]. The CREST approach is largely motivated by this work. Several alternative architectural styles exist to support dynamically evolvable distributed applications. Hereafter we briefly review the most relevant ones and we contrast them with CREST.

Publish-subscribe (P/S) [15,9] is an event-based style where components are not directly connected, but communicate through a common middleware system, which takes any new event notification and dispatches it to any component subscribed for that specific event. This structure is highly dynamic since nodes may be added and removed while the system is running; communication is asynchronous and components can operate independently of each other.

Map-reduce (M/R) [10] is a style used to parallelize a computation over a large data set by distributing work over a collection of worker nodes. In the *map* phase each node receives from a master node some amount of data and elaborates it, returning key-value pairs to the master, while in the *reduce* phase the master node takes the answers to all the sub-problems and combines them to produce the output. Because worker nodes may be masters, a tree structure can be easily obtained, increasing scalability. As in the P/S case, M/R nodes are completely autonomous; they may join and leave dynamically as they do not share any data or state directly, and perform their computation in isolation w.r.t. the others.

Similarly to CREST, P/S and M/R architectural styles are oriented to dynamic adaptation, but differently from CREST they are not specifically oriented to supporting Web applications, probably the most important domain for distributed applications today and the one we target.

The two architectural styles that are today competing for becoming a standard in building Web applications are REST and the *Service-Oriented architecture* (SOA) [11]. We already discussed the differences between CREST and

REST in Section 2.1. SOA models a Web application as a composition of different autonomous services, independently developed and existing in different namespaces and execution contexts. Services may be dynamically discovered and compositions may bind to them dynamically. Usually these services operate over HTTP using Web Service protocols supporting standardized discovery and service invocation. Unfortunately, these protocols violate REST principles, as we already discussed in Section 2.1, and this can be a major problem, since REST principles are those that guaranteed the success of the Web.

CREST not only follows the REST principles, but also promises to support dynamic adaptation much better. Indeed, both REST and SOA focus on data as the primary element exchanged among components and this makes it hard to adapt the architecture of the application dynamically, since this usually requires to introduce new components/services. Vice-versa, CREST adopts the computations themselves as the elements exchanged among nodes (i.e., peers) and this makes it straightforward to change the architecture of the application at run time, when required.

Besides architectural styles, another research direction related with the work presented in this paper concerns programming languages. In particular, the identification of features or language constructs that may provide better support to the specific requirement of run-time adaptation. This sometimes leads to extensions of existing languages to support dynamic adaptation. For example, *context-oriented programming* extensions have been proposed and implemented for various languages [2], starting from initial work on LISP [8], up to the initial version of ContextErlang [18] developed by our research group. The features supported by Aspect-Oriented programming languages [24], and in particular Dynamic Aspect-Oriented languages [21], have also been proved to help in this context.

Functional programming languages, and in particular the notions of continuation and closure, have also been revamped in the context of Web programming. A short summary of work upon which CREST-Scheme is rooted can be found in [7], while examples of use of functional programming concepts in Web applications are provided in [20,27].

6   Conclusions

This article presented CREST-Erlang, a new implementation of a Web framework supporting the CREST architectural style. CREST is a promising style, which suggests to move from an Internet of *data* to an Internet of *computations* to cope with the dynamism of distributed applications developed nowadays.

As its name suggests, the new framework adopts Erlang as its reference language, while the original CREST framework adopted Scheme. This choice was motivated by the fact that Erlang provides advanced mechanisms to develop strongly concurrent, fault-tolerant, distributed applications in an easy and effective way. This intuition is confirmed by the experience reported in this paper. Erlang required less effort than Scheme to develop the framework and the resulting prototype performs better than the original one. Also, as we found easier to develop the framework using Erlang than using Scheme, we argue that programmers using the framework to build CREST applications would benefit from a language that eases development of efficient algorithms, by natively supporting an effective form of concurrency (through the actor paradigm), which very well fits current multi-core hardware.

The main drawback we found was the limited support offered by the language and associated library to security, especially the peculiar form of security required when computations are expected to move among nodes. We provided an initial solution to the problem, but more has to be done.

As for our experience in using CREST, we found it an effective architectural style to build Web applications that could follow the somewhat natural evolution from an Internet of data to an Internet of computations.

On the other hand, a few remarks emerge from this experience. The first is about the protocol for CREST specific operations: is HTTP really the best protocol for transmitting computations? HTTP was developed for accessing documents. Although it is now often used as a general-purpose protocol, this was not its original purpose. Even in the case of Web Services, data had to be encoded in some document-like intermediate representation, such as XML, before being moved to clients, with a certain overhead. The same happens when computations, including state, function references, and code have to be transferred.

The second remark is about security. We already see in today's Internet the security issues induced by the code-on-demand features of Web 2.0 sites, with malevolent Javascript code used for stealing users' data. We can easily imagine what could happen if computations are allowed to move around on the backweb. Apart from citing the usual countermeasures, developed for mobile agent platforms and never assessed in realistic, large scale, open environments, the CREST definition does not provide any specific solution to this problem. We are convinced that this could severely limit the adoption of the CREST style until something new is developed.

As for our future plans, we want to continue developing our prototype, by introducing a caching mechanism that may further increase performance. We will also integrate the concept of *subpeer*, introduced in the latest CREST definition [19].

Acknowledgment

This work was partially supported by the European Commission, Programme IDEAS-ERC, Project 227977-SMScom; and by the Italian Government under the projects FIRB INSYEME and PRIN D-ASAP.

References

1. Mochiweb, http://github.com/mochi/mochiweb
2. Appeltauer, M., Hirschfeld, R., Haupt, M., Lincke, J., Perscheid, M.: A comparison of context-oriented programming languages. In: COP 2009: International Workshop on Context-Oriented Programming, pp. 1–6. ACM Press, New York (2009)

3. Armstrong, J.: Making reliable distributed systems in the presence of software errors. Ph.D. thesis, Royal Institute of Technology, Sweden (December 2003)
4. Armstrong, J.: A history of erlang. In: HOPL. pp. 1–26 (2007)
5. Armstrong, J.: Programming Erlang: Software for a Concurrent World. Pragmatic Bookshelf (July 2007), http://www.amazon.com/exec/obidos/redirect?tag=citeulike07-20&path=ASIN%/193435600X
6. Armstrong, J.: Erlang. Commun. ACM 53(9), 68–75 (2010)
7. Byrd, W.E.: Web programming with continuations. Tech. rep., Unpublished Tech. Report (2002), http://double.co.nz/pdf/continuations.pdf
8. Costanza, P.: Language constructs for context-oriented programming. In: Proceedings of the Dynamic Languages Symposium, pp. 1–10. ACM Press, New York (2005)
9. Cugola, G., Margara, A.: Processing flows of information: From data stream to complex event processing. ACM Comput. Surv. (to appear)
10. Dean, J., Ghemawat, S.: Mapreduce: a flexible data processing tool. Commun. ACM 53(1), 72–77 (2010)
11. DiNitto, E., Ghezzi, C., Metzger, A., Papazoglou, M.P., Pohl, K.: A journey to highly dynamic, self-adaptive service-based applications. Autom. Softw. Eng. 15(3-4), 313–341 (2008)
12. Dybvig, R.K.: MIT Press, 4th edn. MIT Press, Cambridge (2009)
13. Erenkrantz, J.R., Gorlick, M., Suryanarayana, G., Taylor, R.N.: From representations to computations: the evolution of web architectures. In: ESEC-FSE 2007: Proceedings of the 6th Joint Meeting of the European Software Engineering Conference and the 14th ACM SIGSOFT Symposium on Foundations of Software Engineering, pp. 255–264. ACM Press, New York (2007), http://dx.doi.org/10.1145/1287624.1287660
14. Erenkrantz, J.R.: Computational REST: a new model for decentralized, internet-scale applications. Ph.D. thesis, Long Beach, CA, USA (2009) Adviser-Taylor, Richard, N.
15. Eugster, P.T., Felber, P., Guerraoui, R., Kermarrec, A.M.: The many faces of publish/subscribe. ACM Comput. Surv. 35(2), 114–131 (2003)
16. Fielding, R.T.: Architectural styles and the design of network-based software architectures. Ph.D. thesis (2000), http://portal.acm.org/citation.cfm?id=932295
17. Fuggetta, A., Picco, G.P., Vigna, G.: Understanding code mobility. IEEE Transactions on Software Engineering 24, 342–361 (1998)
18. Ghezzi, C., Pradella, M., Salvaneschi, G.: Context oriented programming in highly concurrent systems. In: COP 2010: International Workshop on Context-Oriented Programming, co-located with ECOOP 2010, Maribor, Slovenia (2010) (to appear)
19. Gorlick, M., Erenkrantz, J., Taylor, R.: The infrastructure of a computational web. Tech. rep., University of California, Irvine (May 2010)
20. Graunke, P., Findler, R.B., Krishnamurthi, S., Felleisen, M.: Automatically restructuring programs for the web. In: Proceedings of the 16th IEEE International Conference on Automated Software Engineering, ASE 2001, p. 211. IEEE Computer Society, Washington, DC, USA (2001), http://portal.acm.org/citation.cfm?id=872023.872573
21. Greenwood, P., Blair, L.: L.: Using dynamic aspect-oriented programming to implement an autonomic system. Tech. rep., Proceedings of the, Dynamic Aspect Workshop (DAW04, RIACS (2003)

22. Hewitt, C., Bishop, P., Steiger, R.: A universal modular actor formalism for artificial intelligence. In: Proceedings of the 3rd International Joint Conference on Artificial Intelligence, pp. 235–245. Morgan Kaufmann Publishers Inc, San Francisco (1973), http://portal.acm.org/citation.cfm?id=1624775.1624804
23. Kaminsky, M., Banks, E.: Sfs-http: Securing the web with self-certifying urls
24. Masuhara, H., Kiczales, G.: Modeling crosscutting in aspect-oriented mechanisms, pp. 2–28. Springer, Heidelberg (2003)
25. Oreizy, P., Medvidovic, N., Taylor, R.N.: Architecture-based runtime software evolution. In: ICSE, pp. 177–186 (1998)
26. Oreizy, P., Medvidovic, N., Taylor, R.N.: Runtime software adaptation: framework, approaches, and styles. In: 30th International Conference on Software Engineering, pp. 899–910. ACM Press, New York (2008)
27. Queinnec, C.: The influence of browsers on evaluators or, continuations to program web servers. In: Proceedings of the fifth ACM SIGPLAN International Conference on Functional Programming, ICFP 2000, pp. 23–33. ACM, New York (2000), http://doi.acm.org/10.1145/351240.351243
28. Taylor, R.N., Medvidovic, N., Oreizy, P.: Architectural styles for runtime software adaptation. In: WICSA/ECSA, pp. 171–180 (2009)
29. Vigna, G. (ed.): Mobile Agents and Security. LNCS, vol. 1419. Springer, Heidelberg (1998)
30. Zachary, J.: Protecting mobile code in the world. IEEE Internet Computing 7(2), 78–82 (2003)

Efficient Retrieval and Ranking of Undesired Package Cycles in Large Software Systems

Jean-Rémy Falleri[1], Simon Denier[2], Jannik Laval[2], Philippe Vismara[3], and Stéphane Ducasse[2]

[1] Université de Bordeaux
[2] Rmod - USTL - INRIA Lille Nord Europe
[3] LIRMM, UMR5506 CNRS - Université Montpellier 2
MISTEA, UMR729 Montpellier SupAgro - INRA

Abstract. Many design guidelines state that a software system architecture should avoid cycles between its packages. Yet such cycles appear again and again in many programs. We believe that the existing approaches for cycle detection are too coarse to assist the developers to remove cycles from their programs. In this paper, we describe an efficient algorithm that performs a fine-grained analysis of the cycles among the packages of an application. In addition, we define a metric to rank cycles by their level of *undesirability*, prioritizing the cycles that seems the more undesired by the developers. Our approach is validated on two large and mature software systems in Java and Smalltalk.

1 Introduction

Large object-oriented software projects are usually structured in *packages* (or *modules*). A package is primarily used to group together related classes which define a functionality of the system. Classes belonging to the same package should be built, tested, versioned, and released together. Martin consequently proposed to see the package as the software release unit [3]. Design guidelines state that cyclic dependencies between packages should be avoided [6,3]. Indeed, packages depending cyclically on each other are to be understood, tested, released, or deployed together.

Several tools and approaches have been developed over the years [11,5,7,2] to help the developers to detect cycles. Yet, an exhaustive experimental study [4] shows that in a lot of programs, classes are involved in huge cyclic dependencies. It seems therefore plausible that the way cycles are detected is not sufficient to help the developer to remove them.

We claim that the existing approaches have two main issues. First, some focus on cycles between classes, when cyclic dependencies at the package level should have the priority. Indeed classes are not deployment units, and a lot of cycles among classes are due to the associations, being thus totally expected. Second, and most important, existing approaches are all based on the same algorithm by Tarjan [9]. This algorithm finds the maximum sets of packages depending (directly or indirectly) on each other, called *strongly connected components* (SCC)

J. Bishop and A. Vallecillo (Eds.): TOOLS 2011, LNCS 6705, pp. 260–275, 2011.

in graph theory. Within a SCC, a package is in cycle with all other packages, and there can be multiple cycles in one SCC. In our experience, we have seen software systems with a single huge SCC containing dozens of packages. The above algorithm becomes useless in such cases as it does not provide further information to understand and remove the cycles.

A dependent problem which is not well addressed in current approaches is ranking cycles so that the most "undesired" ones are given top priority for removal. Indeed, not all cyclic dependencies have the same importance. In a hierarchical system of packages (as in Java), a package such as *ui.internal* can be in cyclic dependency with *ui* without much consequences, since they both implement the same functionality. On the contrary, a cycle between *ui* and *core* packages should be avoided as it hampers reuse and deployment of the system. We further discuss this issues as well as the prevalence of packages cycles in four Java programs in Sect. 2.

Our approach advocates the decomposition of a SCC in *multiple short cycles* covering all dependencies of the SCC. Computed cycles usually involve two to four packages. They are therefore easy to understand and to remove, if necessary. Developers can iterate over a set of short cycles and assess them one by one rather than dealing with the single large set of packages contained in the SCC. Moreover, our approach is able to rank the extracted cycles, *prioritizing the ones that seems the more undesired.*

In this paper, we present two major contributions to assist developers in understanding and removing cyclic dependencies in software systems:

- First, we present an efficient algorithm that decomposes a SCC. This algorithm retrieves a set of short cycles that covers all dependencies of the SCC. It has a polynomial time and space complexity (Sect. 3.1).
- Second, we introduce a new metric that evaluates the level of undesirability of a cycle. This metric, called *diameter*, is based upon the notion of distance between packages involved in the cycle (Sect. 3.2).

Our approach is validated against two large and mature programs, in Java and Smalltalk (see Sect. 4).

2 Motivation

This section presents a small study showing why the SCCs are not fine-grained enough to assist developers in understanding and removing cycles in large programs (Sect. 2.1). Then, it explains using an example why some cycles among packages of a software system can be desired by their developers (Sect. 2.2).

2.1 Limitation of the Main Cycle Detection Algorithm

Most of the approaches perform cycle detection by using an algorithm [9] that is capable of finding the *maximum sets of packages that depend (directly or indirectly) on each others.* Such a set of packages is called, in the graph theory, a

Table 1. Measures among packages and package cycles on the Java programs. #**P** is the number of packages, #**LSCC** the size of the largest SCC and **LSCCR** the ratio of packages in the largest SCC.

Program	#P	#LSCC	LSCCR
ArgoUML 0.28.1	79	38	48%
JEdit 4.3.1	29	18	62%
Choco 2.1.0	147	38	26%
AntLR 3.2	31	7	23%

strongly connected component (SCC). In a SCC, each package is in cycle with all other packages, and cycles exists only among the packages of a same SCC. To remove package cycles, it is therefore necessary to remove several dependencies among the packages of a given SCC. We believe that the SCCs are not fine-grained enough to help the developer to understand and remove the undesired dependencies in their programs. Indeed, they indicate *which* packages are involved in cyclic dependencies, but they can not explain *how*. Whenever a SCC contains only a few packages, it remains possible to visualize the dependencies between them and to remove the cycles. On the other hand, when a SCC contains a lot of packages, it does not help the developer at all. Indeed, if it contains dozens of packages, it becomes hard to understand how packages connect with each other to create the SCC.

To show that mature and large programs can contain huge SCCs, we proceed to a small experiment. We select four mature and medium-sized Java programs: ArgoUML (http://argouml.tigris.org), JEdit (http://www.jedit.org), Choco (http://www.emn.fr/z-info/choco-solver) and AntLR (http://www.antlr.org). On these programs we compute: #**P** the number of packages, #**LSCC** the size of the largest SCC and **LSCCR**: the ratio of packages in the largest SCC.

Tab. 1 shows that the programs we selected contains large SCCs. In ArgoUML the largest SCC contains almost half of the packages (see the **LSSCR** measure). Worse, in JEdit almost two third of the packages are in the largest SCC, whereas the total number of packages is not too large. Apart from AntLR, the size of the largest SCC in the programs of our corpus will make their understanding hard (see the #**LSCC** measure).

2.2   Desired and Undesired Cycles

In the introduction, we stated that not every cycle should be removed. In fact, we believe that a significant proportion of the cycles among the packages of a program are desired by the developers. To show this, let us take the example of the JFace (http://wiki.eclipse.org/index.php/JFace) main widget library used in the Eclipse development environment. A great deal of attention has been devoted to its design by several software design experts. We therefore assume that the cycles present in JFace are not accidental. Package *jface.text* is dedicated to the text widgets. This package provides classes such as *TextViewer*.

Package *jface.text.hyperlink* is dedicated to the management of textual hyperlinks. In JFace, there is a cycle between *jface.text* and *jface.text.hyperlink*. The *TextViewer* class is able to display texts containing hyperlinks and therefore *jface.text* depends on *jface.text.hyperlink*. Also, *jface.text.hyperlink* uses a lot of classes and interfaces defined in *jface.text*. For instance an hyperlink is able to trigger text events and therefore depends on the *TextEvent* class, which is defined in the *jface.text* package. Therefore *jface.text.hyperlink* depends on *jface.text*. In this case, the complexity of the hyperlink motivates its isolation in package *jface.text.hyperlink*. Yet it is not necessary to break the cycle with *jface.text* as it would make no sense to release one without the other.

More generally, in several languages such as Java, a package can contain other packages, leading to a package containment tree. It is usual that when a package is too big (i.e. contains two many classes), it is split in several sub-packages. In this case it is very likely that cycles exist between these sub-packages.

3   Our Approach

In this section, we present our two contributions:

- First, we present an efficient algorithm that decomposes a SCC. This algorithm retrieves a set of short cycles that covers all dependencies of the SCC. It has a polynomial time and space complexity (Sect. 3.1).
- Second, we introduce a new metric that evaluates the level of undesirability of a cycle. This metric, called *diameter*, is based upon the notion of distance between packages involved in the cycle (Sect. 3.2).

3.1   A New Cycle Retrieval Algorithm

Intuition of our algorithm. To explain better the intuition of our new algorithm, let us first introduce a sample class diagram, shown in Fig. 1. From this class diagram, we extract the directed graph shown in Fig. 1. This graph shows the dependencies between the packages, therefore we call it a *package dependency graph*. On this graph, the SCCs are rounded by dashed circles.

In the previous section, we stated that the algorithm that computes the SCCs is not fine-grained enough to help the developers to understand and remove cycles from their programs. Fortunately, another algorithm from the graph-theory literature is able to perform a fine-grained analysis of cycles in a directed graph [10]. It computes the set of *elementary cycles*. A cycle is elementary if no node (here no package) appears *more than once* when enumerating the sequence of nodes in the cycle. For instance, in our sample graph of Fig. 1, this algorithm finds the six elementary cycles shown in Fig. 1. Figuring out if an elementary cycle should be removed or not is straightforward, it only requires to decide if the dependencies involved in the cycle are correct. Unfortunately, the number of elementary cycles in a directed graph can be exponential. Therefore, this algorithm does not scale on programs composed of many packages.

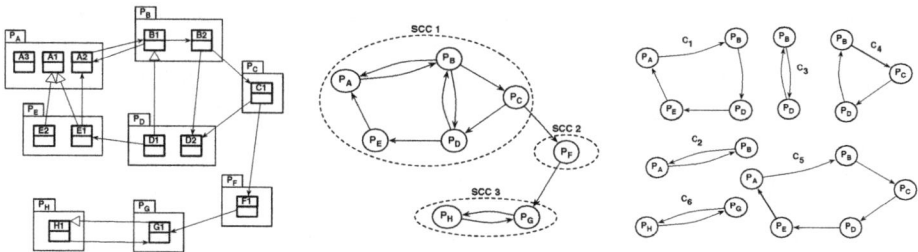

Fig. 1. A sample class diagram (left), the corresponding package dependency graph (midde, the dashed lines round the SCC) and the elementary cycles for this graph(right)

We introduce a new algorithm that still computes elementary cycles in a SCC but that retrieves only a polynomial number of them, reducing time and space complexity. Indeed, some elementary cycles can be seen as redundant. In Fig. 1, cycle C_5 is not useful if we consider cycles C_1 and C_4. Indeed, the dependencies covered by C_5 have already been covered by the two other cycles. We reduce the number of cycles by selecting only a subset of the elementary cycles, ensuring that each dependency of the SCC is covered by at least a cycle. Still, to get all dependencies covered in Fig. 1, it is possible to select cycles C_2, C_3, C_6, and either C_1 and C_4, or the longer cycle C_5. We assume that a long cycle is harder to understand than a short one because it requires the analysis of more dependencies. Therefore our final solution is to select for each dependency **one of the shortest cycles going through the dependency**.

Mathematical model. A package dependency graph G is a couple (P, D) with P a set of nodes (the packages) and D a set of edges (dependencies between the packages). An edge is a couple $(s, t) \in P^2$ where s is the source and t the target package. There is an edge from a package s to a package t iff a class of s uses a class of t. We define the function $\Gamma^+ : P \to \mathcal{P}(D)$ (with $\mathcal{P}(E)$ the power-set of E) which has the following definition $\Gamma^+(x) = \{(x, y) \in D\}$. This function gives all the dependencies where a given package appears as source. Reversely, $\Gamma^- : P \to \mathcal{P}(D)$ is $\Gamma^-(x) = \{(z, x) \in D\}$. This function gives all the edges where a given package appears as target. We denote a path in G by a sequence of nodes, written this way: (a, b, c), where every node has an edge to its successor. We denote a cycle by such a sequence of nodes : $x \to y \to z$, the last node being implicitly linked to the first one.

Details of our algorithm. To understand the algorithm, it is important to notice that cycles exist *only* among the nodes of the same SCC. Also, the set of SCCs of a directed graph is a partition of its nodes. Therefore as a preliminary step to our algorithm, we retrieve the SCCs from the directed graph using the algorithm of [9], remove the inter-SCCs edges, then run our algorithm on each SCC containing more than two nodes (SCCs of size one cannot contain a cycle).

The SCCs of size two contain only one cycle involving the two nodes. Therefore on the graph of Fig. 1, only *SCC 1* is considered by our algorithm, while *SCC 2* is discarded and *SCC 3* directly leads to the creation of the cycle $P_G \rightarrow P_H$. In the following, we therefore focus on what happens in a SCC of size greater than two. To find shortest cycles, we use the well-known *breadth-first search* (BFS) algorithm. This algorithm can be used to find the shortest path between two nodes in a graph where the edges are unweighted. A SCC has the following property: for each possible pair of nodes x, y of the SCC, there is a path from x to y and from y to x. A simple algorithm to find a shortest cycle for every edge of a strongly connected graph is therefore to perform for each edge $(x, y) \in D$ a BFS from target node y going back to source node x. Indeed since there is an edge from x to y, this edge is already the shortest path from x to y. Since we are in a SCC, it is mandatory that at least a path exists from y to x. A shortest path from y to x (found by the BFS) concatenated with the edge (x, y) would therefore be a shortest cycle in which this edge is involved.

The only problem of this simple algorithm is that it requires a BFS for each edge of the graph. Since there are less nodes than edges in a strongly connected graph, it would be better to perform a BFS only for each node of the graph. The idea is therefore to gather the ancestors $A = \{y \in P | (y, x) \in \Gamma_P^-(x)\}$ of a node x, and perform a BFS from x until all its ancestors $y \in A$ are found. This way, only one BFS is performed for each node. The pseudo code of this optimized version is given in Algorithm 1. To avoid the retrieval of identical cycles, we consider that two cycles are equals if the first is a cyclic permutation of the second. For instance $c \rightarrow a \rightarrow b = a \rightarrow b \rightarrow c$. To have a fixed order to represent the cycles and compare them efficiently, we always place the lowest node (using the lexicographic order) at the beginning of the cycle. We call this operation *normalize*. For instance $normalize(c \rightarrow a \rightarrow b) = a \rightarrow b \rightarrow c$.

Let see how this algorithm works on *SCC 1*, shown in Fig. 1. Remember that the edge from P_C to P_F has been deleted because it is a inter-SCCs edge. The set of nodes is $P = \{P_A, P_B, P_C, P_D, P_E\}$. We start with an empty set of cycles: $\mathcal{C} = \{\}$. Here are the steps followed by our algorithm:

1. The first node being picked up is P_A. Therefore, $A = \{P_E\}$. The BFS starting from P_A will find P_E by the following path: (P_A, P_B, P_D, P_E). Since $\mathcal{C}$ is empty, the cycle $\mathcal{C}_1 = P_A \rightarrow P_B \rightarrow P_D \rightarrow P_E$ is added to $\mathcal{C}$. $\mathcal{C} = \{\mathcal{C}_1\}$.
2. The second node being picked up is P_B. $A = \{P_A, P_D\}$.
   - The BFS started from P_B will find P_A by the following path: (P_B, P_A). This cycle is normalized in $\mathcal{C}_2 = P_A \rightarrow P_B$ and added to $\mathcal{C}$. $\mathcal{C} = \{\mathcal{C}_1, \mathcal{C}_2\}$.
   - The BFS started from P_B will find P_D by the following path: (P_B, P_D). The cycle $\mathcal{C}_3 = P_B \rightarrow P_D$ is added to $\mathcal{C}$. $\mathcal{C} = \{\mathcal{C}_1, \mathcal{C}_2, \mathcal{C}_3\}$.
3. The third node being picked up is P_C. $A = \{P_B\}$. The BFS starting from P_C will find P_B by the following path: (P_C, P_D, P_B). After normalization, it becomes $\mathcal{C}_4 = P_B \rightarrow P_C \rightarrow P_D$ and it is added to $\mathcal{C}$. $\mathcal{C} = \{\mathcal{C}_1, \mathcal{C}_2, \mathcal{C}_3, \mathcal{C}_4\}$.
4. The fourth node being picked up is P_D. $A = \{P_B, P_C\}$.

Algorithm 1. Our cycle retrieval algorithm

Data: A strongly connected package dependencies graph $G = (P, D)$
Result: A set of shortest cycles $\mathcal{C}$
begin

    $\mathcal{C} \leftarrow \{\}$;   `// the set of cycles`
    for $x \in P$ **do**

        $V \leftarrow \{\}$;   `// the set of the visited nodes`
        $A \leftarrow \{z \in P | (z, x) \in \Gamma^-(x)\}$;   `// the set of the x ancestors`
        $x.bfs\_ancestor \leftarrow \varnothing$;   `// the path followed by the BFS`
        $Q \leftarrow (x)$;   `// a queue, initialized with x`
        `/* BFS from x that stops when every ancestor of x is found     */`
        while $size(A) > 0$ **do**

            $p \leftarrow pop(Q)$;   `// removes the first element of Q`
            for $(p, y) \in \Gamma^+(p)$ **do**

                `/* if y has not been visited or put on the stack yet    */`
                if $y \notin V \cup Q$ **then**

                    $y.bfs\_ancestor \leftarrow p$;
                    $push(Q, y)$;   `// adds y at the end of Q`

                `/* if an ancestor of x is reached                       */`
                if $y \in A$ **then**

                    $c \leftarrow ()$;   `// the list of the nodes of the cycle`
                    $i \leftarrow y$;
                    `/* builds the cycle                                 */`
                    while $i \neq \varnothing$ **do**

                        $add(c, i)$;
                        $i \leftarrow i.bfs\_ancestor$;

                    `/* adds the cycle to the set of cycles              */`
                    $normalize(c)$;
                    if $c \notin \mathcal{C}$ **then** $\mathcal{C} \leftarrow \mathcal{C} \cup \{c\}$;
                    $remove(A, y)$;   `// removes y from A`

            $V \leftarrow V \cup \{p\}$;   `// p is now visited`

- The BFS started from P_D will find P_B by the following path: (P_D, P_B). This cycle is normalized in $\mathcal{C}_3$ and therefore is not added to $\mathcal{C}$. $\mathcal{C} = \{\mathcal{C}_1, \mathcal{C}_2, \mathcal{C}_3, \mathcal{C}_4\}$.
- The BFS started from P_D will find P_C by the following path: (P_D, P_B, P_C). This cycle is normalized in $\mathcal{C}_4$ and therefore is not added to $\mathcal{C}$. $\mathcal{C} = \{\mathcal{C}_1, \mathcal{C}_2, \mathcal{C}_3, \mathcal{C}_4\}$.

5. The fifth and last node picked-up is P_E. $A = \{P_D\}$. The BFS starting from P_E will find P_D by the following path: (P_E, P_A, P_B, P_D). This cycle is normalized in $\mathcal{C}_1$ and therefore is not added to $\mathcal{C}$. $\mathcal{C} = \{\mathcal{C}_1, \mathcal{C}_2, \mathcal{C}_3, \mathcal{C}_4\}$.

Finally, we have $\mathcal{C} = \{\mathcal{C}_1, \mathcal{C}_2, \mathcal{C}_3, \mathcal{C}_4\}$. We can notice that in contrast to the enumeration of all elementary cycles (see Fig. 1), the long cycle $P_A \rightarrow P_B \rightarrow P_C \rightarrow P_D \rightarrow P_E$ is not retrieved by our algorithm.

Complexity of Algorithm 1. Let $n = |P|$ be the number of nodes and $m = |D|$ be the number of edges. In the worst case, we pick-up a different cycle for every edge, the maximum number of cycles is therefore m. We split the computation of the worst-case time complexity in three parts: worst time spent in the pre-processing step (finding the SCCs), worst time spent in the BFSes, and worst time spent to add the cycles in the cycle set. Since we work with strongly connected graphs, we have $m \geq n$.

1. The worst case time complexity of the algorithm that computes the SCCs in the pre-processing step in $O(n + m)$ [9].
2. The worst case time complexity of a BFS in a graph is $O(n + m)$. Since we perform a BFS for every node of the graph, it leads to a $O(n(m + n))$ complexity for the BFSes.
3. The addition of a cycle in the set of cycles can be done in $O(n \times log(n))$ using appropriate data structures (like a self-balancing binary search tree). In the worst case, we try to add the same cycle involving all packages for each edge. Therefore the worst case time complexity for the additions is $O(m \times n \times log(n))$.

Since $m \geq n$, the overall complexity of our algorithm is $O(m \times n \times log(n))$. Since the number of packages in a program cannot be too large (we consider $1,000$ packages as a fair upper-bound), this complexity is perfectly acceptable to be applied at development-time (for an immediate feedback) as well as maintenance-time (for an in-depth architecture assessment).

3.2   Our Distance-Based Metric to Detect Undesired Cycles

In the previous section, we showed how we efficiently retrieve cycles from a package dependency graph. Unfortunately, there can be many cycles, especially in a large and complex program. A developer is not going to inspect manually all the cycles, because it is a tedious and time-consuming task. Moreover, a significant amount of these cycles is probably *desired*, like we have seen in Sect. 2. To assist in understanding and removing the cycles, it is critical to propose in priority the cycles that seems the most *undesired*. This is the purpose of our *diameter* metric. To define it, we assume that packages are located in a *containment tree*. This is the case in many languages such as Java, C#, Ruby, or PHP. Even when it is not the case as in Smalltalk, such a tree can often be inferred from conventions and names given by the developers to the packages.

To better illustrate the phenomenon described in Sect. 2, let us imagine the sample package containment tree shown in Fig. 2. In this package tree, a cycle between *ui.dialog.wizard* and *ui* seems desired. It is common that a class in a package uses classes of its parent packages. It is also possible that in the parent package, several classes depend on the classes of the sub-packages (such as factory classes). In our example, *ui.dialog.wizard* is likely to use several classes defined in *ui*, like a *Widget* class. It is also likely that *ui* furnishes a factory class to create wizards (such as *WizardFactory*), that uses the different wizards defined *ui.dialog.wizard*. In this case this cycle would be totally desired since

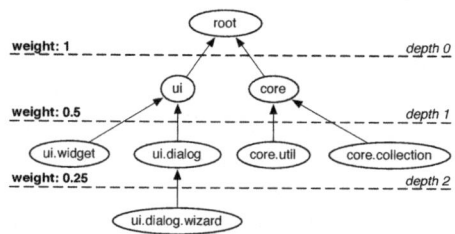

Fig. 2. A sample package containment tree, with the weight associated to the edges

the developer would neither use nor deploy *ui* without *ui.dialog.wizard*. On the other hand a cycle between *core* and *ui* seems strongly undesired. Although the dependence from *ui* to *core* seems normal, it is unlikely that a package such as *core* requires *ui* to be used or deployed.

We do not want the developers to have the burden of inspecting all the desired cycles. We prefer to show them the cycles that seem the most undesired first. To do so, we use the package containment tree to define a distance between two packages: for instance the number of edges required to go from a package to the other package. We assume that the further away are the packages involved in a cycle, the more undesired the cycle seems. Unfortunately, with this definition of distance, the packages *ui.dialog.wizard* and *ui* are at the same distance from each other as *core* and *ui* (two edges). To deal with this problem we add a second assumption: the farther away the common ancestor between two packages is from the root of the tree, the less the distance between them is significant. For instance, the common ancestor between *ui.dialog.wizard* and *ui* is *ui*, while the common ancestor between *core* and *ui* is *root*.

To deal with the two previously described assumptions, we define a weighting function that assigns a high weight to the edges close to the root and a low weight to the edges far from the root. The weight of an edge depends on its depth. For an edge e at depth d, the weight $w(e) = \frac{1}{2^d}$. Fig. 2 shows a sample package containment tree with weights associated to its edges. The distance between two packages $D_P : P^2 \to \mathbb{R}^+$ is then equal to the sum of the weights of the edges that lead from the first package to the second one. For instance $D_P(core, ui) = 2$, $D_P(ui.widget, ui.dialog) = 1$ and $D_P(ui.dialog.wizard, ui) = 0.75$.

We can now define our metric that indicates the level of undesirability of a cycle, called *diameter* (denoted by $\mathcal{D}$). It is defined as the worst possible distance between two packages contained in the cycle. More formally, let $\mathcal{C}$ be a cycle, and let $P_\mathcal{C}$ be the set of packages contained in the cycle. $\mathcal{D}(\mathcal{C}) = \max(\{D_P(x, y) | \{x, y\} \in P_\mathcal{C}^2, x \neq y\})$. Let us imagine that there is the following cycle: $ui \to ui.widget \to core$. The diameter of this cycle is $\mathcal{D}(ui \to ui.widget \to core) = 2.5$ because $D_P(core, ui) = 2$, $D_P(ui, ui.widget) = 0.5$ and $D_P(core, ui.widget) = 2.5$. We also have: $\mathcal{D}(ui \to ui.widget \to ui.dialog) = 1$ because $D_P(ui, ui.widget) = 0.5$, $D_P(ui, ui.dialog) = 0.5$ and $D_P(ui.dialog, ui.widget) = 1$. As one can notice, the larger the diameter is, the more undesired it seems to be.

4   Validation

We validate our approach on two large programs with an experiment involving their maintainers. Our approach can be used both at development-time and at maintenance-time. Nevertheless, we believe that it is harder to understand and remove a cycle at maintenance-time, because it is necessary to remember the past design decisions that led to its creation.

To show that our approach is useful we take the use-case where a developer use our tool, called *Popsycle*[1], on his software at maintenance-time. Popsycle uses the algorithm described in Sect. 3.1 to extract the cycles. It ranks them using the metric presented in Sect. 3.2 (cycles with a large diameter being ranked first). If two cycles have an equal diameter, the number of packages contained in the cycle is used to rank the cycles (the less packages it has, the better it is ranked). If two cycles have an equal diameter and number of packages, they are ranked using the lexicographic order. In addition, Popsycle provides a view that ease the understanding of the cycles by showing the underlying dependencies between the classes that create the cycle.

4.1   Preparation of the Data

We chose two different programs to perform our experiment.

RESYN-Assistant. RESYN-Assistant (http://www.lirmm.fr/~vismara/resyn), is a Java program targeting the domain of organic chemistry. It includes several algorithms for perceiving molecular graphs according to their topological, functional and stereo-chemical features. The development of RESYN-Assistant started in 1996 at the LIRMM institute. It received financial support from the Sanofi-Aventis pharmaceutical company and the french Languedoc-Roussillon region. The development team was composed of four persons: two researchers in computer-science, one PhD student in computer science and one PhD student in chemistry. Because of the turnover within the development team, and because it has mostly been developed by students having different resaerch objectives, its architecture has decayed since the initial version.

The characteristics of the RESYN-Assistant architecture are the following:

- 315 classes, 33 packages, 242 package dependencies
- one SCC (of size > 1) containing 29 packages and 221 dependencies

Pharo. Pharo (http://www.pharo-project.org) is an open-source Smalltalk environment. It has been forked from Squeak, a re-implementation of the classic Smalltalk-80 system. Squeak development was started by Alan Kay group in 1996 based on an original Smalltalk-80 implementation. It received financial support from the Apple and Disney companies. There were about 15 active developers and more than 100 committers involved in its development. Squeak

---

[1] http://popsycle.googlecode.com

contains two graphical frameworks, support for advanced sounds and multimedia presentations, kid authoring system, as well as support for networking and web programming. Lot of experimental code was included in the system without attention to the impact on the global architecture. Pharo forked the code of Squeak in 2008. Its goal is to provide a clean and stable version targeting professional companies as well as researchers. Pharo development team involves about 10 active developers and about 50 committers. The system inherits from more than 15 years of development in a monolithic system context.

The characteristics of the Pharo architecture are the following:

- 1800 classes, 102 packages, package dependencies
- one SCC (of size > 1) containing 61 packages and 790 dependencies

Extraction of the dependencies. To extract the dependencies in the Java program, we use the Apache BCEL (http://jakarta.apache.org/bcel) library on the byte-code of the program. With BCEL, we extract most of the dependencies between the classes, but some of them can be missed. In particular when a method is overloaded, the dependency extracted from the byte-code is always the class that defines the method. Also it is possible that some types are erased if they are used only internally in a method. For Smalltalk applications, we use the MOOSE (http://www.moosetechnology.org) reverse-engineering platform. Since Smalltalk is dynamically typed, type information is hard to extract. The Moose environment deals with that situation by providing a type inference mechanism. It is possible to select the level of fuzziness of the type inference. We selected only the dependencies that can be statically resolved: only direct class references are used to identify dependencies. In addition, Smalltalk does not provide a tree structure for the packages. Nevertheless, the developers of Pharo we analyzed use the names of the packages to simulate it (typical package names: *Collections-Stream* or *Collections-Strings*). Therefore, we take advantage of this naming convention to extract a tree from the package names.

4.2 Experiment

When using Popsycle to extract package cycles, one expects that the most undesired cycles will be ranked first and that the desired cycles will be ranked last. He also expects that Popsycle will extract short cycles, which are easier to understand than the long ones. To validate this, we set up the following experiment. For each program, we compute and rank the cycles. First, we compute the distribution of the cycle sizes, to ensure that short cycles are retrieved. We then ask the maintainers of the programs to count how many cycles in the k first ranked by *Popsycle* are undesired, and how many of the k last cycles are desired. Using this information, we compute the precision over the k first cycles $FP_k = \frac{|\text{undesired cycles}|}{k}$. In our experiment, maintainers will compute FP_{10}, FP_{20} and FP_{30}. These measures will show if our ranking metric is able to rank high undesired cycles. But it could be the case that there are only undesired cycles in the programs of our experiment. In this case, any ranking algorithm would

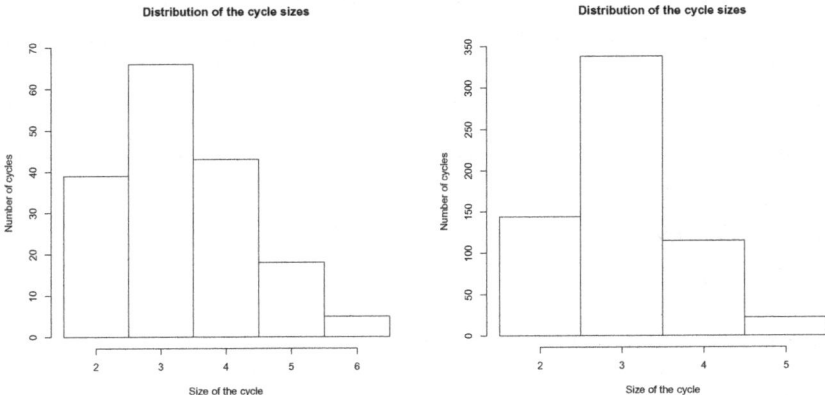

Fig. 3. The distribution of the cycle sizes in RESYN-Assistant (left) and Pharo (right)

have a good precision. To ensure the fact that our ranking metric is able to rank low the desired cycles, we will also compute the precision over the k last ranked cycles $LP_k = \frac{|\text{desired cycles}|}{k}$. In our experiment, the maintainers will compute LP_{10}, LP_{20} and LP_{30}. If both FP_k and LP_k are close to 1, it means that our ranking metric is useful. Lastly, maintainers has been asked to provide a short explanation on why the first cycles were undesired and why the last cycles were desired.

4.3   Results

Size of the cycles. On RESYN-Assistant, our algorithm finds 171 cycles in 17 milli-seconds (mean time computed over 10 runs on a 2GHz Intel Core 2 Duo). The distribution of the cycle sizes is shown in Fig. 3. The largest cycles are of size 6, which is manageable. The majority of the cycles are of size 2, 3 and 4, which are size totally suited for an easy understanding of the cycles. In comparison with the size of the unique SCC (that contains 27 packages), the size of the cycles found by our algorithm is significantly smaller.

Our algorithm finds 619 cycles in Pharo in 40 milli-seconds (mean time computed over 10 runs on a 2GHz Intel Core 2 Duo). The distribution of the cycle sizes is shown in Fig. 3. The largest cycles are of size 5. Like in the previous experiment, the majority of the cycles are of size 2, 3 or 4, even if the size of the SCC is the double of the one in RESYN-Assistant. These sizes are still significantly smaller than the size of the unique SCC of Pharo.

Precision. Tab. 2 shows the precision over the k first and last cycles. Precision is good for the two programs, even with $k = 30$. It means that the first ranked cycles were, as expected, undesired. The last ranked cycles were, as expected, desired.

Table 2. Precision over the k first and last ranked cycles

Program	FP_{10}	FP_{20}	FP_{30}	LP_{10}	LP_{20}	LP_{30}
Pharo	0.9	0.9	0.87	1	1	0.97
RESYN-Assistant 1.0	1	1	1	1	1	1

4.4   Analyze of the Cycles

RESYN-Assistant

First cycles. We found several undesired cycles because the lack of a MVC pattern, creating cycles between the GUI and the algorithms. These cycles have not yet been fixed because they require a significant modification of the code. Several cycles were due to the implementation of an unnecessary interface, and have been corrected instantaneously. A cycle was due to a method that in fact was never called, this cycle has therefore been corrected instantaneously.

Last cycles. Most of them are cycles between packages of the RESYN-Assistant GUI. These cycles are desired since complex graphical components have been developed in the sub-packages and cycles exists between the main window (located in the parent package) and these components. Several other cycles are related to the implementation of an algorithm that was too complex to be implemented in only one package and was therefore split in three packages. Lastly, several cycles are between several packages defining a graph API.

Pharo

First cycles. Most of the first cycles were due to the existence of a multi-purpose package (*System-Support*) that has become huge over the years and contains a lot of misplaced classes. This package creates a lot of undesired dependencies and cycles in the system. We also find several cycles involving the GUI package (*Morphic*), because of the lack of use of an MVC pattern. Several other cycles were due to misplaced methods. Most of the cycles have been corrected in the new version of Pharo.

Last cycles. Most of them are cycles between the *Collection* package and its sub-packages. Several cycles are between the *Network* package and its sub-packages. There is also a cycles between the graphical widget package (named *Morphic*) and its sub-packages.

4.5   Threats to Validity

The methods we use to extract the dependencies extract only a subset of them. Therefore it is possible that at runtime several additional dependencies exist, leading to more cycles. Nevertheless, it is unlikely that it would change the precision results. Another threat to validity is that when we compute the precision, we analyze only a subset of the cycles (35% for RESYN-Assistant and 9.7% for

Pharo). It is very likely that for greater values of k, the precisions LP_k and FP_k will decrease. Lastly, we selected two softwares that have a lot of architectural problems, leading to a lot of undesired cycles. In cleaner software systems, only a few cycles are undesired. In this case, it is possible that they would be missed by our ranking metric.

5   Related Work

Several tools and approaches have been introduced over the years to deal with the problem of cyclic dependencies among packages and classes in a software system. These approaches can be roughly classified using the following criterion: 1) approaches working at the package level, 2) approaches working at the class level, 3) approaches using graph theory algorithms and 4) approaches based on dependency matrix algorithms.

As a general rule, these approaches are concerned with detecting and reporting cycles using Tarjan SCC algorithm [9] or some simpler algorithms. Such approaches do not scale to programs involving large SCCs because they do not provide a deep analysis of how such SCCs arise and how to remove cycles in a SCC. In contrast, we define an algorithm and an approach which computes the information necessary to understand SCCs through subsets of elementary cycles, and that is able to rank cycles by their level of undesirability.

Mudpie [11] is a reporting tool to detect cyclic dependencies between packages in Smalltalk. The paper reports on a single case study performed on packages of the Refactoring Browser in Smalltalk. Classycle (http://classycle.sourceforge.net) is a reporting tool which detects SCC both at class level and package level. Classycle proposes some metrics to characterize cycles but no formal definitions are proposed and their goal is unclear. Both tools rely on Tarjan SCC algorithm for detection of cycles, which make them impractical to analyze large SCCs.

PASTA [1] is a tool for analyzing the dependency graph of Java packages. It focuses on detecting layers in the graph and consequently provides two heuristics to deal with cycles. One views packages in the same SCC as a single package. The other heuristic selectively ignores some dependencies until no more cycle is detected. Thus, PASTA reports on these *undesirable* dependencies which should be removed to break cycles. The paper reports on a case study analyzing the Java core package with effective results. It would be interesting to compare the heuristics for undesirable dependencies with our distance metric for undesired cycles.

JooJ [5] is an approach to detect and remove cyclic dependencies between classes. The principle of JooJ is to find statements creating cyclic dependencies directly in the code editor, allowing the developer to solve the problem as it appears. It computes the SCC using Tarjan to detect cycles among classes. It also computes an approximation of the minimal set of edges to remove in order to make the dependency graph totally acyclic. This NP-complete problem is called minimum feedback arc set in the literature. It highlights therefore the minimum number of statements that one needs to remove to supress all class cycles. However, no study is made to validate this approach : it is possible that the selected dependencies are in fact not to be removed.

Byecycle (http://byecycle.sourceforge.net) is an eclipse plugin to visualize dependencies at class level. It detects and colors in red dependencies involved in cycles. By construction, set of red edges highlight SCC in the visualization. However, the tool does not provide further help for cycle analysis.

JDepend (http://clarkware.com/software/JDepend.html) is a tool for Java which check Martin's principles [3] for package design. In particular, it checks that the package dependency graph is acyclic. Contrary to other approaches, this tool does not detect and retrieve packages in SCCs, but simply reports for each package whether there is a cycle in its transitive dependency graph. For example, with packages A and B in cycle and package C depending upon A, JDepend reports that C depends on a cycle. It can become overwhelming if many packages depends on the same cycle (as each will report separately the cycle) yet is not exhaustive as the tool stops as soon as a cycle is detected (not reporting all cycles in the dependency graph).

Dependency Finder (http://depfind.sourceforge.net) is a set of command line tools to analyze compiled Java code with a focus on dependency graph. One tool detects cycles but at class level only. The algorithm used is not described, although it seems to report elementary cycles.

Dependency structural matrix [8] is an approach developed for process analysis. It visualizes dependencies between some elements (tasks, processes, modules) using the adjacency matrix representation. Several algorithms are defined on the dependency matrices. The main step, called *matrix partitioning*, has a similar output to SCC in a directed graph. Dependency matrices rely on visualization to understand cycles. They make direct cycles easy to spot but indirect cycles are hard to understand with this approach. Lattix [7] and eDSM [2] are two adaptations of dependency matrix to the visualization of package dependencies. They highlight cycles in SCC and can be used as a starting point to understand the architecture of the system. However, due to their limitations in visualizing indirect cycles, they do not benefit from our work which decomposes SCCs in direct and indirect cycles. Instead, we view our work as complementary with DSM as a high level tool and other tools for fine-grained analysis of cycles.

6   Conclusion and Future Work

In this article, we presented two contributions that assist the developers to understand and remove the cycles among packages of a large software system.

- First, we presented an efficient algorithm that decomposes a SCC. This algorithm retrieves a set of short cycles that covers all dependencies of the SCC. It has a polynomial time and space complexity.
- Second, we introduced a new metric that evaluates the level of undesirability of a cycle. This metric, called *diameter*, is based upon the notion of distance between packages involved in the cycle.

Since our algorithm has a low complexity, it can be applied at maintenance-time as well as at development-time, preventing cycles to appear before it is too late. We validate our approach on several case-studies on mature real-world programs in Java and Smalltalk. It shows that our approach has a practical interest and is easy to adapt to various object languages.

To improve our approach we plan to work on the following problems. First we want to define other metrics on the cycles than our distance-based metric. Second, we want to create a visualization that is not a list, but rather a global view of the cycles of the software, it would allow the developers to have a more global vision of the cycles in their programs. Finally we want to adapt and apply our tool to legacy procedural languages like C or ADA, because we believe that cycles are frequent in legacy code. An approach able to help the developers to remove some of them would ease the maintenance effort spent on these systems.

References

1. Hautus, E.: Improving java software through package structure analysis. In: IASTED International Conference Software Engineering and Applications (2002)
2. Laval, J., Denier, S., Ducasse, S., Bergel, A.: Identifying cycle causes with enriched dependency structural matrix. In: WCRE 2009: Proceedings of the 2009 16th Working Conference on Reverse Engineering. Lille, France (2009)
3. Martin, R.C.: Agile Software Development. Principles, Patterns, and Practices. Prentice-Hall, Englewood Cliffs (2002)
4. Melton, H., Tempero, E.: An empirical study of cycles among classes in java. Empirical Software Engineering 12(4), 389–415 (2007)
5. Melton, H., Tempero, E.D.: Jooj: Real-time support for avoiding cyclic dependencies. In: 14th Asia-Pacific Software Engineering Conference, pp. 87–95. IEEE Computer Society Press, Los Alamitos (2007)
6. Parnas, D.L.: Designing software for ease of extension and contraction. In: International Conference on Software Engineering (ICSE 1978), pp. 264–277 (1978)
7. Sangal, N., Jordan, E., Sinha, V., Jackson, D.: Using dependency models to manage complex software architecture. In: Proceedings of OOPSLA 2005. pp. 167–176 (2005)
8. Steven, D., Eppinger, D.A.G.: Methods for analyzing design procedures. In: ASME Conference on Design Theory and Methodology. pp. 227–233, miami (1991)
9. Tarjan, R.E.: Depth-first search and linear graph algorithms. SIAM J. Comput. 1(2), 146–160 (1972)
10. Tarjan, R.E.: Enumeration of the elementary circuits of a directed graph. SIAM J. Comput. 2(3), 211–216 (1973)
11. Vainsencher, D.: Mudpie: layers in the ball of mud. Computer Languages, Systems & Structures 30(1-2), 5–19 (2004)

Seuss: Better Class Responsibilities through Language-Based Dependency Injection

Niko Schwarz, Mircea Lungu, and Oscar Nierstrasz

University of Bern

Abstract. Unit testing is often made more difficult by the heavy use of classes as namespaces and the proliferation of static methods to encapsulate configuration code. We have analyzed the use of 120 static methods from 96 projects by categorizing them according to their responsibilities. We find that most static methods support a hodgepodge of mixed responsibilities, held together only by their common need to be globally visible. Tight coupling between instances and their classes breaks encapsulation, and, together with the global visibility of static methods, complicates testing. By making dependency injection a feature of the programming language, we can get rid of static methods altogether. We employ the following semantic changes: (1) Replace every occurrence of a global with an access to an instance variable; (2) Let that instance variable be automatically injected into the object when it is instantiated. We present Seuss, a prototype that implements this change of semantics in Smalltalk. We show how Seuss eliminates the need to use class methods for non-reflective purposes, reduces the need for creational design patterns such as Abstract Factory and simplifies configuration code, particularly for unit tests.

1   Introduction

Class methods, which are statically associated to classes rather than instances, are a popular mechanism in object-oriented design. Java and C#, for example, provide static methods, and Smalltalk provides "class-side" methods, methods understood by classes, rather than their instances. 9 of the 10 most popular programming languages listed by TIOBE provide some form of static methods.[1] In most of these languages, classes offer the key mechanism for defining namespaces. For this reason, static methods offer a convenient mechanism for defining globally visible services, such as instance creation methods. As a consequence, static methods end up being used in practice wherever globally visible services are needed.

Unfortunately this common practice leads callers of static methods to implicitly depend on the classes that provide these static methods. The implicit

---

[1] TIOBE Programming Community Index for January 2011, http://www.tiobe.com. Those 10 languages are Java, C, C++, PHP, Python, C#, (Visual) Basic, Objective-C, Perl, Ruby. The outlier is C, which does not have a class system.

J. Bishop and A. Vallecillo (Eds.): TOOLS 2011, LNCS 6705, pp. 276–289, 2011.

dependency on static methods complicates testing. That is because many tests require that application behavior be simulated by a fixed script representing a predefined scenario. Such scripted behavior can hardly be plugged in from the outside when static methods are accessed by global names, and thus hard-wired into code. We therefore need to better understand the need for static methods in the first place.

Classes are known to have both meta-level and base-level responsibilities [2]. To see what those are, we examined 120 static methods, chosen at random from SqueakSource, a public repository of open source Smalltalk projects. We found that while nearly all static methods inherited from the system are reflective in nature, only few of the user-supplied methods are. Users never use static methods to define reflective functionality.

Dependency injection is a design pattern that shifts the responsibility of re-solving dependencies to a dedicated dependency *injector* that knows which de-pendent objects to inject into application code [6,11]. Dependency injection offers a partial solution to our problem, by offering an elegant way to plug in either the new objects taking over the responsibilities of static methods, or others required for testing purposes. Dependency injection however introduces syntactic clutter that can make code harder to understand and maintain.

We propose to regain program modularity while maintaining code readability by introducing dependency injection as a language feature. *Seuss* is a prototype of our approach, implemented by adapting the semantics of the host language. Seuss eliminates the need to abuse static methods by offering dependency injec-tion as an alternative to using classes as namespaces for static services. Seuss integrates dependency injection into an object-oriented language by introducing the following two semantic changes:

1. Replace every occurrence of a global with an access to an instance variable;
2. Let that instance variable be automatically injected into the object at in-stantiation time.

Seuss cleans up class responsibilities by reserving the use of static methods for reflective purposes. Furthermore, Seuss simplifies code responsible for configura-tion tasks. In particular, code that is hard to test (due to implicit dependencies) becomes testable. Design patterns related to configuration, such as the Abstract Factory pattern, which has been demonstrated to be detrimental to API usabil-ity [5], become unnecessary.

Structure of the article. In section 2 we analyze the responsibilities of static methods and establish the challenges for reassigning them to suitable objects. In section 3 we demonstrate how Seuss leads to cleaner allocation of responsibilities of static methods, while better supporting the development of tests. In section 4 we show how some creational design patterns in general and the Abstract Fac-tory design in particular are better implemented using Seuss. In section 5 we go into more details regarding the implementation of Seuss. In section 6 we discuss the challenges for statically-typed languages, and we summarize issues of per-formance and human factors. In section 7 we summarize the related work and we conclude in section 8.

2 Understanding Class Responsibilities

Static methods, by being associated to globally visible class names, hard-wire services to application code in ways that interfere with the ability to write tests. To determine whether these responsibilities can be shifted to objects, thus enabling their substitution at run-time, in subsection 2.1 we first analyze the responsibilities static methods bear in practice. Then in subsection 2.2 we pose the challenges facing us for a better approach.

2.1 Identifying Responsibilities

We follow Wirfs-Brock and Wilkerson's [4] suggestion and ask what the current responsibilities of static methods are, for that will tell us what the new classes should be.

We determine the responsibilities following a study design by Ko *et al.* [8]. Their study identifies six learning impediments by categorizing insurmountable barriers encountered by test subjects. The authors of the paper independently categorize the impediments and attain 94% agreement.

We examined 120 static methods and classified their responsibilities from a user's point of view. For example, a static method that provides access to a tool bar icon would be categorized as providing access to a resource, regardless of how it produced or obtained that image. We chose 95 projects uniformly at random from SqueakSource[2], the largest open source repository for Smalltalk projects. We then selected uniformly at random one static method from the latest version of each of these projects. To avoid biasing our analysis against framework code, we then added 25 static methods selected uniformly at random from the standard library of Pharo Smalltalk[3], as shipped in the development environment for developers.

Of the 120 methods selected, two were empty. We randomly chose another two methods from SqueakSource to replace them. Two subjects then categorized the 120 methods independently into the categories, achieving 83% agreement. We then reviewed the methods that were not agreed upon. Most were due to lack of knowledge of the exact inner workings of the API they were taken from. After further review, we placed them into the most appropriate subcategory.

We identified the following three umbrella categories: *Instance creation, Service* and *Reflection*, each further subdivided into subcategories. Whenever a method did not fit into any of the subcategories, we marked it as "other".

Instance creation. (28 of 120) Instance creation methods create new instances of their own class. They are subdivided as follows.

Singleton. (4 of 28) These methods implement the singleton pattern [7] to ensure that the instance is created only once.

Other. (24 of 28) Some methods provided default parameters, some simply relayed the method parameters into setters of the newly created instance.

---

[2] http://www.squeaksource.com/
[3] http://pharo-project.org

Only 3 methods did anything more than setting a default value or relaying parameters. These three methods each performed simple computations on the input parameters, such as converting from minutes to seconds, each no longer than a single line of code.

Services. (86 of 120) Service methods provide globally available functionality. They often serve as entry points to an API. We have identified the following sub-categories.

Install/uninstall a resource. (6 of 86) By resource, we mean a widely used object that other parts of the system need to function. Examples of installable resources that we encountered are: packages of code; fonts; entries to menus in the user interface.

Access a resource or setting. (41 of 86) These methods grant access to a resource or a specific setting in a configuration. Complex settings resemble resources, hence one cannot easily distinguish between the two. Examples include: a status object for an application; the packet size of headers in network traffic; default CSS classes for widgets; a sample XML file needed to test a parser; the default lifetime of a connection; the color of a GUI widget.

Display to/prompt user. (4 of 86) Examples: showing the recent changes in a versioning system; opening a graphical editor.

Access network. (2 of 86) These methods grant access to the network. Examples: sending an HTTP put request; sending a DAV delete request.

System initialization. (11 of 86) These methods set the system status to be ready for future interactions. Examples: setting operation codes; setting the positions for figures; asking other system parts to commence initialization.

Class indirection. (5 of 86) These return a class, or a group of classes, to provide some indirection for which class or classes to use.

Other. (17 of 86) Other responsibilities included: converting objects from one class to another; taking a screenshot; sorting an array; granting access to files; starting a process; mapping roles to privileges; signaling failure and mailing all packages in a database.

Reflection. (6 of 120) Unlike methods that offer services, reflective methods on a class are by their nature tightly coupled to instances of the class. We have found the following sub-categories.

Class Annotations. (5 of 6) Class annotations specify the semantics of fields of their class. All the examples we examined were annotations interpreted by Magritte [12], a framework for adapting an applications model and meta-model at run-time.

Other. (1 of 6) One method provided an example on how to use the API.

2.2   Challenges

Out of the 120 static methods we have analyzed, only 6 belonged naturally and directly to the instances of that class, namely the reflective ones. All other responsibilities can be implemented in instance methods of objects tailored to these responsibilities.

We conclude that static methods are defined in application code purely as a matter of convenience to exploit the fact that class names are globally known. Nothing prevents us from shifting the responsibilities of non-reflective static methods to regular application objects, aside from the loss of this syntactic convenience. In summary the challenges facing us are:

- to shift static methods to be instance responsibilities,
- while avoiding additional syntactic clutter, and
- enabling easy substitution of these new instances to support testing.

In the following we show how Seuss, our dependency injection framework allows us to address these challenges.

3   Seuss: Moving Services to the Instance Side

We would like to turn misplaced static methods into regular instance methods, while avoiding the syntactic clutter of creating, initializing and passing around these instances. Dependency injection turns out to be a useful design pattern to solve this problem, but introduces some syntactic clutter of its own. We therefore propose to support dependency injection *as a language feature*, thus maintaining the superficial simplicity of global variables but without the disadvantages. Dependency injection furthermore shifts the responsibility of injecting dependent variables to a dedicated *injector*, thus enabling the injection of objects needed for testing purposes. Let us illustrate dependency injection in an example.

In the active record design pattern [6, p. 160 ff], objects know how to store themselves into the database. In the SandstoneDB implementation of active record for Smalltalk [9] a Person object can save itself into the database as in Figure 1.

The code of the save method is illustrated in Figure 2. (The actual method is slightly more complicated due to the need to handle further special cases.)

The save method returns the result of evaluating a block of code in a critical section (self critical: [...]). It first evaluates some "before" code, then either stores or updates the state of the object in the database, depending on whether it has previously been saved or not. Finally it evaluates the "after" code.

In the save method, the database must somehow be referenced. If the database were an ordinary instance variable that has to be passed during instance creation, the code for creating Person objects would become cluttered. The conventional workaround is to introduce static methods storeObject: and updateObject: to encapsulate the responsibility of connecting to the database, thus exploiting the global nature of the Store class name, while abusing the mechanism of static methods for non-reflective purposes.

```
user := Person firstName: 'Ramon' lastName: 'Leon'.
user save.
```

Fig. 1. Using the active record pattern in SandstoneDB

```
save
    ↑ self critical: [
        self onBeforeSave.
        isFirstSave
            ifTrue: [Store storeObject: self]
            ifFalse: [Store updateObject: self].
        self onAfterSave.
    ]
```

Fig. 2. The save method in SandstoneDB, without dependency injection

Unfortunately, testing the save method now becomes problematic because the database to be used is hard-wired in static methods of the Store class. There is no easy way to plug in a mock object [10] that simulates the behavior of the database for testing purposes.

The dependency injection design pattern offers a way out by turning globals into instance variables that are automatically assigned at the point of instantiation. We add a method to Person that declares that Person is interested to receive a Store as an instance variable during instance creation by the runtime environment, rather than by the caller, as seen in Figure 3. Afterwards, instead of accessing the global Store (in upper case), save is re-written to access instance variable store (in lower case; see Figure 4).

```
store: anObject
    <inject: #Store>
    store := anObject
```

Fig. 3. Person declares that a Store should be injected upon creation

In the example in Figure 4, we also see that Person does not ask specifically for an instance of a class Store. It only declares that it wants something injected that is labelled #Store. This indirection is beneficial for testing. Method storeObject: may pollute the database if called on a real database object. Provided that there is a mock class TestStore, we can now inject instances of that class rather than real database objects in the context of unit tests.

Avoiding cluttered code by language alteration. The dependency injection pattern introduces a certain amount of clutter itself, since it requires classes to be written in an idiomatic way to support injection. This clutter manifests itself in terms of special constructors to accept injected objects, and factories responsible for creating the injected objects. Seuss avoids this clutter by incorporating dependency injection as a language feature. As a consequence, the application

```
save
    ↑ self critical: [
        self onBeforeSave.
        isFirstSave
            ifTrue: [store storeObject: self]
            ifFalse: [store updateObject: self].
        self onAfterSave.
    ]
```

Fig. 4. The save method from SandstoneDB rewritten to use dependency injection does not access the globally visible class name Store

developer may actually write the code as it is shown in Figure 2. The semantics of the host language are altered so that the code is interpreted as shown in Figure 4.

In Seuss, what is injected is defined in configuration objects, which are created in code, rather than in external configuration files. Therefore, we can cheaply provide configurations tailored for specific unit tests. Figure 5 illustrates how a unit test can now test the save method without causing side effects. The code implies that the storeObject: and updateObject: methods are defined on the instance side of the TestStore class.

```
testing := Configuration bind: [ :conf | conf bind: #Store to: TestStore new].
user := (Injector forConfiguration: testing get: #User).

user firstName: 'Ramon' lastName: 'Leon'.
user save.
```

Fig. 5. Unit test using dependency injection. The injector interprets the configuration, and fills all dependencies into user, including the TestStore

Typically, a developer using dependency injection has to explicitly call only one injector per unit test, and only one for the rest of the application, even though the injector is active during every object instantiation. Section 5 details how the injector is implicitly made available.

4   Cleaning Up Instance Creation

The design patterns by Gamma *et al.* are often ways of addressing language limitations. It is not surprising that by introducing a language change as powerful as dependency injection some of the design patterns will become obsolete. A special class of design patterns that we care about in this section are the creational ones, since we have seen in subsection 2.1 that a considerable percentage of static methods are responsible for instance creation.

The abstract factory pattern has been shown to frequently dumbfound users of APIs that make use of it [5]. Gamma defines the intent of the abstract factory pattern as to "provide an interface for creating families of related or dependent objects without specifying their concrete classes" [7]. Gamma gives the example of a user interface toolkit that supports multiple look and feel standards. The abstract factory pattern then enables code to be written that creates a user interface agnostic to the precise toolkit in use.

Let us suppose the existence of two frameworks A and B, each with implementations of an abstract class Window, named AWindow and BWindow, and the same for buttons. Following the abstract factory pattern, this is how we could create a window with a button that prints "World!" when pressed:

```
createWindow: aFactory
    window := (aFactory make: #Window) size: 100 @ 50.
    button := (aFactory make: #Button) title: 'Hello'.
    button onClick: [Transcript show: 'World']. window add: button.
```

Fig. 6. Object creation with Abstract Factory

Ellis *et al.* [5] show that using this pattern dumbfounds users. When presented with the challenge of instantiating an instance that is provided by a factory, they do not find the required factory. In Seuss, the following code snippet may generate a window either using framework A or B, depending on the configuration, with no need to find (or even write) a factory:

```
createWindow
    window := Window size: 100 @ 50.
    button := Button title: 'Hello'.
    button onClick: [Transcript show: 'World'].window add: button.
```

Fig. 7. Replacing object creation with Dependency Injection

Seuss allows writing natural code that still bears all the flexibility needed to exchange the underlying framework. It can be used even on code that was not written with the intention of allowing the change of the user interface framework.

5 Dependency Injection as a Language Feature

Normally, using dependency injection frameworks requires intrusively modifying the way code is written. The developer needs to make the following modifications to the code:

– Add the definition of an instance variable.
– Specify through an annotation which instance variable gets injected (the inject annotation from Figure 3).
– Provide a method through which the dependency injection framework can set the instance variable to the value of the injected object. This is a setter method in Smalltalk (Figure 3) or a dedicated constructor in Java.

To improve usability, in Seuss we completely remove the requirement of modifying the code in any of the previously mentioned ways. As a result, the code in in Figure 2 is interpreted just as if the code in Figure 4 and Figure 3 had been written.

The feature that allows us to use dependency injection without the invasive modification of source code is a slight change to the Smalltalk language: for every global being accessed, the access is redirected to an instance variable. This instance variable is annotated for injection, made accessible through setters, and then is set by the framework *when the object is created*.

It is not enough to store an object representing the original class in an instance variable. That is because the class usually is not aware of Seuss and thus does not inject dependencies into objects it newly creates.

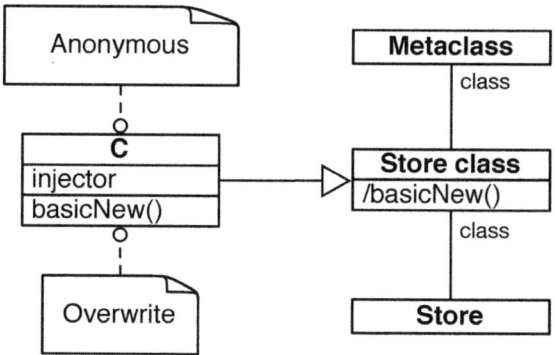

Fig. 8. Instances of C mimic Store, but use the injector when creating instances

Instead, we inject an object that knows the injector and calls it during instance creation. We achieve this by injecting an *instantiator object*. The class of the instantiator is an anonymous subclass of the metaclass of the original method's class. For example, in Figure 3 the object that is injected into instance variable store in is an instance of an anonymous metaclass C. As illustrated in Figure 8, C overwrites method basicNew which is inherited from Store class[4]. It changes basicNew so that it first invokes the injector, asking it to inject all dependencies into the newly created object, and then resets the class of the newly created object to be Store.

In order to change the semantics of a standard Pharo as described above, we use Helvetia [13], a language workbench for Smalltalk. Helvetia lets us intercept the compilation of every individual method. Helvetia requires us to specify our language change as a *Rule*, which is really a transformation from one method AST to another. When changing methods, we also modify the containing class when needed. During the transformation, we also create and update a default

---

[4] basicNew is a primitive that allocates memory for the new object. It is normally not overridden.

configuration, which lets the code run as before, if used. It can also be overridden by the user in unit tests. Algorithm 1 details the transformation.

Algorithm 1. Transforming ordinary code into dependency injected code.

---

1. Replace every occurrence of a global with an access to an instance variable. Add that instance variable if necessary.
2. Generate a setter method for that variable and annotate it so that the dependency injection framework can inject into that variable.
3. If the injected global is a class, act as follows. Generate an anonymous metaclass C as described above, and make its instance known to the default configuration. As described above, the instance should behave just like the original class, but should additionally inject all dependencies into newly created instances of class C.
4. Make the default configuration aware of the referred to global.

Introducing dependency injection as a language feature brings two advantages:

1. *Backwards compatibility.* Dependency injection can be used for code that was not written with dependency injection in mind. We were able to use the unit test from Figure 5 without having to modify the SandstoneDB project, which does not use dependency injection.
2. *Less Effort.* Other frameworks require that all dependencies be explicitly declared through some boilerplate code for each dependency. In our case, by automatically injecting needed dependencies where possible, the amount of code to write was reduced.

6 Discussion

We briefly explore the challenges for implementing Seuss in statically-typed languages like Java, and we summarize issues of performance and human factors.

6.1 Challenges for Statically Typed Languages

In a language where classes are reified as first-class objects, such as Smalltalk, classes can simply be injected as objects. In other languages, such as Java, a proxy must be used.

Seuss works by replacing access to globals by access to instance variables. In a statically typed language, the question arises what type injected instance variables ought to be. To see if our small language change would be feasible in a typed language, we ported part of Seuss to Java. In the following transformation by JSeuss, our Java version of Seuss, the access to the global Store is replaced by an instance variable store (note the lower case initial letter) of type ICStore.

```
class Before {
    void save() {
        Store.storeObject(this);
    }
}
```

is transformed into

```
class After {
    @Inject
    ICStore store;
    void save() {
        store.storeObject(this);
    }
}
```

The interface ICStore is a generated interface. Our Java transformation generates two interfaces for every class, one for all static methods, and one for all instance methods. The interfaces carry the same name as the class, except for the prefixed upper-case letters IC, or I, respectively. During class load time, all occurrences of type Store are then replaced by type ICStore, and so with all classes. All new calls on Store return instances of type IStore. On the other hand, existing interfaces are not touched.

The object of type ICStore serves as a proxy for the class ICStore. This is necessary since classes are not first class in Java, and thus cannot be injected directly. To avoid expensive recompilation, we use Javassist to modify all code at the bytecode level, during class load time.

The current implementation of JSeuss enables unit testing of the save method above, but is otherwise incomplete, thus currently prohibits meaningful benchmarking. We nevertheless learned from the experience that while Seuss for Java is complicated by the static type system of Java, it is still feasible.

6.2   Performance and Human Factors

Seuss impedes the performance of applications exclusively during object instantiation when there is some performance penalty for injecting all dependencies. In all other cases, a pointer to a global is replaced by a pointer to an instance variable, which is not slower than accessing a global in many languages, although it can prohibit inlining. Since every access to a global requires a new instance variable to be added, the memory footprint can grow considerably. However, space penalties can be ameliorated by introducing nested classes to a language, as demonstrated in Newspeak [3]. This should also improve performance during instantiation time, as dependencies can be moved to outer classes and thus need to be injected fewer times.

One might also argue that the new level of indirection may lead to confusion as to which object is being referred to, when an injected variable is referenced.

However, we believe that proper tool support can bring sufficient clarity. An IDE should be able to gather all configurations and use them to display which literals are bound to what.

6.3   Using Seuss to Sandbox Code

If Object's reflective methods are removed, then all objects can only find other classes through their dependencies or method parameters. Thus, any piece of code from within a configuration that does not include access to the File class prevents that code from reading or writing files. This concept of security by unreachability was described by Bracha [3].

7   Related Work

Dependency injection [6,11] is a design pattern that decouples highly dependent objects. Using it involves avoiding built-in methods for object construction, handing it off to framework code instead. It enables testing of components that would ordinarily be hard to test due to side-effects that would be intolerable in unit tests. There are other frameworks that support dependency injection like Google Guice [14] and Spring, after which Seuss's dependency injection capabilities are modeled. In contrast to Google Guice and Spring, Seuss turns dependency injection into a language feature that works even on code that was not written with dependency injection in mind. By superficially allowing the use of standard language constructs for object creation while using dependency injection under the hood, Seuss programs look in large parts like conventional source code.

Achermann and Nierstrasz [1] note that inflexible namespaces can lead to name clashes and inflexibilities. They propose making namespaces an explicit feature of the language and present a language named Piccola. Piccola does not get rid of using global namespace, but makes it a first-class entity. First-class namespaces in Piccola enable a fine degree of control over the binding of names to services, and in particular make it easy to run code within a sandbox. While Seuss sets the namespace of an object at that object's instantiation time, Piccola allows it to be manipulated in the scope of an execution (dynamically) as well as statically. Similarly, some mocking frameworks, such as PowerMock[5], allow re-writing of all accesses to global namespace to access a mock object. Piccola and PowerMock do not attempt to clean up static method responsibilities, but rather add flexibility to their lookup.

Bracha presents the Newspeak programming language [3], which sets the namespace of an object at that object's instantiation time, just like Seuss. However, while Seuss provides a framework that automatically injects individual dependencies into the dependent object during instantiation time, Newspeak leaves this to the developer. Bracha shows that by restricting a module to accessing the set of objects that were passed in during instantiation time, untrusted software

---

[5] http://code.google.com/p/powermock/

can be sandboxed reliably by not passing in the dependencies that it would need to be harmful, such as file system access modules. The same argument holds for Seuss so long as reflection is disabled. While the rewiring of dependencies is a strong suit of dependency injection, and while Newspeak makes it technically possible, the system's design makes it costly in lines of code to run a unit test in a new configuration. By manually searching for a module instantiation that happens in a unit test, we could not find a single unit test in Newspeak that makes use of Newspeak's capabilities to change namespaces.

8   Conclusion

Static methods pose obstacles to the development of tests by hardwiring instance creation. A study of 120 static methods in open-source Smalltalk code shows that out of the 120 static methods, only 6 could not equally well be implemented as instance methods, but were not, thus burdening their caller with the implicit dependency on these static methods.

Dependency injection offers a partial solution to separating the responsibility of instantiating application objects or test objects, but still entails tedious rewriting of application code and the use of boilerplate code to fulfill the dependency injection design pattern. We have shown how introducing dependency injection as a language feature can drastically simplify the task of migrating class responsibilities to instance methods, while maintaining code readability and enabling the development of tests. Moreover, a language with dependency injection as a feature becomes more powerful and renders certain design patterns obsolete.

We have demonstrated the feasibility of the approach by presenting Seuss, an implementation of dependency injection as a language feature in Smalltalk. We have furthermore demonstrated the feasibility of our approach for statically-typed languages by presenting JSeuss, a partial port of Seuss to Java.

Acknowledgments

We gratefully acknowledge the financial support of the Swiss National Science Foundation for the project "Synchronizing Models and Code" (SNF Project No. 200020-131827, Oct. 2010 - Sept. 2012). We also thank CHOOSE, the special interest group for Object-Oriented Systems and Environments of the Swiss Informatics Society, for its financial contribution to the presentation of this paper. We thank Simon Vogt and Ahmed S. Mostafa for their help in implementing JSeuss. We thank Toon Verwaest and Erwann Wernli for their input.

References

1. Achermann, F., Nierstrasz, O.: Explicit Namespaces (chapter 8). In: Weck, W., Gutknecht, J. (eds.) JMLC 2000. LNCS, vol. 1897, pp. 77–89. Springer, Heidelberg (2000)

2. Bracha, G., Ungar, D.: Mirrors: design principles for meta-level facilities of object-oriented programming languages. SIGPLAN Not. 39(10), 331–344 (2004)
3. Bracha, G., von der Ahé, P., Bykov, V., Kashai, Y., Maddox, W., Miranda, E.: Modules as objects in newspeak. In: D'Hondt, T. (ed.) ECOOP 2010. LNCS, vol. 6183, pp. 405–428. Springer, Heidelberg (2010)
4. Brock, R.W., Wilkerson, B.: Object-oriented design: a responsibility-driven approach. SIGPLAN Not. 24, 71–75 (1989)
5. Ellis, B., Stylos, J., Myers, B.: The Factory Pattern in API Design: A Usability Evaluation. In: 29th International Conference on Software Engineering (ICSE 2007), pp. 302–312. IEEE Computer Society Press, Washington, DC, USA (2007)
6. Fowler, M.: Patterns of Enterprise Application Architecture. Addison-Wesley, Reading (2002)
7. Gamma, E., Helm, R., Johnson, R., Vlissides, J.M.: Design Patterns: Elements of Reusable Object-Oriented Software, 1st edn. Addison-Wesley, Reading (1994)
8. Ko, A.J., Myers, B.A., Aung, H.H.: Six Learning Barriers in End-User Programming Systems. In: Proceedings of the 2004 IEEE Symposium on Visual Languages - Human Centric Computing, VLHCC 2004, pp. 199–206. IEEE Computer Society Press, Los Alamitos (2004)
9. Leon, R.: SandstoneDb, simple ActiveRecord style persistence in Squeak, http://www.squeaksource.com/SandstoneDb.html
10. Mackinnon, T., Freeman, S., Craig, P.: Endo-testing: Unit testing with mock objects, ch.17, pp. 287–301. Addison-Wesley Longman Publishing Co., Inc, Boston (2001)
11. Dhanji Prasanna. Dependency Injection. Manning Publications, pap/pas edition (August 2009)
12. Renggli, L., Ducasse, S., Kuhn, A.: Magritte – A meta-driven approach to empower developers and end users. In: Engels, G., Opdyke, B., Schmidt, D.C., Weil, F. (eds.) MODELS 2007. LNCS, vol. 4735, pp. 106–120. Springer, Heidelberg (2007)
13. Renggli, L., Gîrba, T., Nierstrasz, O.: Embedding languages without breaking tools. In: D'Hondt, T. (ed.) ECOOP 2010. LNCS, vol. 6183, pp. 380–404. Springer, Heidelberg (2010)
14. Vanbrabant, R.: Google Guice: Agile Lightweight Dependency Injection Framework. Apress (2008)

Extensive Validation of OCL Models by Integrating SAT Solving into USE

Mirco Kuhlmann, Lars Hamann, and Martin Gogolla

University of Bremen, Computer Science Department
Database Systems Group, D-28334 Bremen
{mk,gogolla,lhamann}@informatik.uni-bremen.de

Abstract. The Object Constraint Language (OCL) substantially enriches modeling languages like UML, MOF or EMF with respect to formulating meaningful model properties. In model-centric approaches, an accurately defined model is a requisite for further use. During development of a model, continuous validation of properties and feedback to developers is required, since many design flaws can then be directly discovered and corrected. For this purpose, lightweight validation approaches which allow developers to perform automatic model analysis are particularly helpful. We provide a new method for efficiently searching for model instances. The existence or non-existence of model instances with certain properties allows significant conclusions about model properties. Our approach is based on the translation of UML and OCL concepts into relational logic and its realization with SAT solvers. We explain various use cases of our proposal, for example, completion of partly defined model instances so that particular properties hold in the completed model instances. Our proposal is realized by integrating a model validator as a plugin into the UML and OCL tool USE.

1   Introduction

Unlike traditional code-centric approaches, model-centric and model-driven software and hardware development relies on comprehensive and in particular flawless models. Modeling languages like UML, MOF or EMF are substantially enriched by the Object Constraint Language (OCL) which allows precise definitions of model properties. However, complex models increase the need for extensive validation and verification. Our work focuses on discovering implied model qualities and properties early in the development cycle, i. e., properties which follow from the given UML and OCL model constraints. During the development, continuous validation of properties and feedback to the developers is required, since many design flaws can then be directly discovered and corrected. Lightweight validation approaches which allow developers to perform automatic model analysis are thus particularly helpful (in contrast to strongly interactive theorem proving approaches). In our work, we automatically confirm wanted and find unwanted model properties (features and bugs) by examining the existence or non-existence of specific model instances, i. e., snapshots representing concrete states of the modeled system.

J. Bishop and A. Vallecillo (Eds.): TOOLS 2011, LNCS 6705, pp. 290–306, 2011.
© Springer-Verlag Berlin Heidelberg 2011

For this purpose, we developed a method which we call OCL2Kodkod. By translating UML and OCL concepts into the relational logic of Kodkod [23], our method enables an efficient SAT-based search and generation of partial and complete snapshots with user-specified properties. The user has not to deal with any details of relational logic, but employs UML and OCL concepts only. We integrated OCL2Kodkod as a plugin into our UML and OCL tool USE (UML-based Specification Environment) [10] adding various new validation options.

In order to realize a modular architecture, the USE system was recently modified in order to support a flexible incorporation of new functionality via plugins. The plugin architecture is well-suited for research and teaching projects like student or PhD theses. The first plugin which realizes the method OCL2Kodkod is called 'model validator'.

The rest of the paper is structured as follows. Sect. 2 introduces the tools and methods handled within the paper. In Sect. 3 we present the principles of the USE plugin architecture and the particularities of the model validator plugin. Section 4 discusses the principles of model validation wrt. the model validator and explains the principles in the context of a concrete UML and OCL model. Section 5 gives an overview of the translation from UML and OCL to Kodkod. Related work is presented in Sect. 6. We conclude with Sect. 7.

2   Background: The Tools USE and Kodkod

In order to assist developers in model-driven techniques, our group puts forward the tool USE [10]. USE is basically an interpreter for a subset of UML and MOF and OCL. The main task of USE is to validate and verify specifications consisting of class diagrams together with OCL invariants and pre- and postconditions. USE further supports object diagrams and sequence diagrams. Commands for atomic snapshot manipulation (object and link creation/deletion and attribute modification) allow to construct states. Also part of the USE system is a so-called snapshot generator based on 'a snapshot sequence language' (ASSL) [9]. We distinguish the built-in snapshot generator from the new model validator plugin in Sect. 4.

Kodkod [23] implements relational logic [13] which is purely based on relations, that is, sets of tuples. Independent from their nature, all values are uniformly handled as relations. Atomic values like integer values are represented by unary singleton relations (e. g., $[(2)]$). Sets of atomic values are relations with possibly more than one unary tuple (e. g., $[(a),(b),(c)]$). Relationships between atoms are specified with n-ary relations (e. g., a function $[(a,2),(b,8),(c,2)]$). The structure of a relation can be freely defined. Kodkod's logic provides a large set of operations for handling relations, including common set operations like union and subset. The most important means for extracting information and merging different relations is the so called 'join' expressed by a dot (e. g., $[(a,2),(b,3)].[(2,c)] = [(a,c)]$). Often, the join emulates a function call (e. g., $[(a)].[(a,2),(b,8),(c,2)] = [(2)]$). In order to perform calculations based on integer values, the relational logic additionally includes the corresponding

operations. Naturally, the relational logic brings boolean operations for building relational formulas which are evaluated in the context of concrete relation
instances.

Kodkod is designed as an API allowing developers of other tools to easily use
its features. Its most important feature is the possibility to efficiently find specific
instantiations of the underlying relations which fulfill the specified relational
formulas. This task is achieved by translating the formulas from the relational
logic into boolean logic. The resulting boolean formulas can in turn be explored
by proprietary solvers for boolean satisfiability (SAT). If the applied SAT solver
finds a solution, the solution is translated back into respective relation instances.

3   Integrating SAT Solving into the USE Tool

The USE tool provides a way to add new features to the USE system without
altering the internal USE sources. In the following subsection we dwell on the
principles of this plugin architecture. After that, we consider the new 'model
validator' plugin and its features.

3.1   The USE Plugin Architecture

Since the first release of USE, several extensions to the system were made. Some
of these extensions were the result of diploma theses supervised in our group. One
example of such an extension is the snapshot generator mentioned before. When
unexperienced developers are involved — which is the common and natural case
with students — it is hard to maintain several concurrent feature branches.
Students are normally not interested in the overall USE development road map,
nor do they care about system changes done during their diploma work. This
makes the (re)integration of their results a labor-intensive task. Therefore, we
enriched USE to support extensions to the system by plugins which allows us to
decouple the various extensions from the system core maintained by our group.
Also the users of our tool will benefit from the plugin architecture, once a greater
variety of USE plugins well be available. Users can then customize USE to their
needs focussing the functionality required to solve their specific tasks.

Several commonly used applications support extensions by plugins, AddOns
or AddIns, respectively. Eclipse may be seen as an application in which nearly
every feature is realized by a plugin whereas modern browsers provide more core
functionality but allow the user to customize and extend them via plugins. We
evaluated some popular plugin frameworks (Eclipse, NetBeans and Mozilla) to
possibly reuse them but came to the conclusion that many of their features are
unnecessary in the context of USE. Therefore, we newly designed a small and less
complex but sufficiently powerful framework. Like other frameworks, the USE
plugin framework provides so-called extension points which plugin developers can
use to add features to the system. The following extension points are available:

Action. This extension point allows a plugin to add new information and interactive elements to the graphical user interface of USE, e. g., for providing
new menu commands to open windows or for executing functions offered by
a plugin.

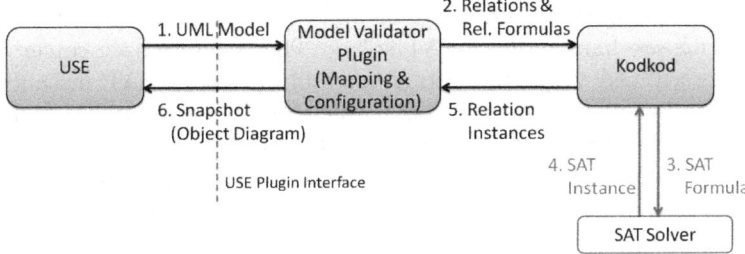

Fig. 1. Translation process involving the USE model validator plugin

Shell. In USE, most of the tasks can be invoked by shell commands. The respective extension point enables plugins to add new commands, for example, with respect to validation tasks.

Model. In order to integrate new model elements into the model browser of USE, this extension point can be used.

These extension points can be seen as controlled hooks to the system which are automatically invoked at runtime to add new functionality and to allow the plugins to execute calculations. This kind of controlled execution is often called the Hollywood Principle ("don't call us, we'll call you" or applied to a framework "don't call the framework, the framework will call you") which distinguishes the plugin framework from a library which does not take care of any execution process. USE plugins can rely on other plugins which is supported by services a plugin may provide. The registration and initialization process of the plugins at the system start up requires that each plugin provides a configuration file with meta data about it. The latter includes information about the main class of the plugin, the provided extensions to the described extension points and information about the offered services. Whereas USE does not know anything about the concrete plugins, a plugin itself can make use of all public features of the USE system which are accessible in a specific context, e. g., the current system state (snapshot) or a parent window.

3.2 The Model Validator Plugin

The model validator plugin connects the UML and OCL side with the world of pure relations and the related logic. On the one hand, it includes Kodkod for the relational part. On the other hand, it utilizes the USE plugin interface to access the UML and OCL part as well as to extend the USE GUI. Generally speaking, the plugin is used to find snapshots fitting the given UML class diagram and fulfilling all further specified OCL constraints.

The resulting translation process is shown in Fig. 1. The plugin is first requesting the model information from USE. Then it maps the UML model including the OCL constraints into relations and relational formulas. It also adds configuration information given by the user within the USE GUI. This information determines the search space as it needs specific bounds. Kodkod performs the task of translating the given relations and relational formulas into boolean formulas which are handled by a SAT solver. The concrete SAT solver to be used can be determined via the plugin. A possibly returned SAT instance is translated into a set of relation instances which fulfill the relational formulas. The plugin maps these relations to objects, attribute values and links, i. e., a snapshot which is forwarded to the USE system and in the end is displayed in form of an object diagram. The UML and OCL concepts currently supported by the model validator are shown in Tab. 1.

Table 1. UML and OCL features supported by the USE model validator

Language	Concepts
UML	classes and attributes (enumeration, object, integer, boolean, string type)
	associations and association classes (binary, n-ary)
	inheritance and abstract classes
OCL	attribute access and navigation
	sets, bags, sequences, ordered sets
	Set, OclAny, Boolean, String and Integer operations

4   Automatic Validation with the USE Model Validator

Within this section we examine multiple alternatives for analyzing a UML and OCL model with the aid of the USE tool and in particular the new USE model validator which considerably enhances the existing USE validation scope.

4.1   Validation Principles

USE helps developers during design and analysis of their models. Common validation purposes in the context of the USE system are the following:

1. Create and check positive model snapshots which are valid in the eyes of the developer. If USE does not accept the given snapshot as valid system state in the context of the OCL constraints, the model is too restrictive, i. e., the constraints are too strong.
2. Create and check negative (i. e., invalid) snapshots. If USE accepts them as valid model instances although the developer does not, the given constraints are too weak.
3. Check model consistency in general. If there are conflicting constraints, it is not possible to create a meaningful snapshot at all, i. e., all snapshots which are valid in the developers' eyes are forbidden by the UML and OCL model.
4. Check constraint independency, i. e., if each OCL constraint adds essential information to the model and is not implied by other constraints (avoid redundancy). When a constraint is independent from the others, there must be at least one snapshot which fulfills all but the considered constraint.
5. Check user-defined properties of the model, i. e., if the model implies a user-specified property given as an OCL expression.

The built-in USE snapshot generator which executes user-defined ASSL procedures adds further validation possibilities, since it allows to automatically generate new system states. It also helps to perform the aforementioned validation aspects by searching system states with specific properties. In [9] we introduce the ASSL language and the generator features. In [11] we apply the generator for checking model consistency, constraint independency and further model properties (consequences).

An ASSL procedure must be manually defined. Through 'try' statements a procedure can describe a complete set of snapshots, that is, a snapshot space. Starting such a procedure with the USE generator, it creates one snapshot conforming to the procedure after another until a valid one was found (invoking backtracking if the found snapshot was invalid). The main disadvantage of the built-in generator is its enumerative nature, as it has to create and check each snapshot if the procedure's snapshot space does not include a snapshot fulfilling all model constraints. As a consequence, larger snapshot spaces which for instance comprise more than a few objects and attribute values or all possible link constellations cannot be handled.

We remove this problem with the model validator which substitutes the enumerative search by an efficient SAT-based approach. In the context of the plugin, a snapshot space to be searched is not determined by an ASSL procedure, but by general bounds to the number of objects, links and attribute values, making the configuration considerably less time-consuming. In the following, we present the main features of the model validator.

Completion of partial snapshots. In many validation scenarios, a developer has concrete situations of the modeled system and related properties in mind. The model validator enables an automatic analysis based on concrete situations which are manually specified as partial model snapshots. Given a snapshot and an optional property to be checked explicitly (specified in form of an OCL expression), the model validator can automatically complete the snapshot so that all model constraints and the optionally examined property are fulfilled (provided that the searched snapshot space includes a fitting snapshot), while leaving the predefined snapshot elements unchanged.

Complete snapshot generation. The model validator also allows the users to generate complete snapshots which do not base on a partial solution. This way, the generated snapshots purely depend on the user-specified snapshot search space, the model constraints and given OCL properties to be examined.

Search space configuration. The search space of the model validator needs to be bounded with respect to the number of the snapshot elements. More precisely speaking,

- the number of objects for each class,
- the number of links for each association, and
- the range of values for each class attribute

can be restricted through lower and upper bounds. Whereas all classes need an explicit upper bound, the maximum number of links can be left open (indicated by the value -1), since the number of all possible link combinations is restricted by the number of existing objects. If a partial snapshot is pre-defined, the lower bounds are automatically adapted and existing attribute values are kept. Furthermore, the existing OCL invariants can be individually activated, deactivated and negated before invoking the snapshot search.

4.2 Explanation of the Model Validator Features

Our following examinations base on a small but nontrivial UML model shown in Fig. 2. We play the role of a developer who created the model with USE and aims to validate the current version.

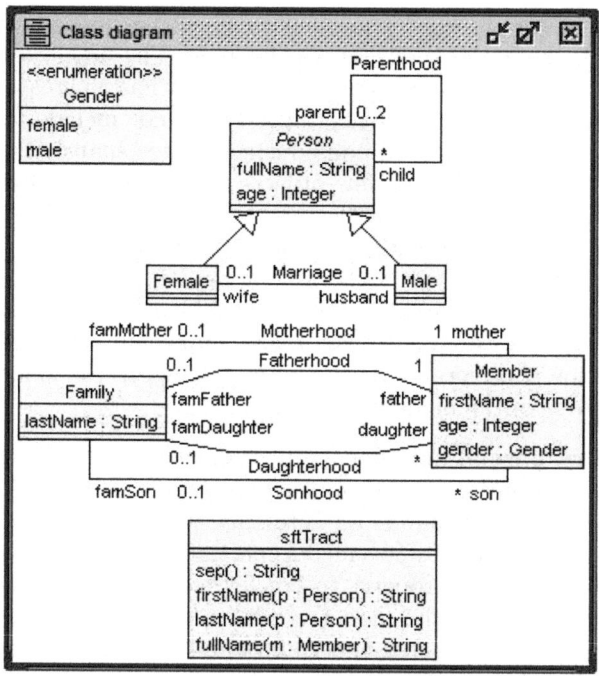

Fig. 2. Class diagram of the example UML model

Running Example. The model declaratively describes a model transformation. The classes Person, Female and Male as well as the associations Parenthood and Marriage represent the source side (source meta model) of the transformation. Instances of the source side are to be transformed into instances of the target meta model consisting of a family and family members who can take four different roles. The full name of a person (source side) is thereby split into a last name (Family) and a first name (Member). Furthermore, the gender of a member is given by an attribute in the target model. The third part of the UML model is a 'simple family tree' (sft) class which observes the source and target models and checks them with respect to the transformation's correctness, i.e., it enforces the transformation contract. The class diagram is supplemented by the following OCL invariants. The first constraint applies to the class Person of the source meta model. We have already explained it in Sect. 2.

```
context Person inv SMM_parentsFM:
  parent->size()=2 implies
    parent->select(oclIsTypeOf(Female))->size()=1 and
    parent->select(oclIsTypeOf(Male))->size()=1
```

The second invariant constraints the target meta model. Mothers and fathers must be female or male, respectively. This invariant has the same purpose as the former invariant at the source model side.

```
context Family inv TMM_mumFemale_dadMale:
  mother.gender=#female and father.gender=#male
```

The transformation contract class adds constraints regarding the transformation. A source model must have the following property. All full names must consist of a first name and a last name separated by a blank character. The invariant makes use of user-defined OCL query operations (sep, firstName and lastName).

```
sep():String= ' '
firstName(p:Person):String=
  p.fullName.substring(1,p.fullName.indexOf(sep())-1)
lastName(p:Person):String=
  p.fullName.substring(p.fullName.indexOf(sep())+1,p.fullName.size)
```

```
inv SRC_fullName_EQ_firstSepLast:
  Person.allInstances->forAll(p|
    p.fullName=firstName(p).concat(sep()).concat(lastName(p)))
```

A further OCL query operation calculates a family member's full name by concatenating the family last name and the member's first name (independent from the member's role in a family). This operation is used in the main invariant which constraints the actual transformation from a source to a target model.

```
fullName(m:Member)=
  let fam=
    if m.famSon.isDefined() then m.famSon else
    if m.famDaughter.isDefined() then m.famDaughter else
    if m.famFather.isDefined() then m.famFather else m.famMother
    endif endif endif in
  m.firstName.concat(sep()).concat(fam.lastName)
```

Each person must have exactly one family member counterpart. The person's and respective member's full name are identical. Their age and gender must coincide. The number of children with respect to persons and members must be equal. Children must be sons or daughters, respectively, at the target side. Married persons imply members who are a mother or father, respectively.

```
inv SRC_TRG_forPersonOneMember:
  Female.allInstances->forAll(p| Member.allInstances->one(m|
    p.fullName=fullName(m) and p.age=m.age and m.gender=#female and
    (p.child->notEmpty() implies (let fam=m.famMother in
      p.child->size()=fam.daughter->union(fam.son)->size())) and
    (p.parent->notEmpty() implies m.famDaughter.isDefined()) and
    (p.oclAsType(Female).husband.isDefined() implies
```

```
      m.famMother.isDefined()) )) and
  Male.allInstances->forAll(p| Member.allInstances->one(m|
    p.fullName=fullName(m) and p.age=m.age and m.gender=#male and
    (p.child->notEmpty() implies (let fam=m.famFather in
      p.child->size()=fam.daughter->union(fam.son)->size())) and
    (p.parent->notEmpty() implies m.famSon.isDefined()) and
    (p.oclAsType(Male).wife.isDefined() implies
      m.famFather.isDefined()) ))
```

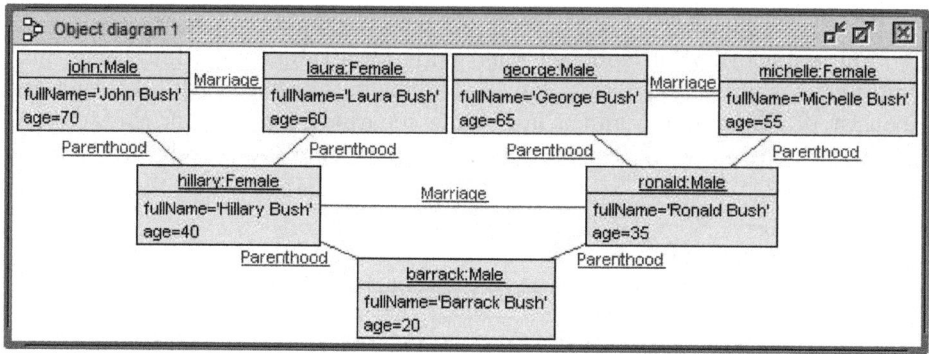

Fig. 3. Manually defined source model (partial snapshot)

Validation Based on a Partial Snapshot. In order to check the main transformation properties, we provide a concrete source model, i.e., an instance of the source meta model, in form of a snapshot displayed in Fig. 3. To keep the diagram clear, we hide the role names, since they follow from the family tree structure. Instead of manually defining a fitting or non fitting family target model, we order the model validator to automatically search a valid target side which we can in turn contrast with our expectations.

Figure 4 depicts a screenshot of the USE GUI which contains configuration windows provided through the model validator plugin. The screenshot shows all information necessary for the first invocation of the validator including the partial snapshot (shown in the USE screenshot with hidden attributes and roles). Since we do not want the source model to be extended by further male and female objects or links we equalize the corresponding classes' and associations' lower and upper bounds. String type attributes are bounded by determining the minimum and maximum string length. However, the settings for the attributes of class Female and Male are not relevant in the current validation context because they would only apply to newly generated Female and Male objects.

Finally, we activate all available invariants ordering the model validator to respect them in the solving process. About ten seconds after starting the search process (on an ordinary desktop pc), we obtain the target model shown in Fig. 5. We hide the source model because it remained unchanged as well as the generated sftTract object. The target model and with it the whole transformation represent a valid system state, since all UML and OCL constraints are fulfilled. But we immediately see several unwanted properties like members taking more than one

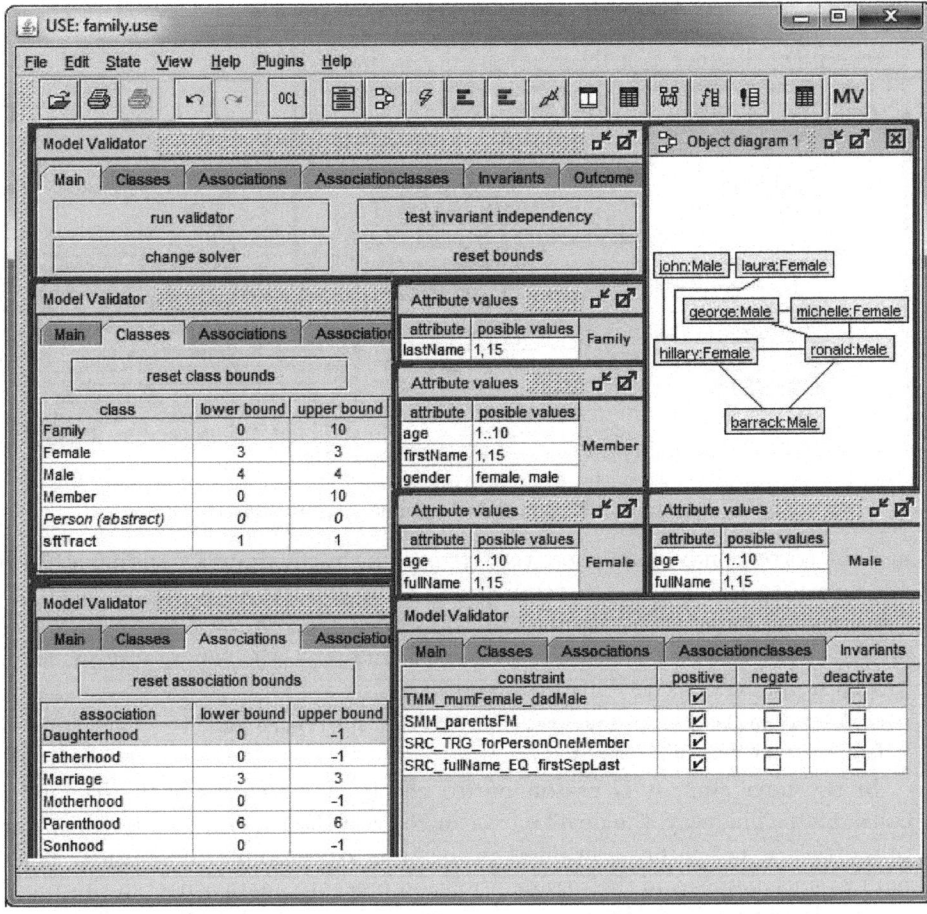

Fig. 4. Graphical user interface of the OCL2Kodkod plugin within USE

role in one family indicating a too weak set of constraints. Thus, we extend the model by the following invariant which forbids more than one link from one member to a family object.

```
inv TMM_oneRoleInOneFamily:
  Family.allInstances()->forAll(fam|
    fam.mother<>fam.father and
    fam.daughter->union(fam.son)->excludesAll(Set{fam.mother,fam.father})
    and fam.daughter->intersection(fam.son)->isEmpty())
```

A second searching run with unchanged bounds yields a target which looks fine at first view (Fig. 6). However, in the eyes of the developer this result should be still invalid because Laura and Michelle switched their husbands during the transformation. As a consequence, George's child is Hillary instead of Ronald. The transformation constraint SRC_TRG_forPersonOneMember accepts this situation because it just enforces the same number of children of a person (source)

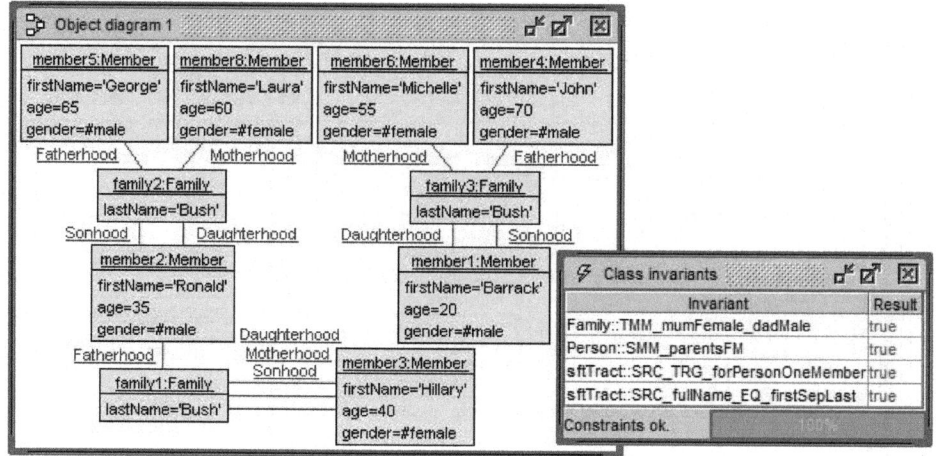

Fig. 5. Automatically generated target with unwanted properties

and the corresponding member. We strengthen the invariant by adding a further restriction to the 'same size' requirement. The children of a person must have the same full name at both transformation sides. Generating a new target based on the adapted model yields the intended result, i. e., the same target as shown in Fig. 6 but without switched husbands.

```
p.child->forAll(c| fam.daughter->union(fam.son)->one(mc|
  fullName(mc)=c.fullName))
```

In the next step, it is reasonable to check consequences from the model's constraints. This way, the developers can check if their model implies the proper properties or not imply unwanted properties. We exemplarily consider person names, since names and their transformation present a main aspect in this model. We would like to check if our model allows family trees with different last names. At first, we change the full names of George and Michelle to 'George Obama' and 'Michelle Obama' in the predefined partial snapshot (Fig.3). These changes lead to the fact that the model validator does not find any valid target model in a search space with up to 10 members and 10 families, thus different last names are in this context not allowed.

The validation by complete snapshot generation can be performed the same way as described before except that no object diagram is given as a partial solution. In [12] our example model is explained in greater detail, including a discussion of validation of models and model transformations.

5   Translation from UML and OCL into Kodkod

In this section we sketch the translation of UML concepts (outlined in Tab. 2) and OCL operations into relational structures and formulas. We illustrate selected translations on the basis of the concrete UML elements Person (class), age (attribute) and Parenthood (association).

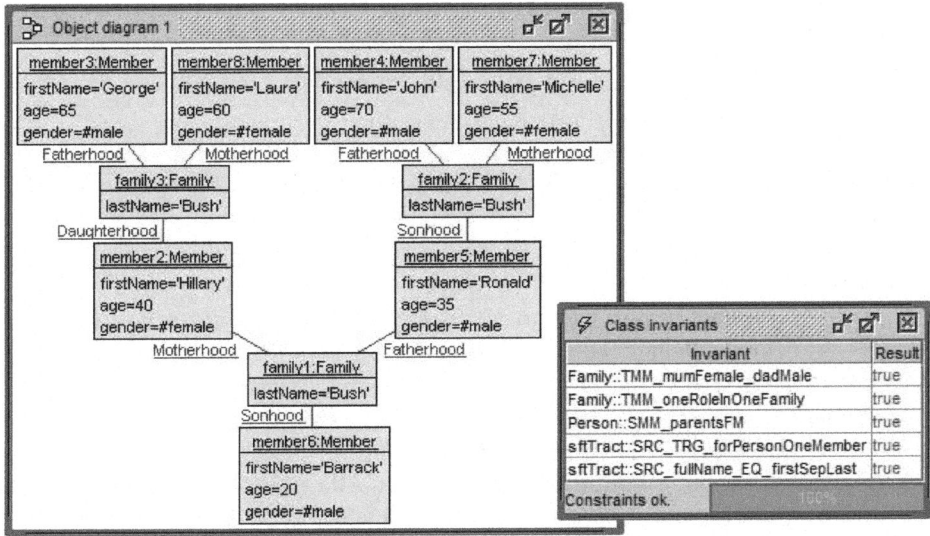

Fig. 6. Automatically generated target with switched husbands

Table 2. Overview of the mapping from UML concepts to relations and formulas

UML	Relation	Formula
class	unary $([[object_1],\ldots])$	no formula
enumeration	unary $([[literal_1],\ldots])$	no formula
n-ary association	n-ary $([[obj_{11},\ldots,obj_{1n}],\ldots])$	typing, multiplicity
n-ary association class	n+1-ary $([[assoc\_obj_1, obj_{11},\ldots,obj_{1n}],\ldots])$	typing, multiplicity
attribute (basic, object, enumeration and set type)	binary $([[obj_1, val_1],\ldots])$	typing, multiplicity
attribute (string type)	ternary $([[obj_1, pos_1, char_1],\ldots])$	typing, multiplicity
class inheritance $(A < B)$	unary (B), unary $(B-A)$	subset

Translated UML concepts result in relations whose tuples hold elements with a specific meaning. The assumption that, for example, class relations consist of objects, enumeration relations comprise enumeration literals, or integer type attribute relations yield pairs of objects and integer values must be made explicit, since the elements of a tuple are originally just plain atoms of the Kodkod universe. Bound declarations generally type the relations by assigning atoms to the corresponding relations, e. g., relating Person objects (e. g., ada, bob and cyd) to the Person relation, to the relation of the attribute age, and to the Parenthood association relation. A concrete Kodkod solution yields all elements of the lower bounds and a subset of the upper bounds. The upper bounds comprise all fitting atoms and all possible resulting tuples (i. e., the Cartesian product of the atoms) if no concrete tuples are defined in the lower bounds. Thus, the types and multiplicities of the association ends, as well as the attribute domains and values must be further constrained using formulas which apply to concrete relation instances in a solution.

Bounds: (relation name, lower bound, upper bound)

Person: $[[ada]]$ $[[ada], [bob], [cyd]]$
ints: $[]$ $[[1], [2]]$
age: $[[ada, 1]]$ $[[ada, 1], [bob, \bot], [bob, 1], [bob, 2], [cyd, \bot], [cyd, 1], [cyd, 2]]$
Parent $[]$ $[[ada, ada], [ada, bob], [ada, cyd], [bob, ada], [bob, bob],$
hood: $[bob, cyd], [cyd, ada], [cyd, bob], [cyd, cyd]]$

Formulas:

age (domain/type): $(age.univ)$ in Person & $(univ.age)$ in $(ints + \bot)$
(multiplicity): all c : Person | one $(c.age)$
Parent (type) $(Parenthood.univ)$ in Person &
hood: $(univ.Parenthood)$ in Person
(multiplicity): all $c2$: Person | $\#(Parenthood.c2) <= 2$

The given example bounds determine that Ada must be included in a valid solution, while the existence of Bob and Cyd is optional. There may be two integer atoms representing the numbers 1 and 2. Ada must be one year old. Bob's and Cyd's age is not constrained, it may be undefined ($\bot$). UML associations are translated into Kodkod relations in which each association end takes one position (cf. Tab. 2). The example bounds of the Parenthood relation allow all parenthood constellations. As a consequence, a solution may yield the Parenthood tuple $[ada, bob]$ (representing the UML link $(parent : ada, child : bob)$) and at the same time a Person relation which does not include the atom bob. This type inconsistency is prevented by the shown formulas which demand that (1) the tuples of the age relation yield Person objects at the first position and integer atoms or the undefined value at the second position (the expression $univ$ represents the relation including all atoms existing in the universe), (2) the relation age connects each person object existing in a solution to exactly one (un)defined value, (3) both positions of Parenthood tuples hold Person objects, and (4) the Parenthood relation connects each Person object at the second position (child) to at most two Person objects (parents).

The translation of OCL operations profit from the large collection of operations provided by Kodkod. Thus, many OCL operations (e. g., integer and set operations) have a counterpart in the relational logic (e. g., the OCL expression set->size<=2 can be expressed as $\#(set) <= 2$ in Kodkod). However, some OCL peculiarities like the undefined value which can occur in all OCL expressions often result in more complex translations. In the following we present the translation of an example navigation which is a central feature in OCL.

In OCL we navigate from a person p to her parents through the expression p.parent. Analogously, her children are calculated with the expression p.child. At the Kodkod side, we have no explicit role names. Thus, the association ends are determined through the positions of the tuple elements, i. e., the first end (parent) takes the first position, the second end (child) takes the second. Consequently, the navigation from a person to the parents yields the relational join $Parenthood.p$. The navigation to the children results in $p.Parenthood$. This straightforward translation is only applied in the case of binary associations. However, the respective Java method implementing the navigation in Kodkod must respect all kinds of associations (n-ary and association classes) and any possible navigation from association end x to end y including the navigation from and to association class objects.

6 Related Work

The relational language of Kodkod directly corresponds to the relational logic of Alloy [13]. The Alloy language is implemented in the Alloy Analyzer which currently bases upon the Kodkod tool. The UML2Alloy approach [1] translates UML and OCL concepts into the Alloy language which is in turn translated by the Alloy Analyzer into Kodkod structures. Our direct approach of translating UML and OCL into the Kodkod relations and formulas is not limited by modeling restrictions of the Alloy language. Thus, we are able to handle several concepts which are not realizable with Alloy like multiple inheritance or a proper treatment of undefined values (e. g., OCL2Kodkod distinguishes between empty sets, undefined sets and sets including an undefined value). UML2Alloy further does not support concepts like n-ary associations and association classes, OCL sequences and bags, or string and integer operations.

Approaches like [27] (specification of enterprise architecture models based on ontologies) and [15] (definition of modeling languages and their formal semantics) directly specify and analyze with Alloy. Kodkod has also been successfully applied in different fields, e. g., for executing declarative specifications in case of runtime exceptions in Java programs [21], reasoning about memory models [24], or generating counterexamples for Isabelle/HOL a proof assistant for higher-order logic (Nitpick) [3]. Whereas Nitpick searches instances to disprove given lemmas (e. g., through the assignment of free variables to concrete values), the model validator is intended for finding snapshots which conform the UML and OCL constraints, as well as snapshots violating constraints. Both kinds of snapshots can help the developer to reveal specific model properties.

Other approaches do not employ Alloy or Kodkod for connecting SAT techniques with UML and OCL. A direct mapping of UML and OCL concepts into SAT has been addressed in [22]. However, while a direct translation is not limited with respect to the peculiarities of an intermediate language, it cannot benefit from existing translation mechanisms like the sophisticated symmetry detection and breaking scheme which enables an efficient handling of partial solutions, or the detection and exploitation of redundant structures in formulas which are implemented in Kodkod [23]. Several other (non-SAT-based) techniques support the analysis of UML and OCL models. A translation of specific UML and OCL features into constraint satisfaction problems (CSP) is done in [5,25]. Furthermore, the constructive query containment (CQC) method [20], rewriting-based techniques [7] or answer set programming (ASP) [19] is applied for analyzing static and dynamic model aspects. In [2] the authors use description logic for reasoning about UML class diagrams. An approach to explicitly checking properties of metamodels is presented in [18] . UMLAnT [26] allows for analyzing model behavior by animating object and sequence diagrams. Beside model animation and simulation Dresden OCL [8] supports constraint verification by code generation and execution, but like the UML tools OCLE [6] and RoclET [14], it does not support automated snapshot generation producing model instances with user-defined properties. In the context of the Eclipse Modeling Framework (EMF) the Epsilon Language [16] provides for model validation based on constraints similar to OCL. The named approaches differ from more interactive approaches like [4] involving formal verification by theorem proving.

Our approach is unique with respect to the use of Kodkod as a conceptual intermediate language for translating the source languages UML and OCL into boolean formulas.

7 Conclusion and Future Work

With the method OCL2Kodkod and its realization as the USE model validator we presented an automatic SAT-based approach for efficiently finding snapshots in large search spaces, i. e., a lightweight way to validate UML and OCL model properties resulting from complex constraints and their often intransparent interdependencies. By immediately translating found SAT solutions back into snapshots displayed in form of object diagrams the model developers receive a detailed feedback on the UML and OCL modeling layer.

Future work comprises the enhancement of supported UML and OCL features like qualified associations, subset relations between association ends as well as OCL operations on sequences, bags, ordered sets and tuples. We will also further optimize the translation into the relational logic as well as the model validator's GUI options allowing developers a more comfortable configuration. Larger case studies are planned, in particular for model transformations employing the completion abilities of the model validator (both for the transformation source or target). Beside analyzing static model properties, we aim to involve behavioral features (operations) through transformation of UML and OCL application models into so-called snapshot models.

The flexible plugin architecture of USE is well-suited for further open-source development in research institutes. USE plugins for various purposes are planned, for example, with respect to special user-interfaces for particular diagrams (e. g., object histories in object diagrams or OCL assertions on lifelines in sequence diagrams), or the realization of domain-specific languages like an RBAC DSL [17].

*Acknowledgements.*We would like to thank the referees for their constructive comments.

References

1. Anastasakis, K., Bordbar, B., Georg, G., Ray, I.: On challenges of model transformation from UML to Alloy. SoSyM 9(1), 69–86 (2010)
2. Berardi, D., Calvanese, D., Giacomo, G.D.: Reasoning on UML class diagrams. Artif. Intell. 168(1-2), 70–118 (2005)

3. Blanchette, J.C., Nipkow, T.: Nitpick: A counterexample generator for higher-order logic based on a relational model finder. In: Kaufmann, M., Paulson, L.C. (eds.) ITP 2010. LNCS, vol. 6172, pp. 131–146. Springer, Heidelberg (2010)
4. Brucker, A.D., Wolff, B.: HOL-OCL: A Formal Proof Environment for UML/OCL. In: FASE, pp. 97–100 (2008)
5. Cabot, J., Clarisó, R., Riera, D.: Verification of UML/OCL Class Diagrams using Constraint Programming. In: Proc. 2008 IEEE Int. Conf. Software Testing Verification and Validation Workshop, pp. 73–80. IEEE Computer Society Press, Washington, DC, USA (2008)
6. Chiorean, D., Pasca, M., Cârcu, A., Botiza, C., Moldovan, S.: Ensuring UML Models Consistency Using the OCL Environment. Electr. Notes Theor. Comput. Sci. 102, 99–110 (2004)
7. Clavel, M., Egea, M.: ITP/OCL: A Rewriting-Based Validation Tool for UML+OCL Static Class Diagrams. In: AMAST, pp. 368–373 (2006)
8. Demuth, B., Wilke, C.: Model and Object Verification by Using Dresden OCL. In: Proc. Russian-German Workshop Innovation Information Technologies: Theory and Practice, p. 81. Technical University, Ufa (2009)
9. Gogolla, M., Bohling, J., Richters, M.: Validating UML and OCL Models in USE by Automatic Snapshot Generation. SoSyM 4(4), 386–398 (2005)
10. Gogolla, M., Büttner, F., Richters, M.: USE: A UML-Based Specification Environment for Validating UML and OCL. SCP 69, 27–34 (2007)
11. Gogolla, M., Kuhlmann, M., Hamann, L.: Consistency, independence and consequences in UML and OCL models. In: Dubois, C. (ed.) TAP 2009. LNCS, vol. 5668, pp. 90–104. Springer, Heidelberg (2009)
12. Gogolla, M., Vallecillo, A.: Tractable Model Transformation Testing. In: France, R., Küster, J.M., Bordbar, B., Paige, R.F. (eds.) Proc. 7th Int. Conf. Modelling Foundations and Applications (ECMFA 2011). LNCS, Springer, Berlin (2011)
13. Jackson, D.: Software Abstractions - Logic, Language, and Analysis. The MIT Press, Cambridge (2006)
14. Jeanneret, C., Eyer, L., Markovic, S., Baar, T.: RoclET- Refactoring OCL Expressions by Transformations. In: Software & Systems Engineering and their Applications, 19th International Conference, ICSSEA 2006 (2006)
15. Kelsen, P., Ma, Q.: A lightweight approach for defining the formal semantics of a modeling language. In: Busch, C., Ober, I., Bruel, J.-M., Uhl, A., Völter, M. (eds.) MODELS 2008. LNCS, vol. 5301, pp. 690–704. Springer, Heidelberg (2008)
16. Kolovos, D., Rose, L., Paige, R.: The epsilon Book, http://www.eclipse.org/gmt/epsilon/doc/book/
17. Kuhlmann, M., Sohr, K., Gogolla, M.: Comprehensive Two-level Analysis of Static and Dynamic RBAC Constraints with UML and OCL. In: Baik, J., Massacci, F., Zulkernine, M. (eds.) Fifth International Conference on Secure Software Integration and Reliability Improvement, SSIRI 2011, IEEE Computer Society, Los Alamitos (2011)
18. de Lara, J., Guerra, E.: Deep meta-modelling with METADEPTH. In: Vitek, J. (ed.) TOOLS 2010. LNCS, vol. 6141, pp. 1–20. Springer, Heidelberg (2010)
19. Ornaghi, M., Fiorentini, C., Momigliano, A., Pagano, F.: Applying ASP to UML model validation. In: Erdem, E., Lin, F., Schaub, T. (eds.) LPNMR 2009. LNCS, vol. 5753, pp. 457–463. Springer, Heidelberg (2009)
20. Queralt, A., Teniente, E.: Reasoning on UML class diagrams with OCL constraints. In: Embley, D.W., Olivé, A., Ram, S. (eds.) ER 2006. LNCS, vol. 4215, pp. 497–512. Springer, Heidelberg (2006)

21. Samimi, H., Aung, E.D., Millstein, T.: Falling back on executable specifications. In: D'Hondt, T. (ed.) ECOOP 2010. LNCS, vol. 6183, pp. 552–576. Springer, Heidelberg (2010)
22. Soeken, M., Wille, R., Kuhlmann, M., Gogolla, M., Drechsler, R.: Verifying UML/OCL Models Using Boolean Satisfiability. In: Müller, W. (ed.) Proc. Design, Automation and Test in Europe (DATE 2010). IEEE Computer Society Press, Los Alamitos (2010)
23. Torlak, E., Jackson, D.: Kodkod: A relational model finder. In: Grumberg, O., Huth, M. (eds.) TACAS 2007. LNCS, vol. 4424, pp. 632–647. Springer, Heidelberg (2007)
24. Torlak, E., Vaziri, M., Dolby, J.: MemSAT: checking axiomatic specifications of memory models. SIGPLAN Not. 45, 341–350 (2010),
    http://doi.acm.org/10.1145/1809028.1806635
25. Treharne, H., Schneider, S., Grant, N., Evans, N., Ifill, W.: A step towards merging xUML and CSP ‖ B. In: Abrial, J.-R., Glässer, U. (eds.) Rigorous Methods for Software Construction and Analysis. LNCS, vol. 5115, pp. 130–146. Springer, Heidelberg (2009)
26. Trong, T.D., Ghosh, S., France, R.B., Hamilton, M., Wilkins, B.: UMLAnT: An Eclipse Plugin for Animating and Testing UML Designs. In: Proc. OOPSLA workshop Eclipse technology eXchange, pp. 120–124. ACM Press, New York (2005)
27. Wegmann, A., Le, L.S., Hussami, L., Beyer, D.: A Tool for Verified Design using Alloy for Specification and CrocoPat for Verification. In: Jackson, D., Zave, P. (eds.) Proc. First Alloy Workshop (2006)

Author Index

GPSR Compliance

The European Union's (EU) General Product Safety Regulation (GPSR)
is a set of rules that requires consumer products to be safe and our
obligations to ensure this.

If you have any concerns about our products, you can contact us on
ProductSafety@springernature.com

In case Publisher is established outside the EU, the EU authorized
representative is:

Springer Nature Customer Service Center GmbH
Europaplatz 3
69115 Heidelberg, Germany

Batch number: 09485837

Printed by Printforce, the Netherlands